Teaching Business Sustainability

Volume 1: From Theory to Practice

Edited by Chris Galea

The companion volume to this book,
Teaching Business Sustainability. Volume 2: Case Studies
is available in 2005.
Check www.greenleaf-publishing.com for details.

Teaching Business Sustainability

VOLUME 1:
FROM THEORY TO PRACTICE

EDITED BY CHRIS GALEA

Greenleaf
PUBLISHING
2 0 0 4

© 2004 Greenleaf Publishing Limited

Published by Greenleaf Publishing Limited
Aizlewood's Mill
Nursery Street
Sheffield S3 8GG
UK
www.greenleaf-publishing.com

Printed on paper made from at least 75% post-consumer waste
using TCF and ECF bleaching.
Printed in Great Britain by William Clowes Ltd, Beccles, Suffolk.
Cover by LaliAbril.com.

British Library Cataloguing in Publication Data:
    Teaching business sustainability
        Vol. 1: From theory to practice
        1.Business education 2.Sustainable development - Study and
        teaching 3.Business ethics - Study and teaching
        I.Galea, Chris
        650'.071

    ISBN 1874719543

Contents

Acknowledgements

I thank all the authors who submitted so many suggestions, proposals and papers; without their hard work and dogged dedication this volume would not have been possible.

My thanks also go to Stephanie Roberts whose editorial help and suggestions improved many of the papers. I also extend my thanks to John Stuart and the staff at Greenleaf Publishing who show much patience and dedication when dealing with wayward editors . . .

Lastly I thank my good friends and neighbours Sean Day and Kingsley Brown who were always there whenever I needed their support throughout this process. I also acknowledge the profound influence of my father, Dr Charles Galea Enriquez, who is always with me in spirit.

Dr Chris Galea
South Side Harbour
Antigonish, Nova Scotia
Canada

5 April 2004

Introduction

Chris Galea

Saint Francis Xavier University, Canada

One of the main challenges facing educators is that of creating an environment where student learning moves beyond theory and becomes instinctive practice. We have all had experiences in our lives where some theoretical concept is instantly grasped because it addressed some immediate concern or solved some pressing practical problem. Although such fortuitous 'eureka' moments are welcome, they are also infrequent. As such, the task of the educator is to make such opportunities emerge in the classroom and to create an environment where theory blends in seamlessly with practice.

The challenge outlined above is especially relevant to the area of teaching business sustainability. This is because educators in the field need to combat the unstated but often underlying assumption that much business sustainability is non-value-added effort—it is work that needs to be done to meet regulatory standards or to stay out of trouble with various stakeholders. Although it is not the purview of this volume to combat this widely held belief—much fine work has recently emerged that challenges this assumption—to deny its existence is to make the educator's task that much harder and the educational outcomes less successful. In light of this, a number of the contributors to this volume bring up this tension and outline various ways of addressing it. The key approach is to acknowledge the dichotomy and to help students explore the various ways in which the theoretical aspects of business sustainability can result in valuable and value-added practical outcomes.

Another consideration about teaching business sustainability is the realisation that the field is, relatively, still in its infancy. As such, there is the added challenge of teaching material that is still evolving and that is constantly in a state of being superseded by more developed concepts and ideas. As a result, the challenge to educators is to teach less of the actual nuts and bolts of business sustainability and more of the various tools and approaches by which students can continue to teach themselves. Although this advice applies to many other disciplines, it is especially relevant to the field of business sustainability, since educators and practitioners continue to make great strides in core areas of the discipline.

This results in another tenet that is especially relevant to our field: the need to use a mix of approaches when teaching business sustainability. This can be seen from the variety of different pedagogies taken by many of the educators who have contributed to this volume. Although many of the approaches are experimental and at the leading edge of management learning, there are some core elements that tie the approaches together. One is that they all share an experiential approach to teaching—a pedagogy that is well grounded in management learning literature. This approach fits in well with the point made earlier that the teaching of business sustainability needs to bring together the theory in a way that makes it relevant to practitioners in the field. The implication is that, whenever possible, educators need to link the learning to the students' immediate and pressing 'real-world' realities. This applies equally to undergraduates or to high-level executives. However, failing the existence of such real-world realities (as may often be the case in undergraduate settings), educators need to introduce experientially based approaches that re-create such settings in the classroom.

Another common element to the learning styles and approaches outlined in this volume is the desirability of holistic and interdisciplinary learning. It is clear from much of the literature on sustainability that the concept does not easily lend itself to being pigeonholed and that it crosses many of the functional areas of business. Indeed, it goes beyond just business learning to encompass many fields such as ecology and biology. If students are to move beyond the narrow perspective that conventional business study often entails, they need to be introduced to the wider vision that an interdisciplinary approach engenders.

Another common theme that one can discern from the various submissions is the desirability for learning to happen in a team-based setting. This is especially relevant because the field of business sustainability is such that there is rarely one optimum way of proceeding. In this kind of setting the collective thinking and experience of a functional group of students will result in much greater learning than if they work in their own individual silos.

The final point that emerges from this collection is that the experiential learning of business sustainability often can, and should be—dare one say this in an academic work—fun! Be it a heated exchange in a case-study discussion, a role-play exercise or a hands-on student consulting project, much experiential learning seems to excite the imagination of the students and to release their creative juices. In such circumstances, learning is a lot more 'fun' compared with the absorption of dry lectures. We can all attest, from personal learning experiences, how effortless and long-lasting such 'fun-based' learning can be.

The rationale for this book

Most readers of this book probably believe that the issue of sustainability and the role that business plays in it is of paramount importance. We also probably all share a notion that much remains to be done to make sustainability a driving force in today's business world. As such, most would agree that there is a great need to infuse business leaders of today and tomorrow with the key ideas behind business sustainability and to equip them with the tools to help them deal with its challenges. This book—and its forthcoming companion volume, consisting of exercises—has been developed directly with that objective in mind. It is meant to equip educators in the field with the tools by which they, in turn, can impart to business practitioners the knowledge and confidence to tackle the issues of sustainability.

Moreover, this collection of essays on business sustainability aims to unite the somewhat disparate efforts of pioneering educators. While the field of business sustainability is still relatively young, much teaching material has been developed and is being used in various business programmes and executive training. This material has emerged on a rather ad hoc basis as various educators have developed new pedagogies to suit their particular teaching needs. While there have been considerable efforts to collect and distribute such material, there has been little academic work done that puts it into a theoretical context. This book is a timely attempt to initiate such a process and to put together in one volume a number of such contextual perspectives.

In addition, the development of the book draws together a nucleus of leading-edge thinkers in the field and thus provides the various educators who are scattered across the globe with the sense that they are part of a larger group of like-minded colleagues. It is hoped that these efforts will spread the ultimate goal of developing business leaders who are ready to face the challenges and also benefit from the opportunities posed by sustainability.

The contents of this book

The 23 submissions to this first volume of *Teaching Business Sustainability* have been divided into three thematic groups. In Part 1, 'Theory, critique and ideas', the authors explore and critique some of the overarching ideas and thinking behind the teaching of sustainability. Part 2, 'Learning from current practice', contains the experiences of a number of educators and the successful and leading-edge approaches that they have used. The final part, Part 3, then outlines, as the title suggests, the tools, methods and approaches that can be used to teach business sustainability. This final section also serves as an introduction to the upcoming second volume that will provide educators of sustainability with a series of case studies, role plays and experiential exercises.

Part 1: Theory, critique and ideas

The book opens with a chapter by John Adams in which he outlines how our mental models—that is, our beliefs, assumptions, expectations and attitudes—exert a powerful effect on our behaviour and therefore on the results we get from our efforts. By extension, he contends that if we do not address 'mental models-in-use' in the teaching of sustainability it is doubtful that many of the technical and management practice ideas contained in this volume will ever be fully implemented, as they are built from mental models that differ from those presently prevailing throughout society.

John then describes and defines six mental models prevailing in North American organisations. He introduces the concept of 'versatility', meaning 'appropriate flexibility', as being necessary for effective teaching of the technical and management practices needed for a sustainable future. Additionally, a list of questions for contemplation and dialogue are provided that can increase the versatility of the learning experience.

Chapter 2 is by Bobby Banerjee. In this chapter Bobby critiques the concept of sustainability and the ways in which it is deployed in the organisational studies literature. Sustainability means different things to different people and, in this chapter, Bobby discusses the key concepts of sustainability and underlying assumptions behind the concept. Employing a critical perspective, the author argues that we need to be cautious of the populist rhetoric and win–win situations that characterise much of the literature on sustainability. The chapter concludes with a discussion of how we can develop a course on teaching sustainability by taking a critical approach through exploring three perspectives: the theoretical, multidisciplinary and global–local.

Chapter 3 is a provocative paper by Tom Abeles. Tom starts out by asking the pivotal question 'Can a publicly traded corporation be environmentally and socially responsible?' After a wide-ranging discussion that draws on various perspectives he posits that, if the investors are seen only as the stockholders and their measure is only in the increasing value of the stock or the dividend pay-out, then the model has significant cognitive dissonance with respect to environmental and social issues. He concludes that, if the business schools approach these issues by such tactics as screening the social and/or environmental values of applicants or by adding separate curriculum palliatives such as ethics and the environment, the institutions will have failed to address the problems at the core.

Following Tom's contribution is a related chapter by Pep Bardouille. In Chapter 4 Pep asserts that, in the decade since the United Nations Conference on Environment and Development (UNCED), the overwhelming focus of sustainable business efforts has been 'greening'. However, just as the sustainability paradigm goes beyond ecological protection, sustainable business strategies cannot be limited to only environmental management. Pep proposes that the private sector must consider ways in which to address 'fundamental human challenges', including poverty eradication and universal access to basic services (water, energy, healthcare). Pep outlines motivations for business to play a leading role in promoting global sustainable development and explores commercially viable ways in which it can contribute to improving the socioeconomic condition.

In Chapter 5 Suzanne Benn and David Bubna-Litic argue that, based on survey results from Australia and the USA, the typical MBA programme is incompatible with contemporary conditions of reflexive modernity. These call for graduates who are ethically self-reflexive, who recognise values differences and can negotiate the corporate transformations required for sustainability. Suzanne and David then explore the questions of whether the MBA can be rejuvenated through the incremental integration of sustainability themes into existing curricula and teaching techniques or whether we need to acknowledge that a holistic and integrated curriculum requires breaking with the fundamental modernism reflected in many assumptions that underpin the MBA. This thought-provoking chapter explores these options.

In Chapter 6 Homer Erekson, along with Steven Elliott and his colleagues at Miami University in Oxford, OH, argue that, historically, industrialists and environmentalists have not been partners in exploring environmental issues because of a lack of common vocabulary and because of silo-based disciplinary approaches. However, in the 1980s, the concept that a robust economy and healthy environment are not mutually exclusive objectives, but are inextricably linked, gained significant support. The authors then describe the integration of business and environmental education that has resulted and discuss the implications for educators.

Next follows a chapter by David Foot and Susan Ross. In Chapter 7 David and Susan outline why social sustainability has emerged as the third ingredient of a successful sustainable business strategy, along with economic and environmental sustainability. They review the current state of social sustainability as an essential component of sustainable business performance. Ultimately, they conclude that social sustainability considerations need to be integrated into virtually all curriculum elements and business units if a truly successful sustainable strategy in business teaching and practice is to be adopted.

In Chapter 8, the concluding chapter of Part 1, Michael Schaper looks at the question of whether there are any substantial, measurable differences in concern for the environment between students from different countries. He outlines a recent evaluation of environmental concern among business school students in four different countries—Australia, France, Hong Kong and Singapore. He concludes that, in general, students displayed a relatively high level of environmental concern. Moreover, there were no substantial differences in mean scores between students of different nationalities.

The results of Michael's research have important implications for management educators. First, it is clear that most business management students are concerned about environmental issues. This concern is relatively universal, and transcends cultural and national boundaries. Second, whereas previous studies have focused on MBA students, this research indicates that undergraduates are also environmentally aware. This is turn suggests that there may be a high level of unmet undergraduate student demand for courses on sustainability and environmental issues in business. Last, proactive university business schools may be able to seize a competitive advantage by incorporating these topics into their curriculum, given the high level of student concern with such issues.

Part 2: Learning from current practice

Part 2 opens with a chapter by Polly Courtice and Jonathon Porritt, who are co-directors of the Prince of Wales's Business and the Environment Programme based in Cambridge University. In Chapter 9 Polly and Jonathon explain how they established their programme as a world-class body in the domain of teaching sustainability. They explain how they give participants a deep, intensive experience in a constructive environment and how this experience shapes their attitudes, values and aspirations about sustainable development. They believe that this has the potential to radically change the way their organisations do business. They conclude that the success of the programme lies in building a core team of people who share a common concern about the sustainability challenges that we face and a belief that a new paradigm for how wealth is generated in our society can be achieved.

Chapter 10 is a second contribution by Elliott, Erekson *et al.*. In this chapter they describe a unique senior-level undergraduate capstone course developed and offered through the Center for Sustainable Systems Studies (CSSS) at Miami University. This course is team-taught by business and the science faculty and the student numbers consist of roughly half business and half science (or other non-business) students. The content of the course draws heavily on the many parallels between ecology and economics, including systems and resilience, ethics and valuation issues, and information and dialogue as central to the process of sustainability. The course pedagogy is intended to get business students to help science students with advanced business concepts and to get science students to help business students with advanced science concepts.

In Chapter 11 by Diane Holt a longitudinal study of a group of 52 business school students is used to examine the effectiveness of environmental education programmes in universities. The focus of the chapter is to examine whether the environmental learning experiences the students undergo have made a difference to their environmental actions, knowledge and attitudes and what factors may have been influential in any changes.

In Chapter 12 Kariann Aarup shares her experience of teaching a course called 'Social Context of Business' at McGill University. This course deals specifically with social and environmental issues and is unique as a core course in undergraduate business school curricula in Canada. Kariann focuses on the pedagogy used to achieve the teaching objectives of the course and the intention behind the assignments given, and outlines the effects that the course has had both on students and on the institution itself.

In Chapter 13 Gillian Rice and Amy Sprague explore the value of experiential learning activities in MBA programmes through an evaluation of the World Resources Institute's Environmental Enterprise Corps (EEC). The EEC matches teams of MBA students with environmental small and medium-sized enterprises (SMEs) in Latin America for specific projects, such as market studies or financial analyses. As a result, students gain an understanding of sustainability and conservation issues in the small-business context of emerging markets and have the opportunity to make a real, measured impact on the business.

Tom Eggert and co-authors, in Chapter 14, describe a partnership between a business school class at the University of Wisconsin and Baxter International, a global healthcare company. The projects that arose from this partnership were developed on the premise that leadership toward sustainability will come from the business community as Western society struggles to come to grips with the challenges of living and acting sustainably. Student teams from a class on 'The Greening of Business Strategy' each worked with a Baxter contact to research various aspects of sustainability such as socially responsible investing, energy conservation and extended producer responsibility. As a result of the programme, students gained a more practical knowledge of sustainability than they would have done had they only studied sustainability in the classroom. The research also benefited Baxter International in its drive toward sustainability by giving it both a more complete picture of the state of sustainability and focused information on specific areas.

The last paper in Part 2, Chapter 15, is by Judi Marshall. Judi suggests that in educating for sustainability we need to generate forms and practices of education that are congruent with the issues addressed. She describes the development of the MSc in 'Responsibility and Business Practice', a master's programme that has an explicit intent to 'address the challenges currently facing those managers who seek to integrate successful business practice with a concern for social, environmental and ethical issues'.[1] She explains key educational choices made in designing the degree, describes the teaching practices adopted and reviews some key learning, based on staff experiences and participant feedback.

Part 3: Tools, methods and approaches

Part 3 of this volume has eight chapters, starting with Chapter 16, by Sasha Courville. Sasha presents a conceptual framework for integrating tools for social justice and environmental protection, such as environmental management systems, corporate reporting systems, codes of conduct, third-party certification systems and so on into current business practices.

This is followed by Molly Brown and Joanna Macy's work on whole-systems learning, in Chapter 17. Molly and Joanna present an approach to whole-systems learning that helps people experience their innate connections with the self-correcting, self-organising powers of all living systems. In Molly and Joanna's experience, this empowers people to seek out, create and apply sustainable business practices within the workplace and the larger world. They outline methods to teach whole-systems learning that are highly interactive, experiential and enjoyable.

The ensuing chapter is by Trudy Heller. Trudy outlines how environmental managers often speak of the need to disseminate sustainable business thinking throughout a company, of communicating beyond the 'green wall'. Many corporations are conducting educational programmes to enlist employees as partners in addressing the challenge of how to enhance the business while diminishing its environmental footprint. In Chapter 18 Trudy reports on a pilot survey that asked companies, 'What activities are being offered to educate employees in sustainable business thinking?' She then describes specific activities, with examples from the surveyed companies. Common challenges are discussed, and an ideal programme, from an educator's perspective, is also outlined.

Chapter 19, by Beate Littig, puts forward neo-Socratic dialogue (NSD) as a didactic method to teach the ethics of sustainable development in business enterprises and in advanced business training. Beate's approach aims at visioning and explaining implicit values and at clarifying fundamental concepts. A second aim of NSD is to improve the communicative skills of the participants. Besides describ-

---

1   Quote from course details, at www.bath.ac.uk/management/carpp/msc.htm.

ing the more theoretical background, Beate also presents a case study, an NSD held with an interdisciplinary group of students studying sustainable development at the University of Vienna.

Kathleen Wood and co-authors, in Chapter 20, explore the difficulties of introducing and embedding triple-bottom-line approaches in a business environment when demands are consistently exceeding resources. They outline a framework, called 'the five pillars', which they successfully use in their work with clients. To embed sustainability into a business a 'systems approach' must be used, where each piece is critical to the whole—and where the whole is greater than the sum of the parts. The pillars consists of:

- Business alignment
- Sustainability knowledge
- Personal and organisational leadership
- Systems thinking
- Enabling technology and/or process

The authors conclude that triple-bottom-line sustainability, when viewed as a solution to strategic business issues and a source of competitive advantage, will garner the credibility and resources needed over the long term to evolve the current extractive business model into one that is sustainable.

The next chapter, by Bob Willard, concerns the why, what and how of teaching sustainability in business schools. In Chapter 21 Bob argues that the business case for sustainable development should be the cornerstone of an enlightened curriculum in business schools. He contends that business schools are overlooking how a well-executed sustainable development strategy can form one of the greatest contributions to savings, revenue, productivity, innovation, competitiveness, lower risk and new markets. Even hard-nosed business leaders are interested in worthy causes when the business language of dollars is used to quantify the benefits of sustainability strategies. He then proposes a tool called the business-case simulator to assess potential business benefits to companies from sustainability initiatives. Using this tool he demonstrates how companies can truly 'do well while doing good'.

The penultimate chapter, Chapter 22, is a second paper by David Foot on population and pedagogy in sustainability analysis. David outlines how population growth is almost always at the core of most sustainability issues, whether they relate to environmental, economic or social sustainability. He contends that sustaining an increasing population in a world with limited resources characterises the sustainability challenge. He then concludes with the practical approaches that educators can take to teach issues pertaining to population studies.

The last chapter, Chapter 23, by Darcy Hitchcock and Marsha Willard, deals with the challenges, methods and tools of teaching sustainability. Darcy and Marsha provide a framework for dealing with the challenge of getting everyone in an organisation to understand sustainability. Sustainability can seem abstract, overwhelming, too starry-eyed or too dismal. Darcy and Marsha examine the most common challenges in each of three phases of implementation and provide practical advice on how to overcome them.

Conclusions

As can be seen from the varied ideas outlined above, it is clear that there is no one approach to teaching business sustainability. Nevertheless, it is also clear that some approaches are better than others and will result in learning that is more grounded, applicable and fruitful. Educators in business sustainability would do well to follow the intuitive and practical advice offered in the chapters in this book while keeping an open mind to possibilities not yet explored.

Part 1
Theory, critique and ideas

1
Mental models @ work
Implications for teaching sustainability

John Adams
Saybrook Graduate School, USA

1.1 Background: what we say and what we do

Human activity during the second half of the 20th century produced huge challenges that are only now becoming evident to significant numbers of people. The engines driving gains in wealth, technology and the production of goods are using up ever-increasing amounts of non-renewable resources and generating unprecedented amounts of waste. New diseases more complex than any encountered before have appeared and have spread globally. Unprecedented numbers of people are left out of the positive advances of 'Western science' and are living in abject poverty—creating a skewed distribution of a few 'haves' and a majority of 'have nots'. The population of the planet has tripled in the past 50 years, and more than half of the people who have ever lived are alive today.

A higher proportion of the population is involved in warfare (civil and ethnic wars are just as deadly as the global kind) now than at any other time in history. As a result of population pressures, growing aspirations and local warfare, unprecedented numbers of people are migrating to the less densely populated countries of the world. Grain and fish production both peaked in the 1980s and have been level or declining ever since. Meat consumption has become a symbol of affluence, and its production makes huge demands on grain harvests and water supplies. Arable lands are turning into deserts, and aquifers are becoming salty as we try to feed the global population.

Since the 1990s, significant attention has been devoted to what it will take to address conditions such as these and to bequeath a high-quality and equitable future to succeeding generations. Ecologists, economists, population experts, business leaders, academics, psychologists and spiritual leaders have all weighed in with their suggestions. Most predict a less than rosy future if we do not make significant changes quickly; some say it is already too late.

Now we have entered a new century, and so far there is no indication that any of these problems has abated. In fact, some of the trends (e.g. emission of greenhouse gases) are growing even faster than was predicted at the beginning of the 1990s. The various global environmental challenges we are facing are well documented and widely reported by the media. More and more people are expressing alarm and are agreeing that 'something should be done'.

As is often the case, however, what people espouse and what they actually do are frequently quite different (for a more comprehensive development of espoused and behaved values, see Argyris and Schön 1978). Widespread changes in consumption patterns and resource usage have not happened. In this chapter I argue that people have to become aware of and question widely shared collective thinking patterns, or mental models, before they can act in new ways.

1.2 Why attention to prevailing mental models is essential

Whatever outcomes we realise in describing and implementing sustainable practices, it is clear that the future quality of life will be dictated by human behaviour, which is driven by human thought. We have no choice about whether we will play a role in creating the future. Our only choice is whether to create the future consciously or unconsciously!

The relevance of generating awareness and choice about mental models in teaching sustainability can be summarised by the following three statements. The first is from Marilyn Ferguson:

> If I continue to believe as I have always believed, I will continue to act as I have always acted. If I continue to act as I have always acted, I will continue to get what I have always gotten.[1]

This statement supports the notion that how we think strongly influences how we act, and our actions, in turn, influence the results we get. Trying to get different results (e.g. more sustainable management practices) while continuing to think in the 'same old ways' is not likely to lead to much change. Our mental models tend to be self-reinforcing and self-fulfilling.

The second statement is a paraphrase of an idea often expressed by Albert Einstein:

> You cannot expect to be able to solve a complex problem using the same manner of thinking that created the problem.

---

1   Comments in a seminar, July 1982.

Einstein's famous statement reminds us that if we do not adopt new mental models we will at best only be able to put short-term band aids on symptoms arising from unsustainable human activities.

Ferguson tells us that our thinking influences the results we get, and Einstein reminds us that a different consciousness will be needed, but the real challenge to teaching sustainability is represented by an observation from R.D. Laing, who suggested:

> The range of what we think and do is limited by what we fail to notice. And because we fail to notice that we fail to notice, there is little we can do to change; until we notice how failing to notice shapes our thoughts and deeds (Abrams and Zweig 1991: xix).

This third statement places the others within the reality that we are generally unaware of the mental models we use. So, an early priority in any sustainability education programme must be to raise awareness of the mental models being used and then to encourage responsible and conscious choice for adopting more appropriate mental models. If our attempts to teach sustainability in academic and corporate classrooms are to lead to significant action, we must help learners to understand and address their own default mental models and then show them how to diagnose and nurture versatility in the thinking of those they seek to influence.

A further implication for teaching sustainability is that the agent of change moving towards increased sustainability, whether she or he is an employee or a consultant, needs to be able to vary her or his mental models to exert successful influence. For example, if her or his opening message comes from mental models similar to those of the receiver, then less defensiveness is generated. Once discussion is under way, the agent of change can gradually shift her or his mental models and those of the person being influenced towards outlooks more appropriate to generating sustainable practices.

Mental models are with us from the very beginning. Owing to continual, normal repetitions and reinforcements, each of us gradually develops persistent ways of thinking that are assumed tacitly to be accurate reflections of reality and that operate, for the most part, unconsciously. Let us turn our attention now to some of the most prevailing collectively held mental models.

1.3 Prevailing mental models in North American organisations

Over the past several years, I have regularly asked people in my graduate courses and in private corporate workshops to brainstorm about their experiences of the commonly held mental models in their organisations, asking them to use adjectives to describe the widespread norms and outlooks. After collecting dozens of these lists and thousands of descriptive adjectives and then sorting the items into themes, I have found that most of the items fall near the left extreme of the six dimensions portrayed in Figure 1.1. Please note, I do not think that these six dimensions provide a complete description of the consciousness needed for a truly sustainable future, but they certainly give us a running start.

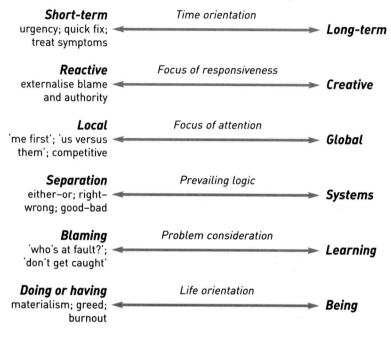

Figure 1.1 Six key dimensions of a sustainable consciousness

Unanimously across every one of my classes and workshops, people have located the present default mental models in business at or near the left-hand side of these dimensions, with a rather narrow 'zone of comfort' around each. When asked what sort of scenario we will create in 20 years if these defaults continue unchanged, the responses are always gloomy—and decidedly unsustainable. When asked if these default mental models are driving the major ecological challenges and economic disparities that exist around the world, there is a unanimous 'Yes!' Although we already know what is needed, the autopilot nature of our prevailing default mental models is very persistent.

What would happen if we were able to shift the defaults significantly to the right, and generate wider 'zones of comfort'? Would we not be better able to create the kind of future we really want? For that matter, would we not also be able to bring our own lives into better balance today if we made these changes?

The challenge is that our mental models have a way of protecting themselves from change and usually operate like an autopilot. As far as we know, we are the only species on Earth that has the capacity to think about *how* we think. Most of the time, however, we do not engage this capacity. We reinforce our outlooks by repeating the same thoughts day after day. To take responsibility, we must move from autopilot to choice. In this respect, we have done a reasonably good job of preparing for the future technologically, but we have a long way to go psychologically and emotionally. Box 1.2, at the end of this chapter, lists some of the success factors needed to bring about real change in deeply ingrained habit patterns such as mental models.

In the workplace, we often find that plans are created but not followed. We are constantly faced with examples of low integrity and questionable ethics in the arenas of business, finance, government and even childcare. When it comes to the environment, relatively few—although their numbers are growing—organisations *voluntarily* restrict themselves with regard to toxic emissions and solid waste disposal and, where regulations exist, minimum compliance—or finding loopholes—unfortunately still prevails.

At the individual level, it seems too few people feel *personally* responsible for their lot in life. The act of taking personal responsibility for other than personal economic gain, although increasing, is still not widespread. Not enough of us recognise how small and endangered the Earth has become, and even fewer of us realise the many things we can do locally to address, even in a small way, some of the larger challenges.

Are people by nature self-destructive? Do people generally not care if they degrade the environment until vast tracts become uninhabitable? Are people unconcerned about the legacy they appear to be leaving for their grandchildren? Do people really think that their lifestyle habits will not have any consequences? Do wealthy Westerners really feel that it is appropriate for four billion fellow humans to live on less than US$2 per day? For most people, the answer is 'No!' to each of these questions, and yet the problems continue to grow.

I think the reason for this contradiction lies in our way of thinking. But mental models are not immutable. With conscious choice they can become more appropriately flexible. **Versatility in consciousness** is a key concept that needs to be introduced into the educational process at all levels if we are to address rising worldwide sustainability issues effectively. I believe that versatility in consciousness is essential for ongoing individual learning and that the only sustainable consciousness is a continual learning consciousness.

Any 'reprogramming' of the autopilot will require the same processes that established the present mental models in the first place—repetitions of messages and experiences. The reiterations of new ideas and intentions must be carried out consciously. Often, to get beyond the status quo maintenance efforts of the old autopilot it is necessary to create structures or mechanisms that require new repetitions be carried out.

It is easiest to change one default message at a time. Wholesale changes of one's consciousness, a complete personal transformation, is possible and sometimes happens, but step-by-step change is likely to be a lot easier for most people to assimilate.

1.4 Implementing the six dimensions of a sustainable consciousness

On each of the dimensions of sustainable consciousness introduced in Figure 1.1, education and ongoing socialisation reinforce default mental models near the extreme left-hand side of the continuum. I propose that the kind of thinking that fosters continual learning and inquiry, **sustainable consciousness**, is that which operates easily and appropriately all the way across each dimension.

Pressure and stress can compress or narrow one's zones of comfort and push the default further towards the left-hand side of the continuum. For example, someone who seems always to be in a hurry may become panic-stricken and overwhelmed by mounting deadlines and feel an absence of enough time. Someone who is mildly prejudiced against certain groups may become more closed-minded and more radically hateful.

Conversely, appreciative processes such as Appreciative Inquiry (Cooperrider and Whitney 1999), Future Search (Weisbord and Janov 1995), Dialogue (Senge 1990), Open Space (Owen 1992) and The World Café (Brown 2002) can help broaden one's zones of comfort by providing new insights and unexpected vantage points in a safe environment. A series of questions is provided at the end of this chapter, in Box 1.1, that is intended to help people focus on building versatility.

Table 1.1 provides examples of how to reinforce or bring attention to the left-hand side of each dimension. Table 1.2 provides examples of how to reinforce or

Focus	Reinforcing messages	Questions to bring focus here	Positive value of focusing here	Consequences of over-using this focus
Short-term	Don't fix it if it ain't broke Just do it	What needs attention now? What are your immediate priorities?	You can: • Establish priorities • Act with efficiency	You may: • Lose the big picture • Overlook the long-term consequences • Merely put bandages on the symptoms
Reactive	Do as you're told If it feels good, do it Life's a bitch and then you die	What is the established policy, procedure or practice? What has been done before in this kind of situation?	You can achieve: • Consistency • Responsiveness • Loyalty	You may: • Become stuck in a rut • Be unable to flow with change

Table 1.1 **Working with the left-hand side ('left-end') focuses (see Fig. 1.1)**
(continued over)

Focus	Reinforcing messages	Questions to bring focus here	Positive value of focusing here	Consequences of over-using this focus
Local	Look out for 'number one' You've got to expect that from a _____ !	What makes you different or unique? What is special about this situation?	You can: • Enhance your survival • Achieve a better level of protection • Maintain your position	You may: • Lose perspective • Tend towards ethnocentrism • Lose diversity
Separation	The best way to understand it is to take it apart A place for everything, and everything in its place	What are the relevant facts in this situation? What do you get when you 'crunch the numbers'?	You may: • Achieve convergence • Enhance specialisation • Increase rationality	You may: • Create fragmentation • Achieve low synergy • Get lost in minutiae
Blaming	It's not my fault! All right, who's to blame here?	What are your reasons for your actions? What's wrong with this picture?	You can increase judgement, law and rule enforcement	You may: • Create a win–lose polarisation • Tend towards risk aversion
Doing or having	What's in it for me? Faster, cheaper, better!	What is the most cost-effective thing to do? What's the bottom line?	You may increase: • Financial performance • Material comforts	You may: • Gain an attachment. to possessions • Lose human sensitivity • Burn out

Table 1.1 (continued)

Focus	Reinforcing messages	Questions to bring focus here	Positive value of focusing here	Consequences of over-using this focus
Long-term	Create a vision Plan ahead	What do you anticipate? Where are we headed? Where do we want to go?	You can increase: • Accuracy of anticipation • Accuracy of prediction • Possibilities • Contingencies	You may: • Lose timely responsive-ness • Ignore pressing realities
Creative	Take responsibility for yourself You can be anything you want to be	Is there a different or better approach? What would you do about this situation if you had a magic wand?	You may: • Increase innovation • Uncover new ideas • Open up new directions	You may: • Overlook proven processes • Reinvent the wheel
Global	Look at the big picture. Let's think about the consequences of this decision	What's best for the organisation as a whole? How can you make a difference in the world?	You may increase your ability to: • Take a comprehen-sive view • Achieve inclusiveness • Value diversity	You may be prone to: • Idealism • Loss of initiative or drive • Inattention to detail
Systems	Solving one problem almost always creates others The whole is more than the sum of its parts	Who are the key stakeholders? If we take this action, what consequences can we predict?	You will achieve an approach that is: • Divergent • Holistic • Able to incorporate key inter-relationships	You may tend to: • Equate models to reality • Get lost in the clouds of complexity or theory

Table 1.2 **Working with the right-hand side ('right-end') focuses (see Fig. 1.1)**
(continued over)

Focus	Reinforcing messages	Questions to bring focus here	Positive value of focusing here	Consequences of over-using this focus
Learning	Let one who is without sin cast the first stone Here's another learning and growth opportunity	What can you learn from this experience? How might you benefit from letting go of that grudge?	You may: ● Increase ease of exploration ● Seek growth and learning	You may be: ● Taken advantage of ● Self-sacrificing ● Prone to loss of discipline
Being	You'll never walk alone Trust the process As ye sow, so shall ye reap	What really matters in your life? What does your 'higher self' say about this?	You can: ● Increase self-realisation ● Achieve a 'greater good' point of view	You may: ● Become ungrounded ● Lose touch with the 'mainstream'

Table 1.2 (continued)

bring attention to the right-hand side of each dimension. These two tables also indicate the positive aspects of each focus and the liability that accrues from too much of each focus.

Course time can be spent on working with these two tables to raise awareness of prevailing mental models and to enhance the choice of more sustainable alternatives. Individuals can also work with these two tables (especially with Table 1.2, which is likely to be less familiar) as part of their personal planning or self-directed personal development work, to increase their versatility of thinking. For example, suppose you find that you have a strong attachment to reactive and short-term thinking (e.g. too much 'firefighting' and focusing on immediate pressures) and conclude that this focus is not serving you well. To build versatility, you can practise asking the questions and looking for opportunities to reframe situations that will bring your awareness to the creative and long-term ends of these dimensions (e.g. 'What kind of outlook would I create for myself if I had a magic wand?'). With regular practice in shifting awareness back and forth along any of the dimensions, your repertoire for dealing with life will increase dramatically.

Likewise, corporate groups can use these tables as templates for planning and decision-making. In my experience, when businesses find that they must undergo significant transformations to survive in their rapidly changing marketplaces, they usually approach this task in a 'get it over with as quick as we can, with as little effort as possible' mentality that reflects 'left-end' thinking. As a result, more than 80% of large-scale organisational transformational efforts fail, as the effort to change devolves into implementing a few initiatives that do not affect the overall situation at all.

To be successful, 'right-end' thinking is necessary to address the intricacies of cross-person and interorganisational dynamics and the extensive interdependences that pervade contemporary organisations. I believe that the mental models (and subsequent behaviour) of corporate leaders and employees are among the most critical success—or failure—factors in transformational change. Therefore, Table 1.2 is suggested as a tool to assist in the planning of large-scale organisational change.

Also, any organisation interested in a dual- (or triple)-bottom-line concept will find Tables 1.1 and 1.2 helpful. To establish a high-quality environment internally and a sustainable approach externally, 'right-end' thinking is necessary.

1.4.1 Time orientation

- Short-term thinking focuses on immediate deadlines, immediate priorities and a sense of urgency.

- Long-term thinking focuses on long-term consequences and establishing long-term goals.

1.4.2 Focus of responsiveness

- When a person is focused on the reactive end of this dimension, he or she is primarily focused on external stimuli, either adhering to or rebelling against the prevailing rules and authority.

- When a person is focused on the creative end of this dimension, he or she is primarily focused on taking initiatives and will choose to be guided by his or her own inner ideas of how to proceed.

1.4.3 Focus of attention

- The local end of this dimension suggests thinking that is focused on one's self or immediate group.

- The global end of this dimension suggests broad, ecumenical thinking.

1.4.4 Prevailing logic

- The separation, or either/or, end of this dimension emphasises specialisation, and thinking is predominantly in the rational–analytic mode.

- The systems, or both/and, end of this dimension suggests ever-increasing generalisation, and thinking is focused on understanding how the interaction of the parts contributes to the operating results of the whole.

1.4.5 Problem consideration

- At the blaming end of this dimension, one expresses the need for self-protection, and one operates in ways to convince others that one is not to blame when problems or errors become evident.

- At the learning end of this dimension, one expresses the need for learning, and one operates in ways to ensure learning.

1.4.6 Life orientation

- On the doing/having end of this dimension, the quest is to engage in activities that will lead to acquiring tangible goods as the primary vehicle to realising satisfaction and fulfilment.

- On the being end of this dimension, the quest is for the acquisition of insight and understanding of what life is all about spiritually.

1.5 Implications and conclusions

As already mentioned, most people have default settings towards the left-hand sides of these dimensions, and their zones of comfort are narrow. There is obviously no single position on any of these dimensions that is *always* going to be the best or most effective position. The challenge that we face, both individually and in our workplaces, is the need to become more aware of the consequences of nearly always behaving unconsciously from our default settings. When most of us read a book about goal-setting, or participate in a seminar on systems thinking, or attend a lecture on water quality, we immediately think 'Wow! That's really important!' But within a few hours, if we are still thinking about these ideas, most of us are likely to be thinking 'Somebody ought to do something about that', as our temporarily expanded awareness snaps back to its default settings—our autopilot mental models.

With greater awareness of what our default positions are, we can make conscious choices about *how* to think. The issue is not about having or not having the 'correct' default settings but about being aware of them and choosing other ways of responding that may be more appropriate to the situation. Each end of each dimension has pluses and liabilities, as outlined in Tables 1.1 and 1.2.

One of the best ways to promote versatility is regularly to ask ourselves questions that will take our thinking to the more distant parts of each continuum. I believe that questions such as those in Box 1.1 need to be embedded in our educational processes from the earliest years.

Courses in increasing mental model versatility could be built around the six dimensions illustrated in Figure 1.1. They could be included in virtually any adult education or worksite training programme, and, when these questions are

I have found that questions such as the following have been very useful to introduce to students learning about sustainability for either discussion or individual contemplation. Addressing these questions in a focused way seems to foster a greater commitment to building more versatility into thinking patterns.

- How can we involve children more as stakeholders for the future in our work?
- What are the 'right' things to do to foster a sustainable consciousness?
- How can we shift from 'Us versus them' to 'We're all in this together'?
- What are our responses to the Iroquois challenge to consider the implications of our decisions for the next seven generations?
- If we created this system in which economic growth is essential, could we not also create a system in which long-term quality of life is essential?
- How can we discover our interconnectedness across organisations, communities and nations?
- What would it take for my place of work to make the environment a key priority in its annual planning cycle?
- Is 70% of the global population 'hopelessly poor', or are 6% 'hopelessly rich'?
- How do we build the courage to express our views and feelings in places where people do not want to hear them?
- How can I help people become aware that they are able to become aware?
- What practices can I adopt to promote consciousness versatility?
- In what ways is my present lifestyle symptomatic of the challenges to sustainability?
- Why am I working so hard these days—in order to do what?
- How can I move from having all the answers to staying in the question?

Box 1.1 **Some questions for contemplation and discussion**

explored, they will enhance the effectiveness of the course material and promote mental model versatility.

We have the means to create just about any future we desire. We also have the means to bring an end to life on Earth. We know what is contributing to the interacting web of global challenges and we have the means to deal with these challenges. But, to address the global situation that is emerging today, it is my opinion that more and better versatility in our mental models is essential. A good way to promote this flexibility is to get into the habit of regularly asking ourselves, and each other, questions that take our consciousness out of autopilot and into choice before deciding how to proceed.

Changing habits, group norms or larger-system cultures is very challenging. Moving from 'autopilot' to 'choice', whether on an individual or a collective level, requires first becoming conscious of the present mental model and then choosing the appropriate way to think about the situation being addressed.

Several years ago, I conducted an investigation (Adams 2003) into what it takes to accomplish sustainable habit changes and found 12 factors that were regularly present when an individual or a group succeeds in moving from autopilot to choice.

For supporting individual habit change there is a need for:

● Understanding and acceptance of the need for change

● A belief that the change is both possible and desirable

● A heartfelt commitment to succeeding

● A clear goal, vision or outcome, plus a practical first step or two

● Mechanisms or structures that require regular repetitions of the newly adopted habit

● Feeling supported and safe

● Versatility of mental models

● Patience and persistence

For supporting group or organisational pattern change we need to add to this list:

● Clear accountability, with visible, vocal, consistent and persistent sponsors and stakeholders

● Explicit boundary management, clarifying the role of 'others' to ensure success

● A critical mass of people in alignment

● Rewards for the new pattern and withdrawal of rewards from old patterns

Box 1.2 Success factors for deep pattern change

References

Abrams, J., and C. Zweig (eds.) (1991) *Meeting the Shadow: The Hidden Power of the Dark Side of Human Nature* (Los Angeles: Jeremy P. Tarcher).

Adams, J. (2003) 'Successful Change', *OD Practitioner* 35.4: 22-26.

Argyris, C., and D. Schön (1978) *Organizational Learning: A Theory of Action Perspective* (Reading, MA: Addison-Wesley).

Brown, J. (2002) *The World Café: A Resource Guide for Hosting Conversations That Matter* (Williston, VT: Pegasus Communications).

Cooperrider, D., and D. Whitney (1999) *Appreciative Inquiry* ('Collaborating for Change' series; San Francisco: Berrett-Koehler).

Owen, H. (1992) *Open Space Technology: A User's Guide* (Potomac, MD: Abbot Publishing).

Senge, P. (1990) *The Fifth Discipline: : The Art and Practice of the Learning Organization* (New York: Doubleday/Currency).

Weisbord, M., and S. Janov (1995) *Future Search: An Action Guide to Finding Common Ground in Organizations and Communities* (San Francisco: Berrett-Koehler).

Further reading

Adams, J. (2000) *Thinking Today As If Tomorrow Mattered: The Rise of a Sustainable Consciousness* (San Francisco: Eartheart Enterprises).

Harman, W. (1998) *Global Mind Change: The promise of the 21st Century* (San Francisco: Berrett-Koehler).

Henderson, H. (1999) *Beyond Globalization: Shaping a Sustainable Global Economy* (Bloomfield, CT: Kumarian Press).

Needleman, J. (1998) *Time and Soul: Where Has All The Time Gone? . . . And How To Get It Back* (New York: Currency/Doubleday).

Ray, P., and S.R. Anderson. (2000) *The Culture Creatives: How 50 Million People Are Changing The World* (New York: Harmony Books).

Schwartz, P. (1991) *The Art of the Long View: Planning for the Future in an Uncertain World* (New York: Doubleday/Currency).

2
Teaching sustainability
A critical perspective

Subhabrata Bobby Banerjee
University of South Australia

It seems as if the term 'sustainability' can be found everywhere these days—in corporate annual reports, in government policies, in the mission statements of community organisations, in speeches of national and world leaders and in the business press. The buzzword of the 1990s seems to have entered the mainstream discourse. But, as with all buzzwords, we need to exercise some caution in understanding how it is being used, by whom and for what purpose. That corporations play a significant role in the path to sustainability is not in doubt. The question is, are current corporate practices compatible with notions of sustainability or are they mere 'greenwashing'[1] exercises designed to ensure that the corporation maintains a positive public image? Some researchers caution that the so-called greening of industry should not be confused with the notion of sustainable development (Pearce *et al.* 1989; Schot *et al.* 1997; Welford 1997; Westley and Vredenburg 1996). Although there have been significant advances in pollution control and emission reduction, this does not mean that current modes of development are sustainable for the planet as a whole (Hart 1997). Claims of 'ecological sustainable' practices of high-profile 'socially responsible' companies such as The Body Shop and Ben & Jerry's have been questioned in the business press (Entine 1995; Rosen 1995). Sustainability means different things to different

---

1 The *Oxford English Dictionary* (Oxford University Press, 2004, 2nd edn) defines 'greenwash' as 'disinformation disseminated by an organisation so as to present an environmentally responsible public image'. The non-governmental organisation CorpWatch (www.corpwatch.org) has a less charitable definition of greenwash, stating it is 'the phenomenon of socially and environmentally destructive corporations attempting to preserve and expand their markets by posing as friends of the environment and leaders in the struggle to eradicate poverty'.

people, and in this chapter I uncover some assumptions behind the concept and look critically at how it is being deployed in the organisational studies literature. I also suggest a framework that can be used to teach students about the concept of sustainability by taking a more critical approach.

2.1 Sustainability: the concept and its implications

A brief historical overview of the discourses about sustainability is a useful starting point. The term 'sustainability' emerged from debates over sustainable development in the late 1980s and early 1990s. At the global level, more than 50 years of 'development' came at a price, especially for poorer nations: environmental degradation, deforestation, resource depletion, social unrest and wide income disparity were some of the problems associated with this period (Escobar 1995; Esteva 1992; Goldsmith 1997; Guha and Martinez-Alier 1997). During the late 1960s and early 1970s, it was becoming clear to planners that economic growth did not necessarily mean equitable distribution of resources, and that unbridled economic growth had adverse social and environmental consequences.

There are more than 1 billion people on this planet unable to meet fundamental needs for food, shelter, clean water and sanitation (Crossett 1998). The gap between rich and poor continues to widen: on a per capita income basis, the ratio of rich to poor was 2:1 in 1800, 20:1 in 1945 and 40:1 by 1975 (Waters 1995). The richest 20% of the world account for about 83% of global income while the poorest 20% of the world earn less than 2% global income (Waters 1995). The total asset value of the world's richest 225 individuals, estimated at over US$1 trillion, is more than the annual income of the poorest half of the world's population (Crossett 1998). In the newly industrialising countries, economic growth was inevitably accompanied by an increase in income disparity. The effect on rural populations in the third world was even more severe, as industrialisation led to displacement, environmental degradation and social inequities. 'Sustainable development' entered the discourse in the 1980s as an effort to address the environmental and social problems associated with development and as a critique of the 'economic growth at all costs' approach of the past 50-plus years (Banerjee 2003).

It is interesting to speculate why the term 'sustainability' has become more popular these days. It is possible that the term 'development' still carries negative connotations for policy-makers in supranational organisations such as the United Nations, the World Bank, and the World Trade Organisation, whereas the more neutral sounding 'sustainability' may seem less controversial. In any case, there is no universal agreement on what this means. Holmberg and Sandbrook (1992) counted more than 100 definitions of 'sustainable development'—no doubt this number has increased since then. This diversity of opinion indicates more than a little confusion: either no one really knows what 'sustainable development' means or, more likely, it means different things to different people.

The most commonly used definition is that of the Brundtland Commission (WCED 1987). According to the Brundtland Commission, sustainable development is 'a process of change in which the exploitation of resources, direction of invest-ments, orientation of technological development and institutional change are made consistent with future as well as present needs' (WCED 1987: 9). This broad categorisation is at the root of several controversies, and there is considerable disagreement among scholars in different disciplines on how this definition should be operationalised and how sustainability should be measured. The Brundtland definition is really not a definition. Instead, it is a slogan, and slogans, however pretty, do not make good theory. As several authors have pointed out, it does not elaborate on the notion of human needs and wants (Kirkby *et al.* 1995; Redclift 1987). Also, the concern for future generations is hard to operationalise. Given a scenario of limited resources, this assumption becomes a contradiction, as most potential consumers (future generations) are unable to access the present market or, as Martinez-Alier (1987: 17) puts it, 'individuals not yet born have onto-logical difficulties in making their presence felt in today's market for exhaustible resources'.

The agenda of the Brundtland Commission also focuses on social justice and human development within the framework of social equity and the equitable distribution and use of resources. In a content analysis of different definitions of sustainable development, Gladwin *et al.* (1995) identified several themes, includ-ing human development, inclusiveness (of ecological, economic, political, technological and social systems), connectivity (of sociopolitical, economic and environmental goals), equity (fair distribution of resources and property rights), prudence (avoiding irreversibilities and recognising carrying capacities) and security (achieving a safe, health and high quality of life). The major proposals of the Brundtland Commission include changing the 'quality' of growth, ensuring a sustainable level of population, conserving and enhancing the resource base, managing technology and environmental risks and incorporating the environ-ment into decision-making. There is also an underlying assumption that market forces can be relied on to achieve sustainable development, although political interventions, international agreements and national environmental regulation also have a role to play.

As Redclift (1987), however, has noted, most environmental initiatives by gov-ernments and international organisations attempt to minimise the 'externalities' of economic growth rather than outline ways in which development should proceed. As recent events at the international summits in Rio, Johannesburg and Kyoto have shown, environmental considerations do not take top priority when they clash with strategic, political or national interests (Banerjee 2003). When there is a clash between economic and environmental interests, the former trumps the latter. Sustainable development tries to reconcile these opposing interests while simultaneously maximising economic and environmental benefits. Exactly how this can be achieved and who will benefit or suffer from this process is debated all over the world.

2.2 From sustainable development to corporate sustainability

The discussion thus far has been at a conceptual, macro level. A more critical approach to sustainability involves examining how this term is being used, by whom and why. For example, how does sustainability operate at the organisational level? The complexities, contradictions and confusion surrounding discourses of sustainability pose significant challenges for business firms. Although there is plenty of research on economic sustainability—the strategy discipline, for example, focuses primarily on how firms can achieve long-term sustainable competitive advantage—the environmental and social dimensions of sustainability are relatively under-researched (Banerjee 2001).

Given that industry was and continues to be a major cause of global environmental problems, it seems only fair that business firms do everything they can to reduce their environmental impact. However, it is important to realise that a purely business-driven sustainability agenda will not achieve the goals of global sustainability, especially where equity is concerned (Banerjee 2003). For most business firms, sustainability means that something is sustainable only if it is profitable, hence the popularity of cost-saving strategies such as eco-efficiency. This narrow focus excludes other sustainable practices that may not deliver a profit to business; hence the need for intervention by other institutions—governments, non-governmental organisations (NGOs) and international institutions, for example. Critics argue that even these institutions are increasingly employing neoliberal agendas in assessing the parameters of sustainability (Rifkin 1999; Visvanathan 1991). For example, an ongoing United Nations Development Programme project is called 'Global Sustainable Development Facility'. That many of the project's team members are transnational corporations with documented negative environmental and social impacts on indigenous and rural populations strengthens the notion that these international organisations do not and cannot serve community interests (Rifkin 1999; Shiva 1991).

At the organisational level the focus of sustainability has generally been restricted to the environment (Banerjee 2002). Recently, there has been a minor explosion of management articles about 'corporate greening'. Many of these try to fit current notions of environmental sustainability into corporate strategy (see e.g. the 1995 special issue on 'Ecologically Sustainable Organisations' in the *Academy of Management Review*, or the 1992 special issue on 'Strategic Management of the Environment' in *Long Range Planning*) and discuss the emergence of corporate environmentalism and organisational processes of environmental management (Banerjee 2001; Crane 2000; Fineman 1996).

More recent efforts to broaden the scope of greening to include social sustainability are also under way. This 'triple-bottom-line' approach attempts to assess the social and environmental impacts of business, apart from its economic impact (Elkington 1999). Elkington (1999: 73) describes interactions between the environment, society and the economy as three 'shear zones' that produce a variety of opportunities and challenges for organisations. Many of the advances in cleaner technologies and emissions reductions have come from the economic–environment shear zone. It is an area with which corporations are comfortable because it delivers measurable benefits to them. Outcomes of the social–environment and social–economy shear zones are more ambiguous (for corporations, at least), although the assumption is that organisations must integrate these to survive in the long term. Theoretical perspectives of the triple-bottom-line approach focus on maximising sustainability opportunities (corporate social responsibility, stakeholder relations and corporate governance) while minimising sustainability-related risks (corporate risk management, environmental, health and safety audits and reporting). Proponents of the triple bottom line claim that use of these and other parameters enables one to map the environmental and social domains of sustainability and help one to assess how corporations perform on a triple bottom line (Elkington 1999). Nonetheless, research on the environmental and social dimensions of corporate sustainability is in its infancy.

A cursory look at the annual reports of most large transnational corporations, however, indicates that they have begun to discuss sustainability with their stakeholders. For instance, the Dow Jones recently launched a 'Sustainability Group Index' after a survey of *Fortune* 500 companies. A sustainable corporation was defined as one 'that aims at increasing long-term shareholder value by integrating economic, environmental and social growth opportunities into its corporate and business strategies' (Dow Jones 2000). Corporate discourses on sustainability produce an elision that displaces the focus from global planetary sustainability to sustaining the corporation through 'growth opportunities'. What may happen if environmental and social issues do not enable the desired growth remains unclear, but the assumption is that global sustainability can be achieved by corporations only through market exchanges. There is limited awareness that traditional notions of capital, income and growth continue to inform this 'new' paradigm. The uncritical acceptance of the current system of markets is also problematic: although markets are indeed efficient mechanisms to set prices, they cannot reflect true costs, such as the replacement costs of an old-growth tropical rainforest or the social costs of tobacco and alcohol consumption (Hawken 1995).

The debates about the role and extent of corporate sustainability emerge from two distinct assumptions underlying the theory of the firm. The received view of the firm is primarily economic. It focuses on the efficiencies required to maximise rent-seeking opportunities. Conversely, the sociological perspective views the firm as a social entity and focuses on issues of legitimacy. The problem with this polarity is that legitimacy becomes subordinate to efficiency, or the terms of legitimacy are often defined by efficiency criteria. An examination of the corporate sustainability literature shows the rationale and assumptions behind this discourse are: (1) corporations *should* think beyond making money and pay attention to social and environmental issues, (2) corporations *should* behave in an ethical manner and demonstrate the highest level of integrity and transparency in all their operations and (3) corporations *should* be involved with the communities in which they operate by enhancing the social welfare of those communities and providing community support through philanthropy or other means.

The normative core of this discourse is not hard to ascertain: the assumptions are that corporations should do all these things because: (1) being a good social and environmental citizen is positively related to good financial performance (despite very weak empirical evidence, if any) and (2) if a corporation is a bad citizen then its licence to operate will be revoked by 'society'. Both of these are simplistic assumptions with little theoretical or empirical support. For example, large transnational corporations responsible for major environmental disasters and negative social impacts in the third world (Union Carbide, Nike, Exxon, Shell; see Welford 1997) have become stronger and more powerful through mergers, restructures or relentless public relations campaigns.

2.3 Teaching sustainability from a critical perspective

So what implications arise for teaching students about multifarious assumptions behind a complex issue? If the objective is to design a course that not only teaches the basic concepts of sustainability but also exposes and critiques the hidden assumptions, then a multidisciplinary approach is essential. Today's radical concepts become the mainstream topics of tomorrow, and our managers of the future need to develop the ability to think critically, to question the assumptions that inform current literature on sustainability and to go beyond populist rhetoric. In this section I discuss three perspectives that educators can use to develop a course on teaching sustainability critically: theoretical, multidisciplinary and local and global perspectives.

Before I explore these themes it may be useful to define what I mean by being 'critical'. I do not use the term to mark allegiance to a school of thought, such as the Frankfurt School of critical theory (CMSIG 2002). Rather, my aim is to question some fundamental axioms of management in the context of sustainability by using a range of theoretical views. I believe this will enhance our role as teachers in business schools where thoughtful debates about social and environmental issues are rare. If our goal is to develop thoughtful, self-reflexive practitioners, then we must focus not only on developing managerial skills but also on nurturing citizenship skills among our future managers.

Recent corporate scandals in the USA, for example, suggest a larger malaise. They are not just cases of faulty business ethics; they indicate structural problems with corporate governance. These scandals can too easily erode trust in corporations, financial and professional institutions and business schools. That those responsible for the scandals also have corporate citizenship policies and sustainability policies in place strongly suggests that we must examine these issues more closely and more critically. Let us see how we might do this in the context of teaching sustainability in business schools.

2.3.1 First theme: theoretical perspectives

Although the concept of sustainable development has been around for nearly 20 years, theory-building in the context of business firms is still in its infancy. Most research in management has focused on environmental sustainability and the implications for business (Banerjee 2002; Shrivastava 1995). One area focuses on the paradigmatic implications of integrating the environment into strategy. Researchers have called for the re-evaluation of existing neoclassical economic paradigms and have discussed the emergence of new paradigms such as the ecocentric and the sustainable development paradigms (Gladwin *et al.* 1995; Purser *et al.* 1995; Shrivastava 1995). They argue that attention to the natural environment is lacking in the literature and, in cases where environmental issues have been addressed, the underlying mind-set is anthropocentric, where ecological principles are either subsumed under or disassociated from the economic paradigm. Traditionally, environmental costs have been treated as 'externalities' arising from economic activity. These costs are typically not borne by the producer and are thus not included in the market transaction. Public policy actions frequently attempt to bring these so-called externalities closer to home by estimating the outside cost of pollution and by applying pollution taxes (Petulla 1980).

This line of investigation tries to develop operational principles of sustainable development as they relate to organisational activity and proposes changes in managerial and policy mind-set that are needed for a paradigm shift. Gladwin *et al.* (1995) discuss the 'technocentric' paradigm, with its key assumptions of limitless growth and reliance on science and technology to solve environmental problems and contrast it to an 'ecocentric' paradigm, which recognises there are limits to growth and the carrying capacity of the planet. They argue that a 'sustaincentric' paradigm has the capability to mesh the polar positions of the other two paradigms and that sustainable development represents a compromise between unbridled growth and no growth. There is a strong normative current underlying this discourse, and the aim is to develop concepts that define an ecologically sustainable organisation by using the broader principles of sustainable development. Thus, authors talk about 'ecologically sustainable competitive strategies' (Shrivastava 1995) and prescribe a variety of managerial tools and techniques, such as total quality environmental management, design for environment, life-cycle analysis and eco-efficiency.

Critiques of these new paradigms can be found (see e.g. Banerjee 2003; Newton 2002; Newton and Harte 1997). Much of 'green management' literature is what Newton and Harte (1997) call 'technicist kitsch, laced with liberal doses of evangelical rhetoric'. Authors exhort managers to be 'greener'. Articles are replete with phrases such as 'managers *must* do this' or 'corporations *should* do that' with little or no discussion of how or why it would be beneficial for them to do so. Replacing the current paradigm of 'competition and consumption with co-operation and material restraint' (Newton and Harte 1997: 97) is an enormously difficult task and involves structural changes in the political economy rather than a superficial greening of business. Recent research indicates that even the most 'environmental' of companies ultimately select their environmental strategies based on the financial bottom line (Banerjee 2001).

Although we must teach our students about tools and techniques to reduce the environmental impact of business, it is equally important we brief them about the limitations: eco-efficiency might deliver benefits to the firm but it is not necessarily the same as sustainability. A quick look at the course outlines available at the website of the Organisations and the Natural Environment Division of the Academy of Management[2] will show that almost every course or case study on corporate environmentalism and sustainability focuses on win–win situations. It is assumed that if it is good for the company and the environment, then it is good—sustainable—for all society. A critical analysis of this literature will go beyond win–win situations and will integrate more radical alternatives from theoretical perspectives not based solely on models of strategy and competition.

Students could learn, for example, about the historical context preceding the formation of today's corporation and why the discipline of mainstream management focuses only on efficiency criteria for organisations rather than legitimacy criteria addressing why business firms exist. The Critical Management Studies Interest Group in the Academy of Management offers this type of perspective. Its domain statement questions the primary goal of profitability that governs management of the modern corporation and argues that the sole pursuit of profit does not automatically satisfy broader societal interests. It states: 'We believe that other goals—justice, community, human development and ecological balance—should be brought to bear on the governance of economic activity'.[3]

Thus, if we are to understand the implications of integrating these goals into management theory, we must learn from disciplines other than management. We must move away from defining and matching societal goals to meet corporate objectives of maximum profit. This stakeholder approach to organisations might be a starting point for imagining business firms where the main measure is not about creating enough shareholder value to maintain investor commitment but includes a 'fair distribution of value created to maintain commitment of multiple stakeholders' (Kochan and Rubinstein 2000).

Perhaps a critique of the way 'corporate social responsibility' is being researched and taught in business schools might pave the way for alternatives to emerge. As Kelly (2002: 5) argues, the corporate social responsibility movement has accomplished little over the past 40 years because 'the pressure to get the numbers overrides everything else'. The same rule applies to sustainability issues—a purely market-driven strategy will achieve little because the current system is designed to serve certain interests at the expense of others (Kelly 2002). Understanding how corporate and institutional power shapes global economic systems is a good starting point for a critique. Kelly (2002) argues that we need to democratise structures of power to deliver what she calls 'economic democracy'. To do this we need to craft new structures of voice, decision-making, conflict resolution and accountability. This cannot be left to corporations but requires legal changes to systems that regulate the behaviour of corporations.

2.3.2 Second theme: multidisciplinary perspectives

Sustainability has been studied in a number of disciplines, including economics, sociology, anthropology, development studies, cultural studies and the environmental sciences. The current focus on issues around sustainability as taught in

2 aomweb.pace.edu/one
3 aom.pace.edu/cms

most business schools takes a narrow economic perspective. We have seen above how the focus in the business press shifted from sustainable societies to sustainable corporations. What this sustains is the dominant ideology of profit-maximising firms and does not allow the emergence of alternate, perhaps more radical, forms of organising and governance. A multidisciplinary and critical analysis of the way sustainability is theorised and practised in management will question the universality of the assumptions about nature inherent in the 'green' organisational and economics literatures.

For example, in an analysis of the sociology of nature, Macnaghten and Urry (1998: 2) argue that current discourses of nature and the environment all assume the existence of a singular 'nature' rather than emphasise that it is 'specific social practices, especially of people's dwellings, which produce, reproduce and transform different natures and different values'. They identify three 'doctrines' of conventional thinking about nature. **Environmental realism** refers to the transformation of nature into a 'scientifically researchable environment' where modern Western science can identify environmental problems and articulate appropriate solutions. Social and cultural environmental practices are subsumed by the realities of scientific inquiry. **Environmental idealism** analyses nature by examining the range of 'values' held by people about nature; these environmental values are assumed to be stable and consistent. Macnaghten and Urry (1998) refute the notion of investigating environmental values without contextualising the temporal and spatial arrangements of people's lives. Individual valuation of nature, they argue, is ambiguous, contradictory and context-specific. **Environmental instrumentalism** refers to the responses of individuals and groups to environmental problems that are determined by evaluating individual or collective interests versus environmental trade-offs through cost–benefit analysis or other market-based mechanisms. The assumption here is that the individual subject will weigh the costs and benefits of different behaviours and, once presented with the facts, will understand that it is in their interest to behave in an environmentally responsible manner, believing that governments and public institutions will also act to protect the environment. Elements of these three doctrines can be observed in discourses of sustainable development, whether at the level of international and national policy (as manifested in the policies of the United Nations, World Bank, national governments, the Convention on Biological Diversity, and Agenda 21) or regional and local governments (Banerjee 2003).

A more critical analysis of how nature is theorised and valued in the management discipline will question the universality behind the assumptions of assessing market preferences for nature. As McAfee (1999: 133) argues:

> contrary to the premise of the global economic paradigm there can be no universal metric for comparing and exchanging the real values of nature among different groups of people from different cultures, and with vastly different degrees of political and economic power.

Thus, notions of 'scarcity' and 'limits' in natural resources are also rooted in social systems, where a natural resource becomes a 'cultural, technical and economic appraisal of elements and processes in nature that can be applied to fulfill social objectives and goals through specific material practices' (Harvey 1996: 147). By definition, the political, social and cultural aspects of sustainability need to be explored from a variety of disciplinary perspectives and will provide a deeper and broader understanding of its complexities. Sustainability, despite what the business discipline tells us, is not just about managerial efficiency. A multidisciplinary approach might provide the lens that will enable us to see through the 'greenwash' and relentless corporate public relations campaigns. It will pose some uncomfortable questions (at least for management scholars and students) about how discourses of sustainable development allow global capital to appear to address environmental problems while at the same time maintaining legitimacy for 'business as usual' (Bandy 1996). Such a perspective might allow us to see how the

> sustainability of nature is rewritten as the sustainability of capital; the protection of nature is inverted to be the protection of profits; and the morality of democratic multi-generational planning is transmogrified into the pursuit of competitive advantage in the free market of nature (Bandy 1996: 542).

2.3.3 Third theme: global and local perspectives

The third theme underlying a critical approach to teaching sustainability is the issue of units of analysis. When we discuss questions of sustainability we need to specify whose sustainability we are talking about. This can be at the level of the individual firm (e.g. Why do firms cease to exist? How can firms integrate social and environmental issues into their decision-making?), at the industry level (e.g. Is the fossil fuel energy sector a sustainable industry? What factors determine a sustainable fishing industry?), at the community, regional, societal, national or global level (e.g. What is the current level of well-being in a particular society? How can we ensure that the economic, social and environmental well-being of a community, region or nation is sustained?). Recent conflicts over trade and environmental issues between first- and third-world countries highlights the extent of the so-called North–South divide. A critical analysis of the problematic notion of 'global' sustainability and the policies developed by the United Nations, World Bank and the World Trade Organisation (Banerjee 2003) may reveal the colonial and monocultural dimensions of which countries have the privilege to define what is 'global'. Several postcolonial scholars and development anthropologists have pointed out how development policies over the past 50 years continue to be informed by colonial thought, where developing countries, as a result of the 'structural adjustment' policies of the World Bank and International Monetary Fund, are forced to export their natural resources at low cost to sustain the economies of the developed countries (Escobar 1995; Patnaik 1990; Shiva 1991). At the Rio and Johannesburg Earth Summits as well as at the Kyoto Protocol talks, there were deep divisions between the demands of the first- and third-world countries over attempts to impose global environmental regimes (Hawken 1995). Several representatives of the developing nations argued that these policies could result in new forms of colonial dependences (Escobar 1995). The developed countries, they argue, have created their wealth since the Industrial Revolution through uncontrolled economic growth and production with little regard to environmental impact (or to social issues such as the problem of child labour, which was common in Western countries during this period) (Patnaik 1990). How are the developing countries expected to 'catch up' without the corresponding pollution effects, especially if 'greener' technologies are not shared?

Discourses of global sustainability need to be unpacked, because, as some scholars argue, these are attempts to socialise environmental costs 'globally' (McAfee 1999). This assumes equal responsibility for environmental degradation while obscuring significant differences and inequities in resource utilisation between countries. Sustainability of local cultures, especially peasant cultures, is not addressed; instead, discourses of sustainable development tend to privilege Western notions of environmentalism and conservation. Espoused as a solution to the environmental ills facing the planet, 'global' environmentalism remains firmly rooted in the tradition of Western economic thought and de-historicises and marginalises the environmental traditions of non-Western cultures (Bandy 1996; Shiva 1991). Although environmental problems such as pollution do not recognise national or regional boundaries, the 'global' solutions advocated by the industrialised countries perpetuate the dependency relations of colonialism. Images of polluted third-world cities with their 'teeming millions' abound in the media without acknowledgement of the corresponding responsibility of industrialised countries which consume 80% of the world's aluminum, paper, iron and steel, 75% of the world's energy, 75% of its fish resources, 70% of its ozone-destroying CFCs (chlorofluorocarbons) and 61% of its meat (Renner 1997). The poorer regions of the world destroy or export their natural resources to meet the demands of the richer nations or to meet debt-servicing needs arising from the 'austerity' measures dictated by the World Bank. It is ironic to the point of absurdity that the poorer countries of the world have to be 'austere' in their development while the richer nations continue to enjoy standards of living that are dependent on the 'austerity' measures of the poorer nations. The dangers of environmental destruction are not egalitarian—the rural poor who depend on the land for survival suffer disproportionately. Neither are the benefits of environmental protection equally distributed: protection measures continue to be dictated by the industrialised countries, often at the expense of local rural communities (Escobar 1995; Shiva 1991).

Radical revisioning of the structures that govern corporate behaviour need to occur at the institutional and societal levels for the so-called stakeholder corporation to move from rhetoric to reality. Alternative development paths for the poorer countries have been discussed at various international forums by a plethora of NGOs, community organisations, scientists and academics. Redclift (1987) describes one such model, a proposal developed to address imbalances in the Latin American economy. Aspects of this model include: utilising natural resources to generate local employment while requiring few imported inputs; restricting the production and importation of unnecessary goods while stimulating the supply of basic goods such as housing, food, water and clothing; increasing the labour expended in rural conservation; and providing environmental management training to professional groups. This model could deliver economic growth without the accompanying colonial dependency that has plagued much of Latin American and Asian society

(Redclift 1987). However, this is an exceptionally difficult task to achieve, requiring large amounts of external assistance and political and social will. It is easy to dismiss these alternative models as being hopelessly utopian, but there is much to be gained by opening up these avenues for discussion in the classrooms in which our future managers are trained.

2.4 Conclusions

I have raised several problematic issues about the concept of sustainability and the limited way it is currently being taught in business schools. I certainly do not pretend to have all the answers—in fact, I urge all of us as critical scholars and students to be suspicious of glib answers and of the 'gurus' that sell easy solutions to sustainability. What I have tried to do is raise a few questions (this, after all, is the information age, where we have too many answers and perhaps not the right questions) that can inform how we can teach sustainability from a critical perspective, that challenge existing ways of thinking and stimulate debate among our students.

Perhaps some of the issues raised by Paul Adler (CMSIG 2002) and members of the Critical Management Studies Interest Group at the Academy of Management—in light of the recent corporate scandals that have seen the demise of high-profile self-proclaimed 'sustainable' and 'citizen' corporations—might serve as a starting point. In a statement issued to the Academy, the Critical Management Studies Interest Group made the following observations (CMSIG 2002):

> Management academics need to ensure that future managers and accounting professionals receive ethical training as rigorous as that which society demands of its professionals in every other field.

> Classrooms should not become pulpits for ideological celebration of the invisible hand of the market and disdain for government. As part of the university, we should foster energetic debate on the appropriate roles of the market and regulation, but in all too many institutions the other side of this debate has progressively disappeared . . . We have thus helped create a generation of managers many of whom see government regulation as an unwelcome—and well nigh illegitimate—intrusion into the world of business.

> We should be fulfilling our highest mission of helping students acquire the skills needed to participate in ongoing debates on the direction of our society. Many business schools have seen their mission as satisfying their key stakeholders' needs—specifically: to satisfy the needs of business for well-trained managers. But as part of the university, we are accountable to a broader set of stakeholders too. And our students graduate not merely as managers, but as citizens of our polity and as members of their communities.

Some specific suggestions made by this group included strengthening ethics courses in business school programmes by integrating ethical issues into every course; developing required courses on the history of business, government and society in an international context; and broadening the disciplinary range. The future will show if these issues do indeed become integrated into the curriculum of business schools. Or do we, as educators, believe that the sustainability of business schools can be divorced from the sustainability of the society in which they operate?

References

Academy of Management Review (1995) 'Ecologically Sustainable Organisations', *Academy of Management Review* 20.4 (Special Issue): 873-1,089.

Bandy, J. (1996) 'Managing the Other of Nature: Sustainability, Spectacle, and Global Regimes of Capital in Ecotourism', *Public Culture* 8.3: 539-66.

Banerjee, S.B. (2001) 'Managerial Perceptions of Corporate Environmentalism: Interpretations from Industry and Strategic Implications for Organizations', *Journal of Management Studies* 38.4: 489-513.

—— (2002) 'Organizational Strategies for Sustainable Development: Developing a Research Agenda for the New Millennium', *Australian Journal of Management* 27.2: 105-17.

—— (2003) 'Who Sustains Whose Development? Sustainable Development and the Reinvention of Nature', *Organization Studies* 24.3: 143-80.

CMSIG (Critical Management Studies Interest Group) (2002) aom.pace.edu/cms.

Crane, A. (2000) 'Corporate Greening as Amoralisation', *Organization Studies* 21.4: 673-96.

Crossett, B. (1998) 'More Consuming More and the Rich Much More', *New York Times*, 13 September 1998: 13.

Dow Jones (2000) *Sustainability Indexes*, www.sustainability-index.com.

Elkington, J. (1999) *Cannibals with Forks: The Triple Bottom Line of 21st Century Business* (Oxford, UK: Capstone Publishing).

Entine, J. (1995) 'Rain-forest Chic', *Toronto Globe & Mail Report on Business*, 21 October 1995: 41-52.

Escobar, A. (1995) *Encountering Development: The Making and Unmaking of the Third World, 1945-1992* (Princeton, NJ: Princeton University Press).

Esteva, G. (1992) 'Development', in W. Sachs (ed.), *The Development Dictionary* (London: Zed Books): 6-25.

Fineman, S. (1996) 'Emotional Subtexts in Corporate Greening', *Organization Studies* 17.3: 479-500.

Gladwin, T.N., J.J. Kennelly and T.-S. Krause (1995) 'Shifting Paradigms for Sustainable Development: Implications for Management Theory and Research', *Academy of Management Review* 20.4: 874-907.

Goldsmith, E. (1997) 'Development as Colonialism', *The Ecologist* 27.2: 60-79.

Guha, R., and J. Martinez-Alier (1997) *Varieties of Environmentalism* (London: Earthscan Publications).

Hart, S. (1997) 'Beyond Greening: Strategies for a Sustainable World', *Harvard Business Review*, January–February 1997: 67-76.

Harvey, D. (1996) *Justice, Nature and the Geography of Difference* (Oxford, UK: Basil Blackwell).

Hawken, P. (1995) *The Ecology of Commerce: A Declaration of Sustainability* (London: Phoenix).

Holmberg, J., and R. Sandbrook (1992) 'Sustainable Development: What Is To Be Done?', in J. Holmberg (ed.), *Policies for a Small Planet* (London: Earthscan Publications).

Kelly, M. (2002) 'The Next Step for CSR: Building Economic Democracy', *Business Ethics* 16.3 (Summer 2002): 2-7.

Kirkby, J., P. O'Keefe and L. Timberlake (1995) *Sustainable Development* (London: Earthscan Publications).

Kochan, T., and S. Rubinstein (2000) 'Toward a Stakeholder Theory of the Firm: The Saturn Partnership', *Organization Science* 11.4: 367-86.

Long Range Planning (1992) 'Strategic Management of the Environment', *Long Range Planning* 25.4 (Special Issue): 3-122.

McAfee, K. (1999) 'Selling Nature to Save It? Biodiversity and Green Developmentalism', *Environment and Planning D: Society and Space* 17.2: 133-54.

Macnaghten, P., and J. Urry (1998) *Contested Natures* (London: Sage).

Martinez-Alier, J. (1987) *Ecological Economics: Energy, Environment and Society* (Oxford, UK: Basil Blackwell).

Newton, T. (2002) 'Creating the New Ecological Order? Elias and Actor-network Theory', *Academy of Management Review* 27.4: 523-40.

—— and G. Harte (1997) 'Green Business: Technicist Kitsch?', *Journal of Management Studies* 34.1: 75-98.

Patnaik, P. (1990) *Whatever Happened To Imperialism? and Other Essays* (New Delhi: Tulika).

Pearce, D.W., A. Markandya and E.B. Barbier (1989) *Blueprint for a Green Economy* (London: Earthscan Publications).

Petulla, J.M. (1980) *American Environmentalism: Values, Tactics, Priorities* (College Station, TX: Texas A&M University Press).

Purser, R.E., C. Park and A. Montuori (1995) 'Limits to Anthropocentrism: Toward an Eco-centric Organisation Paradigm?', *Academy of Management Review* 20.4: 1,053-89.

Renner, M. (1997) *Fighting for Survival: Environmental Decline, Social Conflict and the New Age of Insecurity* (London: Earthscan Publications).

Redclift, M. (1987) *Sustainable Development: Exploring the Contradictions* (London: Methuen).

Rifkin, J. (1999) *The Biotech Century: How Genetic Commerce Will Change The World* (London: Phoenix).

Rosen, H. (1995) 'The Evil Empire: The Real Scoop on Ben & Jerry's Crunchy Capitalism', *The New Republic*, 11 September 1995: 22-25.

Schot, J., E. Brand and K. Fischer (1997) 'The Greening of Industry or a Sustainable Future: Building an International Research Agenda', *Business and the Environment* 6: 153-62.

Shiva, V. (1991) *The Violence of the Green Revolution: Third World Agriculture, Ecology and Politics* (London: Zed Books).

Shrivastava, P.(1995) 'The Role of Corporations in Achieving Ecological Sustainability', *Academy of Management Review* 20.4: 936-60.

Visvanathan, S. (1991) 'Mrs Brundtland's Disenchanted Cosmos', *Alternatives* 16.3: 377-84.

Walley, N., and B. Whitehead (1993) 'It's Not Easy Being Green', *Harvard Business Review* 72.3: 36-44.

Waters, M. (1995) *Globalisation* (London: Routledge).

WCED (World Commission for Economic Development) (1987) *Our Common Future* (The Brundtland Report; New York: Oxford University Press).

Welford, R. (1997) *Hijacking Environmentalism: Corporate Responses to Sustainable Development* (London: Earthscan Publications).

Westley, F., and H. Vredenburg (1996) 'Sustainability and the Corporation: Criteria for Aligning Economic Practice with Environmental Protection', *Journal of Management Inquiry* 5.2: 104-19.

3

Can publicly traded companies achieve environmentally and socially sustainable operation?

Tom P. Abeles

Sagacity Inc., USA

3.1 Prologue

When Mother Nature created humans, she took a chance. Intelligence is not necessarily a survival characteristic.

When we examine the actions taken by individuals, organisations, and corporations we need to understand their impact over both space and time. Dams for flood control, power and water use later prove harmful to fish populations. Computers were once thought limited in application, but are now ubiquitous. Conservation concepts once opposed as destructive to businesses are now embraced as profit centres. Change comes hard, particularly to complex systems such as corporations and humans.

Corporations are given life by the state, which also defines, to some extent, the scope of operation. And the state has the ability to end the corporation's life or modify it, as was the situation with England's presence in India through the East India Company. Regulations, taxes and similar actions comprise other control measures. Like other members of society, the corporation seeks to optimise conditions for its own benefit. Often it seeks such benefits with the petulance of a spoiled child; and and at other times with intimidation, given the size and wealth of some.

In fact, corporations, in many ways, have taken advantage of the fact that nations, like estranged parents, have focused so much on their own internal differences that they have neglected to consider the child left to grow on its own. Given a global economy and the transnational nature of corporations, it is not clear whether governments can achieve sufficient harmony to regain control.

Additionally, one must remember that corporations, as organisms, exist within a larger social and environmental context. Their footprints on Earth are not measured just by the waste that they produce or the natural resources that they consume. Neither of these, in and of itself, is necessarily a useful measure of sustainability when considered only within the boundaries of the corporation, or even the local community in which the business might exist. Small actions taken at one location may and do have dynamic and noticeable affects on the other side of the world. A chemical plant in one country may dispose of its by-products outside of that state, and its products may be distributed globally.

Today, few businesses convert their ideas from raw materials to finished product, whether services or manufacturing, and few have responsibility for all materials and by-products created along this path. Germany's 'green' manufacturing process begins to take this into account, but we are only just starting to understand the complex webs, as knowledge grows over time and the systems evolve. The issue becomes even more difficult as the process for manufacturing and materials used or discarded can change almost overnight.

As an example, rope manufacturers used to extract fibre from sisal and then dispose of the pulp. Today, the pharmaceuticals in this 'waste-stream' far outweigh the value of the rope produced. In contrast, open-pit mining has left large scars across the landscape, with no alternatives for use. Whereas these examples are easily identified, issues such as global warming are more subtle and uncertain. The 'business' of modelling global warming is a growth industry. Groups on both sides compete for funds to validate their respective models, leaving great uncertainty over whether this phenomenon is part of a natural cycle, whether human intervention is the major cause, or some combination of the two.

Nature's inherent rules, 'red in tooth and claw', determine whether individuals or species survive, evolve or are replaced. Nature moves inexorably forward, seemingly indifferent to a singularity in event space or the sustainability of one species, homo sapiens. Humans have a very short history on Earth—thus far a fraction of the time that dinosaurs prevailed. Human constructs such as cities and corporations have even shorter histories.

Peter Ward, in *Future Evolution* (2001), suggests that human ingenuity will prevent humans from becoming extinct. But there is no guarantee in what form humans will evolve, or what type of world will be passed on. Thus, the concerns that humans and their creations—corporations—have to face include the consequences of irreversible actions. Could the very legal structure that gave birth to and that sustains corporations be one of those factors that is a fundamental issue and precipitates the problems?

Corporations exist within a multidimensional construct, bound by the rules of nature and the laws of humans. At present, we think we understand the laws of humans. Yet we really do not, as evidenced by the kaleidoscope of evolving laws within countries and across national boundaries designed, on the one hand, to enhance the rights and opportunities of the creation of humankind, the corporation, and at the same time to attempt to temper those activities for the public good. Like King Midas, we are cursed with the blessing and the anguish.

Steve Keen (2001: xiii), one of a growing number of 'heterodox' economists, said:

> Worse still, over the past 30 years, politicians and bureaucrats the world over have come to regard economic theory as the sole source of wisdom about the manner in which a modern society should be governed. The World has been remade in the economist's image.

Thus, relations between countries and 'peoples' have been recast in economic terms, and the determination of the directions of countries has been defined by current economic thought. The World Trade Organisation (WTO) has taken this thinking one step further and has placed the corporation and its demands as the central engine of progress—economic progress—in many ways displacing the idea of political bodies, such as countries, or smaller subdivisions within these states as determinants of a population's future.

The changes towards the end of the 20th century, which subsequently set a corporation's course as one that must be responsive to 'shareholder value', in turn set a determinant course for the planet and its inhabitants in the hands of those who control the stocks, almost to the exclusion of the voice of the public at the voting booth regardless of the form of government within a country. Not only are the employees within a corporation subject to the whimsy of shareholder value but so too are persons whose lives are touched, globally, by the actions of multi-national and transnational corporations.

3.2 Thinking about the corporation

Ideas do have consequences.

Marjorie Kelly 2001, in *The Divine Right of Capital*

In this context the concepts of time and space remain less than fully appreciated. Space is the easier to comprehend, since we are familiar with the problems of cross-border cultural issues in a global society. What has not been clearly understood, though, is the time dimension. This is particularly true in a digital age that tends to give us both time and space compression.

There is the story of the forester who sent his son on a mission of several years. Each year the forester continued to cut down the trees around his home. When the son returned, he was amazed to find wide, empty fields surrounding the home. The father, on the other hand, saw very little difference in the external environment because he was part of the evolving change.

Has our creation, the corporation, as it exists today, outlived its usefulness? If we think about humans, we have different sets of rules and expectations for our 'youth', where consequences for violating social norms are often forgiven as part of a learning process; but, once past a certain age, the rules change and the consequences for violating the public trust involve penalties. Even as youths, consequences often cannot be avoided both by the child and by the parents. Yet stockholders today often are removed both from oversight responsibilities and from consequences, except for a loss of equity. The penalty for lack of oversight for a corporate transgression stops at the border.

With its charter from the Crown of the time, the East India Company not only traded with India but also was effectively the ruler of the subcontinent. Eventually, for complex reasons, the Crown took back its charter and control of the colony. The question that is never asked today is whether or not the corporation, in its current embodiment, especially in a global society, has outlived its usefulness. A corporation is a child of the government. Its form, tax status and even its charter are granted by governments.

We have seen corporations fail financially and have seen these charters 'go dark'. However, we have seen corporations thrive and exercise many of the same rights and privileges that are afforded individuals, as citizens. And, in a global environment, the ability of the corporation to amass great wealth and carry out business, internationally, often gives it more power and influence than a country and, additionally, the ability to override the influence of the citizens within a country.

In the USA, the collapse of Enron, once the seventh-largest firm on the New York Stock Exchange, and its accounting and consulting firm, Arthur Andersen, suggests, at a minimum, the need to examine the balance between regulation and the entrepreneurial spirit of youth. The growing concern about the influence of transnational corporations raises questions, not about being able to facilitate the conduct of international business but about the balance between corporations and civil society, particularly in countries where the gross national product severely tilts the negotiating table in favour of corporates.

Additionally, the growing concern over employee rights and vested interests in the corporation, coupled with the balance between equity and stockholder returns, is raising issues that did not loom as large in the past as they do today. Time can change how citizens view their institutions and what is considered best for the political will. The USA faced these issues, in part, when it first passed antitrust legislation. This was an attempt to bring a recalcitrant child under some vestige of control. The recent confrontation between the USA and Microsoft Corporation has, in part, caused this issue to be revisited and has seen efforts to seek a specific accommodation without broaching the larger issues of corporations in general. Global ramifications were not on the agenda.

The issues before us seem to transcend the traditional approach to the corporate sector—regulatory changes and independent oversight. It seems to call for a refocusing of the purpose of the corporate body more on becoming a good citizen, since it demands the rights and privileges of citizenship. It also requires a repositioning of the investor, who, up to the present time, has been passive, demanding and unresponsive to the larger corporate vision except as it might affect the expected return on investment. This is particularly important in today's environment where stock values are not congruent with the hard assets but depend heavily on the value attributed to the intellectual capital of the employees.

Where have rights, privileges, rewards and responsibilities fallen in the past between stockholders, employees and the public at large? Like the forester cutting trees, has the landscape changed, the context evolved? Are the patches, compromises and negotiations mere palliatives, reducing the pain without addressing the underlying problems?

Most people forget that Adam Smith wrote two volumes. The first, and often overlooked, volume, *The Theory of Moral Sentiments* (1759), the ethical basis of his work, lays the foundation. It represents the 'spirit of the law', the larger canvas on which we paint. His *Wealth of Nations* (1776) has been considered the foundation of today's ideas about the free-market economy. It is like the outlines within which we apply paint. Today, these lines have become the dominant focus. How close can we paint without colouring outside of the lines? How clever can we get by repositioning these lines without destroying the picture, never mind the larger canvas? Since the state granted life to corporations to serve a public good, perhaps it is time to revisit this contract, regarding both the purpose of the corporation and its underlying values.

Marjorie Kelly's critical insight, expressed in her book *The Divine Right of Capital* (2001), is that there needs to be a major correction in the relationship between the owners of stock in a corporation and the distribution of rewards from corporate growth and success. Allan Kennedy discussed similar issues, but not, in my opinion, with the same clarity and vision as Kelly, in his volume, *The End of Shareholder Value* (2001). Both authors conclude that the capital stock does not always represent the total investment in the company, and the current value of the enterprise is better distributed across the invested capital and the added value from the contributions of the employees, as reflected in the corporate book value against the initial capital invested, regardless of how the stock has appreciated in the marketplace.

Kennedy is more concerned with the abuse that arose in the 1980s when investment bankers were able to convince the public that the total value of the company should be distributed among the traded shares and thus provided control of the assets by these shares, leading to the leveraged buy-out problems that confronted the capital markets. Kelly takes a much broader and more far-reaching view when she points out that, as companies grow, the value of the initially invested capital represents a decreasing portion of the total corporate net worth. This difference in value is the equity created by the employees.

The current investor-driven corporations are obliged, or almost mandated, to generate the appearance of growth so that the investors' portfolios reflect an appreciated or future value of the stock, in many cases almost separate from the value of the company based on assets or earnings. At one time a 10:1 price–earnings ratio seemed reasonable. Today the ratio can be ten times this amount, a value that could never yield a reasonable return on earnings alone. Thus the market has been effectively decoupled, being driven purely by speculation and not on the underlying value; rather, the presumption is that the company will not collapse and be removed from the trading floor.

The other issue, in an era of intellectual capital, is the fact that the survival and profitability of the firms depend on the knowledge of the employees—those who often perceive themselves as being expendable as companies strive for lowered costs of operations—yet the appreciation created internally is not valued equally when weighted against the initial capital investment, separate from the price of the stock in the market.

The argument might be moot if there were no examples of corporations who take such concerns seriously. Kelly cites several examples regarding companies both inside and outside the USA. These corporations provide reasonable returns both to the invested capital and to the increased capital basis created by the employees.

Today, the evaluations of corporations are contradictory. On the one hand, the investors want the sense that the pricing reflects some reasonable value and is not hanging on a 'skyhook', like the cartoon character Wile E. Coyote suspended over a canyon. On the other hand, investors—and, hence, management—want to contain the largest cost factor in knowledge companies: labour (i.e. the employees, who are credited with creating the value), representing corporate intellectual capital.

The analysis is made even more difficult because of the cognitive dissonance that is created between theory and praxis. Today, when many corporations have a market valuation that is several multiples of its hard assets, accountants are busy developing rationales such as 'intellectual capital', or the value provided by the knowledge workers. At the same time, corporations, driven by Wall Street demands for profitability, are trying to strip out costs because growth cannot continue to increase the spread between income and overheads. This, of course, results in staff reduction, removing the very assets that accountants are using to claim the spread between market valuation and hard assets.

Management and financial analysts are trying to explain the distribution of income by claiming that corporations are not entities but a nexus of contracts between parties, particularly stockholders, knowledge workers and management, where accounting practices mask compensation, such as salaries, bonuses and stock options for management and creative knowledge workers, which then becomes an incentive above base compensation, distorting the earnings picture. Not only does this increase the separation between all vested parties but also it confuses the picture of the corporation and the larger, often global, community.

Essentially, the actuarial analysis, used as a means to rationalise stockholder values and distribution of returns between stockholders and employees, clouds the responsibility of the corporation and the individual employees for the actions of the enterprise in financial transactions and with regard to responsibility for impact on the larger social and biophysical and physical environment, much of which is either not monetised or does not appear directly in cash flow analysis.

As Kelly (2001) points out, the actual value of stockholder investments diminishes as corporations grow. Looking at the larger stock market, the invested capital has actually decreased as corporations have bought back their equities. Outside the USA, stockholder influence is tempered by that of other participants on corporate boards; and the larger community, through regulation, often has greater influence on the behaviour of corporations. For example, in Germany labour is strongly represented, and recent environmental regulations make manufacturers responsible for their materials 'from cradle to grave'. In England, pension funds are required to have a percentage of their portfolios vested in socially and environmentally screened investments.

Paul Hawken, and Amory and Hunter Lovins have written a volume, *Natural Capitalism* (1999), in which they suggest ways in which companies can turn environmental problems into profit centres or can create business opportunities from better resource management or the production of environmentally beneficial products and services. Hawken *et al.* attempt to show why being 'environmentally friendly' creates potentially higher returns than doing 'business as usual'. Kenneth Lux, in his presentation to the International Society for Ecological Economics, pointed out that as long as the company is driven by shareholder demands this will only be a temporary approach. Lux also states that, on questioning, Hawken admits that the environmental shift avoids major structural issues that need changing (such as those suggested by Kelly) but that corporations and the 'market' are not ready to confront these larger issues.[1]

John Elkington, in *Cannibals with Forks* (1998), sets forth the concept of the 'triple bottom line' for sustainable business—that is, socially responsible, environmentally sound and economically viable business. In each of these models, the corporation is still seen as an entity separate from the larger environment—biophysical, physical and socioeconomic. The organism lives for the investors or stockholders, and its measure of success is the earnings and the increased value of equity in the marketplace. It may treat employees well and provide grants and financial support to the larger community, but the corporation is designed to extract wealth from the community. This may be in dividends for stockholders or profits from sales in the area or, perhaps, the extraction of resources in a manner that, having depleted them, leaves the community like diners with an empty plate at the dinner table.

At one time there was a movement where investors selected certain companies for their portfolios either because they appreciated the social and environmental values represented or they wanted access to stockholders' meetings to protest issues such as the environment or social inequities. The movement was strongly questioned, particularly by fund managers for whom the primary obligation was to increase the value of their portfolios for investors. This led to a focus on whether one could find 'green' investments that would equal or outperform the market and eventually to funds in which portfolios were labelled as being environmentally or socially screened. A number of screening indices were created, including the venerable Dow Jones Social Group Index (DJSGI) and the London FTSE's FTSE4Good.

Most of these indices supposedly develop their screening criteria independent of the stock market and then seek to see how the companies rank with respect to each other from a 'screened' perspective and how this correlates with market performance. The problems with these indices are manifold, including questions over what is to be measured, how it is to be measured and how information is to be collected. But, in the end, the measure has to do with its ability to reach some correlation with the market valuation of the stock, making investment performance the primary arbiter of the corporation's position in the global economy.

If one follows markets, their ebb and flow over time, one wonders how these 'screening' variables change with the valuations. In other words, does the reverse hold? Do companies really become better citizens or lose ground in the same manner in which their stocks change, or do they float up and down with all stocks as the economic tide shifts, and what does this imply?

---

1 Personal communication with the author.

The collapse of Enron is a good example. Analysis prior to the implosion painted the corporation as forward-thinking, with creative management as well as being a corporation that was 'doing well by doing good'. The postmortem revealed not only that the diagnosis was seriously flawed but also that those carrying out the examination were unable to detect the signs of disease.

One senses that the flaws are more fundamental than those that were internal to Enron and lie not merely with the actuarial practices but are to be found within the heart of the Academy—with those responsible for providing the foundational knowledge to those who will eventually be the 'captains of industry'.

3.3 The finite planet Earth

It is not every truth that sounds so sweet as a birdsong, not every discovery that is welcomed among the occult, not every light that is approved from within the shadows.

Philip Kerr 1992, *A Philosophical Investigation*

David Gelernter, in his volume *1939: The Lost World of the Fair* (1996), points out that at the end of World War II every technological wonder envisioned at that pre-war event was realised and even exceeded. Yet, if we look at the condition of the planet and its inhabitants, the big issues have not been conquered, some new problems have been added and others have been exacerbated. One would not deny the benefits of technology advancements, but many of these have had unintended consequences, others have presented different opportunities from those anticipated and still others, in the long run, might prove less beneficial than hoped. It is this last issue that is of interest here. Technology provides humans with a strange lever, one that not only can impact on the biophysical and physical world but one that can make that impact felt more quickly. A message that took months to cross the Atlantic now travels globally in fractions of a second, from desktop to desktop. Thus, human actions can precipitate large changes at a distance and almost at the speed of light.

The benefits in the case of responding to natural disasters can be gratifying; but the fiscal *tsunami* that hit Asia and Mexico as a result of investor whimsy, coupled with international money movements, proved a frightening experience. Enterprises and national economies, driven like ships caught in a gale on the high seas, are abandoned or left for governments to rescue. This often results in the fiscal stress being shifted to the lower and middle classes, the least able to tolerate such burdens. Regardless of whether these failed enterprises were deemed socially and environmentally responsible, the dispassionate capital markets, unfettered by such geopolitical or moral boundaries, have no mandates to exhibit fiscal compassion.

Thus, one of the first lessons to be gleaned here is that corporations in a global economy may be driven by value systems that are not globally congruent, and their fate can be determined by the winds of fiscal whimsy. The problems facing planet Earth are manifest and amplified by technology, but the underlying causes are not ones that yield readily to technological solutions: 'technologies are neither the naïve product of disinterested science nor the deterministic bearers of social process. They are shaped by existing social relations' (Fortier 2001).

Public corporations, investors in which are afforded a status different to other stakeholders, are caught in the middle, whether we look at the enterprise as a separate entity or as a nexus of contracts between a variety of parties, each with its own agenda. Employees, communities in which corporations have a presence and those who are beneficiaries of the products and services need to find common ground. Investors who are moved by whim to acquire or sell equities have no such need, but currently exert disproportionate influence on the direction and impact of the business. One entrepreneur, who took his company public, has lamented that he now has less control over his business.

Thus we are faced with a time–space problem. If, like a mayfly, we see the world through a short window of time then human actions may not appear to cause change, good or bad, and we can concentrate on short-term benefits to ourselves. However, if, like a redwood tree, we view human actions over a larger time-plane then we might raise issues of concern.

Corporations, like computers, are human constructs. Although we often discuss environmental impact statements for physical projects, we have never conducted a social or environmental impact for the establishment of a corporation. Although we have identified biology gone awry, and we worry about genetic experiments loosed on the planet, we do not seem to have questioned whether a similar case might apply to a socially constructed organism. We construct corrals in the form of laws, but even global attempts at containment, such as those of the WTO, have never seriously addressed the larger issue of transnational corporations—ones that roam freely, grazing the fiscal high grounds

In Ray Kurzweil's recent, and controversial, volume, *The Age of Spiritual Machines* (2000), he suggests that machines will transcend human 'intelligence'. In a voice of concern, David Korten has cogently raised similar issues regarding socially constructed 'beings' in his volume *When Corporations Rule the World* (2000). Although Kurzweil's efforts, focusing on technology, may be written off as speculative, bordering on science fiction, his ideas carry currency within the scientific and philosophical communities. Korten's analysis, juxtaposed with work by others, also suggest that his ideas cannot be easily dismissed, particularly in light of the recent protests surrounding the WTO.

What the recent confrontation between the US government and Microsoft has shown, though, is that it is difficult to conceive of containment strategies for socially constructed creatures whose fiscal resources exceed that of many countries. And it becomes obvious that many other smaller species can thrive adumbrated by a few mega fauna. One might wonder if the science fiction story of the Borg, in Star Trek,[2] might not be prescient.[3]

---

2 Star Trek is a trademark of Paramount Pictures.
3 The Borg 'assimilates' individuals of other species, incorporating their bodies and knowledge into the 'Borg collective', destroying the individualities of those assimilated.

3.4 Back to the future

A large majority of this year's college graduates report that their professors tell them there are no clear and uniform standards of right and wrong . . . In light of the issues about contemporary business ethics generated by the Enron scandal, such opinions raise serious doubt about how well our colleges are doing their job to shape the ethical sensibilities of their students.

National Association of Scholars (NAS) 2002, in *Ethics, Enron and American Higher Education*

Robert Sternberg, a psychologist at Yale University, recently edited a volume, *Why Smart People Can Be So Stupid* (2002), wherein he and his colleagues try to articulate how highly intelligent and degreed individuals can carry out acts ranging from the Nazi atrocities to the frauds perpetrated recently on Wall Street. Although the reasons are complex, Sternberg has identified some critical characteristics of the entrepreneurs heading the corporate leadership.

3.4.1 The belief in invulnerability

'Too big to fail' is a familiar term on the 'Street'. White-collar crimes, globally, committed on the 'Street' carry almost no penalty compared with those felonies committed 'on the street' on much smaller scales and with a far narrower impact.

The current mood in the USA is to 'carry a big stick', to increase the penalties, increase the risk and thus deter corporate fiscal abuses. No one appears to be asking whether there might not exist 'carrots' that would act as drivers for both the entrepreneur and the corporation. The current pain-driven approach lacks both the insight and the wisdom that might be offered from a different approach. It may represent the lack of the creative synthesis advocated by Sternberg.

3.4.2 A substantive sense of omniscience

Armed with an international legal staff and the ability to access seats of political power, multinational corporations have come to believe that their myths are the ones that are needed to provide the guiding principles, globally. Political influence on environmental issues is a paradigmatic example in the USA.

Corporations and those that head them have a finely tuned and singular vision that they have sold to the public at large through a simple, well-defined mantra. In contrast, the larger public is divided on its vision or set of values that could accrue from a revised vision of a mature corporation. Rather than seeing this diversity as a strength, as forming a multiple, flexible and negotiable platform that could be mixed and matched on an individual corporate basis, its diffuse nature has been internally divisive. It is a vision that is cohesive only to the extent that there is a common 'enemy'.

The recent protests at the WTO meetings and at similar summits has awakened governments to the concerns but has shifted the focus from direct negotiations with the corporations to an indirect approach through governmental representation. In many ways, these have had less lasting impact than the direct approach through the stock markets, but, in all cases, internal dissonance reduces both the force and the focus of the argument, returning the solution to shoring up a system in need of restructuring.

3.4.3 Omnipotence as a foundational belief

The case of the US government versus Microsoft over Microsoft's Windows® operating system is, perhaps, a paradigmatic example. The move to weaken antitrust laws in the USA while the multinationals easily transcend political boundaries has led entrepreneur and arbitrageur George Soros to publicly demand governmental action on an international scale to regulate the flow of money and wrest the global fiscal landscape from an almost Wild West mentality of the international investment banking community.

Some insightful observers have pointed out that these characteristics are the very elements that have allowed entrepreneurs to turn an idea into an international success. But these may not be the critical or untempered values that one needs within a mature business. Nor may these be the values that are important for the larger society and the environment.

The USA has gone from corduroy roads to transcontinental rail to global air transport in less than 200 years. In the same period, medicine has progressed from quack remedies to the advanced technology of hearts regulated by microchips. Perhaps it is time that the corporation realises that it has passed puberty. Perhaps society, as it does in its legal system, must recognise when a corporate 'youth' needs to be treated as an 'adult' and that the rules need to be written and enforced differently, particularly in a global environment.

Sternberg (2002) believes that wisdom can be taught. His efforts in this arena are in the primary schools and not where he resides, in the post-secondary education community. In the USA, K-6 institutions integrate all subjects within a single classroom. Across the K-12 system, there are programmes being developed based on the demonstrated competency of students.

The opportunity lies within these institutions and not in the arena of post-secondary education, where students arrive with different expectations and the programme separates knowledge into short, often disconnected, modules or courses. Here the objective is to pass and obtain credit for these units separately, and integration, if any, is left for students to synthesise.

If knowledge and wisdom can be compartmentalised as suggested by the post-secondary education experience, then we can take a reductionist approach to the materials. It is the process that is more telling than the content. It is much like giving a person several medicines and ignoring the potential for drug interactions that can either be positive or have fatal consequences. In the case of academic knowledge and disciplines, without some integrative process the knowledge, as on research campuses, is parsed into ontological cubicles in both the corporate and the governmental world—the familiar silos. Thus, many of the issues surrounding social and environmental concerns will remain unresolved while appearing to satisfy the needs of the community at large.

In the same way that the Academy can compartmentalise and avoid issues, the graduates of the institutions can move into their postgraduate occupations by, essentially, 'colouring within the lines'. Unlike Einstein and his colleagues who struggled with the moral issue of revealing to the US government the potential to create the atomic bomb, few today have to grapple with such issues of conscience. Like Tennyson's horsemen, they ride forth, daily, repeatedly, 'theirs not to reason why'.[4]

What if the goal of a corporation were not to maximise quarterly profits as defined by the current shareholder mantra, or what if the 'profits' had different metrics such as improved local quality of life or increased life-cycle costing for a product line? What if employee ownership were of higher benefit than a high price–earnings ratio?

3.5 Epilogue

> The 'bottom line' of profit as the constantly scrutinised criterion of success in the unregulated marketplace is a major quantity that enslaves the corporate sector and prevents the transition of most companies to a condition of freedom and creativity . . . This suggests that the present business practice, with its rigid focus on maintaining constant high profits, has resulted in severe proneness to the economic equivalent of sudden cardiac arrest.
>
> Brian Goodwin 2000

Over 30 years ago, George Land published a small volume, *Grow or Die* (1986), which presaged the interest in chaos and complexity in the management community. His simple thesis, regarding organisms, biological and socially created, was that they needed to grow continually. The key point, though, was that this growth must be transformative. In complexity theory, we would say that there must be bifurcations where the type and quality of the growth take a path different from that currently pursued. Stability of heart rhythm, as the medical community has shown, is a forerunner of cardiac arrest; and continual growth without transformation follows a path epitomised by cancer's rampant path.

Land's model was the simple sigmoid growth curve, where failure to transform leads to a return to a period where the organism sensed growth. In effect, a failure to make a transition to a new form of growth yields a path that resembles a simple hysteresis loop that we see in magnetic materials (see Fig. 3.1). In other words, when the upper level of the growth curve is reached (the slope approaching zero) we are at a decision point. If we cannot make the leap or transformation to a new growth curve, we return to a point on the rapidly rising slope of the old curve to give us the illusion of growth, but without the transformation.

Kelly and Kennedy and many of those whom they reference (see Kelly 2001; Kennedy 2001) sense that we are at such a decision point in the evolution of

---

4 From the poem, 'The Charge of the Light Brigade'.

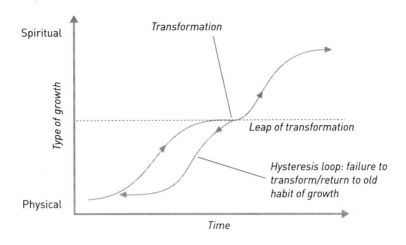

Figure 3.1 A hysteresis loop observed in a failure to make a leap of transformation

corporations. Yet those such as Elkington, who argue for the 'triple bottom line' (see Elkington 1998), and Hawken, with his school of 'natural capitalism' (Hawken 1999), espouse a philosophy that will push corporations back down the traditional curve. The alternative philosophy is represented by those who are pushing for expansion of the growth model, particularly under the rubric of 'globalisation'.

In these times, universities are caught in the middle. As Robert Bates Graber (1995) suggests, few parents or students want to underwrite a college education that does not have prospects for graduates to enter the employment market at sufficient income to offset the expenses of education. Business schools represent one path. Few, if any, of these schools are willing to explore programmes that might produce graduates who will challenge potential employers. Education is a lagging indicator. Its programmes are historical, by design. Like Polonius's repartee with Hamlet, they are designed to 'please', as are students thinking about potential markets for their skills.

Michael Milken, who was convicted on a number of counts of fraud during the collapse of the 'junk bond' market, was to be offered a faculty appointment at a prestigious business school. When the larger campus became very concerned, the business school students, interested in understanding the arcane nature of the investment banking trade, could not understand why there should be such concerns raised, and it is obvious that the faculty's ethical vision was also myopic.

The recent bankruptcies of Enron, Global Crossing and others led to the arrest of many whose education was received in some of the best business schools. And many of the faculty in these institutions seem in a quandary as to why one might be concerned that academics, who had consulting arrangements with these firms, did not see potential conflicts of interest even when writing up their clients as case studies for students to use in their education, and even when their corporate compensation often equalled or exceeded their salaries as professors.

As mentioned in Section 3.2, a set of case studies on environment and socially responsible businesses was being prepared, with Enron as the core example. One must wonder how those preparing such analyses succeeding in overlooking the obvious in favour of the superficial. And it gives one pause to question the substance of similar 'case studies' that are the backbone of many courses in business schools and in scholarly publications. Perhaps it is a case of 'selective vision'?

It is as if Adam Smith's first volume along with universities' humanities departments have been relegated to some dim set of stacks in the academic library, only to be dusted off because, occasionally, they acquire a sudden relevance. In a 'slower' world, the idea of using case studies as a way of helping students to understand the corporate world in which they plan to work might make sense. But what happens when the case studies of academics turn out to have a very short half-life or, in the present situation, to be based on knowledge that was incomplete or faulty, though 'full access' was granted?

Currently, one international consulting firm is promoting a multi-client study for major corporations to address the dynamic management issues confronting these entities during times of rapid and complex change in a global society. What are the issues that these corporations consider, and what happens when this information is developed internal to the corporations while the academic institutions are providing a lagging curriculum? If these corporations are undergoing transformational change at many levels, when are they no longer corporations as defined by their original charter and mission? Can academic programmes even begin to ask these hard questions?

Knowledge transmission is Lamarckian. We do not have to wait for the information to be passed forward through the genes of the survivors. What we learn is immediately available to past and future generations as they are able to access it. This is crucial because we grow and learn only by taking risks and making mistakes. The places where failure can occur are where knowledge is created, discoveries are made and change occurs. Examples abound in the biophysical and physical arenas as well as in the socioeconomic arena. The works of Ilya Prigogine and his former research team provide ample examples as does the work of the Santa Fe Institute (see e.g. Prigogine and Stegners 1983; www.santafe.edu). A study of complex dynamics points out that we cannot run the same model twice, nor step into the same river a second time. As James Carse (1994) has pointed out, life is an infinite game. We do not win as a species if it is finite. Where are the rules for an infinite game? What happens when answers are not in 'case studies' or found in the back of a textbook?

3.6 Where to?

But this long run is a misleading guide to current affairs. In the long run we are all dead. Economists set themselves too easy, too useless

a task if in tempestuous seasons they can only tell us that when the storm is long past the ocean is flat again.

J.M. Keynes 1924

At the turn of the 19th century, Henri Poincaré developed a mathematics for the study of physical systems. The systems of equations lay almost dormant until the advent of low-cost, high-speed computation, resulting in what now we call complex dynamics. It was not until 1984 that the United Nations University assembled an interdisciplinary symposium to explore the impact on all disciplines, including economics. From this arena, as well as more qualitative research, models have been developed that challenge the underpinnings of neoclassical economic thought.

In early 2003, *The Chronicle of Higher Education* ran a feature on the rise of this heterodox economics, or, as it is becoming to be called, 'post-autistic economics'. It is interesting that this movement gained international attention first with a revolt of students in France over the teaching of neoclassical economics, a teaching that not only seemed to fail to take into account current realities but also seemed to have patches and 'fixes' that lacked a coherent rationale. The movement has rapidly spread, from France to England and the USA.

When students, as with the youth in the Han Christian Andersen story of the 'Emperor's New Clothes', can clearly point out that the theory is naked, it raises serious questions about the curriculum, particularly one that sits at the core of most business programmes. It particularly raises questions about casting most problems in economic terms. But, more importantly, we are at a point in time where parochial thinking may cause emerging and fragile ideas to be still-born.

Of potentially greater interest is the fact that it raises questions about the reductionist models of post-secondary education that separate the business programmes from the larger, liberal studies community and force the students to synthesise their experience from fragmented courses that are being driven even deeper into specialisation and which in many cases exist in support of an inward-looking publish-or-perish model for faculty survival. In fact, it is understood that scholarly, peer-approved research creates barriers to theories that may appear orthogonal to current thinking. Although many in the business community have written nobly about the merits of liberal studies, the sentiments found in many academic programmes and among undergraduates can be reflected in Robert Bates Graber's observation that 'the liberal arts may be defined . . . as essentially those areas of knowledge in which practical-minded parents hope their children will not major' (1995: 1).

The call for socially and environmentally responsible corporations did not arise from creative ideas emerging from business schools or, in general, from the Academy. In fact, with the traditional 'case study' approach, I believe the Academy is a lagging indicator trying to use a past that never was in order to extrapolate to a future that never will be. This is particularly true in a dynamic, evolutionary, global society where warnings of the need for change have often been driven from within the industry and by a segment of the larger, external community such as emerged in response to the WTO talks in Seattle or who first pushed for, and developed, social and environmentally responsible 'screens' and used these to influence corporate behaviour.

The Academy has lost its hegemony as the 'public intellectual'. Yet it is these intellectuals, the faculty, who should have commanded the moral and intellectual high ground with regard to environmental and socially responsible business models. Change is arriving at Internet speed. 'Lessons learned', although providing insight, are not the lessons to be learned in a rapidly changing, global society. Process is no longer a minor variable in a changing world.

Education's semantic roots differ from the idea of 'instruction', yet the significance seems to have been lost in the post-secondary community, students and faculty. Change comes hard when the focus is on the faculty. The growing concerns in the arena of socially and environmentally responsible corporations cannot be addressed from an 'instructional' perspective. Complex, non-linear, evolutionary systems demand a different set of ideas, ones that require different thinking in the 'field' and that do not yield readily to traditional instructional modes of learning or teaching. As Robert Bates Graber has said (1995), 'the valuing of "useless knowledge" appears as nothing less than humankind trying to save itself'.

References

Carse, J.P. (1994) *Finite and Infinite Games: A Vision of Life as Play and Possibility* (New York: Ballentine Books).

Elkington, J. (1998) *Cannibals with Forks: The Triple Bottom Line of 21st Century Business* (Stony Creek, CT: New Society Publishers).

Fortier, F. (2001) *Virtuality Check: Power Relations and Alternative Strategies in the Information Society* (New York: Verso Books).

Gelernter, D. (1996) *1939: The Lost World of the Fair* (New York: Avon Books).

Goodwin, B. (2000) 'Out of Control into Participation', *Emergence* 2.4: 40-49.

Graber, R.B. (1995) *Valuing Useless Knowledge* (Philadelphia, PA: Thomas Jefferson University Press).

Hawken, P., A. Lovins and L.H. Lovins (1999) *Natural Capitalism: Creating the Next Industrial Revolution* (New York: Little Brown).

Keen, S. (2001) *Debunking Economics: The Naked Emperor of the Social Sciences* (Annandale, NSW, Australia: Pluto Press).

Kelly, M. (2001) *The Divine Right of Capital: Dethroning the Corporate Aristocracy* (San Francisco: Berrett-Koehler).

Kennedy, A.A. (2001) *The End of Shareholder Value: Corporations at the Crossroads* (New York: Perseus Books).

Kerr, P. (1992) *A Philosophical Investigation* (London: Vintage Books).

Keynes, J.M. (1924) *A Tract on Monetary Reform* (London: Macmillan).

Korten, D.C. (2000) *The Post Corporate World: Life after Capitalism* (San Francisco: Berrett-Kohler).

Kurzweil, R. (2000) *The Age of Spiritual Machines* (New York: Penguin USA).

Land, G. (1986) *Grow or Die: The Unifying Principle of Transformation* (New York: John Wiley [1973]).

—— and B. Jarman (1998) *Breakpoint and Beyond: Mastering the Future Today* (New Brunswick, NJ: Leadership 2000 Inc.).

Monaghan, P. (2003) 'Taking On Rational Man', *The Chronicle of Higher Education*, 24 January 2003; chronicle.com/prm/weekly/v49/i20/20a01201.htm, accessed 6 April 2004.

NAS (National Association of Scholars) (2002) *Ethics, Enron and American Higher Education* (Princeton, NJ: NAS, 2 July 2002; www.nas.org).

Prigogine, I., and I. Stegners (1983) *Order Out of Chaos* (New York: Bantam Books).

Smith, A. (1759) *The Theory of Moral Sentiments* (Buffalo, NY: Prometheus Books, 2000 edn).

—— (1776) *An Inquiry into the Nature and Causes of the Wealth of Nations* (Buffalo, NY: Prometheus Books, 1991 edn).

Snow, C.P. (1993) *The Two Cultures* (Cambridge, UK: Cambridge University Press).

Sternberg, R.J. (ed.) (2002) *Why Smart People Can Be So Stupid* (New Haven, CT: Yale University Press).

Ward, P. (2001) *Future Evolution* (New York: W.H. Freeman).

Further reading

Aida, S., *et al.* (1985) *The Science and Praxis of Complexity* (Tokyo: The United Nations University).

Allen, P.M. (2000) 'Knowledge, Ignorance and Learning', *Emergence* 2.4: 78-103.

Bonabeau, E., and C. Meyer (2001) 'Swarm Intelligence: A Whole New Way To Think About Business', *Harvard Business Review*, May 2001: Reprint R-105G.

Brockman, J. (1996) *The Third Culture: Scientists on the Edge* (New York: Touchstone Books).

Browning, L. (2002) 'MBA Programmes Now Screen for Integrity, Too', *New York Times*, 15 September 2002: 4 (Business Section).

Dixon, D. (1990) *Man after Man: An Anthropology of the Future* (New York: St Martin's Press).

Dobbin, M. (1998) *The Myth of the Good Corporate Citizen: Democracy under the Rule of Big Business.* (Toronto: Stoddart).

Evans, P., and T.S. Wurster (2000) *Blown to Bits: How the New Economics of Information Transforms Strategy.* (Boston, MA: Harvard Business School Press).

McCloskey, D.N. (1998) *The Rhetoric of Economics* (Madison, WI: University of Wisconsin Press).

McMurtry, J. (1999) *The Cancer Stage of Capitalism* (London: Pluto Press).

Mangan, K.S. (2002) 'The Ethics of Business Schools', *The Chronicle of Higher Education*, 20 September 2002: A14-16.

Sull, D.N. (1999) 'Why Good Companies Go Bad', *Harvard Business Review* On Point, Number 4,320 (July/August 1999).

Tainter, J.A. (1988) *The Collapse of Complex Societies* (Cambridge, UK: Cambridge University Press).

4

The business of development
Linking profits and principles to
address global development challenges

Pepukaye Bardouille
McKinsey & Company, Denmark

Concern over the consequences of industrial development for ecological well-being and human health is far from novel: indeed, from the 1962 landmark publication of *Silent Spring* (Carson 1962) and leading up to the 2002 World Summit on Sustainable Development (WSSD), a time-line representing increasing unease about anthropogenic impacts on the environment[1] can be drawn. To highlight causes of disquiet and the need for a socially and ecologically conscious global development path, the term 'sustainable development' was coined in the 1980s and subsequently popularised following the 1992 United Nations Conference on Environment and Development (UNCED). It is now widely accepted that the essence of the sustainable development proviso is that of affording equal importance to economic, ecological and social considerations in meeting the needs of present and future generations.

Although international agencies and governments have customarily been viewed as the drivers for 'sustainability' initiatives, the private sector is increasingly recognised as a major actor. Certainly, the sheer number of companies implementing environmental management systems and publishing 'sustainability reports' leaves little doubt that substantial progress has been made in drawing the attention of business to the topic since the UNCED. The standard motivation given for engaging in 'sustainable business' efforts relates to the benefits to be gained from product and process improvement, waste minimisation and tapping growing 'green markets'. Oft-cited success stories include the 3M Pollution Prevention Pays

---

1 Herein, the term 'environment' refers to society and the ecosystem.

programme that averted the release of 857,000 tonnes of toxic substances into the environment while saving more than US$894 million since the mid-1970s (3M 2004), and the Xerox Reduce Re-use Recycle initiative that diverted 73,000 tonnes of material from landfill in 2002, resulting in savings of tens of millions of dollars (Xerox 2004).

Thus far, though, the focus has primarily been on how products and manufacturing processes can be 'greened'. The socioeconomic aspect of sustainable development has been largely marginalised. Although 'corporate social responsibility' is a more comprehensive emerging concept that addresses ethics, investment in local communities, corporate governance, natural resource management, human rights and worker health, when it is put into the context of achieving global sustainable development more is required. Given its technological know-how and financial strength—two areas that must be effectively tapped if the most essential human development goals are to be achieved—the private sector must consider ways in which to tackle the fundamental challenges of sustainable development, including, among other things, poverty eradication, meeting basic human needs (universal access to safe drinking water, energy services and health-care) and building human resource capacity through improved access to education. Without working to improve the living conditions of the most disadvantaged populations around the world, it would seem that discussion of 'corporate sustainability' per se is extraneous in the wider scheme of things.

Yet beyond ethical reasons are critical business-oriented rationales for the private sector to drive sustainable development. First, in addition to a growing range of legislative and market-based obligations, there is mounting societal pressure for corporations to play a larger socially oriented role—one that has historically fallen within the realm of government. Since the now-infamous proposed sinking of Shell's North Atlantic Brent Spar oil platform it has become increasingly difficult for companies acting (or seemingly so) without heed for ecological well-being to avoid ending up the focus of public outcry. In the past few years, an increasing number of multinational corporations have also been exposed for direct and indirect human rights misconduct, as a result of, for instance, manufacturing products under sweatshop conditions (Nike, Gap, McDonald's, Mattel, Disney; Business & Human Rights 2004) or purchasing so-called 'conflict diamonds' (United Nations 2001). Moreover, added to concern for ending such practices is the growing call for business to proactively contribute to improving the living standards of communities in which they operate. For example, there are escalating demands that companies provide not only social benefits to employees but also extend educational, medical, water, energy and sanitation services to communities living near their facilities.

In addition to stakeholder pressure, there is an array of troubling social and ecological issues—from business inefficiencies linked to corruption in countries of operation and the loss of skilled workers to the HIV/AIDS epidemic, to the impact of poverty and inequity on global security—with the potential to further significantly impact how businesses operate in the future. These trends have direct and indirect consequences for the way business is done. Note the scramble to reduce dependence on Middle Eastern oil by increasing exploration and production in 'more stable African states' such as Equatorial Guinea, Gabon and Chad (Servant 2003).

Finally, perhaps the strongest motivation relates to the potential benefits from developing innovative products and services for new markets that seldom feature on the radar screens of business. In the coming two decades, population growth in the North[2] will flatten out, whereas significant increases will continue in low-income to medium-income countries, where 80% of the world's population lives. By developing creative products and services to meet needs in the South, companies will be able to establish footholds in unserved markets which, given their size, hold the potential to generate significant earnings, attract talent and motivate increasingly values-oriented workforces and gain the trust of stakeholders who see a key moral obligation for business in contributing to sustainable development.

In the following sections I explore justifications for business to drive sustainable development—specifically from the socioeconomic angle. Given the expertise and resources of larger companies, the chapter speaks primarily to the role of larger companies, but it is also appreciated that fundamental to the sustainability paradigm is the promotion of local-level entrepreneurship, capacity-building and institutional development. Thereafter, focusing on energy services provision, I present examples of how the private sector can and is gainfully tapping new markets and contributing to meeting the basic needs of hitherto unserved 'energy-poor' populations. However, recognising that with business opportunities inevitably comes a range of challenges, particularly related to ensuring the viability of capital-intensive infrastructure operations in often-unstable developing markets, I briefly explore ways to reduce economic risks and attract private-sector investment.

4.1 Business as a driving force for sustainable development: moral calling or enlightened self-interest?

4.1.1 Stakeholder pressure: changing the business of business

In the past, the greatest pressures that companies have faced related to the business of increasing profits and satisfying shareholders with a good bottom line: in other words, financial performance pressure. Although this is still true, the growing influence of 'wider stakeholders', from government regulators and workers to the general public, means that the private sector faces broader challenges than those set solely by managers and board members. Today, irrespective of geographical location, industrial sector, product or service focus, organisational type or company size, business is increasingly financially affected by external stakeholder

2 Industrialised countries are also referred to as the 'North', whereas the term 'South' is used interchangeably for developing countries.

demands. There are escalating legislative[3] and market-based[4] pressures, as well as calls from the public and non-governmental organisations (NGOs) for industry to significantly improve its environmental performance. White (1999: 38) observes that:

> in today's business community, the weight of public opinion is an inescapable reality . . . News about problems with new products is disseminated the same day on the Internet and the next day in the business press. As a result, for global companies, hardly any decision is purely local any more.

Numerous examples illustrate how business has been negatively affected by stakeholder pressure: the 1989 *Exxon Valdez* oil spill of about 40 million litres of crude oil over approximately 250 square kilometres into Alaska's pristine Prince William Sound (NOAA 2003), for instance, resulted in billions of dollars of clean-up costs and the payment by Exxon of US$300 million in damages (BBC 2002c). Public outcry and calls for boycotts following controversies such as the 1995 execution of human rights activist Ken Saro-Wiwa and eight others for campaigning against the involvement of Shell and the Nigerian government in environmental destruction in the oil-rich Niger Delta (Sierra Club 2004) and the launch of genetically modified seed by Monsanto (Price 2003) have also highlighted the need for a systematic rethinking of corporate ethics and accountability.

There are also demands for business to provide services in communities in which they operate, as well as generally to support global social causes. In 2001, there were worldwide protests against pharmaceutical companies that had taken the South African government to court to block legislation giving the state power to import or manufacture cheap versions of brand-name drugs, thus putting profits before the lives of millions of people in the developing world who are unable to afford life-saving drugs. But, following this pressure, the 39 companies unconditionally dropped the case (Kasper 2001).

Similarly, in July 2002, hundreds of unarmed women in the Niger Delta took control of at least four ChevronTexaco oil facilities, demanding that the company increase employment opportunities and improve standards of living in poverty-ridden local communities. Halting oil production for weeks, the protests cost the company US$2.9 million daily in lost revenue (*Times* 2002). Nigeria is a country of enormous natural wealth, but lack of action from multinational companies to reduce the disparity between the 'haves' (notably those profiting from lucrative oil contracts) and 'have nots' frequently leads to hostage-taking and sabotage and has tarnished the reputations of a number of companies.

3   Legislation includes: regulations covering emissions levels; packaging recovery and recycling schemes; and extended producer responsibility.

4   Market-based instruments include: market-based and economic instruments, such as carbon taxes, to encourage a positive response to environmental concerns; peer pressure and leadership in the form of competitors acting ahead of legislation; the sectoral integration of life-cycle approaches in product design and development, leading, in turn, to corporate responsible care programmes; competition from a more cost-effective response to legislation and customer demands, and a higher profile in 'green markets' from 'greener competitors'; and preferential investment by financial markets in companies with low environmental liability risks.

Beyond the direct consequences of stakeholder action, reputation costs associated with bad press are hard to quantify. Still, as the Enron and WorldCom scandals show, evidence indicates that equity markets do respond to environmental and moral indiscretions (Grieg-Gran 2002). Furthermore, the emergence of ethical mutual funds and sustainability indicators, such as the Dow Jones Sustainability Indexes (DJSI) and FTSE4Good, points to rising interest by investors and financial institutions in corporate social responsibility.

In the past decade or so there has been a clear increase in the number of companies dealing with the negative impacts of their activities. Many corporations have sought to address environmental concerns by implementing management concepts,[5] developing best-practice sustainability reporting guidelines through the Global Reporting Initiative (GRI, www.globalreporting.org); publishing annual environmental reports; and engaging in local and international stakeholder dialogue. Community development efforts are also becoming more widespread, especially in the extractive sector. Through participation in such voluntary initiatives, there is a general view that companies are progressing from pure compliance with environmental regulations towards 'fully fledged sustainable business strategies'.

Although this is a step in the right direction, the adoption of a sustainable development path implies more than a reacting to ecological mishaps and social gaffes or increasing one's visibility in environmental debates to appease public pressure. Proactive involvement in advancing the proviso is also needed. A more holistic approach to social and ecological issues is critical if one is to claim to be supporting sustainable development. But, from a business-profitability perspective, there is logic in this: in a globalising world, ensuring long-term growth requires that the private sector considers more comprehensively how it is directly and indirectly affected by—and has the potential to affect—the overall global development path.

4.1.2 Poverty: from moral quandary to corporate challenge

Since World War II considerable progress has been made in improving the lives of millions of people. Life expectancy rose from 55 years to 64 years in the developing world between 1970 and 2000 (and by 44–51 years in the less-developed countries [LDCs]); the level of immunisation has increased; and illiteracy levels have fallen, as have infant and maternal mortality rates (United Nations 2002b). Considerable increases have also been seen in economic growth: in China, for example, per capita income rose more than tenfold, from US$270 to US$3,940 between 1975 and 2000 (United Nations 2002a). However, much still remains to be achieved in the sphere of socioeconomic development and quality of life: 1.6 billion people

5 The focus has been primarily on concepts such as Responsible Care® (www.icca-chem. org/section02a.html), the Valdez Principles (now the CERES Principles; www.ceres.org/ our_work/principles.htm), the European Eco-Management and Audit Scheme (EMAS; www.europa.eu.int/comm/environment/emas/index_en.htm), design for environment (DfE), life-cycle assessment (LCA) and the International Organisation for Standardisation (ISO) 14000 series of standards (www.iso.ch/iso/en/prods-services/otherpubs/iso14000/ index.html).

continue to live on less that US$1 dollar a day, and 2.8 billion people subsist on just double this amount (United Nations 2002b). In the poorest countries, 150 out of every 1,000 children die before their first birthday, and more than 240 of every 1,000 before the age of five (as compared with 6 per 1,000 in the rich world) (United Nations 2002a).

In an effort to address these issues, which constitute the crux of the sustainable human development challenge, in September 2000 the member states of the United Nations outlined a set of eight Millennium Development Goals (MDGs). Drawing from agreements and commitments emerging from global conferences held during the past decade, the MDGs aim at: (1) halving, between 1990 and 2015, the number of people whose income is less than US$1 per day, (2) achieving universal primary education, (3) promoting gender equality and empowering women, (4) reducing by two-thirds, between 1990 and 2015, the under-five mortality rate, (5) reducing by three-quarters, between 1990 and 2015, the maternal mortality rate, (6) halting and beginning to reverse, by 2015, the spread of HIV/AIDS, malaria and other major diseases, (7) integrating the principles of sustainability into country policies and reversing the loss of natural resources, and (8) developing a global partnership for development (United Nations 2004).

The MDGs have become widely accepted as a framework to measure progress toward sustainable development. In this context, poverty eradication is rapidly emerging as an objective the achievement of which will determine that of the others. It is also clear that achievement of targets such as the MDGs is not just a moral obligation confined to the realm of bilateral or multilateral development agencies, NGOs and/or intergovernmental processes. In a world of crumbling borders, challenges facing the South are of significance for society as a whole, including the private sector—for local and multinational companies alike.

Take, for instance, poverty and inequality. Millions of people in developing countries live in extreme poverty and do not enjoy the economic benefits of globalisation; this results in inequity and injustice, which in turn breeds conflict. Ever more global, the media broadcasts images of a flourishing industrialised world, increasing the sense of hopelessness of the marginalised, which, in turn, is often manifested through anger directed at those who have prospered. As people voice their discontent at a system that favours the rich, the implications for business begin to show, extending from noisy street protests at World Trade Organisation and World Bank meetings, to targeted disruption of business operations and on to wide-scale politically motivated violence that threatens global security, shaking international markets and dampening consumer spending.

Then there is the issue of contagious diseases, notably HIV/AIDS, which affects an estimated 40 million people worldwide (37.2 million adults and 2.7 million children younger than 15 years) (UNAIDS 2001). Again, poverty—and its links to lack of access to education and healthcare—is a major factor influencing the spread of the disease. Although, worldwide, 1 in 100 adults aged 15 to 49 years is HIV-infected, over 8% of all adults in this age group are infected in Sub-Saharan Africa (UNAIDS 2001): more than 70% of infected people live in Sub-Saharan Africa, and 15% are in South and South-East Asia. Going against the global tide, life expectancy in the Sub-Saharan African region declined from 50 to 47 years between 1990 and 2001 (United Nations 2002a). Only 30,000 of the 30 million Africans with AIDS have access to anti-retroviral drugs. The statistics are staggering and depict a global crisis that the public sector is struggling to control. But is this of consequence to business? Certainly.

In South Africa, for example, 20% of the workforce is infected (UNAIDS 2001). In addition to the traditional 'high-risk groups', infections among migrant workers such as miners and truck drivers are increasing at alarming rates (UNAIDS 2001)— with implicit financial implications for companies involved in these sectors. The extractive sector is being particularly hard hit. One South African mining company, Gold Fields, projects that over a quarter of its 50,000 workers has contracted the virus (BBC 2002a). The financial result is a lowered productivity that adds an estimated US$10 to the cost of each ounce of gold produced. These figures are significant for a company mining 4.7 million ounces of gold annually at an average cost of US$170 per ounce (BBC 2002a).

Recognising that AIDS is noticeably affecting profitability, Anglo-American, Southern Africa's biggest mining group and the largest employer in South Africa, became the first company in the world to provide free anti-retroviral treatment to its employees (*Financial Times* 2002). With 23% of its 134,000 employees infected with the disease, in mid-2002 Anglo-American began negotiations with Glaxo-SmithKline, Merck and Boehringer Ingelheim to supply medications at a cost of US$2.5–5 million in the first year of distribution, and is looking into options for buying generic drug versions (*Financial Times* 2002). Grappling with the same problem, mining giants Anglo-Gold and De Beers are implementing parallel policies (Kaira 2003).

Other sectors are also being hurt. South Africa's financial industry is struggling to manage the growing incidence of HIV/AIDS and related diseases among its clients. A report from the country's Banking Council notes that the sector must identify ways to improve life coverage for mortgage holders, given the number of homeowners succumbing to the disease. The industry council estimates that losses from HIV/AIDS-related deaths could cost banks up to US$3 billion over the next ten years (BBC 2002b).

It is evident, then, that there are corporate financial consequences associated with failing to address global prosperity. Nonetheless, this is only part of the issue. Depending on one's perspective, the billions of people without access to goods and services that the private sector can provide either could be ignored or could be seen as potential markets for products and services from which both sides benefit.

4.1.3 Doing well by doing good: the business of development

Presently, 1.2 billion people worldwide do not have safe drinking water, 2.4 billion people lack adequate sanitation and more than 3 billion people do not have access to electricity or other modern energy carriers (UNDP 2003), yet education, health-care, clean water, infrastructure, energy and sanitation are all critical for improving the human condition: 6,000 children die each day from preventable diseases stemming from lack of access to clean water (UNDP 2003). Availability of basic services is also fundamental in reducing income poverty. Alleviation requires a move away from subsistence towards surplus-generating activities, which in turn requires that the scale of production and the productivity of the workforce be improved. Productive factors include personal assets, such as good heath and education and skills, as well as resources for direct production, such as capital, materials, water, energy and transportation. Given these links, it is increasingly recognised that the nearly 3 billion people worldwide living on less than US$2 a day will see little improvement in their situation without access to productive resources that facilitate income generation and improved quality of life.

In the developing world, as is the case in industrialised nations, the public sector has traditionally provided basic social services. Based on a welfare argument, and with the aim of ensuring the fair distribution of wealth among the populace, the state has traditionally owned and run the productive sector, from soap factories to copper mines, in most developing countries. But, improperly managed, many of these enterprises have suffered losses, leading to public-sector deficit, particularly in the highly indebted poor countries. This has constrained governments' ability to provide satisfactory social services. Moreover, with the implementation since the 1970s of structural adjustment programmes (SAPs) in many poor countries, the role of the state in the direct provision of goods and services is being reduced, further limiting its ability to meet citizens' fundamental needs. Adding to an already difficult situation has been the decline in the past decade of official development assistance (ODA) that previously bridged the national investment gap, as well as a shift in ODA structure towards the social sector at the expense of the productive sector and infrastructure development. ODA went from US$60.9 billion in 1992 to US$53.1 billion in 2000. The share for LDCs fell from US$16.6 to US$12.1 billion between 1995 and 1998 (United Nations 2002b).

Although the decline in aid has been counteracted by steadily increasing foreign direct investment (FDI), which doubled between 1990 and 1997 from US$209 to US$473 billion, and further tripled to US$1,118 billion in 2000, the developing-country share declined from 35% in 1997 to 17% in 2000 (in absolute terms, total world FDI inflows increased marginally from US$178 billion to US$190 billion over this period) (United Nations 2002b). Moreover, in 2000, only ten countries— primarily with large economies such as China, India and Brazil—accounted for 75% of FDI. Consequently, the widely touted benefits of globalisation are not reaching the majority of the world's poor. Limited private-sector investment along with diminishing ODA means that many LDCs are being left behind.

Bridging the gap between rich and poor requires action on several fronts, including increased aid and FDI and improved trade conditions, particularly for LDCs. At the same time, it is becoming more evident that, given the sheer scale of the challenges with which we are faced, governments and development institutions will not be able to make a significant dent in human suffering on their own. As has been the trend with ODA, the emphasis of the public sector is now more on building human resource capacity (education, healthcare). Hence, the involvement of the private sector in implementing development programmes is becoming important.

From a private-sector perspective, the fundamental rationale for 'becoming involved with the poor' would be the allure of increased markets and, of course, profits. However, regardless of the potential market size, without adequate purchasing power the billions of poor 'latent customers' are, understandably, of little attraction. To convince companies to proactively participate in supporting sustainable development in poor countries, a business case must be made. This can be done. Improvement in productivity and, thereby, surplus production is fundamental for income generation and long-term poverty alleviation. As disposable income increases, potential markets for goods and services develop. In this regard, the creation of markets involves addressing several challenges, including that of augmenting productive factors such as access to credit for starting or scaling up production. By investing small amounts of capital in local communities to encourage productive activities and thus to generate income it is possible to open up new markets for appropriate goods and services.

There are numerous illustrations of the potential of even very limited sums of capital (typically about US$50–100) lent through microcredit programmes to individuals or groups to support entrepreneurial activities. The Grameen Bank (Bangladesh; a pioneer in the field), SHARE (India) and Banco Ademi (Dominican Republic) began as non-profit ventures but have, over time, generated significant returns. Other initiatives, such as Bank Dagang Bali (Indonesia), Basix (India), Banco del Desarrollo (Chile), SEWA Bank (India), ProFund (Panama), Aureos (UK) and AFRICAP (Senegal) follow a commercial model as profit-making schemes.[6] ProFund, Aureos and AFRICAP, for instance, seek high returns by promoting the growth of regulated and efficient financial intermediaries whose main target markets are local small and medium-sized enterprises (SMEs): they infuse equity and quasi-equity resources into eligible financial institutions to facilitate expansion and improve operations on a sustainable and large-scale basis (ProFund 2002). Ventures such as ProFund capitalise on the market potential for providing financial services, using their knowledge of the region and local industries to benefit more than 320,000 entrepreneurs and to create jobs and contribute to poverty reduction.

These examples demonstrate that the poor are bankable (loan repayment rates from microcredit schemes are typically 97%—well in excess of Western commercial banks) and are testament to the case for poverty reduction as a business opportunity. From the financial point of view the benefits are twofold: first, meeting the demand for microcredit and larger capital investment for SMEs presents valuable business opportunities for the private sector and, second, by increasing purchasing power a marketplace for goods and services is created.

There is a role for smaller local and larger national and international companies in this area. Indigenous institutions that, starting on a small scale, have rapidly grown to meet increasing demand for credit have dominated the microfinance sector. SEWA Bank (India) is an example: established in 1974 as a co-operative bank focusing on savings and lending products for low-income women in an industrial town, the bank now has 100,000 members—all women.[7] International retail banks are also becoming interested in the area: Citibank has launched lending services that target low-income customers in Bangalore, India, as has Standard Bank in South Africa (Prahalad and Hart 2002).

6 Source: interviews conducted with these organisations in September/October 2002.
7 Source: interviews.

A second dimension to the poverty-reduction challenge involves infrastructure access: energy, water, telecommunications and transportation are critical for the development of viable economic enterprises, notably in the manufacturing sector. In addition, when implemented well, such services contribute to the development of local enterprise, co-operatives, small businesses and community-based initiatives, which, in turn, also generate income (World Bank 2002). Indirectly, too, infrastructure is fundamental for the provision of basic services such as education and healthcare, themselves key productive factors. Finally, in much the same manner as providing capital to individuals and businesses, infrastructure development presents vast opportunities for the private sector to provide services for growing markets.

If the goal is to increase the market for goods and services in the developing world, then, by virtue of its links to improving purchasing power, increasing access to productive resources (capital and the infrastructure that provides basic services) is an essential means to this end. Meeting the demand for credit and infrastructure offers business-building opportunities. As an illustration, the next section centres on options for the private sector to contribute to socioeconomic development through energy service provision while simultaneously benefiting financially.

4.1.4 Profitable principles: partnerships for energy service provision

Access to affordable, adequate and appropriate energy services is a prerequisite for sustainable development and for achieving the MDGs. However, at present rates of grid extension, for 1.5 billion people worldwide electricity connection within their lifetime seems unlikely, thus hampering access to education, modern communications technologies and health services. A further 1.5 billion individuals are dependent on traditional fuels such as wood and agricultural waste for cooking and heating. Among other concerns, use of these fuels results in respiratory disease from indoor and local air pollution (it is estimated that half a million women and children die each year in India as a result of burning traditional fuels), drudgery (the daily transport effort of rural women in Sub-Saharan Africa is equal to carrying a load of 20 kg for distances of up to 5 km), reduced productivity, limited educational opportunities, constrained income generation and land degradation (World Bank 2002).

Despite the importance of energy for socioeconomic development, as discussed in Section 4.1.3, emergent public-sector deficit combined with SAP conditions and declining ODA have resulted in it being difficult for the governments of many developing countries to meet the needs of growing populations for energy services. Given these constraints, the private sector can and is becoming involved in providing services. Indeed, the past decade has witnessed significant growth in the contribution of the private sector to expanding infrastructure. Between 1990 and 1999, 76 developing countries introduced private participation in the energy sector,[8] awarding more than 700 projects,[9] representing more than US$180 billion

8 This sector relates to electricity and natural gas transmission and distribution.
9 Global developers, including AES Corporation (USA), Electricité de France (EDF, France)

in investments, to private firms (Izaguirre 2000). Building on opportunities following energy-sector reform, one successful approach is output-based contracting in which private firms are given subsidies to increase the reach of energy services on behalf of the state. Output-based contracting offers operators flexibility to meet consumer demands with low-cost options, thereby encouraging innovation (Tomkins 2002).

In the early 1990s, 97% of Chile's urban areas were electrified. In rural areas, it was just over 50% (Jadresic 2000). Aiming to provide electricity to the more than one million rural 'energy-poor', the government launched a rural electrification programme in 1994, setting targets of 75% coverage by 2000 and 100% coverage by 2004. The programme provides subsidies through a fund that allocates one-time grants to private electricity distribution companies. It aims to minimise the cost of electrification for the state and to give the private sector an attractive business opportunity. Each year, interested companies propose projects to the regional government for funding consideration. Projects are selected based on cost–benefit, the amount of investment covered by the company and the overall social impact. Regional governments then receive funds based on progress made in rural electrification over the previous year and the number of households in the region still lacking access to electricity. By 1999, some 76% of rural dwellings were electrified, with an estimated state contribution of US$112 million, and private investment of US$60 million (Jadresic 2000).

Similar efforts have been undertaken in Gabon. In 1997, La Société d'Energie et d'Eau du Gabon (SEEG), a privately owned multi-utility company providing electricity and water services to major urban centres, entered into a 20-year output-based concession contract with its government (Trémolet 2002). The contractual obligations involve operating and renewing (investing a minimum of US$135 million in rehabilitation) the electricity and water networks and expanding services to previously unconnected areas (by increasing density where the network exists presently or by expanding it to new centres) to meet regional coverage targets. The government provides subsidies for major network investments; however, SEEG has informally committed itself to investing US$130 million over the life of the contract. In the case of both services, targets for 2000 by percentage of population with connections were exceeded in all regions, except in isolated centres that were not served at all in 1996. The quality of services provided has also consistently improved and tariffs have dropped. Furthermore, from a business standpoint, significant profits have been posted since the initiation of operations: shareholder dividends rose from the guaranteed 6.5% in the first year, to 20% in 2000 (Trémolet 2002).

With appropriate policy frameworks and economic incentives, the private sector can contribute to meeting social development goals in a cost-effective manner and, simultaneously, profit from such ventures.

and Endesa (Spain) were the ten largest sponsors in terms of investment and were involved in a fifth of projects. The middle-income countries of Latin America and South-East Asia have led the growth of private-sector participation, accounting for over 40% and 30%, respectively (Izaguirre 2000).

There are other ways that the public and private sectors can join forces to expand energy services. Focusing on clean fuels, The LP Gas Rural Energy Challenge is a joint venture between the United Nations Development Programme (UNDP) and member companies of the World Liquefied Petroleum Gas Association (WLPGA) that concurrently addresses the UNDP goal of increasing access to modern energy carriers for socioeconomic development and the WLPGA aim of expanding fuel markets. The objective of this initiative is to bring liquefied petroleum (LP) gas to peri-urban and rural populations by addressing availability and affordability. In terms of availability, the critical first cost barrier to the poor is associated with the purchase or lease of a gas cylinder and appliances. Here, UNDP can bring to the partnership knowledge of developing appropriate financing mechanisms for target communities, international expertise in capacity-building for governments in outlining targeted policies and experience in collaborating with local organisations to stimulate investment and employment creation in target areas. In terms of increasing local fuel availability, industry counterparts are well placed to contribute to the partnership by establishing safe storage and bottling facilities near the target markets, by expanding the storage capability for imported gas in order to capture economies of scale in shipping in order to lower the price to users and by addressing recurring user costs through investment in the production of smaller, more affordable gas cylinders (UNDP 2002).

In addition to government-driven and donor-driven initiatives, the private sector is beginning to identify opportunities for long-term growth in developing countries. Electricité de France (EDF), for example, is actively strengthening its African presence in an effort to meet targets of at least 50% revenue from outside France by 2005. One of EDF's successes in Africa is the 294 MW Azito facility in the Ivory Coast, which generates electricity using indigenous gas resources (Akumu 2002). The company has also ventured into large-scale generation partnerships in Egypt and Morocco. However, EDF is also seeking to broaden its reach to rural areas and, to this end, is involved in exploratory studies in Kenya, Burkina Faso, Mali, Gambia, Gabon, Central African Republic, Mozambique, Chad, Sudan and Senegal, where it plans to expand its presence into equity participation through such strategies as: the creation of independent power producers, the use of opportunities arising from privatisation, use of concessions and other transitory arrangements and the creation of private–public partnerships (Akumu 2002).

Exemplary of EDF's initial ventures into the rural electrification market is La Société de Services Décentralisés (SSD), based in Koutiala, Mali. This locally based decentralised energy service company is a result of Accès, an EDF programme to expand access to electricity in developing countries with use of an economically viable service-provider model which, following an initial public subsidy for capital investments, requires payment by users for all operating costs. Held in equal parts by EDF and Dutch operator Nuon, SSD complements the activities of national energy provider, Electricité de Mali, which is unable to electrify most rural areas. The Koutiala SSD, which employs 33 people, began operating in mid-2001 and was serving 250 families in 20 villages using photovoltaic panels by early 2002, with plans to expand to 6,700 customers within two years. Targeting small craft industries (mills, workshops), institutions (health centres, local administrations, schools) and households of 5–10 people with an monthly income of between

US$30 and US$60, of which US$6–10 are presently dedicated to relatively low-quality energy carriers such as kerosene and dry-cell batteries, EDF is developing and launching several more commercial initiatives across Africa (Bal 2002).

E&Co is another example of a commercially oriented initiative that promotes access to energy services for sustainable development. The company's objective is to demonstrate the economic viability of renewable energy and energy-efficiency projects through enterprise development, which involves providing modest amounts of debt and equity (US$50,000–250,000) to allow new enterprises the opportunity to develop their business strategy to attract second-stage investors. Since 1995, E&Co has invested US$6.6 million in more than 50 enterprises in 25 countries. One of its ventures, the Noor Holding Company, focuses on developing and financing small energy enterprises in the 40,000 unelectrified villages in Morocco. With US$255,000 from E&Co in the form of risk capital, Noor secured US$750,000 of equity investment from two Moroccan investors and Shell International Renewables (SIR). Noor has a contract with the national utility for the installation of 7,000 solar home systems in Taroudant, to be sold on credit over three years (E&Co 2002; Willemse 2000).

Given the scale of capital investment required, these examples show that mostly large indigenous or multinational companies venture into infrastructure activities. Still, there is potential for smaller, local businesses to contribute to providing services, particularly in rural areas. The decentralised services model used by EDF relies on small-scale, home-grown outfits to serve communities of limited size. Likewise, the approaches adopted by E&Co and by UNDP and WLPGA involve: establishing local firms; supporting capacity-building for policy-makers, technicians and financiers; and institutional development.

4.2 Going forward: implications for teaching sustainability

As discussed in Section 4.1, business can benefit by supporting sustainable human development. The initiation of energy service activities by corporate giants such as EDF and Nuon, coupled with ventures into renewable energy markets by the likes of BP and Shell (People and Planet 2003), suggests that the private sector is recognising this and beginning to look further afield for long-term growth opportunities. But, owing to economic risks, many companies are cautious of involvement in developing countries.

Because the private sector can substantially help advance sustainable development, barriers must be addressed. Conditions necessary to attract corporate participation and ensure success must be put into place. In this respect, there are several implications for teaching sustainability. These relate to the need to (a) move beyond equating sustainable development with corporate environmental management, (b) adopt tools and methods for assessing the long-term economic attractiveness of potential business opportunities, (c) concretise opportunities for private-sector involvement in meeting human needs and (d) mitigate risks for business related to investment in developing markets.

The first implication—the rationale for business to look at a broader range of issues when discussing sustainability—has been discussed in Section 4.1. When teaching sustainability it is critical to adopt a comprehensive method that highlights issues of socioeconomic and ecological relevance: the emphasis cannot stay on slight improvements to environmental performance of business processes.

Another area requiring attention is the need to enhance the capture of business risks and growth potential: that is, without clearly understanding the implications of, and opportunities related to, today's global development path, private-sector interest in the agenda will remain limited. Methods such as total-cost accounting, financial analysis and decision-making must be better linked to social and ecological trends and associated external threats to profitability. The same holds for value creation: this involves identification of socioeconomic and ecological trends, estimation of direct and indirect implications pertaining to reduced profits or growth potential and development of solutions to address opportunities and threats. Unless a broader approach is adopted business will continue to undervalue the import of driving—and thus benefiting from—sustainable development.

Furthermore, national governments and the international development assistance community must provide real opportunities to business. Fortunately, this is beginning to happen, but, in the short term, private capital will not be forthcoming for most developing countries, particularly LDCs, to the degree needed for widespread socioeconomic development. Thus, public funds, ODA, concessionary loans and government and agency partnerships will remain imperative.

With a growing move towards output-based aid, there is a role for the private sector to provide cost-effective services, such as healthcare and clean water and energy. In teaching sustainability, links between the public and private sectors should be explored with a view to crafting a role for business in services provision, thus maximising effectiveness and impact.

Yet, if opportunities for infrastructure and the provision of basic services in developing countries are increasing, then why were private capital flows for 2001 at half the levels of the mid-1990s? Furthermore, why has FDI disproportionately benefited only a handful of the larger economies, thus marginalising LDCs? As Pearce (1997) observes, private flows are a direct function of risk. In view of this, it is important to recognise that the private sector cannot be expected to jump into markets suffering from political instability, foreign exchange crises, corruption in obtaining contracts or lack of commitment from the state —not least where capital-intensive investments typical of infrastructure development are concerned. A final implication for teaching sustainability, therefore, is that the economic viability of private-sector investments must be assured.

Options for raising confidence in these investments include the integration of infrastructure projects into well-structured regulatory reform for the industry as a whole, co-investment in projects by host-government agencies through loans and minority equity ownership, initiatives to provide risk capital using a mix of preferred private capital and subordinated public funds, and provision of political risk insurance and greater use of targeted enhanced political risk insurance aimed at major specific risks.

Closely tied to this is the need for good governance. Corruption impedes progress. Likewise, poor governance constrains investment in developing countries. Hence, multilateral and bilateral agencies must tie assistance more closely to the implementation of good management practices. In this context there are a number of broader advantages of public–private partnerships. Partnering on specific infrastructure development projects with government institutions, international agencies and NGOs that are situated in and understand local conditions can help ensure programme success and should therefore be supported as a means of further boosting private-sector involvement in development.

4.3 Conclusions

In this chapter I have argued for business to adopt a role in achieving sustainable development, to involve not only managing or minimising the ecological impacts of products and production systems but also, and more importantly, addressing the broader socioeconomic aspects of global development. The private sector is critical for operationalising sustainable human development because it has the required resources, skills and technology for wealth creation and because the role of the public sector is declining. Furthermore, I have shown how business can suffer when the goals of sustainable development are compromised. In contrast, catering to basic social needs offers prospects for business-building.

The development and implementation of solutions to global challenges will necessitate collaboration among a wide range of actors: just as the onus cannot be placed on a single player, the search for appropriate responses will require teamwork. With growing interest in output-based aid, the space for business to provide social services innovatively and cost-effectively is opening. Accordingly, interested parties should focus on how to link public-sector and private-sector efforts to maximise effective service delivery and to minimise the risk of political and economic instability. If the private sector can identify issues relevant to business and then work with public institutions it will be able to develop the synergies necessary to contribute to global sustainable development while doing good business.

References

3M (2004) 'More about Pollution Prevention Pays', www.3m.com/about3m/sustainability/policies_ehs_tradition_3p.jhtml, accessed 26 March 2004.

Akumu, W. (2002) 'French giant gears up for Africa push', *Kenyan Daily Nation: Business Week*, 9 July 2002.

Bal, J.-L. (2002) 'Sustainable Development in Rural Areas: Energy Services and Populations' Needs', paper presented at World Bank Energy Forum, Washington, DC, 5 June 2002.

BBC (British Broadcasting Corporation) (2002a) 'Mining firm reveals cost of HIV', BBC News website, 16 April 2002, news.bbc.co.uk/1/hi/business/1933750.stm, accessed 25 July 2002.

—— (2002b) 'South African banks face Aids crisis', BBC News website, 21 June 2002, news.bbc.co.uk/2/hi/business/2057613.stm, accessed 27 July 2002.

—— (2002c) 'Exxon Valdez damages reduced', BBC News website, 17 December 2002, news.bbc.co.uk/2/hi/americas/2553441.stm.

Business & Human Rights (2004) 'Mattel', www.business-humanrights.org/Categories/IndividualCompanies/M/Mattel, accessed 26 March 2004.

Carson, R. (1962) Silent Spring (London: Penguin Books, 1999 edn).

E&Co (2002) 'Noor Photovoltaics', www.energyhouse.com/p_morocco.htm, accessed 30 September 2002.

Financial Times (2002) 'SA Mining Group to give staff free Aids treatment', Financial Times, London, 7 August 2002.

Grieg-Gran, M. (2002) Financial Incentives for Improved Sustainability Performance: The Business Case and the Sustainability Dividend (London: International Institute for Environment and Development; Geneva: World Business Council for Sustainable Development).

Izaguirre, A.K. (2000) Private Participation in Energy (Public Policy for the Private Sector, Note 208; Washington, DC: The World Bank Group, May 2000).

Jadresic, A. (2000) Promoting Private Investment in Rural Electrification: The Case of Chile (Public Policy for the Private Sector, Note 214; Washington, DC: The World Bank Group, June 2000).

Kaira, C. (2003) 'AngloGold to offer free AIDS drugs at Navachab', Namibia Economist, www.economist.com.na/2003/18jul/07-18-01.htm.

Kasper, T. (2001) 'South Africa's Victory for the Developing World', Médecins Sans Frontières, www.accessmed-msf.org/prod/publications.asp?scntid=3182001040389&contenttype=para&.

NOAA (National Oceanic and Atmosphere Administration) (2003) 'The Exxon Valdez Oil Spill', response.restoration.noaa.gov/spotlight/spotlight.html, accessed 26 March 2004.

Pearce, D. (1997) 'Incentives for Private Sector Financing of Sustainable Development', in Bridges to Sustainability: Business and Government Working Together for a Better Environment (Bulletin Series 101; New Haven, CT: Yale School of Forestry and Environmental Studies).

People and Planet (2003) 'The Coming Energy Revolution', www.peopleandplanet.net/doc.php?id=522&section=728 April 2003.

Prahalad, C.K., and S.L. Hart (2002) 'The Fortune at the Bottom of the Pyramid', Strategy and Business 26 (1Q 2002).

Price, T. (2003) 'Farmers fight to keep Monsanto's genetically modified wheat out of Canada', CorpWatch, 5 March 2003, www.corpwatch.org/article.php?id=5790.

ProFund (2002) 'Profile', www.profundinternacional.com, accessed 16 September 2002.

Servant, J.C. (2003) 'The New Gulf Oil States', Le Monde Diplomatique, January 2003.

Sierra Club (2004) 'Human Rights and the Environment', www.sierraclub.org/human-rights/nigeria, accessed 26 March 2004.

Times (2002) 'This Day [Lagos]', The Times, 18 July 2002, www.thisdayonline.com, accessed 25 July 2002.

Tomkins, R. (2002) Extending Rural Electrification: A Survey of Innovative Schemes (Washington, DC: The World Bank).

Trémolet, S. (2002) Multi-Utilities and Access: Can Private Multi-utilities Help Expand Service to Rural Areas? (Public Policy for the Private Sector, Note 248; Washington, DC: The World Bank Group, June 2002).

UNAIDS (Joint UN Programme on HIV/AIDS) (2001) Global Summary of the HIV/AIDS Epidemic (New York: United Nations, December 2001).

UNDP (United Nations Development Programme) (2002) 'Public–Private Partnership Information Sheet: The LPG Challenge', World Summit on Sustainable Development, www.johannesburgsummit.org/html/sustainable_dev/p2_managing_resources/1208_lpg_challenge.pdf.

—— (2003) Clean Water and Sanitation for the Poor: Fast Facts (New York: UNDP).

United Nations (2001) 'Conflict Diamonds: Sanctions and War', www.un.org/peace/africa/Diamond.html, accessed 26 March 2004.

—— (2002a) *Human Development Report 2002* (New York: United Nations).

—— (2002b) *Outcome of the International Conference on Financing for Development* (New York: United Nations).

—— (2004) *UN Millennium Development Goals*, www.unmillenniumproject.org/html/dev_goals.shtm.

White, A.L. (1999) 'Sustainability and the Accountable Corporation: Society's Rising Expectations of Business', *Environment* 41.8: 30-43.

Willemse, J. (2000) 'E&Co', paper presented at the International Solar Energy Society (ISES) Seminar on Rural Electrification in Africa, Johannesburg, April 2000.

World Bank (2002) 'Making Infrastructure Work for the Poor', press release, 19 February 2002, The World Bank Group, Washington, DC.

Xerox (2004) 'Environment, Health & Safety', www.xerox.com/environment, accessed 26 March 2004.

Further reading

Schmidheiny, S., with the BCSD (Business Council for Sustainable Development) (1992) *Changing Course: A Global Business Perspective on Development and the Environment* (Boston, MA: The MIT Press, 1st edn).

——, R. Chase and L. DeSimone (1997) *Signals of Change: Business Progress towards Sustainable Development* (Geneva: World Business Council for Sustainable Development).

Suez (2002) *Bridging the Water Divide* (Paris: Suez).

WCED (World Commission on Environment and Development) (1987) *Our Common Future* (The Brundtland Report; Oxford, UK: Oxford University Press, 1st edn).

Worenklein, J.J. (2002) 'A Private–Public Initiative for the World's Poorest Countries', paper presented at the World Bank Energy Forum 2002, Washington, DC, 5 June 2002.

5

Is the MBA sustainable?
Degrees of change

Suzanne Benn and David Bubna-Litic
University of Technology, Sydney, Australia

It is inevitable that sustainability will be the defining issue of this new century, requiring public-sector and private-sector organisations to introduce major changes in management.[1] Successful organisations of the future will define 'high performance' as including the fulfilment of human needs and support for the survival and renewal of the planet. For corporations this will mean new ways of doing business (Dunphy *et al.* 2003). But is our leading business education programme, the MBA, up to the task? If not, then how can it be changed?

5.1 Imperatives for corporate change

Unlike the natural disasters of early industrial society, such as disease and famine, contemporary chemical, nuclear and ecological threats are the result of our own endeavours (Beck 1992). Technological and industrial developments are now seen as a source of risk, insecurity, hazard and uncertainty (Beck 1992; Giddens 1990; Lash 2002; Tsoukas 1999). There are recent indications that companies and governments may become liable for the effects of global warming (Cortese 2002). Other examples, such as the BSE (bovine spongiform encephalopathy) crisis in the United Kingdom the effects of toxic chemicals and genetically modified organisms

---

1 In this analysis, we take the term 'sustainability' to imply that, at a minimum, 'activities and behaviours are ecologically sound, socially just and economically viable and that they will continue to be so for future generations' (Clugston *et al.* 2002: 547).

(Vogel 2003) and the ongoing consequences of the *Exxon Valdez* oil spill[2] and of Bhopal (Shrivastave 1987) and Chernobyl (Clarke 2002) demonstrate the massive uncertainties and risks that governments and corporations face in managing social and environmental issues. Each of these episodes has served to play out the prescriptions of leading social theorists who for more than a decade have argued that enhanced knowledge and information flow will increasingly confront society with the negative side-effects of its own modernisation.[3] True to these predictions, governments and corporations have come under increased scrutiny, and trust and credibility have become key factors for corporate survival (Tsoukas 1999).

The emergence of what Beck has labelled the 'risk society' has a number of implications for corporations (Beck 1992, 1999). Increases in the socially responsible investment industry (in Australia the number of managed funds in this area increased by 61% between 2001 and 2002) and new rules for corporate disclosure and financial advisors concerning labour standards and environmental, social and ethical considerations are examples (ASIC 2002). As national governments are seen as unable to deal with global issues of environmental risk and social deprivation, global corporations are increasingly required to collaborate with non-governmental organisations (NGOs) and governments in the alleviation of such issues (Post *et al.* 2002). Under these conditions, developing a high-performance organisation is about developing shared values with stakeholders as much as it is about economic success (Dunphy *et al.* 2003; Zadek 2001).

The management profession is expressing considerable concern at these trends. A recent US survey showed that 77% of corporate recruiters think it important to hire students that are aware of social and environmental issues (Alsop 2001). The editorial of a recent US Academy of Management newsletter called for the development of a more 'ethically self-reflexive community of practice' (*AMN* 2002: 1). But, if the management profession is to change, business education—in particular its flagship, the MBA—must change. What evidence do we have that this is occurring?

5.2 Is the MBA showing the way?

5.2.1 Historical review

Since its inception in 1908, the MBA has proliferated. More than 700 business schools in the USA offer MBA programmes, conferring more than 100,000 degrees annually (US Department of Education, National Centre for Education, quoted in Finlay and Samuelson 1999). The popularity of the MBA with students appears to be its ability to attract a premium in the labour market (Ashenden and Milligan 2001). In turn, employers associate skills gained in an MBA programme with an ability to generate a healthy profit stream (Maxwell and Guanhuang 1998). These

---

2　Some 13 years on, there are many species of wildlife that still have not recovered from the *Exxon Valdez* oil spill in Prince William Sound on the coast of Alaska (EVOSTC 2003).

3　According to these theorists, the conditions of self-confrontation characterise the conditions of 'reflexive modernisation' (Beck 1992, 1999; Giddens 1990).

are values that hark back to earlier periods of industrial growth when social and environmental consequences of corporate activity were ignored and the corporation was judged solely by its ability to make a profit (Dunphy *et al.* 2003; Orr 1992; Shrivastava 1995). Indeed, the MBA has long been charged with resistance to change. Many critics have noted that its curriculum and teaching methods are reminiscent of 1960s thinking (Mintzberg and Gosling 2002; Neelankavil 1994; Pfeffer and Fong 2002; Ross-Smith *et al.* 2002).

Prominent management academics have recently fuelled this criticism. Mintzberg and Gosling (2002) argue that the MBA continues to produce functional specialists drilled in analytical decision-making rather than collaborative, worldly and reflective managers needed to provide leadership and foster success in today's business environment. Pfeffer and Fong (2002) point out that business schools appear to be unable to generate responsive curricula that are sensitive to local issues. They argue that, although the generalist nature of sociology and organisation studies has enabled major theoretical advances in these fields (Weick 1989, cited in Pfeffer and Wong 2002), an over-emphasis on functional specialisation in the MBA has inhibited the research that would translate into relevant teaching practice. Essentially, critics charge that the MBA remains fixed in a modernist paradigm of unitary functionalism and is unable to deal with postmodernist concepts of localism and context.

5.2.2 The MBA and sustainability

Given the recent major advances in environmental sociology (Beck 1999; Dryzek 1997), corporate citizenship (McIntosh 2000; Zadek 2001) and corporate sustainability (Dunphy *et al.* 2003; Ehrenfeld 2000; Hart 1997; Shrivastava 1995), how has this research been integrated, if at all, into the teaching of the MBA? To what extent has the programme responded to the themes of sustainability and more contemporary perspectives, such as the goal of a sustainable economy (Pearce and Barbier 2002)?

A recent survey reported in Benn *et al.* (2001) indicates the extent to which sustainability themes are being incorporated in the principal MBA programmes of management schools in Australia. The survey, first conducted in 1999 and updated in 2000 and 2001, was sent to co-ordinators of MBA programmes at 46 institutions. A total of 25 responded. Four of the responding institutions (Monash Mt Eliza, Royal Melbourne Institute of Technology [RMIT] and the University of South Australia) have core subjects in a general MBA programme that deal with sustainability or matters such as corporate, environmental and social responsibility. Seven MBA programmes (James Cook University, University of Central Queensland, University of Tasmania, University of Queensland, Australian Graduate School of Management [AGSM] at University of New South Wales [UNSW], Deakin RMIT, University of Technology [UTS]) have elective subjects in the areas of environmental or social responsibility. Another three of the responding institutions (University of Southern Queensland, Griffith, and Murdoch) have a specialised MBA in environmental management. Six MBA programmes mentioned ethics-based subjects as areas with environment or sustainability themes.

Very few MBA programmes incorporated environmental and social sustainability themes with environmental electives or subjects commonly regarded as 'stand-alone' units or as aspects of a specialised degree. Clearly, environmental management has been relegated in the MBA to the technical, as distinct from the social realm of decision-making. Only one respondent (RMIT) said that sustainability is an objective in each subject of its programme. Several others said that student project work is expected to show concern for ethics and sustainability. Only six respondents offered any subject dealing with sustainability from an integrated perspective.

From these results, assuming that co-ordinators of MBA programmes that are concerned about sustainability would be most likely to respond to the survey, fewer than 25% of our managers of the future are given the opportunity to increase their understanding of one of the most important and contested management issues of the day. The results also showed that ethics remains a popular vehicle to introduce environmental or sustainability-related material. We argue, however, that the field of business ethics cannot encompass the issues associated with business management for sustainability either at a strategic or an operational level. The average MBA student is not being confronted with the reality that a significant number of firms are moving down the track of resource efficiency or long-term planning to engage with more sustainable products and processes (Elkington 1997; Hart 1997). Such initiatives reflect a broader-based strategy to develop corporate sustainability by using the full potential of humans for innovation (Dunphy *et al.* 2003).

The survey also asked respondents how, if at all, environmental, social responsibility or sustainability-related material featured in other areas of their MBA programme. Only two respondents nominated action learning or other teaching and learning activities in their programme, thus indicating limited awareness of the pedagogical advantages of active learning techniques for sustainability.

The Australian findings are similar to those of recent US studies. In a 1999 survey of the leading graduate business schools in the USA, only 20% reported activity on environmental or social topics (Finlay and Samuelson 1999). Repeated surveys there show a similar pattern to that in Australia: stand-alone environmental electives, ethics used to introduce concepts of social stewardship, lack of meshing of social and environmental themes into an holistic understanding of sustainability and poor integration of sustainability themes into core curricula (Klusman 2000; WRI/AISI 2001). The most recent US survey estimated that environment-dedicated courses in MBA programmes number fewer than 20%, and courses dedicated to social impact management numbered about 38% (WRI/AISI 2001).

5.3 Integration or new generation?

The research presented here shows limited recognition by business schools of the social, economic and environmental considerations required to incorporate sustainability into management education. It supports the criticism noted in Section 5.2.1: that the MBA is resistant to change.

As public opinion has moved towards a more 'ecocentric' ideology (Beder 1996; Harding 1998), the MBA appears stuck at the 'technocentric' end of the sustainability spectrum, linked to a set of values that play down the possibility of negative social, cultural or environmental impacts of business activity (Cotgrove 1982, cited in Harding 1998). From this perspective, ecological processes can be substituted with either human or built capital, and nature is judged against its worth to humans (Harding 1998; Pearce 1991). If the programme remains underpinned by these values, associated with centralised decision-making and technological determinism, the MBA will remain insensitive to demands that corporations contribute to the needs of a more communal and collaborative society and to those of future generations. For Australia, one of the most ecologically vulnerable nations on Earth (ACF 2001; Yencken and Williamson 2000), and for the USA, where the management profession is acutely aware of the need for more responsible, responsive and ethical corporate behaviour, we argue that this ideological position of the MBA will act as a significant barrier to its continuing relevance.

Educators are faced with two generic strategies to incorporate issues of sustainability into management education. The programme can be rejuvenated by incrementally integrating sustainability themes across existing curricula and by using teaching and learning techniques that enable students to engage actively with sustainability issues. The alternative is to adopt a more transformational approach to the development of an integrated and holistic curriculum. This becomes possible if the programme is separated from the belief in material values and technological progress reflected in most assumptions that currently underpin the MBA.

5.4 Integration across curricula: business education *for* sustainability

The first approach, based on the argument that 'average' managers and their corporations must be targeted if sustainability is to be achieved, is to integrate sustainability into the existing curriculum of the MBA. Pedagogically, it recognises the need to reposition sustainability issues into the mainstream curriculum if student interest is to be piqued. Emphasis is also placed on using teaching and learning techniques that foster active engagement (CEEFHE 1993). This approach derives from the premise that interdisciplinary inquiry is essential to address issues such as social and environmental sustainability and racial and gender inequality (Bartlett and Eisen 2002; Cortese 2002; Orr 1992).

Educating *for* sustainability is quite distinct pedagogically from education *about* sustainability (Fien and Tilbury 1996). Education for sustainability aims to promote explanation and understanding of sustainability across the curriculum.

If the whole MBA programme is approached as a means of developing personal and professional responsibility, sustainability should be considered where relevant across all subjects. Each subject area should use examples and activities that raise sustainability issues. Holistic integration encourages active learning, using, for example, Kolb's learning cycle. Kolb's steps include concrete experience, reflective observations, abstract conceptualisation and experimentation (Kolb 1978, cited in Benn 1999). An active learning environment would encourage the development of generic skills such as systems thinking, teamwork, ability to manage change, oral and written communication, negotiation and time management (Benn 1999).

5.4.1 Ideas for integration

Traditional accounting is limited to descriptions of financial transactions taking place within and between organisations. A first step towards sustainability is to incorporate measures of social and environmental impact such as triple-bottom-line accounting (Elkington 1997). Concepts from environmental accounting could also be introduced into other aspects of the curriculum, if environmental impact is taken as a factor to be considered in corporate decision-making.

Sustainability concepts could be integrated into organisational analysis and design subjects—core curricula in many MBAs. Reframing exercises could examine the implications of ecologically resonant metaphors, such as the 'organisation as organism' metaphor for organisational change and leadership strategies (Bolman and Deal 1997; Morgan 1997).

Dematerialisation concepts could also be introduced into operations management, organisational analysis and design curricula. These concepts focus on decoupling profit-making from materials use. Students could be introduced to a range of sustainable business strategies, such as leasing rather than selling goods, or sharing various goods and services by companies on a network basis. For example, Fuji Xerox leases rather than sells photocopiers. It has also introduced eco-manufacturing as a highly profitable venture. Thus, faulty photocopier parts are remanufactured to be better than new, which greatly reduces materials use and lowers operating costs (Benn *et al.* 2002). The shift from quantity to quality and the principles of industrial ecology could be introduced to students as themes that require new organisational structures based on collaboration, not competition, and on re-use rather than obsolescence.

Organisational change courses could show a firm moving from compliance to eco-efficiency to strategic sustainability as an example of change processes (Dunphy *et al.* 2003). In other examples, marketing curricula could focus on the environmental consumer, product stewardship and stakeholder analysis could be introduced into strategic management, and economic assumptions about human nature, such as rational egoism, could be examined as part of a traditional economics course.

5.4.2 Challenges faced by the incremental approach

Integration of environmental literacy and social responsibility across all subjects within degrees, educational programmes and campus provision has been attempted at several institutions of higher education (see Filho 1999). Educators acknowledge the difficulties in dislodging the dominant world-view of exploitation of nature and acceptance of social inequity in existing programmes; this is a problem the students may confront if aspects of their personal life, such as family or group values, seem contrary to the sustainability agenda. Rowe, for instance, argues that change agent skills, such as optimism, efficacy, futuring and implementation, are essential features of education *for* sustainability (Rowe 2002: 84-90).

Another challenge with integration is that, unless the examples and subject matter are closely linked to the core curriculum, the course may be perceived as either too generalised or too self-contained. Already-overloaded lecturers may resist having to introduce new examples and unfamiliar teaching methods (Benn 2000). The organisational changes required to incorporate sustainability themes into existing courses may be frustrated by academics who are unwilling or unable to change their ways of thinking and who actively resist changes towards sustainability that they see as impossible and perhaps irrelevant. Exposure to relevant sustainability concepts, such as interdepartmental mentors and campus 'greening' activities, can help in this case.

5.5 The argument for a new-generation degree

Incremental integration may not be enough to achieve the shift to sustainability. A second option is to create a revolutionary new MBA—one designed from the bottom up to address the needs of 21st-century business to transform itself. Such a degree would acknowledge the difficulty of changing established orders. As Kuhn (1970) observed, paradigmatic change tends to be revolutionary. This second, new-generation, approach to change is based on the argument that the design, pedagogic rationality and content of today's MBA is interwoven with modernist assumptions that engender a 'technocentric' way of thinking. To break out of this world-view, students need to be exposed to an entirely different approach.

5.5.1 Questioning the core assumptions behind an MBA

Bateson has observed that we may continue to function for quite some time even with deeply incorrect premises:

> The [erroneous] premises work only up to a certain limit, and, at some stage or under certain circumstances, if you are carrying serious epistemological errors, you find that they don't work any more. At this point you discover to your horror that it is exceedingly difficult to get rid of the error, that it's sticky. It is as if you had touched honey. As with honey, the falsification gets around; and each thing you try to wipe it off on gets sticky, and your hands still remain sticky (Bateson 1972: 479).

Reviewing the reasoning behind the structure of the MBA reveals many crucial epistemological errors. One key error is in the basic assumptions that justify the MBA. The four foundational disciplines of accounting, economics, organisational behaviour and quantitative methods on which the MBA is built are based on assumptions that these disciplines are unitary, coherent and uncontested. Embedded in this pragmatic approach is the belief that a simple appreciation of the dominant view of a particular discipline is sufficient for MBA graduates to negotiate the world of business. Similarly, the foundations of the physical sciences remained uncontested until Kuhn and the sociology of science emerged to challenge long-held assumptions.

This approach can be problematic. Such a reductive perspective on subject matter has major limitations. For example, it does not allow for the debates that make up the dynamic of a discipline to be encompassed (Keen 2001). A geography of critiques that falls under the rubric of postmodernism suggests a fundamental questioning of most of the core disciplines of a management education. However, the complex, ambivalent, self-questioning and thus 'subversive' conditions (Beck 1997: 22) engendered by the ecological and social imperatives of sustainability are those that must eventually have the most tangible and powerful impact, presenting philosophical and practical challenges to the managers of the future.

The epistemological error that management is a value-free, functionalist activity is deeply embedded in MBA programmes. MBA courses built on old assumptions are increasingly unable to bridge the gap between managers' beliefs and hopes as human beings and the reality of their working lives. Furthermore, the very structure of an MBA based on a selection of core disciplinary areas has the dangerous consequence of training future managers in a 'technocentric' world-view, an outdated perspective of the knowledge base of the society in which they operate.

This lack of critical reflection has negative implications for society and for business. Perhaps most importantly, it does not foster creativity in management or problem-solving. Nor is it conducive to the introduction of the emergent concepts of cyclical ecological thinking, biomimicry and the social and cultural construction of knowledge.

To illustrate this dilemma with a simple example, many subjects in the MBA programme teach from the paradigmatic perspective that organisations have a unitary purpose or mission. This view is characteristic of a certain school in organisation theory popular in the 1960s. The major reason for this lag is that a significant revision of the entire subject would be required to fully explain the advances. This presents a difficulty because the complexity of the issue brings in a range of other arguments that make up an almost paradigmatic shift in the discipline. This is far beyond the scope of an introductory overview. Sustainability likewise calls for the questioning of numerous assumptions, each of which has substantial implications for each subject in the course. For a coherent and consistent approach to sustainability to be incorporated, a concerted effort to track corresponding changes across the various subjects would need to be instituted. To introduce paradigmatic changes in economics, for example, would mean the complete reconceptualisation of existing subjects. Obviously, this would cut across the interests of significant constituencies in existing MBA programmes. This is particularly problematic where these constituencies do not necessarily share the same paradigmatic assumptions or the same world-views (Gladwin *et al.* 1995).

This new approach cannot be unilateral. Rather, it must find a middle ground not only in what is taught but also in what is done. The significant opportunity for a 'green-fields' approach is based on creating a new constituency able to integrate the assumptions and ideas of sustainability into the existing business culture. This requires an entirely different way of conducting business (Harman 1993).

For example, simple formulaic methodologies for strategic thinking (Porter 1980, 1985) could be balanced with more complex approaches that acknowledge how pre-existing mind-sets and interpretive frameworks structure and guide strategic choices (Bate 1995; Chaffee 1985; Stacey 1992). These have an impact at all stages of strategy creation. Organisations that adhere to 'environmentally friendly' values have been found to be more proactive in developing sustainable practices (Hood and Bubna-Litic 2000). This research also shows that less environmentally concerned organisations are unlikely to divert the attention of management to exploring sustainable practices unless the practices coincide with clear and significant cost advantages.

5.5.2 Challenges in the creation of the new degree

It is crucial in dealing with the epistemological errors of the existing MBA, as discussed in this chapter, that such a degree should not fall into the same pit of unreflexivity and selectivity of subject matter. It must not take just one set of assumptions, discard them for another and create an oppositional degree that ignores graduates' needs for skills relevant to contemporary corporate life. The ecology of modern society will not provide a hospitable habitat for graduates unless they can reframe everyday business problems in ways that are understood and perceived as valuable. This means the need to develop graduates able to span both worlds and who have the ability to think critically and act creatively and reflectively to transform current business practices.

5.5 Conclusions

Today's MBA programme cannot meet the needs of management in an increasingly interconnected information-rich society, in which we are confronted with the effects of ongoing modernisation and industrial development. This chapter has explored the need for sustainability to be incorporated into management education by incrementally integrating sustainability into all aspects of the current curriculum through the inclusion of activities that foster systems thinking and critical thinking. It has also considered a revolutionary design for a new and separate MBA that addresses sustainability by incorporating existing discourses critically and reflexively.

Underpinning the argument is the understanding that the MBA is value-laden and contested (Beder 1996; Dryzek 1997; Harding 1998) and that sustainability themes exemplify 'new' knowledge, characterised by transdisciplinarity, heterogeneity, social accountability, reflexivity and issues of legitimation (McDonell 2001). If sustainability is integrated across the curriculum, then active engagement via self-examination and debate may be approached from many sub-disciplinary areas of the MBA. Active engagement enables reflexive assessment of performance now required of our leaders and managers.

The argument for the alternative degree is based on evidence of a new interpretative understanding of reality and the need for new curricula that can incorporate contemporary provisional interpretations of the world. A crucial aspect of sustainability is recognising meaning in its geographical, political, economic and cultural context. A new degree freed from the constraints of determinist and technical understandings of management education would address the needs of a new model of doing business that embraces the temporary and multiple environments of postmodern society (Novo 2002).

Ultimately, both approaches seek the same goal of reflexivity. This pedagogy prepares students for management in a business climate where demands for sustainability will mean a greater emphasis on meaning and values, where knowledge is negotiated and where knowledge claims are significant arenas for competition (Tsoukas 1999). Hence, the question is not whether it is necessary to make these changes but how to make them. It is possible that both approaches can be used to take students beyond 'reflex' action to an active reflection on the traditional institutions and norms of society, including corporate responsibilities and purpose (Beck 1999).

References

ACF (Australian Conservation Foundation) (2001) *Australia's Report Card* (Melbourne: ACF).

Alsop, R. (2001) 'Career Journal: Corporations still put profits first, but social concerns gain ground', *Wall Street Journal*, 30 October 2001: B12.

AMN (*Academy of Management News*) (2002) 'Positive Professional Practice: A Response to Ethical Dilemmas in our Profession', *Academy of Management News* 33.4: 1.

Ashenden, D., and S. Milligan (2001) 'Australian "Mutants" Flourishing', *Sydney Morning Herald*, 24 May 2001: 17.

ASIC (Australian Securities and Investments Commission) (2002) *Socially Responsible Investing Disclosure Guidelines?* (Discussion paper; Traralgon, Vic., Australia: ASIC, December 2002).

Bartlett, P., and A. Eisen (2002) 'The Piedmont Project at Emory University', in W. Filho (ed.), *Teaching Sustainability at Universities* (Frankfurt am Main, Germany: Peter Lang): 61-78.

Bate, P. (1995) *Strategies for Cultural Change* (London: Butterworth-Heinemann).

Bateson, G. (1972) *Steps to an Ecology of Mind* (New York: Ballantine).

Beck, U. (1992) *The Risk Society* (London: Sage).

—— (1997) 'Global Risk Politics', in M. Jacobs (ed.), *Greening the Millennium? The New Politics of the Environment* (Oxford, UK: Basil Blackwell).

—— (1999) *The World Risk Society* (Molden, MA: Polity Press).

Beder, S. (1996) *The Nature of Sustainable Development* (Newham, Vic., Australia: Scribe Publications).

Benn, S. (1999) *Education for Sustainability* (Kensington, NSW, Australia: Institute of Environmental Studies, University of New South Wales).

—— (2000) 'Progress towards Education for Sustainability at UNSW', in W. van den Bor, P. Holen, A. Wals and W. Leal Filho (eds.), *Integrating Concepts of Sustainability into Education for Agriculture and Rural Development* (Frankfurt am Main, Germany: Peter Lang): 231-44.

——, D. Bubna-Litic and D. Eckstein (2001) 'Is the MBA Sustainable? Degrees of Change', paper presented at the Australian and New Zealand Academy of Management Conference, Auckland, New Zealand, December 2001.

——, D. Dunphy and S. Wilson (2002) *Fuji Xerox: A Case Study in Human and Ecological Sustainability* (WP-25/02; Sydney: School of Management, University of Technology).

Bolman, L., and T. Deal (1997) *Reframing Organisations: Artistry, Choice and Leadership* (San Francisco: Jossey Bass).

CEEFHE (Committee on Environmental Education in Further and Higher Education) (1993) *Environmental Responsibility: An Agenda for Further and Higher Education* (London: Department of Education and the Welsh Office).

Chaffee, E.E. (1985) 'Three Models of Strategy', *Academy of Management Review* 10.1: 89-98.

Clarke, R. (2002) 'Risky Future', *OECD Observer* 235 (December 2002): 66-68; www. oecdobserver.org/news/fullstory.php/aid/891/Risky_future.html.

Clugston, R., W. Calder and P. Corcoran (2002) 'Teaching Sustainability with the Earth Charter', in W. Filho (ed.), *Teaching Sustainability at Universities* (Frankfurt am Main, Germany: Peter Lang): 547-64.

Cortese, A. (2002) 'As the Earth warms up, will companies pay?', *New York Times*, 8 August 2002: 6.

Cotgrove, S. (1982) *Catastrophe or Cornucopia? The Environment, Politics and the Future* (Chichester, UK: John Wiley).

Dryzek, J. (1997) *The Politics of the Earth* (Oxford, UK: Oxford University Press).

Dunphy, D., A. Griffiths and S. Benn (2003) *Organisational Change for Corporate Sustainability* (London: Routledge).

Ehrenfeld, J. (2000) 'Industrial Ecology', *American Behavioral Scientist* 44.2: 229-45.

Elkington, J. (1997) *Cannibals with Forks: The Triple Bottom Line of 21st Century Business* (Oxford, UK: Capstone Publishing).

EVOSTC (*Exxon Valdez* Oil Spill Trustee Council) (1990) 'Spill: The Wreck of the *Exxon Valdez*: Final Report, Alaska Oil Spill Commission', www.evostc.state.ak.us/facts/details.html, accessed 28 January 2003.

Fien, J., and D. Tilbury (1996) *Learning for a Sustainable Environment: An Agenda for Teacher Education in Asia and the Pacific* (Bangkok: United Nations Educational, Scientific and Cultural Organisation [UNESCO]).

Filho, W.L. (1999) *Sustainability and University Life* (Frankfurt am Main, Germany: Peter Lang).

Finlay, J., and J. Samuelson (1999) *Beyond Grey Pinstripes: Preparing MBAs for Social and Environmental Stewardship* (Washington, DC: World Resources Institute).

Giddens, A. (1990) *Modernity and Self-identity: Self and Society in the Late Modern Age* (Cambridge, UK: Polity Press).

Gladwin, T., J. Kennelly and T. Krauss (1995) 'Shifting Paradigms for Sustainable Development: Implications for Management Theory and Research', *Academy of Management: The Academy of Management Review* 20.4: 874-96.

Harding, R. (1998) 'Value Systems and Paradigms', in R. Harding (ed.), *Environmental Decision-Making: The Roles of Scientists, Engineers and the Public* (Sydney: The Federation Press): 61-81.

Harman, W. (1993) 'Approaching the Millennium: Business as a Vehicle for Global Transformation', in M. Ray and A. Rinzler (eds.), *The New Paradigm in Business: Emerging Strategies for Leadership and Organisational Change* (New York: P. Tarcher/Putnam).

Hart, S. (1997) 'Beyond Greening: Strategies for a Sustainable World', *Harvard Business Review*, January/February 1997: 67-76.

Hood, P., and D. Bubna-Litic (2000) 'Three Colours Green: Drivers of Environmental Change in Organisations', paper presented at the Asia–Pacific Researchers in Organisation Studies Conference, Sydney, 2000.

Keen, S. (2001) *Debunking Economics: The Naked Emperor of the Social Sciences* (Annandale, NSW, Australia: Pluto Press).

Klusman, T (2000) 'MBA: Making Business Accountable', *Business Ethics*, May/June 2000: 9-14.

Kolb, D. (1978) *Learning Style Technical Manual* (Boston, MA: McBer and Co., rev. edn).

Kuhn, T. (1970) *The Structure of Scientific Revolutions* (Chicago: University of Chicago Press).

Lash, S. (2002) 'Foreword', in U. Beck and E. Beck-Gernshein *Individualisation* (London: Sage).

McDonell, G. (2001) 'On Choosing . . . The Nearest Amenable and Illuminating Lie: The Spread of Transdisciplinarity', paper presented at the Conference on Inter-disciplinarity, 'No Sense of Discipline', Brisbane, Australia, 11–12 June 2001.

McIntosh, M. (2000) *Living Corporate Citizenship: Strategic Routes to Socially Responsible Business* (London: Financial Times Prentice Hall).

Maxwell, P., and L. Guanhuang (1998) *The MBA in Australia: Why Has It Been Such A Success?* (working paper; Perth, Australia: Division of Business and Administration, Curtin University of Technology).

Mintzberg, H., and J. Gosling (2002) 'Educating Managers beyond Borders', *Academy of Management Learning and Education Journal* 1.1: 64-77.

Morgan, G. (1997) *Images of Organization* (Thousand Oaks, CA: Sage, 2nd edn).

Neelankavil, J.P. (1994) 'Corporate America's Quest for an Ideal MBA', *Journal of Management Development* 13.5: 38-52.

Novo, M. (2002) 'Higher Environmental Education in the XXI Century: Towards a New Interpretative Paradigm', in W. Filho (ed.), *Teaching Sustainability at Universities* (Frankfurt am Main: Peter Lang): 429-58.

Orr, D. (1992) *Ecological Literacy* (Albany, NY: State University of New York Press).

Pearce, D. (1991) *Blueprint 2: Greening the Economy* (London: Earthscan Publications).

—— and E. Barbier (2002) *Blueprint for a Sustainable Economy* (London: Earthscan Publications).

Penley, L.E., P. Fulton, G.G. Daly, and R.E. Frank *et al.* (1995) 'Has Business School Education Become a Scandal?', *Business and Society Review* 93 (Spring 1995): 4-16.

Pfeffer, J., and C. Fong (2002) 'The End of Business Schools? Less Success than Meets the Eye', *Academy of Management Journal of Learning and Education* 1.2: 78-95.

Porter, M. (1980) *Competitive Strategy: Techniques for Analyzing Industries and Competitors* (New York: The Free Press).

—— (1985) *Competitive Advantage: Creating and Sustaining Superior Performance* (New York: The Free Press).

Post, J., L. Preston and S. Sachs (2002) 'Managing the Extended Enterprise: The New Stakeholder View', *California Management Review* 45.1: 6-29.

Ross-Smith, A., S. Clegg and P. Agius (2002) 'Cashed Up and Complacent: A Diagnosis of the Present Condition of Management Education in Australian Universities', paper presented at the Australia New Zealand Academy of Management Conference, La Trobe University, Victoria, Australia, December 2002.

Rowe, D. (2002) 'Environmental Literacy and Sustainability as Core Requirements: Success Stories and Models', in W. Filho (ed.), *Teaching Sustainability at Universities* (Frankfurt am Main, Germany: Peter Lang): 79-104.

Shrivastava, P. (1987) *Bhopal: Anatomy of a Crisis* (Cambridge, MA: Ballinger Publishing Company).

—— (1995) 'Ecocentric Management for a Risk Society', *Academy of Management Review* 20.1: 118-30.

Stacey, R. (1992) *Managing the Unknowable* (San Francisco: Jossey-Bass).

Tsoukas, H. (1999) 'David and Goliath in the Risk Society: Making Sense of the Conflict between Shell and Greenpeace in the North Sea', *Organization* 6.1: 499-528.

Vogel, D. (2003) 'The Hare and the Tortoise Revisited: The New Politics of Consumer and Environmental Regulation in Europe', *British Journal of Political Science* 33.4: 557-81.

Weick, K.E. (1989) 'Theory Construction as Disciplined Imagination', *Academy of Management Review* 14: 516-31.

WRI/AISI (World Resources Institute/Aspen Institute for Social Innovations) (2001) 'Beyond Grey Pinstripes: Preparing MBAs for Social and Environmental Stewardship', www.beyondgreypinstripes.org/results/past_reports/bgps2001.cfm, accessed 23 March 2004.

Yencken, D., and D. Williamson (2000) *Resetting the Compass* (Collingwood, Vic., Australia: CSIRO Publishing).

Zadek, S. (2001) *The Civil Corporation* (London: Earthscan Publications).

6
Integrating business and environmental education

Steven R. Elliott, Raymond F. Gorman,
Timothy C. Krehbiel and Orie L. Loucks
Miami University, USA

O. Homer Erekson
University of Missouri–Kansas City, USA

H. Gregory Hume
TECHSOLVE, USA

6.1 Business confronts environmental change

Environmental awareness has grown immeasurably among the US general public since the first Earth Day in 1970. The scientific community working on the National Ecological Observatory Network (NEON) project argues that 'human-induced changes in our environment are expected to increase greatly over the coming decades, causing environmental issues to be one of the greatest challenges of the 21st century' and that 'study of direct effects and feedbacks between environmental change and biological processes is inherently interdisciplinary' (Committee on the National Ecological Observatory Network 2003: 1-2). But formal programmes in environmental education have only recently reached the periphery of a crucial audience—graduate and undergraduate students in business schools. Given the control of vast resources by modern industrial organisations, meaningful progress towards sustainable development seems unlikely unless this student audience develops a thorough understanding of principles that link ecological and business systems. Edward Hennessy, former CEO of Allied-Signal Inc., notes that, 'If we are to preserve the environment and at the same time continue to enjoy the benefits of advanced technology, we must educate tomorrow's leaders to think in new ways about protecting the environment' (quoted in

Smart 1992: 146). The National Wildlife Federation Corporate Conservation Council (NWFCCC 1992) observed that societal and private-sector benefits arising from investments in business school environmental education would have a significant multiplier effect in terms of positive benefits to society, nationally and internationally.

Moreover, the thrust to understand and measure the sustainability of business development will have to be data-driven, holistic and interdisciplinary as modern ecological dysfunction results from the long-term 'failure to see things in their entirety' (Orr 1993: 10). The step of appending brief environmental issues to traditional business school curricula, although useful for certain problems, cannot be effective in the long term (Clark 1991). Conversely, there are a mounting number of interdisciplinary degree programmes in higher education generally, suggesting an increasing awareness of the interdependency of traditional academic disciplines. Traditional business education, however, is typically 'silo-based'. It emphasises more specialised knowledge within a unique disciplinary niche such as accounting or marketing. We contend that higher learning also must advance students' appreciation of a complex, interconnected world and a moral vision sufficient to ensure a high quality of life across multiple generations in a dynamic world.

Based on this premise, several questions arise. The goal of this chapter is to address them. Given the historical antagonism between environmentalists and business leaders, would an interdisciplinary, ecological approach to business education be welcomed by either group? What about in higher education—what would motivate business students to respond to such an initiative? What structures and organisations are emerging to encourage business schools to add interdisciplinary, sustainable development approaches to the business canon?

6.2 The waning entrenched antagonism toward environmental concerns

The traditional relationship between industrialists, responsible for the continuing flow of goods and services that constitute the material basis of society, and environmentalists, concerned with the inimical effects of this process, has been largely oppositional. To an environmentalist of the 1970s and 1980s, the business executive epitomised the worst aspects of a capitalistic society: corporate greed, exploitation of natural resources, habitat loss and uncontrolled pollution. Conversely, an environmentalist often was viewed by the business community as a modern-day Luddite, with a predilection for unreasoned regulation and bureaucracy.

The account of demand-side management in the electric utility industry related by Bradford (1992) is illustrative of industrialist–environmentalist tensions. Utility growth was based primarily on increasing investment in the construction of generating stations. Economies of scale led to increased utility income and decreasing electricity prices relative to cost-of-living adjustments. Relative price reductions provided an incentive for more consumption, resulting in a positive feedback loop that was reinforced by tax policy changes in the early 1970s. It was not surprising that the utility industry summarily rejected suggestions that consumer interest would be better served by conservation. By the end of the 1980s, however, closer relations between the two camps was becoming evident in their shared agreement on the role of market-based incentives. A growing number of environmentalists recognised the potential of the market to serve environmental objectives when price signals properly reflect the total environmental cost of producing a specific pollutant or of exploiting a particular resource (Alper 1993). At the same time, industrialists, facing mounting scientific evidence of environmental damage and stiffer penalties for regulatory non-compliance, saw the opportunity to engage in meaningful dialogue based on economic and ecological considerations. Moreover, both factions could ill afford to ignore the increasing public belief that economic growth and environmental protection should be compatible (Rice 1992).

Today, industry leaders acknowledge that it is good business to be environmentally responsible. For instance, then Dow Chemical chairman and CEO Frank Popoff noted that protecting the economy and the environment are compatible objectives and that less-wasteful production saved the chemical industry 'hundreds of millions, if not billions of dollars in costs' (quoted in APN 1992). Bruce Smart (1992: ix), the former CEO of the Continental Group, has suggested the term 'eco-industrial revolution' to describe the technological transformation necessary to bring the impact of human activities 'back into balance with nature's regenerative powers'. He provided an extensive compilation of corporate best practices that sustain the economy and the environment through pollution prevention technology.

6.3 Business school students and the need for environmental education

The upsurge in environmental interest by industry in the 1980s was not answered immediately by a corresponding trend among business schools. Synodinos (1990) found that business students' verbal commitment, actual commitment and knowledge about environmental issues were significantly lower than those seen in previous studies of students from other disciplines—hardly surprising given that as late as 1987 not a single business school offered an environmental course (MEB 1992).

The failure of business education to incorporate environmental content is partially a problem of specialisation of academic inquiry and partially a problem of rhetoric. Higher education is organised chiefly, in its teaching and research, along disciplinary or even sub-disciplinary lines. This compartmentalisation is indicative not just of higher education but of other organisations and of society itself. Wheatley has noted:

> It is interesting to note just how Newtonian most organisations are. The machine imagery was captured by organisations in an emphasis on structure and parts. Responsibilities have been organised into functions. People have been organised into roles . . . Knowledge was broken into disciplines and subjects, engineering became a prized science, and people were fragmented—counseled to use different 'parts' of themselves in different settings . . . Until recently, we believed we could study the parts, no matter how many of them there were, to arrive at knowledge of the whole . . . A world based on machine images is a world filled with boundaries (Wheatley 1992: 27-28).

Following suit, the study of environmental issues has too often been relegated to the science and engineering sub-disciplines or to specialists within a disciplines such as environmental and natural resource economics. The inherent danger in this balkanised approach is that disciplinary specialists define environmental problems from a limited perspective. The learnings from each discipline ignore the feedback effects or constraints that the physical system may impose on the social system, or vice versa. As Orr (1995: 44) has stated, 'the fact that we see them as disconnected events or fail to see them at all is evidence of a failure to educate people to think broadly, perceive systems and patterns and live as whole persons'.

The problem of rhetoric confounds this disciplinary isolationism. To a great extent, the language of discourse used in intellectual inquiry or in public policy determines the probable outcome of that discussion. If discussions of the potential effects of global warming are held using scientific vocabulary, the apparently carefully reasoned and scientifically verified 'facts' about global warming are persuasive. However, if this same discourse uses the language of an ethicist who discounts the validity of science, very different questions are permissible.

Environmental education has often been criticised for focusing on efforts that are 'doomsday oriented, fear generating, activist and devoid of science teaching' (Kwong 1995: 1). The argument follows that environmentalists are advocates, often 'issue-driven rather than information-driven' and based on 'emotionalism, myths and misinformation' (Kwong 1995: 3). On the other side, business executives and physical and social scientists are regarded as opposing responsible environmental behaviour and accused of 'the willful dismissal or distortion of fact, logic and data in the service of ideology and self-interest' (Orr and Ehrenfeld 1995: 985). It was in this contentious culture that business schools were faced with linking business and environmental concerns and recognising the limitations of tackling environmental questions from a disciplinary perspective. They also saw the necessity for developing language that provides a basis for common discussion between those from within business, science or other areas of inquiry.

6.4 Environmental education and business school curricula

As noted in Section 6.3, as late as 1987 not one business school offered course work with an integrated environmental approach. Individuals interested in studying business and the environment had the option either of pursuing multiple degrees, such as an undergraduate technical degree coupled with an MBA, or of ranging somewhat far afield by picking up an incidental elective for which little theoretical groundwork had been laid. Neither approach was widely accepted.

As early as 1982, however, the National Wildlife Federation had established the Corporate Conservation Council to provide a forum for frank and open discussions with corporate executives about emerging environmental and natural resources issues. In 1988, the NWFCCC conducted a survey of business school faculties to determine the status of environmental education in business schools and the outlook for the future. The survey results suggested that there were no established electives focusing on environmental management issues at graduate schools of business. If discussed at all, environmental issues were addressed in the context of business law, business ethics or regulatory issues. Although faculty respondents agreed with the need to focus more attention on environmental matters, there was no consensus on the best way to accomplish this. A majority did agree that environmental concerns must be taught within a multidisciplinary framework (NWFCCC 1992). James Post of Boston University's School of Management summarised the results of the study, noting that business schools are years behind corporate practices. To the extent that business schools do address issues of natural resources and environmental risks, those questions are posed primarily in business and society courses (Post 1990: 70-71).

Based on its survey results, the NWFCCC commissioned a three-member academic team to develop graduate-level pilot courses at Boston University, the University of Minnesota and Loyola University in New Orleans. Functional topics that emerged included the history of environmental concerns, ecological concepts, environmental ethics, issues and policy and corporate environmental strategies. Lectures were supplemented with case studies, videos, outside speakers and class projects (NWFCCC 1992).

This initial work was an important catalyst for other business school initiatives. In the 1990s, a limited number of programmes began to emerge, exploring boundary-expanding approaches that linked scientific or technical approaches with business and/or economic approaches. At the University of Michigan, the Corporate Environmental Management Program (CEMP), a joint venture between the School of Natural Resources and the Business School, developed a new MBA course, 'Strategies for Environmental Management'. This course was designed to provide graduate students with a solid grounding in ecological concepts, environmental policy and management practice. At the University of Maryland ecological economics was introduced as an international transdisciplinary field of study to address the relationships between ecosystems and economic systems in the broadest sense (Costanza *et al.* 1991). At Tufts University, the Centre for Environmental Management took a more applied approach and focused on pollution prevention, health research, policy analysis and education.

Each of these and similar initiatives throughout the USA and beyond began to provide links whereby business students could examine environmental issues and relate them to business decision-making. In Sections 6.4.1–6.4.3 we highlight three programmes we believe have significantly advanced the integration of business and environmental education.

6.4.1 Management Institute for Environment and Business: Business–Environment Learning and Leadership

As reported by the World Resources Institute (WRI) website[1] in late 1990 Dirk Long met with an old friend, Matt Arnold, who talked about his dreams. He had been thinking about corporate environmental performance and the relationship between companies and environmentalists. He argued that there must be an alternative to the existing conflict-based relationships and that perhaps business students would be best able to identify new courses of action for corporations to deal with environmental issues.

To make this vision a reality, the Management Institute for Environment and Business (MEB) was founded in 1990 to educate current and future business professionals about opportunities presented by sustainable development. At this point, the concept behind the MEB was powerful but unrefined. Long and Arnold received puzzled looks from friends, who saw risks in the strategy, but the pair remained inspired by the vision of improving the private sector's approach to environmental challenges. They also understood that it is the nature of almost any good concept that it does not begin complete. Rather, it must be revised and reshaped continually.

Long and Arnold faced the same problems as their private-sector friends when they tried to convince financiers and customers to work with them. By late 1991, however, they began to experience success. AT&T and the Rockefeller Brothers Fund took a gamble by supporting them. Then, they asked business schools at five universities—Stanford, the University of Michigan, Northwestern University, the University of Texas–Austin and the University of Virginia—to join in an experimental partnership to develop models for integrating environmental issues into business school education. Early academic adopters—James Patell, Alan Beckenstein, Thomas Gladwin, Stuart Hart and Max Bazerman—showed that their educational efforts could yield results in company strategy and individual behaviour.

The number of universities invited to join in the partnership soon expanded to 25 and became the Business–Environment Learning and Leadership (BELL) network. Today, the BELL network includes professors and programmes from most of the top business schools in North America. These schools now offer more than one environment and business elective, and many include this subject in required courses.

The continuing objective of the BELL project is to integrate environmental and sustainability issues into the curricula of business schools worldwide. It focuses on

1   Go to www.wri.org/meb.

greening management education by training business professors and providing environmental curricula. The programme publishes a biennial report, *Beyond Grey Pinstripes*, that rates business schools' environment and social content in MBA programmes and offers field-study opportunities to MBA students to work with sustainable enterprises in Latin America.

The annual BELL Conference convenes more than 200 innovative business school faculty and WRI staff members, as well as representatives from the private sector, governments and other non-governmental organisations (NGOs) interested in sustainability. The conference features teaching case presentations, panel discussions of emerging environmental topics important to business education and presentations of innovative business and environment teaching initiatives.

The growth in the BELL network mirrored the growth in the MEB. In 1995, the MEB began thinking about its own sustainability and investigated alliances as a path to accomplish longer-term goals. It found a partner in the WRI and its president Jonathan Lash. He and his team understood the ideas of the MEB and the needs of its people. The merger was launched with a seminar, 'Sustainability and the Private Sector: From Vision to Action', in September 1996 in Washington, DC. More than 60 business, government and NGO leaders came to listen to WRI's Lash, MEB's Arnold, WRI board member Bruce Mart, and Michael Hartnagel from E.I. du Pont de Nemours & Company discuss strategies for sustainable development. 'MEB's business expertise will enable WRI to engage the private sector with practical and innovative solutions to environmental challenges', said Mr. Lash. 'The merger sets us on a course toward our vision of sustainability by evolving as an organisation.'

The merger with the WRI provided the MEB with new resources: a much larger library that increased its research ability, an online network that enhanced its communication internally and externally and the expertise of colleagues in science, development, technology, policy and economics. These additional resources allowed the MEB to improve and expand the BELL, LA-BELL and China BELL programmes (described below) to reach more stakeholders. The collaboration also resulted in innovative new programmes in sustainable forestry, new ventures and sustainable enterprise.

In September 2001, the MEB changed its name to the Sustainable Enterprise Program (SEP). Among its current programmes are:

● BELL (Business–Environment Learning and Leadership). BELL is SEP's flagship project. It focuses on building environmental concepts into the core curricula of North American business schools. It works with universities to provide educational materials, faculty training and outreach.

● LA-BELL (Latin America Business–Environment Learning and Leadership). Over the past three years, the SEP has built a network of more than 20 business schools in Latin America similar to those of the BELL programme. It also provides training materials to this network of schools and tries to build closer linkages between these schools and local industry.

● China BELL. by moving aggressively to extend the network to China, SEP is working with Asian business schools to meet the challenges and opportunities resulting from Asia's growing economies and the concomitant stresses on its environment. As government control of Asian businesses diminishes, greater decision-making power will be in the hands of those trained in business schools. BELL is ensuring that this training takes advantage of educational resources being developed in the rest of the world.

● Sustainable Forestry. This project, funded by the MacArthur Foundation, allows the SEP to continue its development of business case studies on sustainable forestry management. These efforts are being co-ordinated with the WRI Forest Frontiers Initiative, which promotes responsible forest management.

● New Ventures. The SEP and the WRI will explore the potential for developing an incubation service fund, providing business planning and market development for young, socially oriented entrepreneurs in the USA and Latin America who seek to build businesses consistent with a vision of sustainability. This work is based on the belief that a key bottleneck in the creation of more green businesses is the scarcity of entrepreneurs and business plans and that funding could be readily mobilised for high-potential management teams.

● Sustainable Enterprise. A core team of people from 5–10 companies will develop a set of tools and best practices that address sustainability in design, profit-and-loss management and performance measurement. An outreach group of up to 50 more companies will also be established to promote dialogue and the adoption of the tools and best practices developed by the core team.

By sustaining its commitment to industry and education, the SEP has helped leaders in both sectors transform the constraining perspective of environmental performance as a cost to business into a profit-enhancing concept in which environmental initiatives are viewed as a potential source of competitive advantage.

6.4.2 Miami University Sustainability Project, and the Center for Sustainable Systems Studies

At a dinner in Oxford, OH, during November 1989 two Miami University scientists—Norman Grant from the geology department and Orie Loucks from the zoology department—began to talk about how to teach sustainable development by emphasising real-world problems and solutions. Grant and Loucks focused on ways to address sustainability issues in the context of economic market realities. They envisioned an interdisciplinary method that would synthesise ecological and economic concepts for students.[2]

---

2 See Chapter 10 in this volume for more details regarding the Center for Sustainable Systems Studies.

Further conversations led to the creation in 1990 of the Miami University Sustainability Project (MUSP), comprising a group of seven faculties from two colleges—Business Administration, and Arts and Science. The goal of the MUSP initially was to foster collaboration among business and science professors interested in sustainable resource use, corporate public policy, benign production technology, corporate public policy and the implications of each of these for business and science education. This was seen as a good way of promoting sustainability, as more than 250,000 undergraduate business degrees are granted by US colleges and universities each year.

MUSP needed a text and other materials that documented the shift by industry to low-impact technologies and recycling in order to teach the subject. It sought outside funding and received a substantial grant from the Cleveland Foundation in 1992 to prepare a monograph on principles and case studies. Next, MUSP developed an interdisciplinary capstone course in sustainability perspectives for senior students of business, science and other fields, taught for the first time in spring 1996. Today, this initiative is still unique at the undergraduate level in the USA. The goal has been not only to develop and test teaching materials at Miami but also to promote the teaching of sustainability in other business schools. Some of the accomplishments of MUSP made possible by the Cleveland Foundation grant include:

- A textbook, comprising eight chapters describing principles and 11 case studies

- A course first tested as an honours seminar that has since been adopted as a senior capstone experience by the Liberal Education Council and the School of Business and is now cross-listed by 11 departments

- A thematic sequence, 'Sustainable Systems', which has been accepted by the Liberal Education Council

- A series of statewide workshops, through which MUSP engaged faculty at 12 Ohio and Midwestern institutions

- A seminar series featuring about two speakers from business and academe per semester which seeks to enrich student and faculty experience by adding interdisciplinary experience in business and the environment

- Collaboration with two external groups:
  - It was one of the first 25 universities in the Business–Environment Leadership and Learning (BELL) programme of the MEB in Washington, DC (see Section 6.4.1)
  - It collaborates with the Council for Ethics in Economics, based in Columbus, OH

- The hosting of two federal agency teleconferences on sustainable development

- Facilitated teaching of a spin-off course, 'Practicum in Community Environmental Management and Sustainability' in 1995 (through the

Institute of Environmental Science [IES] using an instructor trained by her involvement in MUSP

- A biannual newsletter, *Sustainability Issues,* which is circulated to more than 1,000 people throughout the world

The Cleveland Foundation and Miami University's support also helped maintain the focus and timetable, run a central office, support up to five graduate students per year and involve faculties in which scholarship was influenced by work in, or linked to, the project. However, by 1996, the feeling was that, although MUSP had been useful over the previous six years, new opportunities and responsibilities were emerging that required a new framework. To continue to be committed to an expanded programme, a university centre dedicated to sustainability was needed.

Thus, in 1997, Miami University established a university-wide Center for Sustainable Systems Studies (CSSS) to help meet the needs of the colleges involved, as well as the university's mission of leadership in environmental education and research.

Its principal objectives are:

- To develop, support and help the teaching of one or more inter-college interdisciplinary courses on sustainability perspectives for students in business, design, natural sciences, engineering and natural resources and to help develop curriculum materials for intra-course modules at the business–science interface appropriate for introductory or intermediate courses in many fields of the colleges involved

- To expand the opportunities for faculty research in sustainable development by seeking external funding for projects, faculty scholarship and interdisciplinary graduate training on issues of sustainable business planning, Earth resource development and re-use, tax and other policy instruments, and lifestyles

- To provide a meeting point at which industry leaders and faculties from other universities can be brought to exchange information, attend conferences and speak at seminars

Today, the CSSS continues to enable the important cross-fertilisation among business, science and policy scholars to develop unique perspectives on sustainability. The CSSS also plans to become a focus for some of the graduate theses or reports done in the MBA programme in the IES and in the Special Committee PhD offered at Miami University. Undergraduates are still involved with the CSSS. Research has been expanded now to several major projects, many publications and several seminar speakers each year. A strategic plan and an external advisory council guide this work. More than 20 faculty members from five of the university's divisions have become associates of the CSSS.

6.4.3 Organisations and the Natural Environment

In 1991, a small group attending a caucus meeting at the Academy of Management convention in Miami, FL, created Organisations and the Natural Environment

(ONE), according to their website.[3] Since then, ONE has grown from a few impassioned scholars around a table in Miami into a dynamic interest group with more than 400 members. Over a period of three years, a core of energetic scholars led by Paul Shrivastava of Bucknell University took professional risks to ensure that the environment would be properly recognised by scholars in the management community. They were engaged in spirited debates from many quarters and had to overcome many obstacles. In 1994, their efforts paid off when the ONE Interest Group was officially sanctioned by the Academy of Management.

The visibility of ONE in the Academy has been disproportionate to its size. It has brought in to speak notables such as Anita Roddick and Peter Senge and has sponsored many symposia and pre-conference events designed to encourage Academy members to debate the relationships among organisations and the natural environment.[4]

The rapid growth in membership has forced ONE to become more structured and to address consequent issues of leadership and finances. There has also been an ongoing struggle for professional legitimacy in the field of management. The Academy of Management has twice reaffirmed ONE as an interest group, most recently in April 2002, but ONE is still hopeful that at its next review in 2005 it will be elevated to division status.

6.5 Conclusions

The necessity for business school students to understand environmental issues has intensified as scientific inquiry reveals the implications of modern consumer society for the environment and human welfare. Business school students and graduates must fully grasp the economic, ethical and ecological aspects of sustainability if they are meaningfully to talk about and contribute to policy-making on these issues.

Some 15 years ago there were few environmental management courses offered in business schools at either the graduate or undergraduate level. Thanks to the vision and efforts of a handful of people, today's students are studying the role of the environment in business decisions at top business schools around the world. Furthermore, the topic is the focus of research by some of the most renowned scholars. The Association to Advance Collegiate Schools of Business (AACSB International) now lists the environment as a mandatory perspective to be taught in all accredited undergraduate and MBA programmes. However, as can be inferred by the difficulty that the ONE management group has had trying to move from interest group to division status within the Academy of Management, infusing an environmental perspective into business curricula remains a daunting task. It will take the continued hard work of the dedicated few in business schools and a clear

3   Go to myaom.pace.edu/DivisionsAndGroups/ONE.
4   See *ONE Newsletter* 4.1 (1998), divisions.aomonline.org/one/one_Spring_1998_Newsletter.htm.

signal from the business community that their efforts will continue to be rewarded.

References

Alper, J. (1993) 'Protecting the Environment with the Power of the Market', *Science* 260: 1,884-85.

APN (American Political Network) (1992) *Media Monitor: Greenwire* (Alexandria, VA: APN, 16 December 1992).

Bradford, P. (1992) 'Foreword', in S. Nadel, M. Reid and D. Walcott (eds.), *Regulatory Incentives for Demand-Side Management* (Washington, DC: American Council for an Energy-Efficient Economy): ix-xi.

Clark, M. (1991) 'Rethinking Ecological and Economic Education: A Gestalt Shift', in R. Costanza (ed.), *Ecological Economics* (New York: Columbia University Press): 400-15.

Committee on the National Ecological Observatory Network (2003) *NEON: Addressing the Nation's Environmental Challenges* (Washington, DC: National Academies Press).

Costanza, R., H. Daly and J. Bartholomew (1991) 'Goals, Agenda and Policy Recommendations for Ecological Economics', in R. Costanza (ed.), *Ecological Economics* (New York: Columbia University Press): 1-20.

Kwong, J. (1995) *Environmental Education: Getting Beyond Advocacy* (Contemporary Issues Series 76; St Louis, MO: Centre for the Study of American Business, Washington University, December 1995).

MEB (Management Institute for Environment and Business) (1992) 'Environmental Education at US Business Schools', *Envirolink*, Summer 1992: 1.

NWFCCC (National Wildlife Federation Corporate Conservation Council) (1992) *Gaining Ground: Environmental Education at US Business Schools* (Washington, DC: NWFCCC).

Orr, D.W. (1993) 'The Problem of Disciplines/The Discipline of Problems', *Conservation Biology* 7.1: 10-12.

—— (1995) 'Educating for the Environment', *Change*, May/June 1995: 43-46.

—— and D. Ehrenfeld (1995) 'None So Blind: The Problem of Ecological Denial', *Conservation Biology* 9.5 (October 1995): 985-87.

Post, J. (1990) 'The Greening of Management', *Issues in Science and Technology*, Summer 1990: 68-72.

Rice, F. (1992) 'Next Steps for the Environment', *Fortune*, 19 October 1992: 98-100.

Smart, B. (1992) *Beyond Compliance: A New Industry View of the Environment* (Washington, DC: World Resources Institute).

Synodinos, N. (1990) 'Environmental Attitudes and Knowledge: A Comparison of Marketing and Business Students with Other Groups', *Journal of Business Research* 20: 161-70.

Wheatley, M. (1992) *Leadership and the New Science: Learning about Organisations from an Orderly Universe* (San Francisco: Berrett-Koehler).

7
Social sustainability

David K. Foot
University of Toronto, Canada

Susan Ross
Golder Associates Ltd, Canada

The concept of sustainability has become more important as businesses, from resource extraction to service providers, compete for advantage in an increasingly global marketplace. In the private sector, sustainability is still often narrowly interpreted as environmental stewardship. Recently, however, sustainability has evolved to add economic and social sustainability as critical components of successful sustainable business strategies.

In many respects, the recent attention of business to sustainability has its foundation in the Brundtland Commission's (WCED 1987: 8) definition of sustainable development: that it 'meets the needs of the present without compromising the ability of future generations to meet their own needs'. This definition embraces the triple requirements of environmental quality, economic prosperity and social justice.

Economic prosperity has been the cornerstone of most post-war economic development. Attending to current needs, particularly in the private sector and in developing or depressed regions, has been the crucial test of any private or public investment. A timely revenue stream for current participants was almost always required of any project.

The Brundtland Commission's contribution emphasised that economic development benefiting the current generation (through profits, jobs, taxes and so on) should not be at the expense of the ability of future generations to do likewise. This implies that economic benefits must be sustained for subsequent generations, either from the current project or, in the event of its eventual demise perhaps as a consequence of resource depletion, from the economic infrastructure created from the direct and indirect income streams generated by the project. It is easier to sustain economic benefits if environmental quality is maintained, thus environmental stewardship became closely associated with sustainable economic prosperity.

The requirement of inter-temporal equity in the Brundtland Commission's definition extended the sustainability focus of the development assistance community on equity through poverty reduction and conflict prevention, thereby integrating social justice into sustainability. Social sustainability has emerged as the third ingredient of a successful sustainable business strategy, along with economic and environmental sustainability. This chapter reviews the current state of social sustainability as an essential component of sustainable business performance.

7.1 Background

Why has social sustainability become essential to the definition and practice of sustainability? First, social sustainability is inextricably linked to economic and environmental sustainability (Royal Dutch/Shell 2001). A stable social environment supports the achievement of economic and environmental sustainability. In contrast, war—the antithesis of social sustainability—produces unsustainable economies and environments, especially when associated with competition for scarce or diminishing essential environmental resources (Homer-Dixon 1999).

Second, for a variety of reasons, there are increasing demands for businesses to proactively address many social issues in sustainable ways (WBCSD 2002). Such demands can come from suppliers, from investors requiring a corporate commitment to ethical behaviour, from regulators mandated to ensure that benefits continue to flow to the community, from governments that promote responsible self-regulation by business or from business's own workforces where retention and productivity may depend on enlightened employment practices. In all cases, an appropriate response contributes to long-term business success. Conversely, an inappropriate response ultimately leads to failure. Consequently, sustainable business success requires acknowledging and understanding social sustainability as perceived by the participants who look to business to demonstrate its practice (Graves and Waddock 2000).

Although the broad characteristics of social sustainability can be inferred from committed business practices, a precise definition remains elusive. In Section 7.2 we trace the evolution of the concept and outline the essential characteristics in any particular business context. In Section 7.3 we present the business case for a commitment to social sustainability. In Section 7.4 we discuss the modalities for successful implementation. What social sustainability is, why it is important and how it can be implemented are essential issues for any business or student of business to understand. Finally, in Section 7.5 we present some conclusions.

7.1.1 Teaching social sustainability

It is important to recognise that sustainability is inherently a multi-dimensional concept (for discussions of sustainability in business school curricula, see Springett and Kearins 2001; Wheeler *et al.* 2001). So too is social sustainability. It contributes to, and is an integral part of, any business discipline that is taught and practised in a stand-alone format, such as human resource management, financial analysis, marketing or strategic decision-making. Many of the ideas presented in this chapter have relevance for almost every business course or practice. Ultimately, social sustainability considerations need to be integrated into virtually all curriculum elements and business units if a truly successful sustainable strategy in business teaching and practice is to be adopted.

7.2 Definition

Social sustainability has proved difficult to define in a way that is both comprehensible and meaningful to business and to the range of external stakeholders[1] in government and society with which it interacts. Broad definitions seldom provide guidance on how to achieve social sustainability or even how to discuss the concept. Definitions to meet specific needs often use the same vocabulary to express different ideas, and different words can have similar meanings. Inconsistency in the use of terms creates confusion and misunderstandings among stakeholders. A mutually comprehensible vocabulary to facilitate communication among participants affected by sustainability initiatives has not yet emerged.

7.2.1 The development assistance approach

Sustainability as a concept originated in development assistance by governments and multilateral agencies such as the World Bank. The World Commission on Environment and Development[2] (WCED 1987) was established by the United Nations to explore alternative approaches to development assistance that would reduce poverty in developing countries. As noted, the now familiar definition of sustainability that resulted from its work has become the foundation for modern approaches to the definition of sustainability.[3] Although the definition did not

---

1 Stakeholders are defined as participants or parties either that are affected by the operations of any particular enterprise or that are in a position to affect those operations. Potential stakeholders include suppliers, customers, regulators, workforces, governments, civil-society groups such as non-government organisations (NGOs) or other self-identified interest groups (e.g. these might be neighbourhood associations or an activist individual).

2 This is often referred to as the Brundtland Commission after its chairperson, Gro Harlem Brundtland.

3 Carson (1962) made an earlier contribution to the understanding of sustainability issues and unsustainable practices but did not provide a definition.

explicitly differentiate between the different elements of sustainability, it was clear from the report that it encompassed environmental, economic and social sustainability.

The report was used as the groundwork for organising the 1992 United Nations. Conference on Environment and Development (UNCED) in Rio de Janeiro. The resulting 'Rio Declaration' (UNCED 1992) identified a global, multi-participant responsibility for sustainable development. However, the global imperative to deal with emerging environmental problems by governments and non-governmental organisations (NGOs) of the developed world overwhelmed the agenda of development assistance professionals concerned with sustainable economic and social development in the developing world as well as environmental protection.

The environmental focus of the Rio conference resulted in a widespread interpretation of sustainability as environmental stewardship. For the development assistance community,[4] however, sustainability could be used to reduce poverty in developing countries. Recognising that years of development funding had not produced lasting change for the better, sustainability became a filter through which future assistance programmes were viewed.

The development assistance concept of sustainability, consistent with the Brundtland Commission definition, focuses on environmental (protection), economic (poverty reduction) and social (conflict prevention) objectives. Their interdependence is clear. Usually the poor depend disproportionately on environmental resources. Their livelihood, therefore, is more affected by the degradation of resources. Scarce and degraded resources have great potential to create conflict, particularly in those environments where dependence on these resources is extreme (Homer-Dixon 1999). Conflict exacerbates poverty. For the very poor, there is an imperative to extract the short-term maximum to survive. This is rarely consistent with good environmental management. A continuing downward spiral begins.

This describes the essence of the development assistance sustainability problem, but none of the three components is one-dimensional. Particularly in the economic and social spheres, a broad range of policies must be addressed to break the downward spiral. These may include preserving the cultures of indigenous communities, increasing the capacity to satisfy basic human needs, enhancing equity and supporting transparency and accountability in government.

Thus, in development assistance, the three pillars of sustainability (environmental, economic and social) have been identified and elaborated, particularly in relation to specific problems and contexts. For example, infrastructure projects cannot be considered sustainable if the capacity to manage and cover recurrent costs in recipient organisations is lacking. So the provision of training in infrastructure projects enhances sustainability by developing economic infrastructure. Equity within and across regions (space) and generations (time) reduces poverty, so targeting interventions to particularly vulnerable groups enhances sustainabil-

---

4 This community includes national development assistance agencies such as the Canadian International Development Agency (CIDA), multilateral agencies in the United Nations family, international financial institutions such as the World Bank, and international and national NGOs working in development assistance.

ity. Capacity-building—the strengthening of social capital through education and training—is an integral aspect of most development assistance projects (Putnam 2000 provides elaboration on the characteristics of social capital; Sobel 2002 provides a critique). However, the sustainability goals of environmental stewardship, poverty reduction and conflict prevention remain fundamental.

7.2.2 The triple bottom line

The sustainability foundations established by the Rio conference and the development assistance community were reinterpreted and applied to the economic and social roles of business in the 1990s. Probably the best application is Elkington's (1997) triple-bottom-line definition of sustainability, which includes environmental, economic and social components. It moves beyond traditional financial accounting and the dominance of financial value in business decisions to the creation of environmental, economic and social value by business. But, because the triple-bottom-line goal of creating business value is not the same as the development assistance community goals of sustainable development, the associated languages can mean something different.

Only the environmental component is readily transferable from the development assistance literature and practice and has proved straightforward for business to grasp. Environmental sustainability, even when not labelled thus, has been recognised for decades (the first impetus to the adoption by business of good environmental practice is often cited as Carson 1962) through, for example, increasingly sophisticated requirements for environmental impact assessments, moves towards recycling, and legal obligations regarding contaminated sites. Historically, civil-society pressures and regulatory systems have driven improved business environmental practices, although creativity pertaining to product design and industrial processes has often originated in individual businesses committed to protecting the environment.

The economic component in the triple-bottom-line definition refers to the long-term financial performance of business. The logic is clear—without enduring financial viability there is no sustainability. This is comparatively straightforward for business to understand, being the substance of good management. However, the triple-bottom-line definition goes deeper by moving beyond simple short-term financial results into creating longer-term value. Nonetheless, the concept does not fall outside of the normal realm of business thinking.

Of the three components, social sustainability is the least familiar and, therefore, the most poorly defined and least consistently adopted by business. It is generally not conceived as conflict prevention (or even poverty reduction), so the development assistance literature and practices provide little guidance. However, examples are not hard to find. Enlightened human resource policy, health and safety practice consistent with the requirements of the Occupational Health and Safety Assessment Series (OHSAS), adherence to standards from the International Organisation for Standardisation (ISO), meeting the needs of customers for quality goods and services, transparency to shareholders and commitment to philanthropy can all be considered social sustainability initiatives.

Further, particularly for international businesses that may play critical roles both locally and nationally, appropriate economic and political interventions are generally conceived to fall under social sustainability practices. Examples might include the provision of community economic infrastructure, advocacy leading to the empowerment and enfranchisement of communities or public refusal to engage in corrupt practices. These practices are closer to the development assistance concept of social sustainability.

Business has difficulty grasping what precisely constitutes the creation of social value, because it is considered external to the business. Also, it is a broadly conceived yet context-specific concept. Business and its stakeholders define the context. For example, compare a business operating only in a domestic market that determines that its interests are best served by reorganising into an employee-owned company with a multinational company that discovers compulsory vaccination of all project personnel is necessary to protect indigenous peoples in the area of a project from common Western illnesses.

Additional factors complicate identifying what social sustainability entails for a particular business. Social contexts are rarely homogeneous—different groups can have competing interests. Also, business has a multi-dimensional agenda, with objectives that can range from enhancing shareholder value to managing AIDS in the workforce. Trade-offs are likely. Moreover, it is hard to predict or control social dynamics because they depend on individual choice and response to the business and to other actors and events. Impacts are often diffuse and cumulative and sometimes irreversible. Also, there are less best-practice examples to draw on for guidance.

7.2.3 Convergence

Are the development assistance and the triple-bottom-line business interpretations of social sustainability liable to converge? Civil society and governments appear to increasingly expect businesses to take concrete initiatives to improve the well-being of people local to their operations. Permission to proceed is often contingent on achieving specified social results, particularly for new projects in developing countries or depressed regions.[5] In an increasingly global marketplace, more businesses are finding themselves implicated in these expectations as they locate operations in places of lower costs and expanding markets (MMSD 2002).

Perhaps this shift is attributable to the perceived poor performance of paternalistic government and the drive to see central governments divest themselves of responsibility for intervening in the lives of their citizens. Business is seen as having the resources to assume this role. Business is also looked to as the engine of sustainable economic and social development, especially in the developing world, a situation understood by the development assistance community. Certain businesses are accepting this new role, as evidenced by the participation of over 700 businesses in the 2002 Johannesburg World Summit on Sustainable Development (WSSD 2002) compared with their virtual absence from Rio in 1992.

---

5 Permission to proceed can range from formal permission from government authorities to a 'social licence to operate' from the community.

Some recent initiatives have combined the development assistance and private-sector frameworks. For example, the Mining, Minerals and Sustainable Development project report (MMSD 2002) recognised that mining-sector companies must deliver on an obligation to ensure that a mining project directly materially benefit local communities.[6] Therefore, the MMSD framework for defining sustainability includes (under the economic component) not only the financial viability of a mining company but also the 'maximisation of human well-being' (MMSD 2002).

MMSD also includes a governance component that urges mining-sector companies to contribute proactively to democracy, empowerment and probity in their operating environments. The economic importance of mining to the communities in which the mines are located and, in many cases, to national economies makes such a role possible, more so when the participating companies act in concert. This governance role generally is not emphasised in developed countries where a single business or sector rarely has such a predominant role, where government is less problematic and where there are other checks and balances on governance.

Concurrently, in developed countries, stakeholders have begun to examine business performance under the term 'corporate social responsibility' (BSR 2002). This concept arises from recognition that businesses should go beyond simply contributing to the communities as an employer.

Historically, business philanthropy and attention to the welfare of the workforce, however paternalistic, were the cornerstones of corporate social responsibility.[7] With time, expectations have expanded to encompass ethical practices, environmental stewardship and contributions to the economic development and quality of life of the workforces and communities (CDCAC 2002).

Corporate social responsibility and the broader concept of social sustainability, which embraces a wider, time-dependent definition of a benefit to society (such as social capital) and focuses on results rather than standards of behaviour, do overlap. Nonetheless, expanding the interpretation of corporate social responsibility can provide business with a familiar foundation for social sustainability initiatives and a basis for integrating the development assistance and triple-bottom-line concepts of social sustainability into strategies.[8]

---

6 The MMSD project is part of the Global Mining Initiative that was established to improve the social acceptance and performance of the mining sector. This leading strategy toward a more integrated understanding of social sustainability reflects the large scale of operations, the severity of potential impacts and an increasing resource dependence in the most challenging of environments: namely, remote locations in developing countries.

7 Such social contributions of business in fact predate the coining of the term 'social responsibility', which developed to describe what was happening and to provide a framework for increased expectations (for useful reviews, see Carroll 1996; Marcus 1996).

8 Some organisations such as Business for Social Responsibility (BSR 2002) use different language from that of the development assistance or academic communities.

7.2.4 Context specificity

The definition of social sustainability for a business comes from a process that includes articulation of its objectives in committing to social sustainability and a stakeholder engagement process to establish and enable integration of stakeholder interests into its policies and practices. Consequently, social sustainability is context-specific. Tension exists between the requirement to define social sustainability relative to the objectives and constraints of a business attempting to implement the concept and the needs of the stakeholders—workforces, suppliers, customers, governments, civil-society organisations, affected communities and so on—whose interests are being addressed through the initiative.

The company reports of the Royal Dutch/Shell Group are useful to show appropriate business action towards social sustainability.[9] Shell's commitment to environmental and social sustainability is expressed differently and with different levels of resources according to the context.

In Nigeria, in addition to human resource policies, Shell is committed to projects that improve infrastructure, health and education, income potential and agricultural production of the general population and that address human rights in communities local to its operations. Almost 40% of Shell's sustainability spending is disbursed in Nigeria. Shell emphasises results and has contracted independent reviews and evaluations of its activities. The response in Nigeria is motivated partly by the public relations disaster it experienced after Ken Saro Wiwa was executed, but of interest here is the nature of the response rather than the original motivation (for more information, see Boele *et al.* 2001).

In the USA, Shell focuses on workforce issues, including health and safety, equality of opportunity and investigating and responding to the interests and desires of staff.[10] Shell also supports diversity in the larger community by supporting national organisations that work with minorities and women.[11] In Canada, Shell often operates in remote, marginalised communities where native populations face formidable challenges. Social sustainability initiatives not only address workforce issues but also help increase local employment and procurement from aboriginal businesses and support native culture.[12]

7.3 The business case

The business case for social sustainability focuses on reducing risk and creating business value. In many cases, the imperative is to act in order to avoid the costs of not acting! For example, being insufficiently proactive in Nigeria forced Shell to incur significant costs and to implement its current social sustainability policy to avoid future problems (see Section 7.2.4). Beyond avoidance, recent contributions

---

9   See e.g. www.shell.com/shellreport.
10   www.countonshell.com/diversity/index.html
11   www.shellus.com, accessed April 2004
12   www.shell.ca/code/values/reports/sd01.pdf

provide both theoretical and practical reasons for business creation that can result from a social sustainability commitment. In the quest for a competitive edge, many businesses have embraced or accommodated social sustainability as good business. Another motive, then, is simply to stay current—or risk being outpaced.

7.3.1 Drivers

The business case for social sustainability first arises from drivers that require sustainability and the penalties imposed in its absence. Licences to operate, both formal licences granted by regulators and informal licences granted by other stakeholders in society that permit a business to operate without opposition, are generally based on a commitment to meet the requirements and expectations of others.

Standards of performance set by governments or industry organisations represent another driver, with the regulating, monitoring and implementation often being delegated to other civil-society entities, including business. Continued operation has long been contingent on undertakings to minimise and mitigate environmental impacts. More recently, it has also required businesses to demonstrate commitment to ensuring that local people receive a net benefit.

A more aggressive approach to elaborating and enforcing standards is a further impetus to action. For example, the Canadian Environmental Assessment Act, which came into force in January 1995,[13] does not include a requirement to assess and mitigate social impacts except where they result from identified environmental impacts. Developers of large projects, however, are governed by project-specific directives written to ensure that economic and social impacts are assessed and that appropriate benefits are provided. In northern Canada permits are generally conditional on a legally binding contractual agreement specifying the benefits that local communities will receive as a result of resource exploitation. Another example comes from the USA, where government has responded to unscrupulous financial accounting practices with tougher penalties for white-collar crime.

Environmental standards already require companies to identify where activities have negative environmental impacts, to plan mitigation and to allocate resources to implement remediation. To date, social standards are much less developed. Social impacts are harder to predict and mitigate and the means of reversing negative social change are unclear. Environmental standards evolved from the same uncertainties, so it is likely that means will be found to ensure that business cannot walk away from the negative social impacts of its operations. In this event, for example, the mining company not government would be looked to for funding the resettlement of the people left in a 'dead town' after a mine has closed.[14]

---

13 See www.ceaa-acee.gc.ca for details.
14 The town of Murdochville, Quebec, voted to close in August 2002 when its last major employer left. Requests to the provincial government for relocation funds were denied (CBC 2002). However, new developments in remote areas are now required to plan financially for their eventual closure (see e.g. the De Beers Snap Lake Diamond Project in northern Canada, www.mveirb.nt.ca/Registry/EADeBeers/RevisedDeBeersToR.pdf).

Internationally, project financing is harder to obtain in the absence of a clear commitment to social sustainability. The World Bank Group has developed international standards in an effort to ensure that the projects it funds are implemented according to its mandate for poverty reduction (IFC 1998).[15] Private-sector financing institutions have also adopted these standards to minimise lending risk. Furthermore, private-sector companies looking to participate in projects in the developing world are discovering that the participation of the International Financial Corporation (IFC) of the World Bank, which is dependent on documentation of a commitment to environmental and social sustainability (IFC 2002), is the ticket to financing the balance through commercial banks.

More informally, business must operate in ways consistent with community expectations. Globalisation has linked markets for business and communities for action. Increased literacy and democratisation worldwide has empowered people to act. Improved global communication has provided the means, information, resources and assistance that motivates effective action. Stakeholders have the leverage to articulate expectations and to delay or stop projects if those expectations go unmet.

As these drivers get stronger, the costs of ignorance and inaction become larger. Higher financing costs, project delay, loss of markets, reduced shareholder value, remediation and reclamation costs, reputation degradation and, ultimately, bankruptcy can result from failure to acknowledge responsibility for social obligations and considerations, irrespective of good environmental practice.

7.3.2 Evidence

Risk mitigation addresses negative potential. Demonstration of the positive potential to create value specifically through social sustainability initiatives is harder to establish. There has been some success with evidence of better financial performance, increased sales and reduced labour costs through improved workforce productivity in businesses committed to sustainability generally (BSR 2002; WBCSD 2002; WWF 2002), However, as the costs associated with generating these improvements are seldom included, the full business case is incomplete. Moreover, research is not yet available over long enough time periods to determine that the triple-bottom-line approach to sustainability is achieved through appropriate initiatives.

Benchmarking is a business tool that can be used to identify businesses successful at achieving a specified level of sustainability in their operations.[16] This information can be used for business inclusion in sustainability indices such as the Dow Jones Sustainability Indexes (DJSI),[17] in socially responsible investment funds

15 Other organisations, such as Canada's Export Development Corporation and the US Overseas Private Investment Corporation are increasingly using these policies to govern their decision-making (see www.edc.ca and www.opic.gov for details).

16 Benchmarking systems identify criteria by which a business is judged. The characteristics of corporate social responsibility are the basis for most benchmarking (Carroll 1996; Marcus 1996). As noted, this is an incomplete description of social sustainability (see CDCAC 2002).

17 www.sustainability-indexes.com

or in academic investigations into the contribution of sustainability to overall financial performance (Graves and Waddock 2000).[18] The performance of these indices, funds and/or groups of socially responsible businesses is reviewed and tracked over time.

Businesses identified through benchmarking as socially responsible or 'ethical' under the concept of corporate social responsibility can also be considered, at least loosely, to be addressing social sustainability issues. Comparisons of the performance of these businesses with businesses that are not construed as socially responsible have generated some quantitative evidence of superior performance in the socially responsible businesses. Graves and Waddock (2000) found returns on equity to be 10% higher, returns on assets to be 3.5% higher and returns on sales to be almost 3% higher.

Also, some evidence points to enhanced stock performance of socially responsible businesses. For example, the DJSI has outperformed the Dow Jones Global Index and the growth rates for socially screened portfolio assets generally have outperformed professionally managed assets (SIF 2001). Certainly, the growing demand for the shares of socially responsible businesses and for ethical funds, which now constitute over 12% of all professionally managed investment assets, implies increases in the share values of these businesses.

The limited quantitative evidence available, however, does not prove that a commitment to sustainability in general and to social sustainability in particular is linked to improved business success. Standards for choosing socially responsible businesses have been minimal. Businesses that embrace sustainability initiatives are also likely to embrace other leading business initiatives that affect performance. More research is required to establish the link between social sustainability practices and enhanced business performance.

Much of the convincing evidence is anecdotal. Initiatives often categorised as socially sustainable, such as seeking customer input in product design, product servicing or marketing decisions, or enhancing human resource policies, have been shown to improve business performance (WBCSD 2002). For example, Dell's attention to customer preferences and requirements certainly contributed to its establishment as the leader in personal computer sales (Magretta 1998). Nokia's enlightened human resource policies were considered to be fundamental to the quality and stability of its workforce (Masalin 2003), which contributed to an improved quality of production relative to costs and its increased market share. Stakeholder engagement allowed Suez Lyonnaise des Eaux to adapt its design of water-delivery systems and billing to respond to the realities of poor water-users in developing countries which improved its sales and margins.[19]

---

18 Graves and Waddock measure social sustainability in terms of stakeholder relations rather than for a complete range of specific initiatives.

19 In addition, the contribution of social sustainability ideas to corporate strategic planning can be found in such companies as BP and Exxon in the oil and gas sector, Rio Tinto and Placer Dome in mining, Weyerhaeuser in forestry, Coca-Cola and General Motors in manufacturing and The Body Shop in retailing, as well as in the businesses that participate in the World Business Council for Sustainable Development, the Prince of Wales International Business Leaders Forum, Business Partners for Development, the Global Mining Initiative and other similar organisations.

Further evidence, particularly in the area of social sustainability, relates to management of business risk (i.e. avoiding threats to profitability) rather than to the creation of business value (i.e. increasing profitability). Here, case studies are useful. The recent abandonment of a court case on the part of 39 drug companies to prevent the sale of generic equivalents of AIDS drugs in South Africa is a convincing example of how a failure to include social issues in management decisions can impact business performance (BBC 2001). Nike suffered substantial business losses as a result of its failure to ensure good working conditions in its clothing manufacturing plants in developing countries (Nike 2002).

The quantitative, anecdotal and case-study evidence supporting the business case for social sustainability is wide-ranging but limited. It suggests that failure to address social issues can increase business risk, including the risk of loss of sales and reputation. Also, a successful commitment to social sustainability can improve and facilitate strategic planning, enhance corporate reputation as an organisation of choice for customers, suppliers, employees and shareholders, contribute to a healthy, stable and productive workforce and community and build shareholder value.

7.4 Implementation

Although a precise definition and a watertight business case for social sustainability remain elusive, the procedures for implementation are better defined. Tools are available to resolve the challenges for effective planning, implementation, monitoring, evaluation and reporting (for more information on reporting see www.globalreporting.org; WBCSD 2002).

Some tools are well developed. Management theory on methods to develop and motivate a productive workforce is extensive (Marcus 1996). Numerous health and safety standards have been developed and implemented, and certification systems such as those of OHSAS and ISO are in place in many jurisdictions. Stakeholder engagement and consultation best practice, including conflict resolution, is well understood and often used (Carroll 1996). The development assistance community has established best practice related to the economic and social development of communities around the world.

Other tools are available in principle but their use is limited by lack of applied experience in social sustainability. Examples include the incorporation of social sustainability into financial models for project evaluation, the integration of social issues into environmental management plans and the evaluation of cost-effectiveness initiatives from a social perspective where impacts may be difficult to quantify.

The application of such tools often requires the use of expertise not normally found within a business. This expertise may have to be developed internally or outsourced. Outside expertise may be used to develop and support internal capability. Partnerships with organisations that are more experienced with delivering social benefits, within government and civil society, can be used extensively where a business is required to act outside its area of core expertise. This is no different from the use of outside resources for many business functions that are necessary for business to fulfil its objectives.

7.4.1 The implementation process

The implementation process necessarily starts with a commitment from senior management. This is essential to command resources and to motivate business units to internalise the necessary processes. Social sustainability thinking must then be integrated into all decision-making processes within the organisation. The next step is to extend the accountability of staff beyond the financial bottom line to embrace the quality of responsiveness and relationships with all stakeholders. The motivation of staff to be receptive to, if not proactive about, social sustainability is important. However, without a leadership commitment from management to embrace social sustainability the implementation process is destined to fail.

Given the newness of social sustainability and its links to environmental sustainability, the most common organisational structure places responsibility with an environmental manager, with staff that has environmental and social training. Although this can work, effectively managing social issues will be less successful as an adjunct activity to environmental management. Changing expectations and operational realities require a separate unit able to respond quickly and unambiguously.

The establishment of a responsibility centre that develops policies and monitors their success can better support implementation. The scale of this unit depends on the context, but it is essential that it has adequate resources and is led by a senior manager with credibility among all employees and is accountable to the highest level of management. It must be staffed appropriately. Social management is not a 'soft' field in which anyone can achieve success. What may be a perceived lack of method and rigour is likely to be related more to the complexity and unpredictability of human behaviour inherent in a process that embraces the tension among the many objectives and values of the business and its stakeholders. Management of this process demands more, not less, expertise.

Social sustainability is an organisational culture and a function of all relationships with stakeholders, so responsibility cannot be left solely to a designated centre. A centre can champion implementation, but sensitivity and responsiveness to the interests of stakeholders must come from all employees. This is cultural change that requires training and support throughout the organisation.

Training in social sustainability concepts and implementation practices within the organisation inculcates a relevant culture throughout the organisation and ensures consistent and unambiguous responses to stakeholder needs. This is especially important in cross-cultural environments where the people affected by business operations are in demonstrably different circumstances from the business staff. In this case, training is frequently necessary to deepen employee understanding of stakeholder values and to enable levels of responsiveness that might otherwise be difficult to achieve.

Extension of the accountability of staff beyond the traditional financial bottom line helps to motivate broad-based participation in social sustainability. Such accountability is explicit for staff of a social responsibility centre where job descriptions, objective-setting and performance appraisal are consistent with achieving social sustainability. But social accountability must also be made explicit for all staff, irrespective of their role, if only by adding an appropriate line to their performance expectations.

This process is not new to business. For example, in the developed world, experience with integrating gender issues into corporate strategy, operations and customer responsiveness provides some of the best practice on how to operationalise a concept facing internal resistance. Resistance can emanate from unfamiliarity with the concept and its implications, underestimation of its value to business success, uncertainty concerning perceived changes to individual employee status or from other sources. Under these conditions, implementation can be a long process. Nonetheless, the analogy of gender equality provides recent experience for businesses embracing a new commitment to social sustainability.

7.4.2 Stakeholder relationship planning

Consultation, including transparent disclosure to stakeholders of the information they need to provide informed and constructive input, has become the *sine qua non* of social sustainability in international settings (IFC 1998). It is impossible to achieve social sustainability without understanding the values, perceptions and interests of stakeholders through dialogue. Consultation must continue over time. Values may be deep-rooted and comparatively consistent over time, but perceptions and interests are mutable and can change with new information and experience.

This does not imply that business is obliged to accommodate all input that comes from stakeholders. Consultation is a two-way, iterative process that searches for the commonality of interests that satisfies business and stakeholder needs, at least partly. Just as business must understand stakeholders and their expectations, so too must stakeholders understand business and its realities. The role of transparent information disclosure is critical. It not only facilitates mutual understanding but also ensures that such understanding is correct and complete enough to frame socially sustainable initiatives. There is no place for the manipulation of stakeholder opinion through incorrect or withheld information. This is the antithesis of acceptable business behaviour, is untenable in the long run and, therefore, is not socially sustainable.

Consultation best practice can take many forms, including surveys, public meetings and making contacts available for stakeholders if concerns arise about business information or behaviour. Careful consideration must be given to inclusivity: that is, to identifying all stakeholders and differentiating them according to their roles relative to the business and/or to the potential effects they may experience as a result of operations. The type of consultation and information disclosure can be adapted to the particular requirement of each stakeholder. For example, surveys that ensure confidentiality may work well in a literate community but may be inappropriate in the developing world where illiteracy is widespread (UNESCO undated). Alternative approaches are necessary to reach marginalised social groups in ways that provide them with an opportunity to speak freely.

Social assessment is an invaluable complement to consultation, especially in cross-cultural environments. It deepens the knowledge and understanding of stakeholders and their values. It involves collecting and analysing data about the economic and social characteristics of relevant populations and provides quantitative support for consultation results. When available, census information is a logical starting point, but good social assessment goes beyond a census to social surveys and marketing studies. Data collection is guided by relevant past studies (if available) and relevant population experience as well as by the issues identified through consultation. It complements consultation to the extent that analysis, experience and best practice can introduce ideas beyond those identified either by business or by stakeholders.

In contexts where social sustainability is conceived as a contribution to the economic and social development of particularly disadvantaged groups, such as aboriginal groups in northern Canada or indigenous groups in developing countries, a needs analysis should be included in the social assessment. This identifies the specific economic and social needs of the group, usually, but not necessarily, in relation to some prescribed norm or minimum standard of a surrounding or contiguous community. For example, the need for at least subsistence per-capita income levels or for an opportunity to vote or to otherwise anonymously select a group's leaders may be identified through this route.

The development assistance community has used participatory processes to improve the quality of data in social assessment and to engage stakeholders so that they feel some ownership of the social sustainability initiatives. Such processes move beyond consultation to involving stakeholders in decision-making and responsibly implementing social sustainability initiatives as well as in subsequent monitoring and evaluation.

Project planning and management tools are well developed in business and in the development assistance community. Implementing social sustainability should be approached as a programme involving a well-defined series of integrated projects with clear objectives and measurable results that are responsive to business and stakeholder interests. Projects that redirect the actions of employees and the effects of business on its stakeholders must be implemented with the goal of integrating social sustainability into all decision-making and operations. Commitment to social sustainability unsupported by concrete initiatives with clear results-oriented objectives will be perceived as an exercise in public relations.

The two main models for financing social sustainability initiatives are direct and indirect funding. Traditionally, most assistance funding has been direct, requiring social sustainability initiatives to be funded directly by the sponsoring governments or agencies. Sometimes, however, a 'hands-off' mechanism is preferable, particularly in developing countries where complexity of social issues, suspicion of multinational corporations, sponsor unfamiliarity with the culture and lack of infrastructure create special challenges for project management. The establishment of a locally managed foundation, probably with the expectation that it will become fully or even partially self-financing, to implement social and economic development projects can increase credibility, build local capacity and increase stakeholder 'ownership' in the project.

7.4.3 Monitoring and evaluation

Certification systems for social sustainability are less well developed than are those for environmental sustainability, where the ISO 14001 standard is applicable to the full range of environmental initiatives and is the recognised standard of choice across countries and sectors. This situation is partly a result of newness and partly a result of the wide variation of initiatives that contribute to social sustainability. The standards that exist are industry-specific, relate to a particular subset of social sustainability initiatives or are multi-sector but not widely used. For example, the apparel industry has a number of standards intended to ensure that the labour practices used by their suppliers are not exploitative. The OHSAS developed one widely used standard (OHSAS 18001), but it applies only to health and safety issues.

Efforts to develop broader certification systems have been less successful, essentially because they do not capture the full range of a business's sustainability performance. Nevertheless, two systems (Social Accountability standard 8000 [SA8000] and AccountAbility standard 1000 [AA1000] described below) are emerging as social sustainability standards. Certification is applied through a process of social auditing that is comparable to management or environmental audits insofar as they establish whether a particular practice of a business is consistent with its articulated commitments.

The social audit standard SA8000, established by the Social Accountability International (SAI) agency of the Council on Economic Priorities (CEP),[20] focuses on compliance with codes of conduct voluntarily committed to by a business (SAI 2002). These could include codes of conduct governing the use of child labour, health and safety, working conditions and the right to collective bargaining. The codes of conduct are developed by the individual business but are often based on international standards such as the International Labour Organisation (ILO) conventions (www.ilo.org). The SA8000 social audit is concerned primarily with the relationship between the management of a business and its workforce and does not extend to the broader community of stakeholders.

The AA1000 standard of the Institute of Social and Ethical AccountAbility[21] (ISEA 2002) is a social audit approach strongly rooted in stakeholder engagement and business responsiveness to stakeholders. It looks primarily at the quality of the relationships between a business and its stakeholders rather than at the quality of the social sustainability initiatives.

Benchmarking on a subset of standards developed by private-sector consultants and/or industry professionals looks at the presence or absence of criteria, variously defined, considered to indicate social sustainability. But this approach has its limitations. It can be cursory when applied to a range of businesses or sectors,

---

20 Founded in 1969, the CEP is a non-profit public-service research organisation dedicated to studying the social and environmental records of corporations.

21 The Institute of Social and Ethical AccountAbility (ISEA) is an international, non-profit organisation dedicated to the promotion of social and ethical accountability.

qualitative in the sense that intangibles such as 'poor relationship with employees' are judged and reflective of the viewpoint of the benchmarker. For example, it is unclear why the Jantzi Social Index (a component of a benchmarking service provided by Michael Jantzi Research Associates Inc.[22]) excludes only those companies with operations in Myanmar. Benchmarking as currently used, therefore, is less a measure of the quality of the social sustainability performance of a business than it is a binary approach for establishing suitability for inclusion in a sustainability funds portfolio or a credential for public relations purposes.

Evaluation is an important ingredient in social sustainability implementation. Usually, evaluation works by assessing the results of actions with a view to learning how to improve performance. Results identify which objectives are being achieved and which are not and include analyses of successes and failures. Information generated by effective evaluation can guide decision-making and resource allocation and can help to demonstrate objectively the achievement of goals and objectives. Thus, evaluation is an important component of an iterative strategy in implementing social sustainability and provides the content for reporting to stakeholders on social sustainability results.

Evaluation is most effective when it is participatory. In this framework, stakeholders identify their goals and objectives, evaluate whether they are being achieved and participate in identifying improvements. This process improves mutual understanding of the issues and contributes to better resolution of differences. Participatory evaluations extend the partnership and responsibility for social sustainability implementation beyond a business responsibility centre.

Third-party participation in evaluation by a non-participating entity such as a consulting company can provide additional credibility to a wider audience. This may be particularly useful to a business seeking investors and/or financing for new projects. Wide dissemination of credible results also provides evidence of transparency and accountability and can further solidify the iterative process that secures the delivery of a successful social sustainability programme.

7.5 Conclusions

Social sustainability is the 'third leg on the stool' of business sustainability practice. Founded in the work of the development assistance community and the Brundtland Commission and supported by the recent application of the triple bottom line to business, a sustainable business strategy includes environmental, economic and social components. Their interdependence is well established. Although economic and environmental sustainability initiatives have been increasingly identified and embraced by business, social sustainability initiatives are still in their infancy in business applications.

This chapter has reviewed the what, why and how of social sustainability. As with the other components, social sustainability is inherently multi-dimensional.

22 www.mjra-jsi.com, accessed March 2004

This can be problematical because the options for action are as numerous as the expectations and values of a business and all its stakeholders and are dependent on the context in which they are exercised. Thus, a precise definition is difficult, although an emerging consensus of general characteristics is identifiable in the literature and in practice.

The business case for social sustainability currently is based more on minimising risk than on creating value. This observation is supported by quantitative, case-study and anecdotal evidence, although more research is needed to establish an unassailable foundation. A commitment to social sustainability can attract customers, employees, suppliers and shareholders, improve project planning, enhance corporate reputation and contribute to a healthy, stable and productive workforce.

Although a precise definition and a watertight business case for social sustainability remain elusive, the procedures for implementation are better defined. Planning, implementation, monitoring and evaluation business tools have been successfully applied to social sustainability initiatives. Continuing consultation supported by transparency and a supporting corporate culture are the keys to successful implementation. Monitoring demonstrates input delivery and audits report on compliance, and evaluation—with its emphasis on results and on causality—assures stakeholders that businesses are realising their commitments. Credibility solidifies the iterative process that ensures the ongoing success of a business commitment to social sustainability.

Social sustainability is an integral part of any business discipline that is taught and practised in a stand-alone format. Ultimately, social sustainability considerations must be integrated into all curriculum elements and business units if a truly successful sustainability approach is to be achieved.

References

BBC (British Broadcasting Corporation) (2001) 'SA Victory in AIDS Drug Case', April 2001, news.bbc.co.uk/1/hi/world/africa/1285097.stm, accessed September 2002.

Boele, R., H. Fabig and D. Wheeler (2001) 'Shell, Nigeria and the Ogonoi: A Study in Unsustainable Development', *Sustainable Development* 9: 74-86, 121-35, 177-96.

BSR (Business for Social Responsibility) (2002) 'Introduction to Corporate Social Responsibility', www.bsr.org/Print/PrintThisPage.cfm?DocumentID=138, accessed September 2002.

Carroll, A.B. (1996) *Business and Society: Ethics and Stakeholder Management* (Cincinnati, OH: South-Western College Publishing).

Carson, R. (1962) *Silent Spring* (Boston, MA: Houghton Mifflin).

CBC (Canadian Broadcasting Corporation) (2002) 'Quebec Town Votes to Shut Down', August 2002, cbc.ca/stories/2002/08/25/murdochville_020825, accessed September 2002.

CDCAC (Canadian Democracy and Corporate Accountability Commission) (2002) *The New Balance Sheet: Corporate Profits and Responsibility in the 21st Century* (Toronto: CDCAC; available at www.corporate-accountability.ca).

Elkington, J. (1997) *Cannibals with Forks: The Triple Bottom Line of 21st Century Business* (Oxford, UK: Capstone Publishing).

Graves, S.B., and S. Waddock (2000) 'Beyond Built to Last: Stakeholder Relations in the Built to Last Companies', *Business and Society Review* 105.4: 393-418.

Homer-Dixon, T.F. (1999) *Environment, Scarcity and Violence* (Princeton, NJ: Princeton University Press).

IFC (International Financial Corporation) (1998) *Doing Better Business through Effective Public Consultation and Disclosure* (Washington, DC: World Bank Group).

—— (2002) 'Safeguard Policies', www.ifc.org/enviro/EnvSoc/Safeguard/safeguard.htm, accessed September 2002.

ISEA (Institute of Social and Ethical AccountAbility) (2002) 'Introducing AA1000', www.accountability.org.uk/aa1000/default.asp, accessed December 2002.

Magretta, J. (1998) 'The Power of Virtual Integration: An Interview with Dell Computers' Michael Dell', *Harvard Business Review*, March 1998: 74-84.

Marcus, A.A. (1996) *Business and Society: Strategy, Ethics and the Global Economy* (Chicago: Irwin).

Masalin, L. (2003) 'Nokia Leads Change Through Continuous Learning', *Academy of Management Learning and Education* 2.1: 68-72.

MMSD (Mining, Minerals and Sustainable Development) (2002) *Breaking New Ground* (London: Earthscan Publications).

Nike (2002) 'FAQ', www.nike.com/canada/siteInfo/faq.html, accessed September 2002.

OHSAS (Occupational Health and Safety Assessment Series) 'OHSAS 18001 Occupational Health and Safety Zone', www.ohsas-18001-occupational-health-and-safety.com, accessed April 2004.

Placer Dome (2002) 'Sustainability', www.placerdome.com/sustainability, accessed December 2002.

Putnam, R. (2000) *Bowling Alone: The Collapse and Revival of American Community* (New York: Simon & Schuster).

SAI (Social Accountability International) (2002) 'SA8000', www.cepaa.org/SA8000/SA8000. htm, accessed December 2002.

SIF (Social Investment Forum) (2001) '2001 Report on Socially Responsible Investing Trends in the United States', www.socialinvest.org/Areas/research/trends/2001-Trends.htm, accessed September 2002.

Sobel, J. (2002) 'Can We Trust Social Capital?', *Journal of Economic Literature* 40.1: 139-54.

Springett, D., and K. Kearins (2001) 'Gaining Legitimacy? Sustainable Development in Business School Curricula', *Sustainable Development* 9: 213-21.

UNCED (United Nations Conference on Environment and Development) (1992) 'Annex 1: Rio Declaration on Environment and Development', www.un.org/documents/ga/conf151/aconf15126-1annex1.htm, accessed March 2004.

UNESCO (United Nations Educational, Scientific and Cultural Organisation) Institute of Statistics (undated) 'Estimated World Illiteracy Rates', www.uis.unesco.org, accessed March 2004.

WBCSD (World Business Council for Sustainable Development) (2002) www.wbcsd.ch, accessed December 2002.

WCED (World Commission on Environment and Development) (1987) *Our Common Future* (The Brundtland Report; Oxford, UK: Oxford University Press).

Wheeler, D., D. Horvath and P. Victor (2001) 'Graduate Learning for Business and Sustainability', mimeograph.

WRI (World Resources Institute) (2002) 'Governance and Institutions', governance.wri.org, accessed December 2002.

WSSD (World Summit on Sustainable Development) (2002) www.un.org/esa/sustdev/documents, accessed March 2004.

WWF (2002) 'To Whose Profit? Building a Business Case', www.panda.org, accessed September 2002.

8
An international comparison of environmental concern among business students

Michael Schaper
University of Newcastle, Australia

In recent years a number of tertiary institutions have begun to incorporate environmental education into the courses offered by undergraduate and post-graduate business schools. Increasingly, 'green' issues have become part of the business curriculum, although the trend is a recent one, and only a small number of universities currently offer courses on business and the environment (WRI 2001).

Concurrent with this development has been the separate issue of the continuing internationalisation of business school courses and student bodies around the world. Although North American and Western European business schools have traditionally been quite cosmopolitan in their student intake, in recent years there has been a substantial growth in internationalisation by universities from Australia, Asia and other regions. As a result of these changes, universities face increasing pressure to understand and deal with cultural differences in the diverse student body they manage.

In terms of environmental business education, these two trends mean that universities must now begin to understand whether cultural differences also equate to differences in environmental concerns and interest and whether this will impact on the business–environment courses they teach.

In this chapter I report on a study designed to measure the overall level of environmental concern among tertiary business students, using a reliable, cross-national quantitative measurement tool. I sought to determine if any statistically significant differences existed in the scores recorded among different nationalities and to determine if other personal characteristics of students, such as their age or gender, are reliable indicators of the likely level of environmental concern. I conclude by providing some ideas and recommendations for the future development of environmental education within tertiary business schools.

8.1 Concern for the environment

The meaning of the term 'environmental concern' can hold quite different connotations for various observers. Generally speaking, it refers to a view or belief that an individual holds about environmental issues per se or about particular environmental events. Berkowitz (1975) has suggested that the best definition is also the simplest and that 'concern' simply means the way people feel about something. Gifford (1997:47) refers to environmental attitudes as 'an individual's concern for the physical environment as something that is worthy of protection, understanding or enhancement'.

An attitude is very much an indication of a personal set of preferences and views. Indeed, over the years, the terms 'concerns', 'attitude', 'belief', 'intentions', 'values' and 'views' have been the source of semantic argument. Some researchers (such as Azjen and Fishbein [1980]; Cooper and Croyle [1984]) have preferred to assign highly specific meanings to each of these words, whereas others have preferred to treat the terms as largely interchangeable (Gifford 1997; Newhouse 1990). Given the lack of clear consensus in the academic community about how each of these terms might be separately defined, for the purposes of the current study the latter approach has been adopted.

8.2 Predictors of environmental concern

The factors giving rise to environmental concern are many and varied, and different researchers have argued that attitudes are attributable to a number of different causes. Although many of these causes are external factors, Gifford (1997) has suggested that there are also a number of predictor variables drawn from personal characteristics that remain fairly constant over time or that change only in a relatively slow and predictable manner. These can often be used to predict a predisposition towards strong environmental attitudes in certain groups of individuals. Three common possible predictor variables are cultural differences, age-based differences and gender-based differences.

8.2.1 Sociocultural differences

The impact of an individual's culture on his or her environmental perceptions is a significant but relatively unresearched aspect of environmental studies (Berberoglu and Tosunoglu 1995). It has been suggested that different cultures often possess markedly diverse perspectives on environmental issues and that some cultures may generally possess a greater degree of environmental concern than others (Dunlap and Mertig 1996; Holahan 1982). Several researchers have documented examples of substantial cultural differences in environmental concern (see e.g. Dodd 1998; Sarbaugh 1979), although few of these have been quantified empirically.

These variations arise when cultures exist in different ecological systems and are subject to differing environmental pressures, resource limitations and opportunities (Dodd 1998). Over time, a common set of environmental concerns and values arises through socialisation, peer-group activity and vicarious learning (Bandura 1969). As a result, members of particular cultural groups often have similar environmental attitudes that may be significantly different from those of other communities (Cave 1998). Cramer (1998) has suggested that these cultural norms regarding the desirability or otherwise of environmental protection are a significant factor in shaping individual responses and attitudes.

It has often been asserted, for example, that there is a fundamental difference in environmental perceptions and attitudes between Western and Asian societies. Some writers have argued that Asian cultures are generally more supportive of the environment as a result of their long history of Buddhist, Taoist and Hindu religious systems, which stress veneration of and respect for all life (Callicott and Ames 1989). In contrast, Kalland and Persoon (1998: 6) claim that Asian environmental attitudes are generally less romanticised and more pragmatic than are those found in the West and that 'there is nothing in Asian perceptions that prepares people for a more environmentally friendly behaviour than elsewhere'. Finally, a third perspective argues that neither Western nor Asian cultures are inherently 'greener' than the other; instead, environmental concern is in fact a fairly common human trait that can be found in all peoples and nations (Dunlap and Mertig 1996; Rukavishnikov 1996).

In the study reported in this chapter this variable was examined by limiting the selection of respondents to four countries. The two Western nations chosen for the research—France and Australia—are geographically large nations. Both have a deep sense of national identity and history based on the land and environment. In contrast, Hong Kong and Singapore are small, densely populated urban city-states. If there really is a significant cultural difference between oriental and occidental environmental perceptions, then it might be expected to surface in the results from such different nations.[1]

At the same time, the four nations chosen also provided the opportunity to test for differences within Western and Asian cultures. Australia, for example, is a predominantly Anglo-Saxon country with a strong British cultural heritage, in contrast to France. Likewise, Hong Kong is essentially a Chinese community, whereas Singapore contains a mix of Chinese, Tamil and Malay residents. Given these differences, if there is any meaningful contrast in environmental attitudes

---

1   It is acknowledged that Hong Kong is a Special Administrative Region of the People's Republic of China; however, for brevity, the terms 'nation' and 'country' have been used herein.

within Western and Asian societies, then it might be apparent in the results from respondents in these countries.

8.2.2 Age

Age appears to be one of the most easily identifiable factors correlated to environmental attitudes and responsiveness among the general community (Honnold 1984). Indeed, Klineberg *et al.* (1998) have suggested that age is one of the most consistently reliable indicators of environmental attitudes, with younger respondents frequently being correlated with high levels of environmental concern.

This phenomenon appears also to hold true within the business community: studies by Charlesworth (1998) and by Petts *et al.* (1998) have identified younger managers as being more environmentally proactive than their older counterparts. Gifford (1997) has argued that this phenomenon usually occurs as a result of what has been termed the 'true age effect', in which individuals generally become more conservative as they get older. If these studies are accurate, then it would be reasonable to expect that age could be used as a valid predictor of environmental concern within management students as well.

8.2.3 Gender

Gender-based differences in management styles and approaches have been the subject of considerable research in recent decades, with a number of researchers claiming that women operate their businesses in very different ways from those of men and that they go into business for different reasons (Eagly and Johnson 1990). It is often suggested that female managers make a greater effort to address emotional and relational issues than do their male counterparts. As a result, they tend to be more participative, democratic and empathetic supervisors, with a greater focus on 'meaning and quality-of-life' issues rather than just simple task achievement (Robbins *et al.* 2000). At the same time, it is often claimed that women in general appear to be more concerned about environmental issues than are men (Gutteling and Weigman 1993), and this assertion has been supported by the results of other studies (ABS 1998, 1999; Lothian 1994; Schahn and Holzer 1990). This being the case, it would seem reasonable to assume that female management students would also be more environmentally sensitive and supportive than are their male counterparts.

8.3 Measuring environmental concern

The measurement of environmental concerns can be a somewhat difficult proposition, given the many different dimensions of environmental issues and the cultural context of different societies (Ray and Hall 1995). The first problem is in terms of *what* to measure. Most public measures of environmental attitudes have used very simplistic or limited tools to measure people's views. Although Stanton

(1972) has shown that single-question measures can have a relatively high degree of validity and reliability, most researchers have argued that multi-item scales are generally preferable (Maloney *et al.* 1975; Ray and Hall 1995). This is because attitudes towards environmentally related issues are not homogeneous. There are many different aspects to being 'green', and it is entirely possible for an individual to have quite strong environmental views in one area while being antipathetic on other issues (Kuhn and Jackson 1989).

The second difficulty has been whether the same measuring tool can be used with equal validity in different cultures and nations. Most tools developed have been strongly grounded in a specific cultural context and therefore their generalisability has been limited. This is because each culture and each nation has its own set of environmental problems, opportunities and heritage, and this has made it difficult to extend such instruments beyond the country of origin. Many researchers have devised questionnaires to measure environmental concern, although few of them have been extensively used or cross-validated in different countries. As a result, there is still a need for further research to determine which scales can be meaningfully applied internationally.

8.4 Methodology

Data for this study was collected from management students studying at four business schools in the four countries studied (Australia, France, Hong Kong and Singapore). To reduce the number of extraneous variables likely to affect the outcome of the study, respondents were drawn from similar streams of study in each institution. All students were undertaking degree-level business management courses (broadly equivalent to the third year of an undergraduate degree programme in Australia) and studying similar topics (in this case, entrepreneurship and small business) in the English language. The selection of students was through a convenience sample, based on the willingness of institutions to provide access to their students. Data was collected in the classroom at the commencement of lectures.

Environmental concerns were measured by using an adapted version of the questionnaire first used by Weigel and Weigel (1978; the questions asked and the scoring system are given in Box 8.1). Whereas many other scales of environmental concern are written specifically for particular countries, the Weigel and Weigel scale has already been used successfully in a number of countries (Schaper 2001; Holahan 1982). This instrument consists of 16 questions using a five-point Likert scale (see Box 8.1). The maximum theoretical score is 80 and the minimum is 16, with a theoretical mid-point of 48.

Cultural differences were measured by using respondent nationality as a broad proxy measure. Although an individual's nationality does not always equate to his or her cultural background, such an approach is widely used in cross-cultural studies (Smith and Bond 1993).

The age (in years), gender and nationality of each respondent is requested. The respondent is then asked to rate the following statements on a scale of 1–5, with 1 indicating 'strongly disagree', 3 indicating a 'neutral response' and 5 indicating 'strongly agree'. For questions 1, 3, 6, 7, 10, 15 and 16 the score received corresponds to the response given (i.e. 'strongly agree' corresponds to a score of 5, and so on); for questions 2, 4, 5, 8, 9 and 11–14 the scores are given in reverse order (i.e. if the respondent answers that they strongly disagree with the statement 'We should not worry about killing too many game animals because in the long run things will balance out' they will receive a score of 5, and so on).

1 The government will have to introduce harsh measures to halt pollution, since few people will regulate themselves.

2 We should not worry about killing too many game animals because in the long run things will balance out.

3 I'd be willing to make personal sacrifices for the sake of slowing down pollution even though the immediate results may not seem significant.

4 Pollution is not personally affecting my life.

5 The benefits of modern consumer products are more important than the pollution that results from their production and use.

6 We must prevent any type of animal from becoming extinct, even if it means sacrificing some things for ourselves.

7 Courses focusing on the conservation of natural resources should be taught in all schools.

8 Although there is continual contamination of our lakes, streams and air, nature's purifying processes soon return them to normal.

9 Because the government has such good agencies, it's very unlikely that pollution due to energy production will become excessive.

10 The government should provide each citizen with a list of agencies and organisations to which citizens could report environmental problems.

11 Predators, such as crows and foxes, which prey on farmers' grain crops and poultry should be eliminated.

12 The currently active anti-pollution organisations are really more interested in disrupting society than they are in fighting pollution.

13 Even if public transportation were more efficient than it is, I would prefer to drive my car to work.

14 Industry is trying its best to develop effective pollution technology.

15 If asked, I would contribute time, money or both to an organisation such as Greenpeace that works to improve the quality of the environment.

16 I would be willing to accept an increase in my expenses of $100 next year to promote the wise use of natural resources.

Box 8.1 **The questionnaire and scale used in the author's survey to determine the level of environmental concern**

8.5 Results and analysis

A total of 329 responses was collected, the sample consisting of 50 students from Singapore (15.2% of the total respondent set), 51 from France (15.5%), 59 from Australia (17.9%) and 95 from the Hong Kong Special Administrative Region (28.9%). The remaining 74 students (22.5%) were citizens of other nations, which is a reflection of the diverse international composition of each business school. The data set included 117 males and 206 females (6 respondents did not provide gender details). The mean score of all respondents was 58.25, with a median score of 59.00 and a standard deviation of 6.65. A summary of the pertinent descriptive statistics is detailed in Table 8.1.

Statistic	Nationality					Whole sample
	Singa-porean	French	Australian	Hong Kong	Other	
Sample size, N	50	51	59	95	74	329
Environmental concern:						
Mean score	57.54	59.14	59.68	57.93		58.25
Median score	56.00	60.00	60.00	58.00		59.00
Standard deviation	6.91	7.14	7.32	5.22		6.65
Skewness	0.143	0.034	0.166	0.269		0.186
Age (years):						
Mean	27.98	22.33	23.78	31.45		25.88
Median	27.00	22.00	20.00	30.00		22.00
Standard deviation	5.40	1.09	7.62	5.32		6.53
Gender:						
Number of females	43	27	27	72	37	206
Number of males	7	22	32	20	36	117

NB: Six respondents did not provide gender details.

Table 8.1 Summary of descriptive statistics obtained from the author's survey

Reliability was tested by using one of the standard measures of inter-item consistency for multipoint-scaled items, Cronbach's α. The resultant score of 0.7076 (standardised item $\alpha = 0.7161$) was within the range of acceptability (Sekaran 2000). For all tests a confidence limit (α) of 5% was employed.

8.5.1 Nationality and environmental concern

Null hypothesis, H_0: There is no difference between the mean environmental concern scores of different nationalities.

Alternative hypothesis, H_A: There is a difference between the mean environmental concern scores of different nationalities.

This hypothesis was tested by conducting a one-way analysis of variance (ANOVA) between the three nationalities; respondents from other countries were excluded from this test. The result ($F = 1.427$, $p = 0.235$) indicates that there is no significant difference in the mean scores between the groups, and the null hypothesis cannot be rejected (Hair *et al.* 1998).

In general, each of the student groups displayed a relatively high level of environmental concern, with the mean score of each nationality being substantially higher than the theoretical mid-point of 48.

8.5.2 Age and environmental concern

Null hypothesis, H_0: There is no relationship between a student's age and his or her level of environmental concern.

Alternative hypothesis, H_A: Older students have a higher level of environmental concern.

This issue was examined by conducting a correlation between the variables of respondent age and the aggregated total score. As both data sets consisted of interval data, a Pearson correlation was employed; a one-tailed test was used. Results of the test are as follows:

- Sample size, N: 300
- Pearson correlation: 0.105
- Significance: 0.034
- Decision: accept the alternative hypothesis, H_A

In this case a significant statistical relationship does exist between the two variables. However, the correlation coefficient is a comparatively weak one, which tends to suggest that, although there is a link between the age of respondents and the strength of their environmental ('green') attitudes, age may not be a critical determinant. Moreover, the positive correlation indicates that the older the student the higher their environmental concerns. This is in direct contrast to the inverse correlation usually found in most studies (such as Klineberg *et al.* 1998) and suggests that older students are in fact 'greener' than young ones.

8.5.3 Gender and environmental concern

Null hypothesis, H_0: There is no relationship between a student's gender and his or her environmental attitudes.

Alternative hypothesis, H_A: Female students are more likely to display a positive environmental attitude.

This was tested using a one-way Spearman correlation between the variable 'gender' (which was recoded as a dummy variable) and the respondents' aggregate concern score. The results of this procedure are as follows:

- Sample size, N: 323
- Spearman correlation: -0.006
- Significance: 0.456
- Decision: reject the alternative hypothesis

It is not possible to reject the null hypothesis, and it can be concluded that there appears to be no significant link between environmental concern and gender. This contradicts the findings of Schahn and Holzer (1990), who found a tentative relationship between gender and environmental concern, but supports the arguments of the Australian Bureau of Statistics (ABS 1998: 12) that 'there is no great difference between the sexes' with regard to environmental attitudes.

8.6 Implications for management educators

The above results have a number of implications for the teaching of environment and sustainability courses in university business schools.

8.6.1 Student interest in sustainability

There is a general affinity for environmental issues among students. As these results show, student concern in each of the business schools surveyed is quite substantial. The mean scores are well above the theoretical midpoint and about on par with Weigel and Weigel's (1978) original mean score for the general US population ($\bar{x} = 59$). These results mirror the findings of other recent studies that show management students do in fact care about the environment (Aspen Institute 2002).

8.6.2 Concerns transcend culture

A second finding is that concern about environmental issues is a relatively common characteristic not limited by cultural or national boundaries. It would be incorrect to assume that students in particular countries are more receptive to green issues than are others; it matters to them all. The results of this study clearly contradict the assumption that cultural differences translate into differences in environmental concern.

8.6.3 Undergraduates care

Previous international studies into the attitudes of business students towards environmental sustainability have largely been confined to postgraduate participants, usually drawn from MBA programmes (Aspen Institute 2002; WRI 1998, 2001). For a variety of reasons, students taking their initial degree have been overlooked. The data in this study suggests that undergraduates share a similar concern to that of their graduate colleagues: both groups care about environmental and sustainability issues. This need should be taken into account when structuring future tertiary programmes. Instead of providing environmental business courses only for graduate studies, it may well be worthwhile offering such courses for undergraduates as well.

8.6.4 Difficulty in predicting likely 'green' students

It is hard to paint a profile of the 'typical' environmentally conscious student from the basic demographic data tested in this chapter. On the basis of the current study, it appears that neither nationality nor gender are useful predictor variables, as there is no statistically significant relationship between either factor and an individual's level of environmental concern. Only the age of students is positively correlated with level of green concerns, and even then only weakly. It would seem that there is no such thing as an archetypal 'green student'; instead, most students basically are environmentally concerned.

8.6.5 Unmet course demand

Previous assessment of business school course offerings has indicated that there is a relative paucity of courses related to environmental issues and sustainability. Moreover, the majority of such courses currently offered are found in Western Europe and North America; Asian and Australian universities have generally tended to lag behind in providing such programmes (Schaper 2002; WRI 1998, 2001). However, given the high level of environmental concern expressed by all respondents in the current study, there are probably many students who might consider enrolling in a 'business and the environment' unit or sustainability course if it were offered. But since such courses are rarely offered, many students do not have the opportunity to study in this area.

8.6.6 Course differentiation

The points raised in Section 8.6.5 suggest that university business schools may be able to seize a competitive advantage by incorporating the topics of environmental management and sustainability into their curricula. The combination of high levels of student environmental concern, coupled with an existing low supply of courses, suggests an opportunity for entrepreneurially minded educators. There is considerable scope for proactive business schools to become 'first movers' in this field. This would attract potential students interested in studying and working in the area of sustainable development and help differentiate the institution from its competitors.

8.7 Conclusions

Given the relatively small sizes of the samples involved, this study should be treated only as an exploratory initial examination of this topic. Clearly, the area of international differences in environmental business education is one in which more research is needed.

Although at first glance it may be encouraging to find that most students display relatively high levels of environmental concern, there is a caveat: such scores do not automatically translate into environmentally friendly behaviour. Environmental concerns are a possible indicator of likely behaviour but do not provide an all-encompassing guide to what people actually do. There is a large body of research that indicates that people do not always act in a manner that is consistent with their professed attitudes (Cave 1998; Fishbein 1967; Manzo and Weinstein 1987; Triandis 1971), and students are unlikely to be any different.

The existence of a 'gap' or discrepancy between individual concerns and practices is not new. Research in many different disciplines has shown that a substantial gap often exists between attitudes and practices. Indeed, Freire (quoted in Hunter *et al.* 1999: 102-103) has claimed that 'one of the major struggles in every individual is to diminish the difference between what one says and does, between the discourse and the practice'. The goal of effective environmental education in business, then, may be to give students the tools they need to readily convert those concerns into meaningful change in their own world.

References

ABS (Australian Bureau of Statistics) (1998) *Environmental Issues: People's Views and Practices* (Catalogue No. 4602.0; Canberra: ABS).

—— (1999) *Environmental Issues: People's Views and Practices* (Catalogue No. 4602.0; Canberra: ABS).

Aspen Institute (2002) *Where Will They Lead? MBA Student Attitudes about Business and Society* (Queenstown, MD: Aspen Institute).

Azjen, I., and M. Fishbein (1980) *Understanding Attitudes and Predicting Social Behaviour* (Upper Saddle River, NJ: Prentice Hall).

Bandura, A. (1969) *Principles of Behaviour Modification* (New York: Rinehart & Winston).

Berberoglu, G., and C. Tosunoglu (1995) 'Exploratory and Confirmatory Factor Analyses of an Environmental Attitude Scale (EAS) for Turkish University Students', *Journal of Environmental Education* 26 [Online] Electronic Library Australia.

Berkowitz, L. (1975) *A Survey of Social Psychology* (Hinsdale, IL: Dryden Press).

Callicott, J.B., and R.T. Ames (eds.) (1989) *Nature in Asian Tradition of Thought* (Albany, NY: State University of New York Press).

Cave, S. (1998) *Applying Psychology to the Environment* (London: Hodder & Stoughton).

Charlesworth, K. (1998) 'Business needs clear policy on green issues', *Professional Manager,* July 1998: 16-17.

Cooper, J., and R.T. Croyle (1984) 'Attitudes and Attitude Change', *Annual Review of Psychology* 35: 395-426.

Cramer, J. (1998) 'Environmental Management: From "Fit" to "Stretch"', *Business Strategy and the Environment* 7: 162-72.

Dodd, C.H. (1998) *Dynamics of Intercultural Communication* (Boston, MA: McGraw–Hill, 5th edn).

Dunlap, R., and A. Mertig (1996) 'Global Environmental Concern', in P. Ester and W. Schluchter (eds.), *Social Dimensions of Contemporary Environmental Issues: International Perspectives* (Tilburg, Netherlands: Tilburg University Press): 133-64.

Eagly, A.H., and B.T. Johnson (1990) 'Gender and Leadership Styles: A Meta-Analysis', *Psychological Bulletin*, September 1990: 233-56.

Fishbein, M. (1967) *Readings in Attitude Theory and Measurement* (New York: John Wiley).

Gifford, R. (1997) *Environmental Psychology: Principles and Practice* (Boston, MA: Allyn & Bacon, 2nd edn).

Gutteling, J.M., and O. Wiegman (1993) 'Gender-specific Reactions to Environmental Hazards in the Netherlands', *Sex Roles* 28: 433-47.

Hair, J.F., R.E. Anderson, R.L. Tatham and W.C. Black (1998) *Multivariate Data Analysis* (Englewood Cliffs, NJ: Prentice Hall, 5th edn).

Holahan, C.J. (1982) *Environmental Psychology* (New York: Random House).

Honnold, J.A. (1984) 'Age and Environmental Concern: Some Specification of Effects', *Journal of Environmental Education* 16.1: 4-9.

Hunter, D., A. Bailey and B. Taylor (1999) *The Essence of Facilitation* (Auckland, New Zealand: Tandem Press).

Kalland, A., and G. Persoon (eds.) (1998) *Environmental Movements in Asia* (Richmond, UK: Curzon Press).

Klineberg, S.L., M. McKeerer and B. Rothenbach (1998) 'Demographic Predictors of Environmental Concern: It Does Make a Difference How It's Measured', *Social Science Quarterly* 79.4: 734-53.

Kuhn, R.G., and E.L. Jackson (1989) 'Stability of Factor Structures in the Measurement of Public Environmental Attitudes', *Journal of Environmental Education* 20.3: 27-33.

Lothian, J.A. (1994) 'Attitudes of Australians towards the Environment: 1975 to 1994', *Australian Journal of Environmental Management* 1 (September 1994): 78-99.

Maloney, M.P., M.P Ward and G.N. Braucht (1975) 'A Revised Scale for the Measurement of Ecological Attitudes and Knowledge', *American Psychologist* 30: 787-90.

Manzo, L.C., and N.D. Weinstein (1987) 'Behavioural Commitment to Environment Protection: A Study of Active and Non-active Members of the Sierra Club', *Environment and Behaviour* 19: 637-94.

Newhouse, N. (1990) 'Implications of Attitude and Behaviour Research for Environmental Conservation', *Journal of Environmental Education* 22.1: 26-32.

Petts, J., A. Herd and M. O'hEocha (1998) 'Environmental Responsiveness, Individuals and Organisational Learning: SME Experience', *Journal of Environmental Planning and Management* 41.6 (November 1998): 711-31.

Ray, J.J., and G.P. Hall (1995) 'Are Environmentalists Radical or Conservative? Some Australian Data', *Journal of Social Psychology* 135.2: 225-29.

Robbins, S.P., R. Bergman, I. Stagg and M. Coulter (2000) *Management* (Sydney: Prentice Hall, 2nd edn).

Rukavishnikov, V. (1996) 'Methodological Problems of Measurement of Ecological Attitudes and Comparison of Survey Data', in P. Ester and W. Schluchter (eds.), *Social Dimensions of Contemporary Environmental Issues: International Perspectives* (Tilburg, Netherlands: Tilburg University Press): 215-27.

Sarbaugh, L. (1979) *Intercultural Communication* (Rochelle Park, NJ: Hayden).

Schahn, J., and E. Holzer (1990) 'Konstruktion, Validierung und Anwendung von Skalen zur Erfassung des individuellen Umweltbewußtseins' ('Construction, Validation and Application of Scales for the Measurement of Individual Environmental Concern'), *Zeitschrift für Differentielle und Diagnostische Psychologie* 11: 185-204.

Schaper, M. (2001) *Environmental Concern among University Business School Students: An International Comparison* (WP-5; Perth, Australia: School of Management, Curtin University).

—— (2002) 'Educating Ecopreneurs: Environment Studies in Australian Tertiary Business Schools', *Australian Journal of Environmental Management* 9.3 (September 2002): 38-41.

Sekaran, U. (2000) *Research Methods for Business: A Skill Building Approach* (New York: John Wiley, 3rd edn).

Smith, P.B., and M.H. Bond (1993) *Social Psychology across Cultures: Analysis and Perspectives* (London: Harvester Wheatsheaf).

Stanton, H.E. (1972) 'A Comparison of Two Approaches to Personality Measurement', *Australian Psychologist* 7: 33-39.

Triandis, H.C. (1971) *Attitudes and Attitude Change* (New York: John Wiley).

Weigel, R., and J. Weigel (1978) 'Environmental Concern: The Development of a Measure', *Environment and Behaviour* 10: 3-15.

WRI (World Resources Institute) (1998) 'Grey Pinstripes with Green Ties: MBA Programmes where the Environment Matters', www.wri.org/meb/grnties/mba-home.htm, accessed 8 December 2001.

—— (2001) 'Beyond Grey Pinstripes', www.beyondgreypinstripes.org/results/past_reports/bgps2001.cfm, accessed 18 March 2001.

Part 2
Learning from
current practice

9

Sustainability education
The experience of HRH the Prince of Wales's Business and the Environment Programme

Polly Courtice and Jonathon Porritt
Business and the Environment Programme, UK

Like every solid, successful initiative, HRH the Prince of Wales's Business and the Environment Programme (BEP) began as an idea in the mind of someone willing to nudge it into being. In this case it was the Prince of Wales who, in the wake of the Rio Earth Summit in 1992, felt that business leaders needed an active, educational experience to help them grasp the scale and significance of the emerging sustainable development agenda. That the agenda was—and to an extent still is—so difficult to define reveals how innovative and bold his idea was.

After consulting with advisors[1] in 1992, the Prince invited the University of Cambridge Programme for Industry to create an appropriate executive learning programme. The original mandate of the programme was to help business executives develop a greater ability to integrate sustainable development into their thinking and practice without sacrificing profitability. The concept was simple but ambitious: to bring together a world-class team of thought leaders and practitioners to give an annual week-long seminar on sustainable development to senior executives in a retreat-style setting. The Prince appointed an independent management committee to oversee the development and strategic direction of the programme and to ensure its position at the forefront of the debate. The committee included international business leaders and was chaired by the Chairman of the National Westminster Bank in the United Kingdom.

The high level of visibility provided by the Prince and the University of Cambridge, contributions from leading thinkers and practitioners and the

1 Including one of the authors of this chapter, Jonathon Porritt, a sustainability activist and co-founder of Forum for the Future.

innovative formula and continuous development of the content and format adopted by the BEP has attracted a steady demand from senior executives from leading companies around the world. Delegate approval ratings have remained consistently high, with an overall average rating of 84%, and the programme has expanded rapidly and globally over the past nine years. It has served more than 650 delegates from 35 countries in 18 seminars on three continents. As of 2003, it will operate in four regions: the United Kingdom, the USA, continental Europe and Southern Africa.

We believe it is fair to say that the Business and the Environment Programme is now the global leader in its class. In this chapter we will identify the key elements of this outstanding formula and explore their relevance to its success.

9.1 The early years

The first BEP seminar was held in 1994 at Madingley Hall on the outskirts of Cambridge. Some 35 delegates from UK industry joined a team of seven core faculty and an international cast of speakers. Several things differentiated the programme from other models of sustainable development education surfacing at the time:

- Its founding claim—radical at the time—was that the interface between business and the environment was a strategic issue, not a technical one.

- The seminar was, for senior executives, long—four days and nights in a residential setting. This intensive experience was the gateway to membership of an alumni network that still provides support and inspiration.

- The selection of delegates was specific: the seminar was aimed at senior operational executives, *not* their environmental or corporate social responsibility (CSR) managers. Included among the delegates were senior public-sector representatives, in recognition that, by its very nature, sustainable development depends on creative solution-finding between the private and public sectors.

- The seminar was not based around a business school or any locationally bound faculty or institution but instead relied on some of the most prominent experts in sustainable development internationally.

- By drawing together a few of these local and international experts as the BEP's permanent core faculty who shared the week with the delegates, we ensured diverse institutional and individual perspectives and created the continuity that is a hallmark of the programme. The core faculty became, in a sense, 'owners' and shared responsibility—helped by the Cambridge Programme for Industry—for designing and refining each year's seminars.

- The programme was based on the assumption that sustainable development is a way of thinking and taking action that is accessible to everyone rather than purely a body of knowledge to be passed on from expert to newcomer. It recognised that conventional analytical and decision-making approaches cannot address the seemingly intractable problems facing society today. Fundamental mind-set changes and new thinking is required from those with the power to shape the debate and implement the solutions. Thus, the BEP was founded on the understanding that busy executives must undergo a special experience to help them recognise the limitations of conventional approaches and to develop and test their understanding and responses in a trust-based environment with their intellectual peers.

9.2 The basic seminar model

From the outset, the BEP was structured to support a meaningful shift in thinking, beginning with the delegate selection process. We decided to target those who operate at highly strategic levels within their organisations and who are capable of having an impact on long-term and wider strategic planning. The programme is not designed for those who are environmental experts or CSR specialists within their organisations. Most delegates are drawn from business backgrounds, although a few public-sector and non-governmental organisation (NGO) participants are selected each year, adding valuable perspectives and ideas. An outline of the general structure of the BEP follows.

On the first day, some of the world's foremost sustainability thinkers introduce delegates to information that leaves little room for doubt that we are entering an era of unprecedented change, where conventional beliefs will yield ever-shrinking returns. Delegates spend the next three days analysing some of the most critical issues, teasing out their deepest implications for business and society and exploring how alternative models may hold the key to a sustainable future. We never offer pre-packaged solutions. Indeed, we hold that such things do not exist. We maintain that, with fresh thinking and some moral support, executives can uncover the solutions they need.

Perhaps most important of all, plenty of time is scheduled for small syndicate groups. Each group of seven delegates is pre-selected and remains together for the duration. A member of the core faculty is assigned to facilitate each syndicate group, to hold open the requisite space for deep discussion of what they have heard in the plenary sessions. Alumni report that these syndicate sessions are catalytic. In the freedom of intimate debate we find that the base metal of information, challenge and confusion can be transformed into the beginnings of deeper understanding and self-confidence. As each day passes and trust grows, the seeds of 'What I might do about this when I get back to my organisation' can be planted and nurtured.

The core faculty plays an essential role in the success of the process. The strength of this team lies in its diversity and flexibility, combined with continuity and deep familiarity with the BEP's objectives and methods. Not only do members bring their particular field of expertise, they also act as an integrating force, drawing the threads of the debate together and helping delegates relate what they have heard to their organisational and personal roles and responsibilities. About 16 core faculty alternate their geographical participation in seminars and use their knowledge of the programme's underlying purpose and the evolution of the debate to enhance each seminar. They come from different academic, environmental or business institutions, where they have full-time jobs. They meet at least twice during the year to plan seminar content and process and to discuss the strategic direction of the programme.

9.3 The Business and the Environment Programme evolves

Most fundamentally, however, the BEP is a sustainability learning programme that has continued to learn; over the years the format, content and geographical diversity have evolved to meet the needs of delegates and to stay abreast of the rapidly emerging debate. This process of innovation has become one of its greatest assets.

In the early years, and in line with our perceived goal—to raise executives' awareness of the sustainability challenge and help them see its potential threats to, and opportunities for, business—we drew on a variety of inspirational and prominent speakers to address the delegates. Over the years, our invited guest speakers have included industrialists, leading-edge practitioners, entrepreneurs, contrarians, bishops and direct-action campaigners. This exposes delegates to a diversity of opinion and a range of means by which they can engage with sustainable development.

The programme's processes have evolved in response to feedback from delegates and advances in educational learning methods in general. The seminars continue to include diverse formats such as plenary talks, syndicate groups and workshops. Group debates, focus and carousel workshops, shared learning exercises and organisational case histories have replaced many of the original speech-with-Q&A formats. Many of these innovations signal a shift towards a shared learning approach that emphasises balancing the input by the 'expert' with output from 'learners'. This allows delegates to learn from respected experts and experience and to be more active in their learning by sharing with each other and learning directly from the experiences and input of other delegates.

A recent innovation has been the introduction of small group work: delegates discuss sustainability dilemmas that they face in their organisations and explore resolution strategies. This approach underscores the view that the best approach to learning about something as complex as sustainable development is through extended dialogue rather than lecture, thus building on the extensive business acumen and experience that has been brought together at the seminar.

A further development of the original 'visiting expert as talking head' model began with the inclusion in the inaugural Southern African seminar of several sessions in which delegates with specific expertise became 'contributors'. This makes sense. When there is a high level of knowledge in the room, we would rather have that shared than bring in a specialist. This has become increasingly possible, as the issues being discussed are now more likely to pertain to the experience or expertise of some of the delegates.

In 2003 the BEP initiated an exciting effort to clarify what the world's business leaders think 'it's really all about'. Seminar participants discussed three critical questions: What is the fundamental purpose of a good economy? Why do our current economies fail to achieve the fundamental goal? and What can business do to reduce these failings? These Sustainable Economy Dialogues have been introduced into all BEP seminars as well as special events in which alumni can participate. By the end of 2004, a 'BEP Business Work Plan for a Sustainable Economy' will be presented, comprising the most powerful and actionable ideas that have emerged from the Dialogues. The draft Work Plan will be improved through electronic comments to be invited from all BEP alumni, and enriched by further input from future Dialogues.

9.4 Embedding sustainable development: the role of leadership and personal values

Over the years, the BEP has sought ways to respond to a perennial concern of delegates after their participation: the difficulty of implementing some of their new insights as a result of organisational resistance and personal constraints.

Organisationally, we emphasise that delegates, as their name implies, represent larger organisational communities facing the challenge of sustainable development. One of the major syndicate group discussions encourages participants to identify, discuss and confront their company's potential organisational response, or even resistance, and to explore what they can do to start transformational change.

To this end, we have introduced new content, in workshop and plenary format, on leadership and organisational change. We have also used more case histories to explore different approaches that organisations are taking to further 'embed' sustainable development. Sessions from leading business practitioners sharing insights about what is involved in leading a company to a more sustainable future have always been important. Delegates value the opportunity to hear at first hand what individuals have been able to achieve and where they have faced their greatest challenges.

Perhaps even more importantly, the seminar has always paid particular attention to the connection between corporate practice and an individual's personal sense of ethics and responsibility. If delegates leave a seminar having had a professional, but not a personal, experience, then we consider the programme's goals to be unmet. Seminars have increasingly included personal reflection time, journal writing, syndicate and discussion groups and workshops about delegates' personal ethics and values.

9.5 Evolving content: the changing nature of the debate

The concept of sustainable development, with its origins in the 'limits-to-growth' thesis and the oft-quoted Brundtland Commission definition (see page 107) (WCED 1987), has maintained a core definition based in environmentally sound development. Yet, topically, the breadth of the agenda and priorities at any one time have changed over the past decade. The debate for the corporate sector has moved far beyond the concept of eco-innovation that dominated the early 1990s and has grown to encompass issues of poverty and inequality, economic globalisation, human rights, ethics, institutional capacity-building, partnership development and international relations. The sustainability agenda has become more sophisticated as the demands of society have shifted and it has added the successes and failures of the first generation of practitioners to its repertoire.

In 1994, the core content of the BEP focused on natural system pressures, environmental risk management and the science of climate change, market mechanisms and regulation, and the business case for responding to these elements. The social dimensions of sustainability were addressed within each of these themes but were not core themes. This reflected the reluctance of the corporate sector in the early 1990s to engage fully with the social aspects of the sustainability debate, although we always intended to build these issues into the seminar content. By 2002, without losing sight of the criticality of ecological challenges, the content had diversified to include human rights, global health and poverty, corporate social responsibility, social entrepreneurship and the ethical and spiritual dimensions of sustainable development.

9.5.1 A truly global perspective

By inviting delegates and faculty from outside the region to attend each seminar— another productive policy that has emerged during recent years—diverse cultural and political perspectives on sustainable development regularly emerge. These regional nuances are appreciated and critiqued by companies operating in an increasingly complex global environment. The cross-cultural and cross-sectoral perspectives on sustainable development have provided new insights and reinforced the multi-dimensional nature of sustainable development. In terms of diversity of geographical content, for example, the business case for sustainable development contains different components depending on the political and legal environment of the company from which delegates come. In the USA, the debate around the corporate political context of sustainable development inevitably takes greater account of environmental liability law and regulation, whereas in Europe social democracy features more prominently. In Southern Africa it is impossible to address sustainable development without looking deeply into the links between globalisation, poverty and health.

In addition to clear regional variations, the sustainability challenges are different for a chemical engineer than for a media executive, for example. Again, throwing these different disciplines together in the debates and syndicate group sessions has proven time and again that diversity can be the friend of learning, that methods used in one sector constitute transferable knowledge for other sectors. Delegates attach great value to this diversity and to the opportunity to engage in substantive discussions with people from different sectors and from different walks of life. This has particularly been the case where NGOs and business executives are able to explore sometimes radically different views in a constructive and trust-based environment.

Over time, the BEP has embraced these multiple cultural and disciplinary perspectives while realising that organisational and personal change are common challenges for all delegates and that learning to be gained in these areas is universal.

Finally, responsiveness to the changing business needs of sustainable development education and training has been an important part of programme development. The concept of sustainable development is notoriously difficult for business managers to grasp in ways that make it relevant and functional to their business practices. The BEP has avoided the temptation to provide some sort of sustainability 'toolkit' that executives can use when they return to work. Rather, it has sought to provide them with a conceptual framework and 'thinking tools'. These help them to make informed decisions in a context of environmental uncertainty and to engage with a constantly evolving agenda by making better judgements, not just better decisions. Seminars, therefore, include practical sessions on, for example, systems thinking, dilemma resolution and deconstruction of the business-case lens.

Executives are recognising the need to be able to contextualise their decisions and judgements within ethical, social, political, environmental and economic frameworks. The BEP seeks to achieve this by bringing the content of sustainable development to delegates in a way that highlights the rational and the moral and ethical dimensions of sustainable development. There remains a dearth of such frameworks in business schools and executive education curricula, yet, judging from the demand for our seminars, the need has never been more apparent.

9.6 Expanding the scope of the Business and the Environment Programme

As discussed above, sustainable development is, by its very nature, a transnational challenge. Understanding it requires a multi-country perspective, and business leaders must think globally. From very early on in the BEP's history it was clear that this debate could not be limited to its UK location, so we steadily expanded the seminars to Schloss Leopoldskron in Salzburg, Austria (1997), Wingspread in Racine, WI, USA (2001) and Lanzerac Manor in Stellenbosch, South Africa (2003). With new delegates, a flexible core faculty, local partners and an annual seminar in each location, we now host four seminars per year. The cross-fertilisation of knowledge and methods among these extremely dynamic seminars has led us to our most exciting period of development to date. The BEP's geographic expansion has been an exceptionally enriching component of its development and makes it unique in its niche.

Experience has taught us that a mantra for the founding of sustainability education programmes should be the same as that for many entrepreneurial endeavours: 'location, location, location'. Both in the physical setting of the seminars and in the geographic composition of faculty and delegates, location is a crucial consideration. In terms of the immediate location, the retreat-style seminar space has been consistently well received and has been used successfully in each new country.

The BEP began small. It focused on providing an escape-and-reflect location for executives to engage with the idea of sustainability. The first seminar took place in Madingley Hall in Cambridge, which, unlike more functionalist corporate conferencing settings, drew on the ambience and pastoralism of the English countryside and has allowed a retreat for executives whose lives are more normally urban, fast-paced and mobile. The continental European, US and South African seminars have emulated this model. They, too, take place in peaceful and natural spaces that allow delegates to reflect and reconnect with their natural surroundings.

9.6.1 Funding an outstanding global initiative: challenges and benefits

A world-class programme of this kind is difficult to establish on a fully self-funding basis. Not only are the costs of continuously updating the seminars and materials high but also we offer extensive bursaries to delegates from not-for-profit organisations and from developing or emerging economies. We believe that no delegate should be prevented from attending because of cost. This also makes it easier to assemble a well-balanced and representative cohort of delegates for each seminar.

Perhaps the highest costs in running the BEP are those associated with marketing and managing. It is expensive to develop and maintain relationships with corporations internationally while remaining committed to bringing new organisations into the programme. Three to four staff work full-time in marketing and use a sophisticated client relationship management system. Securing the right level and mix of delegates requires individual approaches and extended discussions with interested parties before nominations can be put to the selection committee. Three to four more staff work full-time in programme development, delegate and speaker liaison and venue logistics. Numerous other staff at the Cambridge Programme for Industry work in business and systems management.

There are two sources of funding—delegate fees and sponsorship. Fee income covers about half of the total operating costs. The BEP offers unique sponsorship opportunities to a select group of companies. Its sponsoring organisations are, and will continue to be, drawn from a broad range of sectors and will be genuinely committed to operating more sustainably and to demonstrating their leadership on sustainable development. Many of the BEP's sponsors are long-standing supporters. They clearly benefit from their association with the BEP, in terms of direct reputational benefit and through the participation of their senior executives in the seminars.

9.7 Relationship-building: key to continued success

9.7.1 A thriving alumni network

The BEP has realised the importance of maintaining its relationship with delegates, not least because its network is one of its attractions. A strong and active alumni network exists, comprising more than 650 executives in 35 countries around the world. Individuals who join the programme remain members of the network regardless of their subsequent place of employment. Companies that send delegates remain corporate members of the network.

This community of sustainable development practitioners is enabled by the programme's website, which includes an alumni directory, a library of materials, including executive briefings on sustainable development issues, discussion boards, updates from new seminars and information about alumni activities. Information about alumni events, a newsletter and a web letter are circulated regularly. An internationally distinguished speaker gives a biennial lecture (past speakers have included Mrs Gro Harlem Brundtland and James Wolfensohn), and an annual reunion and update seminar are held at the Prince of Wales's private residence. At these meetings, and through the newsletters, past delegates share their experiences of embedding sustainable development in their organisations. These alumni contributions become a valuable knowledge resource.

We have examined ways to support the alumni. Given how busy most of them are, and how many sources of information are available to them, experience has shown that demand for activities, events and services must come from alumni. If it does not, there may not be sufficient take-up to warrant the investment in planning such activities. We do research periodically to establish what alumni would most value from the network and then concentrate resources in these areas. Recently, there has been a strong demand for sustainability best-practice examples; examples from member companies are now shared at the seminars. In due course these will be extended and available to the whole network.

The BEP thus seeks to operate as a transnational network in which members already have some experience of cross-sectoral, cross-cultural sustainable development problem-solving. We hope that delegates go on to become not only sustainable development practitioners in their minds and in their organisations but also in the cultural, economic and political spheres in which they are influential. As one recent contributor to the programme said, sustainable development is more about 'creating will' than about 'technical wizardry'. This will-creation must be global, co-ordinated and at the highest levels of impact. The executives we serve are experienced in global co-ordination and impact; we try to create a programme that will allow them to uncover and develop that personal will.

9.7.2 The central role of partnerships

From the outset the BEP has worked closely with the World Business Council for Sustainable Development (WBCSD) and the International Business Leaders Forum (IBLF). Many delegates have joined because their organisations have been exposed to the ideas and opportunities of the sustainable development agenda through one of these initiatives. Similarly, having attended a BEP seminar, the newly enlightened executive finds the WBCSD and IBLF offer routes for further engagement and learning. The association is mutually beneficial.

A different sort of partner was considered when deciding where and when to expand the programme. The BEP's founding principles (that it should use leading thinkers regardless of their institutional affiliation and that it should be not-for-profit) have yielded opportunities that would not have arisen easily otherwise. Yet they have also represented a constraint on the nature of the partnerships and affiliations that have emerged. For example, most academic institutions with which such a partnership might have been established would expect to be able to field its own faculty on the programme and would hope to earn some revenue from the seminar to fund research.

The University of Cambridge adopted a broader perspective. It accepted that its faculty would be involved only if it was in the best interests of the BEP. Furthermore, although all the operating costs of the University of Cambridge were met in full, any surplus from the programme accrued not to Cambridge but to the programme's trust fund. This fund has been used to meet ongoing development costs and, importantly, to fund bursaries.

Currently, three of the four seminars are marketed and run by the Cambridge team. The Southern African Programme is also run by the University of Cambridge, but by Cambridge staff located in Cape Town, with the Graduate School of Business at the University of Cape Town and the National Business Initiative in South Africa.

9.8 Conclusions

The Business and Environment Programme has established itself as world-class in the domain of teaching sustainability. Many valuable lessons have been learned over the BEP's life-span, and its continued expansion testifies to its value. It gives participants a deep, intensive experience in a constructive environment. This experience shapes their attitudes, values and aspirations about sustainable development and has the potential to radically change the way their organisations do business.

The difference between a good seminar and a transformative seminar can only partially be explained by its structure, physical setting and calibre of core faculty and presenters. Time has revealed that the magic of the BEP lies in the spirit of the team of people who share a concern about the challenges we face as a society and a belief that we can help to create a new paradigm for the relationship between business and society and make a real difference in how wealth is generated now and in the future.

Reference

WCED (World Commission for Economic Development) (1987) *Our Common Future* (The Brundtland Report; New York: Oxford University Press).

Web addresses

Business and the Environment Programme   www.princeofwales.gov.uk/trusts/busenv.htm
Graduate School of Business, University of Cape Town   www.gsb.uct.ac.za/gsbwebb/home.asp
International Business Leaders Forum   www.iblf.org
National Business Initiative, South Africa   www.nbi.org.za
University of Cambridge Programme for Industry   www.cpi.cam.ac.uk
World Business Council for Sustainable Development   www.wbcsd.org

University of Cambridge Programme for Industry

Nominations and all queries regarding the programme should be directed to: University of Cambridge Programme for Industry, HRH The Prince of Wales's Business and Environment Programme, 1 Trumpington St, Cambridge CB2 1QA, UK. Tel: +44 1223 332772; fax: +44 1223 301122.

10
Approaching sustainability through a business–science synthesis

Steven R. Elliott, Raymond F. Gorman, Timothy C. Krehbiel,
Orie L. Loucks and Allan M. Springer
Miami University, USA

O. Homer Erekson
University of Missouri–Kansas City, USA

10.1 A unified approach to sustainability

We believe that sustainability involves a system whereby economic growth and/or improvements in the quality of life occur in a unified system that is complementary with, rather than antagonistic to, natural capital. Sustainability suggests a paradigm shift in business where resource use today need not jeopardise quality of life in the future. In this new paradigm, profitability and environmental responsibility are viewed as complements rather than substitutes.

In our opinion, sustainability involves building consensus among industry, political institutions and the general populace, supporting policies that will 'close the loop' and reconcile manufacturing and disposal of waste with the need to maintain the Earth's capital, through waste minimisation, recycling, adoption of benign technologies and environmental conservation. Ultimately, sustainable economic development is driven, in part, by the self-interest of consumers, businesses and other stakeholders pursuing individual goals while intentionally considering the impact of their action on the greater unified natural and human subsystems. Such a goal requires a dialogue among the various stakeholders representing these subsystems. The result should be a unified system, able to maintain a dynamic equilibrium and to regenerate itself to maintain its viability (see Loucks *et al.* 1999).

10.2 Sustainability perspectives in resources and business: a capstone course

The traditional university structure that separates business students and faculty from science students and faculty is not well equipped to develop effective leaders in this new era of interdisciplinary decision-making. Science students graduate without a sufficient understanding of the business contexts in which environmental problems occur. Similarly, business students are too often ill-prepared in the sciences to understand the technical side of many environmental issues. An even larger problem is that these two groups of students have not been trained to work together. In a world that requires co-operation and synthesis between business and science, the typical university structure has promoted an atmosphere of isolation and distrust between the two fields of study.

In 1989, faculty members in the School of Business and the College of Arts and Science explored alternatives to teaching sustainability. It was decided that an interdisciplinary undergraduate seminar would be the place to start. In 1992, after three years of development, the course entitled Sustainability Perspectives in Resources and Business was first offered as an honours seminar. At this time, the course was team-taught by six faculty members. Over the past ten years, the course delivery and content has evolved. Today, Sustainability Perspectives in Resources and Business is an interdisciplinary capstone course taught primarily to seniors majoring in business or the natural sciences and taught by one professor from the School of Business and one professor from the College of Arts and Science.

The course requires participants to think critically about (1) how the best scientific knowledge can be used in evaluating resource use options, (2) the parameters of business planning, ethics and profitability and (3) the role and impact of citizens, human values and government or corporate institutions in policy-making. Our course is unique in that it relies on a synthesis between business and science, not just an exposure to the two different viewpoints. Among the areas of study that the course tries to cover are:

- Historical trends, present status and projected futures of critical sociological, economic and ecological systems

- Renewability of the resource system (supply, infrastructure, recycling and regulation)

- Production and process technology and innovation

- Environmental quality and social adjustments

The course contains a combination of lectures, case studies, team projects and discussions of current research projects.

10.2.1 Lectures

Lectures and instructor-led class discussions can vary depending on who is teaching the course. Instructors are able to investigate in some detail their own areas of expertise and interest. For example, one instructor whose interest lies in quality management systems presents a comparison of Deming-based total quality environmental management (TQEM) systems, the American Chemistry Council's Responsible Care® initiative and the ISO 14000 series certification requirements. A finance professor can use the course to challenge the students to think about how catastrophe bonds can be used to mitigate the risks that insurance companies may face from the effects of global warming.

10.2.2 Case studies

Case studies provide students with the opportunity to examine and critique a real-world problem faced by a corporation. By working in teams with business and science students the students begin to experience the multidisciplinary and complex nature of the problems that confront business today. The cases used in a particular semester come from case studies that we have developed. The case studies, which look at companies such as Procter & Gamble, Ashland Chemical Company and Fetzer Vineyard, would not have happened without support of the business community. Corporate leaders have been helpful in providing us with information that truly reflects industry's position on environmental management and highlights the complexities of environmental problems facing executives.

The cases differ with respect to scope and complexity. Although all of the cases introduce business and economic issues related to sustainability they vary with respect to the degree of coverage of these issues. For instance, one case focuses on the issue of pollution prevention (waste minimisation) efforts within the G.E. Aircraft Engine Company. This is a rather straightforward case examining the payback for pollution prevention efforts, mainly from a business perspective. Alternatively, another case involves the production and distribution of wines by Fetzer Vineyard that are produced using organically grown grapes. This case is relatively complex and covers topics such as technical feasibility and desirability of growing grapes organically as well as business issues such as the marketing of the resulting product in a market not overly receptive to organic wine.

10.2.3 Team projects

Teams of students are assigned to work on and present the results from one major team project. Besides being interdisciplinary, the team projects cut across many societal institutions: business, government, consumers, labour unions and environmentalists, to name a few. An example of a team project involved dividing the class into four teams that represented four different perspectives of a forest management problem. Team 1 represented environmentalists, team 2 represented business, team 3 represented government and team 4 represented workers. Among the questions each group was asked to consider included: Who should own the forest? How should the forest be used? What are the costs and benefits of maintaining an old-growth forest instead of a managed industrial forest? To what extent are the needs and culture of the people from timber towns relevant? Are there international considerations (e.g. export sales to Japan)? Are there any ethical issues to consider? Is there a relevant historical perspective?

10.2.4 Integration of current research

The course provides a forum to discuss the research projects currently in progress by faculty in the Center for Sustainable Systems Studies (CSSS; see also Chapter 6). In some cases, lessons learned from the course help inform that same research. For a recent semester in 2002, the focus of a study was the Big Darby Creek watershed. The Big Darby, designated by The Nature Conservancy as one of the 'Last Great Places' in the Western hemisphere, is an example of a high-quality ecosystem in the agricultural Midwest that is relatively free of pollution. We established methods to link valuation of alternative development scenarios with associated changes in relevant ecological, economic and social factors and, in turn, the likelihood of adverse effects on relevant biological end-points. The methods involved characterisation of physical change and risks to biota in a landscape from four development scenarios and then the use of contingent valuation techniques to quantify the monetary value associated with the biotic integrity end-points. Presentation and contingent valuation surveys were presented to three groups of participants: watershed residents, residents near the watershed and non-residents. The 750 participants in the study were 'regular' people, not experts in the sciences or economics, and needed to understand complex concepts and relationships in the physical and social sciences.

Many lessons we learned through the course about communicating sustainability concepts to non-traditional audiences were incorporated into the presentation and survey. Thus, lessons we have learned about communicating sustainability concepts to students informed this research effort. We point out to our students how the research informs the class, and the class informs the research; another example of closing loops.

10.3 Challenges and limitations

The major challenge to offering the course involves resource constraints. We are convinced that team-teaching and limiting the number of students to approximately 30 are critical components of the course. To overcome these self-imposed constraints, administrators must be willing to give instructors full credit for team-teaching, or instructors must be willing to accept an overloaded teaching assignment. A second challenge is that sustainability requires instructors to be multidisciplinary, not only in relation to business and science but also within multiple business and science disciplines. It is a time-intensive struggle for the instructors of the course to remain current and to provide students with up-to-date material.

A major limitation for our course is that we are able to reach only a small percentage of the student population. Although we believe that all students would benefit from the course, requiring the course for all students would necessitate an extraordinary reallocation of university resources to hire and train faculty qualified to teach the course. Second, for the students on the course, the discussion of the principles of sustainability is very broad; an additional course would allow for a greater depth of understanding.

10.4 Outcomes

In spite of the challenges and limitations discussed in Section 10.3, we believe that the outcomes of the course are significant. The faculty members involved with the course have enriched the productivity and impact of their research and have integrated thought-provoking issues into all their courses. Our efforts have helped to bridge the gap between the School of Business and the College of Arts and Science for students and faculty. Perhaps the most significant outcome is that our students have a better understanding of the interrelatedness of business and science and therefore are better prepared to be effective leaders and decision-makers. Today, these individuals realise that the decisions they make in their lives and careers can have profound impacts both on the economic system and on the ecological system in which we live.

10.5 Summary

Sustainability involves a synthesis of science, business and other disciplines. Therefore, an excellent approach to teaching sustainability is a team-taught seminar for business and science students facilitated by business and science faculty. For more information on our course see Krehbiel *et al.* 1999 and the CSSS website at www.sba.muohio.edu/csss2.

References

Krehbiel, T.C., R.F. Gorman, O.H. Erekson, O.C. Loucks and P.C. Johnson (1999) 'Advancing Ecology and Economics through a Business–Science Synthesis', *Ecological Economics* 28: 183-96.

Loucks, O.L., O.H. Erekson, J.W. Bol, R.F. Gorman, P.C. Johnson and T.C. Krehbiel (1999) *Sustainability Perspectives for Resources and Business* (New York: Lewis).

11

Environmental actions, attitudes and knowledge
Making a difference through university education? The case of Middlesex University Business School

Diane Holt

Middlesex University Business School, UK

11.1 Environmental education at Middlesex University

Middlesex University is a multi-campus university based in North London. The University provides a wide range of undergraduate, postgraduate and post-experience courses and serves over 25,000 students from around the world. In the 1996 review of the Toyne Report (Sparks 1997) the University was identified as one of the UK's 'trail-blazing' universities in terms of its environmental initiatives. It is also a member of Forum for the Future and one of the 18 UK universities involved in the Higher Education Partnership Scheme.

Middlesex University's environmental mission statement[1] states that the University seeks to incorporate an environmental ethos into its operations and to promote an environmentally responsible community through teaching and research. This is achieved by integrating green issues into academic work and by demonstrating good environmental practice in the way it operates.

---

1   Go to www.mdx.ac.uk/mission/environment.htm.

11.1.1 Environmental education in the Business School

Middlesex University Business School (MUBS) is based primarily on the Hendon campus in North London and provides a range of undergraduate, postgraduate and post-experience courses to over 5,000 students. The students are drawn from around the world, with over 1,200 non-European students from 88 countries studying in Hendon in 2001. The MUBS teaches in a modular, semesterised structure and includes a law school.

The main constraints to teaching sustainability in a business school such as MUBS have been examined in detail in Holt *et al.* 1999. However these constraints can be summarised as follows:

- The student body at MUBS is international and culturally very diverse. An individual student's perception of the importance and relevance of environmental issues may differ as may his or her previous environmental education.

- Any environmental skills taught to students need to be able to stand the test of time and perhaps focus more on the fundamental concepts underpinning those skills. The majority of students will go into mainstream business and management jobs rather than be involved in an environmental role at the start of their career.

- The modular academic structure allows a high degree of flexibility. However, ensuring that each student receives a balanced environmental education is difficult to control and monitor. This is complicated by the lack of space in programmes (especially those dictated by accrediting professional bodies) making it difficult to add compulsory generic environmental elements.

- The Hendon campus is an urban campus where students tend to 'drop in' and spend large amounts of time working off-campus. This tends to lead to a decreasing concept of 'ownership' or responsibility for the site, unlike the case with some more rural campus universities where students tend to spend most of their time on-site (because they live, study and socialise there) and where students might, therefore, perceive a greater sense of stewardship and responsibility for the care of 'their' campus.

Environmental management at MUBS is managed by the estates division in accordance with the University's environmental polices and guidelines and will not be discussed in detail here. More details can be found on the University website.[2] The curriculum is designed around modules and validated by the University's quality assurance department into programmes, including a highly flexible joint honours pathway. There is no compulsory environmental literacy module in MUBS. The constraints of professional bodies and the timetable have prevented such an inclusion. However, all students have the option of taking one of the level-one introductory classes from the social science and environmental faculty, but these may be on a different campus.

2 www.mdx.ac.uk/www/planning/ap_aps5b.htm

Thus environmental education at MUBS occurs in a discipline-focused manner. It is included in the curriculum of a range of modules, reflecting the emergence of environmental and social responsibility in the corporate environment and therefore the curriculum.

Many of the 'traditional' business and management classes contain case studies that discuss environmental matters. However, there has been no systematic analysis of the environmental content of these traditional business school modules—so knowledge about what environmental topics and case studies are taught in the mainstream modules is available on an anecdotal basis only.

In the general environmental education literature there has been some work undertaken on students' environmental values. However, there is no empirical work that assesses how students' environmental values, knowledge and actions may change over the life-span of their time in education, and how different educational experiences may influence this change. It was in recognition of this that in 1998 MUBS and the School of Social Sciences undertook a longitudinal environmental survey of their student body. This descriptive study aimed to identify students' environmental values, actions and attitudes in their first year at the University and then return to this group at the end of their time at the University to see if the environmental learning experiences the students had been through had made a difference to their actions and attitudes. The study sample is too small to identify definite causal relationships, the aim being to provide an exploratory data set to inform future work.

11.2 Assessing students' environmental knowledge, action and attitude

The first stage of the project consisted of a sample comprising first-year undergraduate students in the two disciplines of social science and business studies. The questionnaires were given out to between 20% and 25% of the first-year cohorts in those schools. Of those returned, a selection of 127 questionnaires from each school were randomly selected and evaluated (Holt and Anthony 2000b). Stage two involved the analysis of a group of 200 employees of a large international telecommunications company (Nortel) with a strong commitment to environmental improvements (Holt and Anthony 2000a).

Stage three involved returning to the first-year MUBS sample at the end of the students' degree course in order to assess the impact of their educational and cultural experiences on their environmental behaviour during their three years at the University. There were 221 questionnaires collected from the MUBS first-years, of which 127 were randomly selected to use in the comparative assessments in stages one and two of the research study. In stage three, a random selection of year-three classes was chosen in which to give out the final questionnaire. There were 52 useable questionnaires returned, where the student had previously completed the first questionnaire and in both instances provided their student identification number (23.5% of the original sample of 221 first-years).

A full analysis of the findings of the first two stages of the study are available elsewhere (Holt and Anthony 2000a, 2000b) but key findings with reference to the *business students* in the longitudinal study are detailed below.

- There was strong agreement not only with ecocentric-oriented attitudinal statements[3] but also with belief in the need for economic growth.

- There was strong agreement with sustainability-oriented statements to do with intergenerational equity and futurity.

- A total of 32% had signed an environmental petition in the previous 12 months, 37% had donated money to an environmental cause, 5% had been involved directly with an environmental project and 6% had actively demonstrated about an environmental issue.

- Environmental actions that carried a cost in terms of time, convenience and money (i.e. that carried the 'green premium') were undertaken less often than those that did not carry such a cost.

- However, those actions that saved money but were inconvenient or required a cost outlay were less popular (e.g. there is a tendency to leave the TV on standby for convenience's sake or to buy filament rather than energy-efficient lightbulbs which require a higher initial cost outlay).

- In addition to the expected high values for products not tested on animals or that are ozone-friendly, 33% of business students would avoid using the services of companies with poor environmental records.

- A total of 51% used a bottle bank, 37% a can bank and 46% recycled their paper.

11.3 Research findings in the longitudinal study

The following is a summary of the research findings; more details are available in Holt 2003.

11.3.1 Data analysis

In the final stage of the project the emphasis was placed on identifying whether or not the specific educational experiences the undergraduate students had been through appeared to have made a difference in their behaviour and attitudes. The data in stage three was compared with that of the identical survey administered three years previously. Of the original 28 questions used in the first survey, 7 were

---

3 O'Riordan (1972) defines a continuum of environmental values and ethics. Ecocentrism is on the left of the continuum and is associated with deep ecology whereas technocentrism is defined to the far right and is associated with use of technology and humans' right to exploit natural resources.

selected to use as indicators of environmental knowledge. Some of the original questions were no longer current or were, in hindsight, ambiguous. The selected questions reflected topics such as global warming, air pollution, water pollution and resources. These seven questions were compared to see if the students' knowledge had changed in the three years. Environmental attitudes and values were assessed by using a selection of the original statements (detailed in full in Holt and Anthony 2000a):

- We owe a duty to our children and grandchildren to preserve the environment.
- I love the peace and quiet of the countryside.
- We have a duty to other people as well as to our families.
- I want my children and grandchildren to see and enjoy those things I enjoyed as a child.
- We owe a duty to animals and nature; they don't exist just for our enjoyment.
- The Earth and nature are fragile and we can easily cause irreversible damage.
- I like to be in the open air.
- We should live in harmony with nature even if it means some sacrifices on our part.
- The countryside is important for recreation.
- A fair society is better than a rich society.
- We have no choice: we have to protect the environment or we will destroy the human race.
- The most important problems today are the threats to the environment.

These statements were scored 5 for 'strongly agree' through to 1 for 'strongly disagree'. The cumulative scores for each survey were compared and then the mean value score identified. The attitudinal statements are all ecocentric and/or sustainability focused.

11.3.2 Environmental curricula studied in degree programme

As discussed in Section 11.2, 52 student questionnaires could be compared with those completed at the start of the students' studies. In addition to the identical questions previously asked, students were asked about their environmental experiences at the University (see Table 11.1). The results indicated that 13.5% of the respondents had studied a dedicated environmental module, and 17.3% had undertaken an environmental piece of coursework. Some 26.9% had covered environmental issues in other modules. There were 13 business school modules that were mentioned as having an environmental component in the classes (in

	Percentage	Number
Have you studied any dedicated environmental modules?		
Yes	13.5[a]	7
No (or no response)	86.5	45
Have you undertaken a coursework assignment with an environment theme?		
Yes	17.3[b]	9
No (or no response)	82.7	43
Are you aware of covering any environmental issues in any other modules?		
Yes	26.9[c]	14
No (or no response)	73.1	38
Do you think you have become more environmentally knowledgeable and aware during the past three years?		
Yes	55.8	29
No (or no response)	44.2	23
If 'Yes', do you think that the University has played a role in this?		
Not at all (or no response)	46.1	24
A little	51.9	27
A lot	2.0	1
What factors, incidents, etc. have contributed to a change in your environmental knowledge and awareness?[d]		
News	7.7	4
Television/documentaries	7.7	4
University classes	11.5	6
Pressure groups	1.9	1
Fellow students/friends	9.6	5
Work experience	1.9	1
Reading generally	5.8	3
Recycling campaigns	11.5	6
No response	59.6	31
Are you aware of the University's mission statement on the environment?		
Yes	15.4	5
No (or no response)	84.6	47
Have you read the University's environmental mission statement?		
Yes	9.6	5
No (or no response)	90.4	47

a Five had studied Environmental Management.
b Courses listed were: Tourism Impacts, Environmental Management, Business Ethics.
c A total of 13 different modules were mentioned: Tourism Marketing, Business Ethics, Travel and Tourism, Introduction to Business, Contemporary Issues in Business, EC Law, Financial Management, Introduction to Marketing, Small Business, GIS for Business, Strategic Marketing, International Business, Tourism Impacts.
d A breakdown of the multiple responses from the open response section.

Table 11.1 Environmental educational learning experiences of the students (sample size *n* = 52)

addition to the two dedicated MUBS undergraduate modules in environmental management and environmental law). Most of these modules are second-year and third-year classes, with a cohort size ranging from 40 to 150, suggesting significant numbers of students in the student body will have some environmental educational input at some point in their undergraduate degree.

Interestingly, 55.8% of the students believed they had become more environmentally aware over the previous three years, and 53.9% of the respondents believed that the University had played a role in this. Twenty-one students identifying reasons for their awareness in the open section of the questionnaire tended to comment on the role of social factors, with only six identifying the University classes as playing a part in this awareness building. The majority of the respondents cited interaction with fellow students, the media, television and work experience as playing a role in their increased awareness. This seems to correspond with the influence of informal societal environmental education as discussed elsewhere (Holt *et al.* 1999).

11.3.3 Environmental knowledge

The sample was analysed by marking the seven multiple-choice environmental knowledge questions and the mean score for the correct responses was 5.3. However, the cumulative improvement (i.e. the new total score minus the original total score) was only 16.0. This score reflects the fact that in 13 instances the number of correct answers in fact decreased between the first and second survey (but only two of these cases involved students who had undertaken an environmental learning experience (an environmental module, coursework or topic in their modules). The biggest improvement in the knowledge score concerned a student who had undertaken all three environmental education experiences discussed, from one correct answer originally to five correct answers in year three.

11.3.4 Environmental actions

The total number of actions taken in both samples is very similar but this result masks large increases and decreases in action. The second survey did indicate an increase in the total number of environmental actions taken (a total of 101 more actions taken in the year-three survey), but this figure would have been significantly higher had there not been a number of negative scores, with individuals' change in number of environmental actions ranging from –11 to +16. The three highest increases in environmental action taken occurred in the group that had undergone the environmental educational experiences. However, although the amount of environmental activity increased over the three years, from 1,017 to 1,118 actions in total, this equates to only an average improvement of 1.9 actions per person from a possible maximum score of 38.

11.3.5 Environmental attitudes

The questions selected for analysis all had an ecocentric or technocentric focus. As can be seen from the summary and discussion of the stage-one results (Anthony and Holt 2000a, 2000b), the students already had a strong affinity with these ecocentric and sustainability statements. However, there was a slight increase in the agreement with the values listed, from an average score of 4.1 to 4.2. However, this increase again masks some sweeping changes, such as a decrease in one person's score from 4.5 to 2.7. Interestingly, the mean score for the group that studied the environmental curricula improved from 4.17 to 4.24; the group that did not undertake an environmental learning experience still improved, but less so (from an average of 4.13 to an average of 4.16).

11.4 Shaping attitudes and actions: success or failure?

The results show that some students have increased their environmental aware-ness, knowledge and actions over time. Certainly, almost 56% believed they were more environmentally aware, and approximately 54% of students thought the University had influenced their environmental awareness. Students' attitudes to the environment—their affinity to ecocentric and sustainability statements that are enshrined in the concepts of sustainable development—remained strong over the three-year time-period and, in fact, on average strengthened slightly (but this cannot be supported statistically with this sample size).

However, the data does show some large decreases in environmental actions and knowledge over time. This suggests that, although third-year students' general atti-tudes remained fairly similar in comparison with when they entered the Univer-sity, some reason(s) exists as to why some students show such a decrease in knowledge and action.

Those students who had undertaken some form of environmental learning experience did appear to have increased their environmental knowledge, actions and attitudes, but this effect was not constant. The biggest changes seemed to occur in those students who had undertaken a discipline-specific learning experi-ence, in comparison with those that had not. However, it could be that this change is not related to their university-based educational experiences at all. The role of informal societal interaction (with the outside media, Internet, television, films and friends) and personal experiences (such as personal health, travel and wide-ranging cultural experiences) may influence an individual's environmental atti-tudes, actions and knowledge.

11.5 Limitations of the study, and future work

It is important to note that the data set analysed in the longitudinal study relates only to MUBS students, representing a sample of the original respondents. The 52 questionnaires were analysed with reference to the original survey completed, thus looking at changes that had occurred. Further work is needed to explore the implications of the data presented. The results have not been cross-tabulated with the demographic data collected, and the data presented does not cover responses to all of the questions posed; some of these tasks remain for further analysis. The results from the study are only indicators of the influence of environmental education; a much larger study would be needed to establish the causal effect of environmental education on students' knowledge, actions and attitudes.

11.6 Conclusions

The study suggests that there were changes over time in the students' knowledge, actions and attitudes, but it does not establish a clear link to the role of the University in these changes. However, since learning does not take place only in the classroom it is important that teachers of sustainability begin to assess the influence the informal (external) environment has on their students and factor this into the teaching of sustainability. This study offers some interesting avenues for further investigation and certainly seems to suggest that the effect of discipline-specific teaching on environmental knowledge, actions and attitudes is worthy of more detailed analysis with a large sample size and perhaps surveying students in different disciplines. The work also raises some questions as to the viability of the 'generic' environmental courses. The (perhaps arrogant) assumption that those students entering the University are a blank canvas needing to be taught 'environmental awareness' and the attempt itself to shape environmental attitudes tends to take no account of previous environmental education experiences or the influence of informal educational experiences.

Students enter MUBS from a wide variety of backgrounds and judging this in order to design a literacy module is extremely complex and will change every year. Thus if an environmental literacy model is chosen it will have to start from a fairly low base level of knowledge. However, all the students surveyed are aware of some issues and have fairly 'sustainable' attitudes, if not actions. Thus, in these circumstances, I would argue against a generic literacy model and argue for discipline-based teaching. Optional modules in different programme areas that make the link to environmental issues could be considered, along with environmental elements in the core subject modules. Environmental topics, themes and examples are taught in at least 15 modules at MUBS at the undergraduate level as part of a business curriculum.

If a business school is to consider integrating environmental issues in a discipline-specific manner, there are a number of key issues to consider (for more details see Holt *et al.* 1999). First, what is already taught? A curriculum audit is needed to assess environmental material currently taught. Second, members of staff need to reflect on their module material and think about how environmental case-study examples might be used. A few examples include such areas as crisis management (e.g. Shell and Brent Spar), strategy (i.e. environmental strategy), green marketing, corporate communications, and finance (e.g. the environmental sections in annual reports). Perhaps curriculum teams should meet and decide where the environment overlaps with their subject areas and plan where in the curriculum different topics could be included. There appears to be little evidence of a systematic assessment of the 'key' university textbooks in business and management to see if they include environmental issues, although anecdotally there does appear to be increasing coverage of environmental topics.

It must be recognised, however, that environmental issues are, in fact, *business* issues. By 1998 the Institute of Management found that only 2% of respondents surveyed were sceptical of the importance of the environment as a business issue (IM 1998). The 1994 survey undertaken by the Institute of Directors (IoD 1994) stated that environmental issues featured on the agenda of 58% of the boards of companies surveyed, with directors expecting an increasing amount of time to be devoted to environmental issues in the future. This is a view endorsed by Stoner *et al.* (1995), who put the environment at the top of the list of workplace issues for managers in this new century. Thus it would be expected that environmental issues (especially environmental management and environmental law) will be taught in the curriculum of any modern business school, irrespective of the institution's mission statement on environmental education. Middlesex University offers opportunities for environmental education within the business curriculum, but its core function is to teach students the skills necessary to operate as business school graduates. It could be argued that as students study core modules and optional choices the starting point in any business school curriculum should be to integrate discipline-specific environmental curricula into the core business programmes through elements of core modules.

References

Holt, D. (2003) 'The Role and Impact of the Business School Curriculum in Shaping Environmental Education at Middlesex University', *International Journal of Sustainability in Higher Education* 4.4: 324-43.

—— and S. Anthony (2000a) 'Exploring Green Culture in Nortel and Middlesex University', *Eco Management and Auditing* 7.3: 143-54

—— and —— (2000b) 'Education for a Sustainable Future? An Exploration of Environmental Attitudes, Actions and Knowledge in a UK University', *International Journal of Business Disciplines* 10.2: 25-34.

——, S. Homewood and D. Kirby (1999) 'Greening a Business School: The Case of Middlesex University', *Journal of European Business Education* 9.1: 111-26.

IM (Institute of Managers) (1998) *A Green and Pleasant Land? A Survey of Managers' Attitudes to, and Experience of, Environmental Management* (London: Institute of Managers, May 1998).

IoD (Institute of Directors) (1994) *IoD Business Opinion Survey: The Environment* (London: IoD).

O'Riordan, T. (1976) *Environmentalism* (London: Pion, 1st edn).

Sparks, A. (1997) 'Sustainable Middlesex', *Environmental Excellence* 4.2 (June 1976): 47.

Stoner, J., R. Freeman and D. Gilbert (1995) *Management* (Englewood Cliffs, NJ: Prentice Hall, 6th edn).

12
Mainstreaming sustainability issues in core undergraduate management education
The 'Social Context of Business' course at McGill University

Kariann Aarup
McGill University, Canada

In this chapter I will share my experience of teaching the 'Social Context of Business' course at McGill University. It is one of only two core courses in the strategy department of the Bachelor of Commerce programme and, dealing specifically with social and environmental issues, is among the very few such core courses in Canadian undergraduate business schools.

Learning is about 'connecting the dots', allowing the learner to establish the meaning and relevance of otherwise abstract notions. Sustainability is also about connections and relationships. The Social Context of Business course has been designed with these in mind. Its underlying pedagogy shows relationships by connecting the dots among management practice, global social and environmental issues and, most importantly, the students themselves—as individuals and as future managers.

The course was developed in the mid-1990s to increase student awareness of and ability to confront social and environmental issues and has undergone several transformations since. As a core requirement of the undergraduate commerce programme, more than 600 management students take the course annually. This large enrolment gives instructors the potential to have a significant impact on a targeted audience. With this potential, however, comes a significant level of responsibility.

In 1999 the course underwent major pedagogical redesign, including the introduction of experiential learning and critical self-reflection. These changes constitute the focus of this chapter.

12.1 Intentional pedagogical design

As a core course the Social Context of Business is designed to be introductory. It covers more breadth than depth of topics. The course is intended to spark students' interest and encourage them to take more advanced courses in related topics also available in the faculty, including Business and Society, Strategies for Sustainability, Business Ethics, and Organisational Politics. The content is structured around four subjects: (a) a brief history of capitalism, (b) consumerism and advertising, (c) critical perspectives of globalisation and (d) sustainability, stakeholder theory and emerging alternatives.

Although sustainability is listed as the fourth and final subject area, it is a common thread that binds the course throughout the whole semester. It is introduced to the students in the first class. Before the recent Rio +10 Summit in Johannesburg in 2002, most had not heard about sustainability.

Sustainability is not a concept that is separate from the learner. Rather, it engages learners and invites them not only to 'know' differently but also to act differently. By focusing on connecting the dots among themselves and the issues, the course invites students to actively participate, in a conscious way, in the world around them. For this transformative process to occur, students' emotions, memories and personal experiences need to be integrated into the formal learning process. Such is the case as well with their awareness of themselves and of the external world. Engaging and learning this way enables students not only to learn about sustainability but also to begin experiencing it.

Some of the pedagogical choices we have made include: (a) using video footage, (b) structuring the class around discussion rather than lecturing, (c) assigning experiential assignments and voluntary reflective writing pieces and (d) introducing critical media exercises. These pedagogical choices are based on the learning objectives set out below. They are to:

1. Increase students' awareness of social and environmental issues and their connection to business

2. Provide concepts and vocabulary for students to better comprehend social and environmental issues and give them the opportunity to use them

3. Make students aware of the personal dimension of the global and macro issues discussed

4. Make students aware of and provide alternative perspectives of the global market economy

5. Create the opportunity for students to discuss and express their feelings about the complex topics covered

12.2 Setting the tone: the first class

The first class is a very important one, for it establishes the foundation for the rest of the semester. It is especially so in this course since it differs so much from most of the students' other management courses. In the first class, all five learning objectives are touched on. It is a bombardment strategy of sorts to make them aware of the radically different nature of the class.

Sustainability is introduced through a video titled *The Next Industrial Revolution* (Bedford and Morhaim 2001). It is an excellent teaching tool that ties together concepts such as eco-effectiveness, stakeholder engagement and 'waste equals food' with industrial processes, manufacturing, factory and product design and so on. The video tells mini-stories about global companies, in various industries, that have deliberately integrated sustainability into their core business operations and decision-making. These stories serve as key reference points for the students throughout the semester, always bringing them back to real examples of sustainability in the context of profitable business.

Another important activity that takes place in the first class is establishing the content of the class itself. Students are asked to identify what faculties and departments they are in, what their country of origin is, where in Canada they are from, where they have lived and so on. Students are surprised at this, but it is crucial to bring about an awareness of the diversity of their classmates and, furthermore, to make them aware of the richness and the value of this diversity. Students have much to learn from each other, and this is often not valued in the classroom itself, especially at the undergraduate level. Throughout the semester, an effort is made to recall countries of origin and ask those students to share their often vastly different experiences with their classmates. Many of the issues we discuss about the developing world are personal for some of the students. This perspective is valuable and addresses, tangibly, the objective of making personal connections to the issues covered.

I also share with the students my background, my business studies, my work experience, my travel experience and, most importantly, my personal struggle with what I was taught in business school and what I experienced in the real world. By admitting that I am perplexed by and care deeply about the issues raised I find that students are more likely to engage in class discussions and likewise to share their feelings.[1]

---

1   There are often at least two, if not three, instructors for this course in any one semester. Although the fundamental pedagogical choices are the same between all classes, some of the approaches may differ somewhat. I will try to make this clear by using 'I' and 'we' where appropriate.

12.3 Using videos as teaching tools

When speaking with colleagues and friends who work in sustainability and social justice sectors, many of them claim that the best education they have had came from travelling. I have had the same experience and have wondered how this can best be replicated in a classroom. The use of videos is one solution that has been successful. We use them to complement assigned texts as they can bring otherwise cumbersome articles to life with colourful, evocative images and personal stories. The visual stimulation arouses students' imaginations and emotions more easily. This is when heartfelt discussions take place.[2]

Despite the international diversity of the student body, our student audience is predominantly Canadian. We choose Canadian-made videos that link Canadian business, Canadian organisations and Canadian issues to the global businesses, organisations and issues we discuss. This is an important element of relevance for local students, as it facilitates their sense of accountability as citizens and consumers. It is important for international students, too, because it increases their knowledge of Canada's role on the world stage. This Canadian content also helps foster students' perceptions of being change agents at a local level. I will highlight some outcomes of this towards the end of this chapter.

Critical teaching issues must be taken into account when using videos. They are not stand-alone tools and, if they are used as such, their effect can be very counterproductive. It is important to harness and guide the emotion and questions raised by the videos lest they be lost or the discussion become chaotic. Creating a common space for sharing students' different impressions is vital to achieving the objectives of showing multiple perspectives and interconnecting the topics: that is, addressing learning objectives (4) and (5) listed in Section 12.1. Although the whole class may have watched the same video, each student will have seen it differently. Sharing these different perspectives is part of the richness of the debriefing period. This may be challenging, depending on the length of the class and of the video. Experience shows, however (and my colleagues concur on this point), that it is more valuable to have a debriefing period and to omit other material than not to have a debriefing period at all. Students are asked to note what shocked, surprised or confused them.

The videos also serve as ideal bridges between subject matters. For example, the complexity of relationships among sustainability, globalisation, consumerism, poverty and so on is well illustrated by the video stories. They show a reality that texts and explanations cannot. Videos should be integrated into the course material as valid sources of knowledge and information.

2   Details of videos mentioned in this chapter and of other useful videos are given at the end of this chapter.

12.4 Experiential assignments

The objective of the experiential assignments is to allow the students to experience what we have been discussing in class. These exercises attempt to introduce students to the 'being' component of sustainability. These are deliberate exercises that get students to engage personally with the issues covered and to demonstrate that the personal dimension is not just about opinions but about personal involvement in systemic processes. Students have a choice of four assignments, each corresponding to the four sections of the course. They are asked to choose and carry out two experiences and then write about them from a first-person perspective. This poses a challenge to management students, whose voices are rarely required in their writing assignments. Many of them lack the practice or perhaps the confidence to freely express themselves. We give two assignments to give them an opportunity to learn over time.

12.4.1 Listening to and hearing the other voices: alternative-perspective learning objective

Throughout the semester students are invited to attend speaking events or seminars on campus or in the city that have some relevance to the course. They are asked to describe the event and the issues discussed and to note who else was there, what they talked about, what their concerns were, how their perspective may have differed from their own, how they perceived the relationships among the participants, panellists and representatives, how they felt being there, what they expected before going and what they learned from having participated in the event themselves. The objectives are to encourage students to be conscious of what is happening and why.

The impacts of this assignment are several. Not only do students attend events that they probably would not have otherwise attended but they also expose themselves to people and groups with concerns often widely different from their own. Attending in person provides a more direct experience. They often become excited by issues. We have also found that management students are reluctant to go to what seem like 'activist' events. Assigning attendance as a course requirement helps them to broaden their perspectives.

Events are recommended to them, or students find events on their own then verify their appropriateness with the instructor. This act of individual selection has had a positive impact in the class. Not only does it make students aware of the variety of relevant events, but the act of seeing their colleagues' awareness of the events also encourages them to become aware too. Assignments are rarely all handed in on the same day because of the many possible events to cover. However, for those attending the same event a common deadline is set. This allows students to share their experience with the rest of the class, ensuring that all can benefit even though they may not have attended the event themselves.

12.4.2 Media moments

When we discuss consumerism and the unsustainable lifestyle of most Western nations, inevitably the role of the media emerges. As a young person today, inundated by media, it is difficult to be critical, to distance oneself and to observe its influence. This assignment is meant to facilitate this critical process.

Students are asked to count the number of times they are confronted by advertising during the course of one day. They note where and when these 'media moments' occur. This assignment helps students become more conscious of the images that fill their perceptual environment. They are asked to reflect on that experience and to convey what they noticed the most, how they felt as they went through the experience, what shocked them and how their impression of advertising may have changed subsequently. They are also asked to focus on one advertisement from a current campaign that particularly struck, disturbed or offended them and to analyse it. They must explain why they chose the one they did, what feelings it evoked, what it may reflect about society and what it may say about them.

This may seem like a tame assignment, but it is especially effective after showing the video *The Ad and the Ego* (CBC Production 1997), which provides students with some useful and important theoretical concepts from notable Canadian media critics. Typically, the most revealing thought that emerges from the discussion is that students see themselves as billboards for company logos, which are plastered on their clothes, shoes and school supplies. They also discuss invasion of privacy with the placement of advertisements in public toilets and the appropriateness of public-service campaigns compared with that of corporate campaigns in such intimate spaces. The objectification and commodification of sexuality and people's bodies is another issue that they often raise.

12.4.3 Where does it all go?

Consumerism and consumer society can be rather abstract notions. It is difficult to make these topics personally relevant in an elite North American university setting without criticising people's choices and lifestyles. Young adults in a commerce programme can be especially protective of the lifestyle to which they aspire. The way we have structured this experiential assignment allows for self-critique as well as self-realisation, without worry of judgement from others.

Students are asked to track all money they spend during one week. They first estimate what they think they will spend and then start their detailed spending log. At the end of the week they are asked to take stock of their log with the following questions: How much did you spend? What categories of items did you spend your money on? Of the items you purchased, what did you really need and what not, and why? What motivated you to buy particular items? We ask them to hand in a rough list, by day, time and cost, of their purchases. We also ask students to reflect on themselves as consumers.

During the debriefing, rather than discuss individual experiences when students hand in their work, we discuss them when the assignment is handed back. While grading, I make note of common themes that emerge from the papers and share them with the class. Experience shows that this helps students to share their own experiences and feel that perhaps they are not alone. Students reveal concerns about some important issues, such as drinking too much, binge shopping sprees to console themselves, blowing parent-set budgets, having massive credit card debts and gambling. This emphasises that many lifestyle issues in North American society are present even in their own peer group.

12.4.4 Just who *are* these people?

This assignment supports the readings about stakeholder theory and stakeholder engagement processes. When we speak about diversity within sustainability, we include the diverse voices within communities. This assignment is based on that concept.

For this assignment, students are asked to pick a local event or issue they are somehow connected to or care about. They are asked to draw a stakeholder map of the issue, including themselves, then to interview two stakeholders other than customers, employees or shareholders to discover how they are involved, what their position is and how they feel about it. Students are then asked to report their reactions to the interviews, to clarify what their assumptions were before the interviews, how they felt during the interviews, what they learned from the stakeholders and how that may have changed their perceptions.

Students often pick something that is happening 'back home' and are able to engage in the exercise out of immediate or personal concern. This powerful motivator adds great quality to their work and brings the notion of sustainability-based processes closer to home. When we carry out the debriefing, students share what is happening in their communities, what the issues are, who they spoke with and so on. Classmates learn not only about each other but also about others in different parts of the country or the world.

12.5 Critical media assignment

The purpose of this exercise is to get students to read their newspapers and follow other mainstream media from a critical perspective. The objective is to make students more aware of how daily, local and world issues that may appear unrelated to their business studies are in fact related.

Students locate an article from local or national newsprint or online news sources that are relevant to the course. They are asked to look for emotionally charged language, positioning of arguments or data that potentially biases them as readers. They are directed to ask themselves who has not spoken or been quoted in the article who might have had a different voice and how that inclusion might have changed the article. Furthermore, students ask themselves what questions are left unanswered, what language is used and how it influences the reader. Who is the journalist and how does that affect the bias of the story? What paper or section of the paper is the piece in and how does that reflect a potential bias?

The purpose is to help students become aware of the unquestioned assumptions they make when reading and, more importantly, to increase awareness of the impressions they are left with after reading the article. Many commerce students read only the business section of the newspaper and thus form narrow ideas of complex current events.

12.6 Reflective writing

This assignment is not compulsory and is not graded. At the end of the semester, students are asked to share their thoughts and feelings as they reflect back over the 13 weeks in the larger setting of their commerce degrees. There are no right answers. There are no specific questions.

Admittedly, not all students choose to do this assignment, as there is no grade assigned to it. However, those that do, which has been up to half of the class, hand in up to five pages of personal reflections, often admitting deep struggles they are confronting in their studies and in their lives, questions they are asking of themselves about work and career and deeper meaning. It is a special way to share that which students otherwise do not experience at university. It validates their internal world and the personal processes they go through. I enjoy and highly recommend the assignment.

12.7 Some effects of the Social Context of Business course

Some of the effects that the course has had at McGill have been individual and institutional. Students have made career choice changes and applied for jobs in sectors that they had not previously considered, such as the Peace Corps, the alternative media organisation in Quebec, voluntary-sector consulting and third-world development. I know this through conversations with them during the semester and in some cases for years following graduation.

Institutionally, the Social Context of Business course has become a vital space of learning and a safe space where students can question fundamental assumptions held within their field of study, confront the many ethical issues prevailing in their discipline and admit that they care about values and problems that otherwise go unnoticed in their programme. The class helps students to become change agents in their own communities. Leaders emerge from the course who become active around those social and environmental issues they care about. Some have led several initiatives that have had a significant impact on the business school. We know this because those of us who teach have stayed in close contact with the students who are most affected by the class. Keeping office hours is particularly important for this course. It is here, on a one-to-one basis, that students open up and express their personal dilemmas, their desires regarding work and their ideas about what could be done to make a difference. As instructors, and this follows from the responsibility that comes with teaching, we are obligated to help students through this questioning process and to support them in their ideas for change. We are not just instructors. We are mentors. Three concrete examples are explained below.

12.7.1 Student club

McGill Business Watch is a student club, the tag line of which for management students is 'You don't have to stop caring!' These students are serious about increasing the awareness of sustainability and social justice issues of their peers and their professors. They also worry about their reputation on campus and the stereotypical idea that many have of them because they are in business school. These student entrepreneurs have organised speaker series, movie nights, a bi-weekly radio show and have a page in the student newspaper. Not only has the club encouraged students to act and participate in their university community but also it has served as a bridge to other like-minded organisations in the greater Montreal community—organisations that otherwise would have no contact with the business school. Probably the most important aspect of the club, yet the hardest to quantify, has been its capacity to serve as a referent community for management students who otherwise feel marginalised in their faculty because of their 'non-mainstream' concerns. Club activities are officially supported by the course. Course instructors also serve as faculty advisors to the students who are the co-organisers. The club emerged from a conversation that two students had, each with a different instructor, about wishing that such a club existed. The instructors spoke to each other, introduced the two students and, over the course of the summer, the website was developed, the club constitution was written, funding was received and the club was launched in the autumn.

12.7.2 Curriculum changes

At the end of the course, several students expressed frustration that more courses did not follow. Bringing this to the attention of the department led to the development of a follow-up course and of a concentration in the strategy department around 'social context'. Although the follow-up course was taught only for two years and was suspended for administrative reasons (much to the dismay of students), the concentration was launched in the autumn of 2002 and includes courses such as Business Ethics, Strategies for Sustainability, and Business and Society.

12.7.3 Career placement activities

One final student-led initiative that I wish to mention is a voluntary-sector career day—the first of its kind in a Canadian business school. Together with a group of MBA students, McGill Business Watch co-organised this successful event, which will now proceed annually with the support and financial backing of McGill's management career centre. Although this was primarily an MBA-led event, the inclusion of undergraduates was essential. The idea developed from students' requests for job opportunities in sectors or organisations that deal with issues addressed in the Social Context of Business and similar MBA courses. The career centre and standard recruiting system did not meet these requests, so students decided to meet their own needs. The career fair is being rolled out in other Canadian cities in association with the Community Experience Initiative (www.cei-iec.ca) and the career centres of local business schools.

12.8 Limitations of the course

Thus far I have highlighted the positive effects of the course and the intentions of its pedagogical design. The overall impact of the course is indeed positive; however, I do not want to create the illusion that it is only, or all, positive.

Each year, several students do not connect with the material or the issues. Some students complain about the 'socialist' nature of the material and its inappropriateness in a faculty of management. Some students express strong negative opinions during class discussion and are adamant about protecting their views. Some students attend only because this is a core course and there is a 20% participation mark. These are all realities that are unavoidable and that must be accepted.

There are further limitations owing to the subjective nature of the assignments. Students complain about the lack of quantitative projects. They complain about not being used to writing essays, not being accustomed to writing in the first person and not believing that they as individuals can effect change. These are important issues that must be addressed and confronted outright with all of the students. For those students who do connect with the material and who do support the issues it is important for them to recognise that there will always be opponents. They must learn to speak with colleagues who hold different values and beliefs, to not disrespect them for it and certainly not to change their own minds simply because they encounter opposition.

Finally, the main limitation of the course is that it is but one class among dozens that students will take throughout their four years in which none of these issues is likely to be raised. Even if students specifically take courses such as Strategies for Sustainable Development, the issues remain isolated from their mainstream concentration courses such as finance, accounting and marketing. Without reinforcement and integration into standard business courses it is likely that many of the notions to which we introduce students will remain unused again on the way to their diplomas.

12.9 Closing remarks: 'limitations are just opportunities in work clothes'

The objectives of the Social Context of Business course are to graduate students with a broader awareness of social justice and environmental sustainability issues, to give them an expanded vocabulary of terms and concepts with which to engage in these issues and to familiarise them with the multiplicity of perspectives that exist in the complex world in which they will be managers. To do so at the undergraduate level of management education—where the foundations of being a manager and practising management are laid—is crucial if the ultimate goal is to integrate the essence of sustainability into management on a comprehensive global level.

Since 1999, more than 2000 management students have graduated from McGill who have heard of and worked with stakeholder theory, who have engaged with and discussed sustainability issues, who have reflected on being global consumers, who have struggled with their concerns about the state of the environment and who have discussed their roles and responsibilities as managers *vis-à-vis* the environment. These students will graduate with a more holistic commerce degree than most others. Only time will tell what type of a difference they will make in the future. In the meantime, they have certainly left their mark on the business school at McGill University.

Videos

Bedford, Chris, and Shelley Morhaim (Dirs.) (2001) *The Next Industrial Revolution* (Earthome Productions, USA). Subject: eco-effectiveness as basis for building design, manufacturing processes and product design.

Bonheim, Harold (Dir.) (1997) *The Ad and the Ego* (CBC Production). Subject: the role of media and advertising in society today.

Fricke, Ron (Dir.) (1992) *The Sprit of Baraka* (excerpt). Subject: changes in society and different cultures through industrialisation. Comment: very powerful.

Nash, Terre (Dir.) (1995) *Who's Counting? Marilyn Waring on Sex, Lies and Global Economics* (NFB [National Film Board of Canada]). Subject: feminist economics and Genuine Progress Indicator.

Poliquin, Carole (Dir.) (1998) *Turbulences* (NFB [National Film Board of Canada]). Subject: links many locals around the world and the global financial markets. Comment: good Canadian content.

Prodanou, George (Prod.) (2000) *Coffee with a Conscience* (Market Place series; CBC Production and TransFair USA Video mix). Subject: globalisation; coffee production; multinational pressure on producer prices; fair trade concept.

Richardson, B. (Dir.) (1987) *SuperCompanies* (NFB [National Film Board of Canada]). Subject: focuses on Alcan aluminium production, globalisation and environmental and social devastation. Comment: excellent Canadian content, historical and contemporary.

Suzuki, D. (2000) *Lost in the Burbs* ('The Nature of Things' series; CBC). Subject: urban sprawl, planning, car culture, sustainability and urban redesign.

SVT Video (1997) *Santa's Workshop, IKEA's Backyard.* Subject: globalisation, sweatshops and subcontracting of labour; focus on IKEA.

Volkmer, Werner (Dir.) (1995) *Bomb under the World* (The Human Race Collection; NFB [National Film Board of Canada]). Subject: globalisation, effects on local communities in India. Comment: provides a very good portrayal of effects of international strategy theory.

13

The Environmental Enterprise Corps
Educating MBA students about sustainability

Gillian Rice
Thunderbird, The Garvin School of International Management, USA

Amy Sprague
World Resources Institute, USA

Experiential learning activities, especially those incorporating the offering of services, are important for educators trying to impart a meaningful understanding of environmental sustainability and conservation issues. Because the private sector is integral to advancing sustainable development, and because MBA students are generally considered tomorrow's most influential business leaders, the World Resources Institute (WRI) developed a programme to match teams of MBA students with environmental entrepreneurs in Latin America to work on consulting projects.[1]

The WRI programme, branded the Environmental Enterprise Corps (EEC), gives business students the opportunity to gain an understanding of the importance and profitability of environmental business and helps entrepreneurs develop the tools they need to succeed and attract investment. WRI identifies Latin America's most innovative entrepreneurs in environmental sectors, such as sustainable

---

1 Although the initial focus of the Environmental Enterprise Corps (EEC) has been Latin America, because of the importance of and threats to the region's areas of biodiversity the WRI expanded the programme to Asia in 2003, starting in China, because of the environmental and social challenges facing that country and the fast growth of the Chinese economy.

forestry, eco-tourism, organic agriculture, renewable energy, cleaner production and sustainable fisheries, through outreach and an annual business plan competition. WRI services for entrepreneurs include participation at the annual Investor Forum, where entrepreneurs present their business plans to international and local venture capitalists and investors, potential partners and buyers. The EEC provides pro bono mentoring by MBA student teams to help the entrepreneurs improve their business plans or strategies to attract investors or increase sales.

13.1 Experiential learning with the small business sector

Environmental partnerships generally involve collaboration between large corporations seeking environmental credibility skills and competence, access to environmental technologies, a presence in 'green' markets or other benefits unavailable to an organisation in isolation (Crane 1998). EEC, however, focuses on small and medium-sized enterprises (SMEs). Entrepreneurs in SMEs often lack the business skills or resources of large organisations to gather relevant market intelligence. MBA students can provide these services, and, because the enterprises are relatively small, they have the opportunity to significantly contribute to the growth of the companies.

Furthermore, because students share their skills and prepare business, marketing and financial plans and tools voluntarily, service-based learning supplements the experiential learning. According to Papamarcos (2002), academic achievement is not the only objective in service-based learning. The experiences gained also enhance the students' skill levels, social responsibility, value development and feelings of self-efficacy. Adapting the framework of Kolenko *et al.* (1996), we applied three dimensions of experiential and service-based learning for student participants in the EEC (see Fig. 13.1). These are (1) the application of skills (business research, marketing planning, communication, teamwork, presentation, and management), (2) understanding environmental issues in business (how business can positively and profitably impact environmental issues, and the emerging-nation perspective) and (3) personal insight (entrepreneurial focus, cross-cultural awareness and environmental awareness, especially with respect to career plans).

Each participating business school has integrated EEC projects into the curriculum in a different area. For example, projects have been woven into the International Multidisciplinary Action Project (IMAP) course at the University of Michigan Business School, into the Emerging Markets course at Fuqua School, Duke University, and into the International Marketing course at Thunderbird. Whether or not the student receives or experiences effective learning depends on the way in which the experiential component is integrated into the course content as well as on the level of active reflection in the applied lessons (Bush-Bacelis 1998).

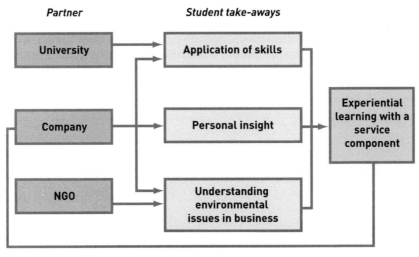

Figure 13.1 Dimensions of experiential and service-based learning for students

13.2 **Gathering feedback**

Feedback on the programme has been positive. To illustrate, 50 of 52 students that evaluated the WRI said they would recommend EEC projects to a colleague.[2] The evaluations also revealed that students overwhelmingly agreed that the best part of the project was its basis in reality (see Table 13.1). They often compared the project to case-study assignments and said they appreciated the advantages of experiential and service-based learning, such as dealing with uncertainty and doing work that will actually be used by someone. Representative student comments were:

> [The best part was] seeing that parts of our recommendations such as travelling to [trade] fairs or improvement of the website had been executed. This showed us that we are doing more that just another case study for class, but adding real value to a business with an ecological vision.

2 Of the remaining two students, one left that question—and many others—blank, and the other student wrote 'possibly'. The WRI project evaluation is sent to all students who have completed EEC projects, which at the time of writing is 181 students (other projects are in process). Of the 181 students, 52 have completed and returned the evaluations to the WRI.

Questions and answers[a]	Number[b]
Are you more likely after the EEC project to tailor your job search to include companies that are clearly concerned with environmental issues?	
'Yes'	8
'Not necessarily', or 'Was already interested'	11
'Possibly'	1
'No'	4
Total	24
Did the EEC project make you more aware or change your attitudes regarding environmental issues in business strategy?	
'Yes'	20
'Not necessarily', or 'Was already aware'	4
'No'	1
Total	25
What was the best part of the project?	
'Real experience'	18
'Suggestions taken by clients'	7
'Getting to know an industry'	4
'Teamwork'	4
'Final results or output'	1
'International aspect'	2
Total	36
What problems did you encounter? What was the worst or most difficult part of the project?	
'Different expectations or unclear objectives'	6
'Lack of time'	5
'Lack of relevant information or information-gathering'	16
'No problems'	3
'Other'	10
Total	40

a Because the questions are open-ended and the purpose was to elicit subjective answers, student responses were highly varied; thus we have grouped student responses into general categories.
b The third and fourth questions appeared in all questionnaires sent out and thus potentially could have been answered in each of the 52 evaluations returned to the World Resources Institute (although some students did not provide responses to these questions). The first and second questions were added at a later time and therefore have a lower number of potential responses (again, the response rate was not 100%).

Table 13.1 **The World Resources Institute (WRI) Environmental Enterprise Corps (EEC) programme: student responses on selected questions from returned project evaluations**

> [The best part was] to learn how difficult it is to make managerial decisions under uncertainty and limited information. It was a real business situation; we cannot experience this sense in the classroom.

Student satisfaction with the reality of the project and the possibility that their recommendations would be implemented and significantly affect a business also reflects that clients benefit from these projects. Feedback from entrepreneurs working with university teams indicates that they do indeed use and benefit from the students' work. One company that manufactures hardwood flooring from managed Amazonian forests reported the benefits of the project almost one year after the students recommended a new distribution channel. After receiving more than US$1 million in investment, which allowed it to implement the recommendations, the company's annual sales improved dramatically. It went from US$800,000 annually with US$250,000 in losses, to US$3 million and a net profit of more than 8%. The company is now one of Bolivia's top 70 exporters. It reported this good news to the former students who helped them, thus showing the students the value of their work.

Another entrepreneur that uses reverse vending machines to promote recycling in Mexico said the projects have provided him with essential data to present to potential partners, investors and clients. The company secured a contract with a major multinational client for US$40,000 and is in negotiations with more clients for amounts more than US$120,000.

13.3 Refining and spreading the programme: challenges and future directions

From a student perspective, a more structured approach could improve the EEC programme. In the post-programme survey, students indicated they would prefer more feedback from their faculty advisors and the entrepreneurs. From a faculty perspective, time is the challenge. Because faculty–team consultations are held outside of class hours, experiential learning activities demand more time, effort and attention than does the traditional instructor format. Faculty members must recognise this before committing to supervise EEC teams.

Teachers must also decide and inform students at the beginning of the process about the extent to which an EEC project can replace another type of team project that may be required for a course. It would be unusual for all students in a particular class to be working on an EEC project; therefore, students must see the work requirements and grading procedures as fair compared with projects being carried out by other students in their class. Owing to confidentiality, EEC students may be unable to discuss their projects during general class discussions or give classroom presentations. Prior permission must be sought from the entrepreneur. Although this is usually granted, in some cases other out-of-class arrangements must be made so that the students will still gain the benefits of integrating an outside project with course material.

Furthermore, difficulties can arise when students eager to work on a 'real' project form EEC teams hastily at the beginning of the semester. The faculty member must interview each team and carefully evaluate its suitability in terms of skills, commitment, language and cross-cultural experience before forwarding a team's application to the WRI for review by the potential client entrepreneur. The teacher must also ensure that a team begins with realistic expectations about data collection, because many of the students have little experience working in entrepreneurial environments in emerging economies. Nevertheless, faculty can also encourage students to develop innovative solutions to these data-collection challenges and can guide them in framing their project in different ways. Because the time available for the projects is short (less than one semester, given the time for the initiation of the process and the final client teleconference presentation towards the end) it is important for faculty to monitor progress continually and to have regular meetings with teams. An additional method to ensure that the project is on track is to require an interim report by the students, to be shared with both the faculty member and the entrepreneur.

The WRI faces challenges in managing the success and growth of the programme to include more schools, more entrepreneurs and more regions of the world. In response to faculty and student feedback over the past two years, the WRI has developed a more 'hands-off' role, which has allowed the WRI to increase the number of projects offered and to foster relationships with various business schools. Student feedback on the role of the WRI is generally positive but also suggests areas for enhancement, including channelling best practices from previous to future projects, providing travel funding to students, since travel depends on whether schools have available resources, and facilitating more meaningful client feedback to the students. Time is again the crucial factor in obtaining more feedback from the entrepreneurs.

WRI facilitators can encourage quick responses from clients to all of the student-initiated communications. The WRI has developed a client evaluation form to be sent to students immediately after the conclusion of a project. Also, students working with companies that have worked with previous teams can benefit from the reports of those teams or, in some cases, may be able to consult with the previous students. These improvements increase the team's effectiveness and contribute to a better sense of their accomplishments after the project.

Although the programme has grown steadily over the past two years to include more than 200 MBA students, the resources of the WRI are not extensive enough to cover the need that exists for MBAs to assist sustainable enterprises in emerging markets. MBA programmes can look to the various ways in which participating universities have incorporated these EEC projects into the curriculum (e.g. in courses on international marketing, emerging markets, global projects, and venture capital and into independent study and field studies). The WRI is one source of projects, but many more organisations exist that have developed similar student programmes. Small business associations or national banks with programmes to help sustainable entrepreneurs are active in many emerging markets. Interested faculty members who see a niche for experiential projects could investigate working directly with these business development organisations.

The EEC programme is still relatively new. Nonetheless, it has successfully enhanced the education of MBA students and assisted environmental entrepreneurs in Latin America. MBAs internalise the experiential, service-based learning lessons, which are further enhanced year after year, by subsequent work with SMEs. Students gain the satisfaction of having a major effect on a business built around environmental protection. The programme is an example of what works in teaching sustainability. Students apply their skills in a real setting, appreciate how business can positively affect the environment and gain personal insights into environmental responsibility and cross-cultural phenomena that could influence subsequent career paths.

References

Bush-Bacelis, J.L. (1998) 'Innovative Pedagogy: Academic Service-learning for Business Communication', *Business Communication Quarterly* 61.3: 20-34.

Crane, A. (1998) 'Exploring Green Alliances', *Journal of Marketing Management* 14: 559-79.

Kolenko, T.A., G. Porter, W. Wheatley and M. Colby (1996) 'A Critique of Service Learning Projects in Management Education: Pedagogical Foundations, Barriers and Guidelines', *Journal of Business Ethics* 15.1: 133-42.

Papamarcos, S.D. (2002) 'The "Next Wave" in Service-learning: Integrative, Team-based Engagements with Structural Objectives', *Review of Business* 23.2: 31-38.

14
Partners in learning
How a business school and a company worked together to advance sustainability

Thomas L. Eggert and Dan Anderson
University of Wisconsin-Madison, USA

Ronald Meissen and Verie Sandborg
Baxter International Inc., USA

14.1 Business–university collaboration

14.1.1 Business school class: University of Wisconsin–Madison

In 1997 Tom Eggert, through the Gaylord Nelson Institute for Environmental Studies at the University of Wisconsin–Madison, developed a class on sustainable development. This class, with an initial enrolment of 28, was geared toward examining societal decisions that have led to society's 'unsustainable' position and considered options to address and improve societal and personal responsibility.

The class drew a number of students from the business school at the University of Wisconsin–Madison during 1997 and 1998. They became convinced that their school should offer a similar class on the impact of business on sustainability and its responsibility for providing leadership for change. With the help of the graduate dean of the business school, they surveyed graduate students for interest. Surprisingly, more than 60% favoured such a class and said they would be interested in taking it.

This interest led to the development of (or rather the evolution into) a new class jointly offered by the business school and the Gaylord Nelson Institute for

Environmental Studies, called Environmental Strategy and Sustainability. We developed the class on the premise that the business community needs to provide more leadership as society struggles to accept the challenges of living and acting sustainably. The development of this class was also aligned with a series of business school surveys done by the World Resources Institute (WRI), which revealed that many top business schools offer classes about the environment.[1]

14.1.2 Business: Baxter International Inc.

Baxter is a global medical products and services company that provides critical therapies for people with life-threatening conditions. The company's products and services include bioscience (biopharmaceuticals, vaccines, biosurgery and transfusion therapies), medication delivery and renal therapy and are used by healthcare providers and their patients in more than 100 countries. Baxter's corporate office is located north of Chicago, IL, about 130 miles from the campus of the University of Wisconsin–Madison. The company has 55,000 employees worldwide, and its sales in 2002 were US$8 billion (see www.baxter.com).

Baxter's sustainability efforts evolved from its strong environmental and corporate responsibility programmes and gained increasing momentum during the late 1990s. Its 1996 environmental policy specifically addressed sustainable development. The company issued its first full public sustainability report in 1999.[2] In the same year, several environmental, health and safety (EH&S) professionals organised a Sustainable Development Team to advance the company's sustainability initiatives. Then, an article on the company's intranet site by the CEO in December 2000 championed sustainability. In 2001, Baxter added sustainability, or Best Citizen as it is called internally, to the company's balanced scorecard[3] to help employees better understand the meaning of the relationship between sustainability and its global strategic goals.[4]

14.1.3 University of Wisconsin–Baxter collaboration

In the autumn of 2001, we met at Baxter's corporate headquarters in Deerfield, IL to explore the possibility of having students from the University of Wisconsin–Madison work on real sustainability projects with Baxter. We were excited about the potential of such collaboration, but time was short. The first class was scheduled for spring 2002. Working together, we developed the necessary procedures, infrastructure and expectations to enable this bold new initiative to move forward. We hoped to create a situation where Baxter would benefit from student

---

1 Three surveys were done, one in 1998, one in 2001 and one in 2003, which asked business schools about how environmental issues were incorporated into the curriculum. The results from these surveys are available at www.wri.org/bschools and www.beyondgreypinstripes.org.
2 Sustainability reports are available as PDF files at www.baxter.com → Sustainability.
3 A balanced scorecard is a concise summary of a company's most important overarching business goals and measurement metrics.
4 See www.baxter.com/ehs for additional information on EH&S sustainability initiatives.

research and where students would benefit from interacting with professionals in a corporation while helping to solve real business sustainability issues.

14.2 Methodology

Early during the semester, Baxter's EH&S Sustainable Development Team sent the Environmental Strategy and Sustainability class an invitation to evaluate Baxter's sustainability progress and direction. The invitation outlined possible project topics, the basic approach to be followed, common elements to be considered for each area of research and the Baxter–University student team relationship. A total of 13 sustainability-related topics of interest to the company were proposed, and student teams were invited to suggest other topics if they wished. After reviewing the suggested topics, each student selected four and ranked them in order of interest. These rankings were used to organise students into nine groups to address the following topics:

- Biodiversity of plant and animal species
- Energy conservation[5]
- Renewable energy
- Product life-cycle assessment and extended producer responsibility
- Recycling plastics and PVC (polyvinyl chloride) materials from customers
- Water resources
- Socially responsible investing
- Stakeholder engagement
- Organisational structure and culture

After the student groups were formed, representatives from Baxter's Sustainable Development team met with each student group individually to provide an overview of their topics and to give them packages of information about Baxter and about their respective subjects. Each group was asked to designate one person to be the main contact with Baxter during the project. Seven Baxter employees with expertise in these topics were identified to act as contacts from within the company. An e-mail was then sent to student team contacts introducing them to their respective Baxter contacts.

Baxter gave the students a basic structure for their research to ensure that the company obtained the information it desired and that the students learned about

---

5 Energy conservation and renewable energy are also very important as they relate to reducing energy-related greenhouse gas emissions, which contribute to global warming and climate change.

some of the issues businesses grapple with as they move toward becoming more sustainable. Each student group was asked to:

- Understand and further research their team's selected topic
- Determine what other large progressive companies are doing to address the subject
- Assess what Baxter is doing and planning to do in the topic area
- Recommend what Baxter could do to strengthen its sustainability posture in each area

A list of companies to act as benchmarks was given to each group. Each team was able to develop an outline of their recommendations by identifying and evaluating state-of-the-art practices at these other companies. Comparing that data with Baxter's initiatives helped teams make a 'gap' analysis of Baxter's sustainability efforts.

On their part, Baxter contacts were encouraged to:

- Interact with the student teams via telephone and e-mail
- Provide additional information on the topics
- Explain what Baxter is doing or intended to do in the topic areas
- Arrange for the student team to visit Baxter or for company contacts to meet the students at the University, if feasible

Company contacts were encouraged to provide students with guidance and support but were cautioned not to do the students' work.

Each student team was asked to read and sign a confidentiality agreement with Baxter that committed students not to disclose any confidential company information. At the conclusion of the projects, each team was expected to prepare a formal report outlining its important findings and main recommendations for Baxter. At the end of the semester, each team made a short class presentation on its research topic. A number of Baxter representatives travelled to the university to hear the presentations, ask questions and thank the students in person for their assistance. In appreciation, Baxter gave each student a small gift and made a US$1,000 contribution, on behalf of the entire class and Professor Eggert, to the Tapanti Foundation. This Foundation, with the support of many Baxter employees, works to protect and enhance the 150,000 acre Tapanti rainforest near the company's manufacturing facility in Costa Rica. The rainforest was initially 'adopted' by Baxter's local facility in the early 1990s.

14.3 Benefits, challenges and lessons learned

14.3.1 Students

Following a presentation of their research, the students were surveyed about their experience with this partnership. A total of 32 students completed the survey. Their responses indicated a high degree of satisfaction with the project and interaction with Baxter employees. The results from this survey are described below.

Two key questions asked in the survey were: 'Did you find the partnering aspect of the project beneficial?' and 'Do you feel that this project is worthy of the time that you invested in it?' Questions were answered on a five-point scale, with 1 indicating the lowest satisfaction, and 5 indicating the highest satisfaction. The average score for the first question was 4.2. The average score for the second question was 4.0. Narrative comments also suggested a high degree of satisfaction with the project. Some sample comments are as follows:

> This project was definitely more interesting than normal homework. I would be interested in following up on the project to see what happens.

> The partnership provides both a compelling dimension of education in practice and a great resource for additional information.

> I got to know my group well, I got to know my material well, and the project taught me how to work well in a group and showed me that I am truly interested in this field.

> I really liked the opportunity to apply my business knowledge to a real-world example.

> I really liked the problem that Baxter assigned us; it was very specific and real-world.

> It's cool to see people actually working on these issues.

This is not to imply that the groups did not run into problems. As might be expected, the contacts between students and Baxter representatives were not always satisfying. We asked two questions in the survey regarding this interaction. The first was: 'Were your contacts at Baxter available and did they promptly return your e-mail or voicemail messages?' The second was: 'Were they responsive to your requests/questions?'

Overall scores for these two questions were 3.7 and 3.8, respectively. The narrative comments, predictably, indicated a breadth of opinion. On the one hand, students wrote:

> We had a great contact. She really wanted to help whenever possible!

> Our contact was very helpful in getting us information and providing some direction for the project.

On the other hand, not all students had such successful relationships with their contacts:

> We had little contact with our designated representative. He seemed often unavailable, uninterested and discouraged us from comparing Baxter with similar organisations—which became an important part of our paper.

> Our contact was out of town for at least three weeks in a row, and when we did reach him he had nothing specific to add to our work.

Some of the trouble establishing contact was probably a result of the different schedules of students and Baxter participants. In addition to regular business travel commitments, for an entire week in mid-March most of the Baxter contacts were out of the office attending Baxter's global EH&S conference. Students were then out the following week on spring break. This meant there was little opportunity for contact for two weeks at the crucial early stage of the project.

14.3.2 Baxter International

Baxter conducted a similar feedback survey of participants and received five responses from the seven professionals involved in this project. Overall, participants found the project worthwhile and interesting. The ranking for the question 'Did you find the partnering aspect of the project beneficial?' was 4.0. Respondents gave a 4.8 to the question 'Do you feel that this project is worthy of the time that you invested in it?'

Favourable comments included:

> The processes of connecting, of dialogue, of working together were valuable and contribute to sustainability. These are the tactics sustainability practitioners must employ as they go forward.

> The content of the students' final reports and their group presentations exceeded my expectations. I was very impressed with the clarity, level of detail and professionalism reflected in the reports.

> The student team provided information I did not have, and I was able to learn something from them that will help Baxter. There were also some follow-up activities that could lead to benefits for Baxter.

> Most of the students were highly motivated and responsive.

> I liked the students' sincerity and freshness.

> I appreciated the interest of the students and the vigilance with which they worked on the project.

Baxter participants generally enjoyed working on the project, but expressed some dissatisfaction. To the question 'Did you receive adequate information and understanding of what the students were working on and the direction they were going with their project?' Baxter respondents rated student groups at 2.8. The comments below shed some light on this below-average score:

> The group didn't let me know what it was doing. I unexpectedly received an e-mail at home from someone, who, because of the way

the group organised its work, was my new contact. We set it up I would call her from my home. When I called her, she wasn't available until an hour later.

I knew the direction the student team was going, but I had no idea of the results it was obtaining until the final project. There were several inaccuracies in the results I could have helped them with.

I would have liked to see some drafts of the report along the way to give better advice.

14.3.3 University of Wisconsin–Madison

From the University's perspective, the overall quality of the student learning experience and the quality of the final projects was higher than at any time during the five years that this class had been taught. Students were enthusiastically engaged in the projects and in many cases the engagement lasted beyond the end of the class.

However, a substantial amount of support was required to make this learning experience valuable. Parts of many classes were devoted to checking in on the teams, office hours were often spent addressing issues that came up with the teams and a substantial amount of out-of-class time was needed to help teams that ran into trouble. Co-ordination with the Baxter contacts also required planning and time. So, although the partnership was very successful, it did take more time than a traditional class with a final project based on research.

14.4 Recommendations for others looking to develop working partnerships

- Start with an interested company. Identify a company that is actively committed to the concept of sustainability and willing to commit employees' time to working on the projects.

- Develop a list of potential projects before class starts. Handing out a list of potential projects on the first day of class helps students to understand the types of projects that they will be working on. This list also is used by students to indicate which projects they would like to work on. The company's contacts for each of the projects should be briefed on the relationship with the university. They should be clear about what kind of support is expected of them.

- Have someone from the company introduce the project from the company's perspective. The project should be introduced by the professor and by a main contact person from the business. The main contact should introduce the company and provide a brief description of the business and also of its efforts in the sustainability area. If a confidentiality agreement is to be used (such an agreement was used in the project described in this chapter), it too should be discussed at this time. The company representative should also describe how the company is likely to use the results of the project. Basic ground rules should be covered, as should the expectations of both parties.

- Give students the opportunity to choose which project they are to work on. We suggest giving the students a choice about which potential projects they will work on so that students use their talents in areas where they may contribute best to the project's success. In our case, students chose nine projects from a list of 13. In all cases, students worked on one of their top three choices.

- Clarity of assignment. The amount of direction each group received varied substantially. In some cases, Baxter made it clear that it was happy to receive any research in the selected topic area. In other cases, the questions were very specific. The student groups did much better when asked to work on a specific, clear, achievable assignment. In the future, all the topics will need to be thoughtfully prepared and presented clearly to the groups.

- Outline process. Most students will never have worked on a project with someone outside of the university. In order to make the project proceed as smoothly as possible, the class should be briefed by the professor on the typical time demands of the company contacts. This briefing should include the differences between a student project and the project expectations of professionals in a large company. In some instances, the typical student approach to this project was to get started early, allow the project to languish for several weeks and then get very frenzied in the last week or ten days. Some students did not have a good sense of how working with people in a corporation is different from working with other students (or even professors). Thus, students should be given a clear indication of what is expected from them and of what they can expect from their contacts. These expectations should include everything from basics such as who makes the first contact to how fast they can expect information to be provided.

- Site visits. If feasible, all students should meet with their contacts and visit the company site. Students benefit tremendously from such a visit. The problems that they are working on become more real to them in this situation. Another benefit of a site visit is that the teams meet their company contact, helping to create a relationship between the teams and the contacts.

- Improve access to competitor information. Many groups had difficulty getting information from Baxter competitors and other companies. Whereas Baxter opened its doors (and filing cabinets) to the students and provided them with the information they needed, other companies were not so forthcoming. Additional work needs to be done on finding alternative ways for students to get access to information from other companies. These could include working with trade associations, non-profit organisations that track a particular industry or personal contacts in the company.

● Provide an opportunity for frequent updates in front of the whole class. Once project teams are formed, class time should be taken each week for quick updates. Developing and checking in on progress toward particular milestones puts continued positive pressure on the students to apply themselves to the project. Though the students do not appear to appreciate this constant pressure during the semester, comments from the students at the end of the semester suggest that they need some incentive to avoid procrastinating. A need to produce draft reports before the end of the semester, as was suggested by several Baxter representatives, would be one option.

● Wrap up the project with a formal presentation of the research results and recommendations. At the conclusion of the project, each of the teams should present its research, not only to the rest of the class but also to their company representatives. This brings a sense of closure, and reminds students that they have produced a report that really will be used.

● Grading. One other twist that was tried in this class was to take the anxiety about a grade out of the equation. This was accomplished halfway through the semester by allowing each team of students to choose the grade that they would receive on their final project. All students chose to give themselves a grade within the 'A' range: namely, from 92 to 100. The most popular choice for a grade was 95, followed by 96 and 92. The highest grade chosen was a 96. Though this was the grade that was ultimately assigned to each student within the group, the professor also independently graded the group projects. In all but one instance, the grade that the students chose was lower than the grade they would have received from the instructor. The high grades can be explained by at least two considerations. First, once a grade was set, students pushed hard to deserve it. Second, the project required real work. Students pressured themselves to produce quality projects because they knew the reports would be used by Baxter. In fact, as noted, the final work of the students represented high-quality work.

14.5 What lies ahead?

Baxter intends to use the students' research to support Baxter's short-term and longer-term sustainability initiatives. The student research will be used to:

- Inform the company EH&S management as Baxter develops its annual EH&S strategic plan

- Help meet evolving Global Reporting Initiative (GRI) reporting requirements.[6]

- Increase knowledge and strengthen efforts to respond better to the growing scrutiny of socially responsible investors as they evaluate the sustainability stance and direction of companies

Feedback from the students and the Baxter representatives was so positive that the University of Wisconsin–Madison will continue to include a final project in this course that will have the students working with Baxter or some other company. In the immediate future, Baxter has invited the next Environmental Strategy and Sustainability class to refine and expand the work of some of the initial student groups and to develop more specific recommendations for the company. These groups of students will use and build on lessons learned and the past research performed by the previous group of students. Continuity with the past allows new groups to probe deeper by starting with work done by previous groups. It also helps to remind students that their work may be built on by others, too, which provides more incentive to work harder.

14.6 Conclusions

In the Environmental Strategy and Sustainability class we talk about win–win opportunities, where both the company and the environment win because of an action a company takes that saves money by producing less waste, which then benefits the environment. The relationship between Baxter and the class also represents a win–win opportunity. Not only did the students benefit by engaging in work that was meaningful, real and valued but also Baxter benefited from the research and recommendations. The following were some unexpected and exciting outcomes from the partnering:

- The 'Guide to Socially Responsible Investment'[7] prepared by one student team was so well done that Baxter has invited members of this team to present its findings to a wider Baxter audience, including the company's investor relations group.

- One of the students involved in researching and preparing the above guide asked and was given permission to share this report with the

---

6 The GRI is 'an international, multi-stakeholder effort to create a common framework for voluntary reporting of the economic, environmental and social impact of organisation-level activity. The GRI mission is to elevate the comparability and credibility of sustainability reporting worldwide' (www.globalreporting.org).

7 A copy is available from the author at teggert@bus.wisc.edu.

management of a financial institution where she worked. She said her company's management needed to know this information.

● One student initiated a meeting between Baxter and one of Baxter's major customers to discuss issues associated with using Baxter's products. This dialogue led to consideration of a new partnership between Baxter and the customer to explore mutually beneficial, innovative solutions. Baxter expects to use this partnership as a pilot for a broader application with other customers.

As we look toward the future, we will continue to refine the approach that was used, and we expect that Baxter, the University and students will continue to benefit from this partnership.

15

Matching form to content in educating for sustainability
The Master's course in Responsibility and Business Practice*

Judi Marshall
University of Bath, UK

Some scholars are seeking to integrate sustainability into core conceptions of business (see e.g. Elkington 1997; Shrivastava 1995a, 1995b; Starik and Marcus 2000; Starik and Rands 1995; Westley and Vredenburg 1996). A parallel area deserving attention, but too seldom addressed, is how and to what extent sustainability, ecology and social justice should be incorporated into mainstream management education (for exceptions, see Bilimoria 1998; Egri and Rogers 2003; Shrivastava 1994).

Training in ethics is sometimes advocated as a solution to concerns about business responsibilities. Although this may be a step forward, it is also a limited, conceptually restricted response unlikely to foster the asking of sufficiently radical questions about the impacts of business on the planet. If, as many argue, sustainability challenges require a fundamental redesign of commerce (see e.g. Hawken 1993), participants in management education programmes would be better served by targeted encouragement and training rather than by being schooled to believe that business should continue as usual

Yet various factors deter educators from addressing sustainability. Some categorise ecological and social justice issues as value-laden while claiming that mainstream management education is value-neutral. Given that all theorising

* With acknowledgements to my colleagues, Gill Coleman and Peter Reason, in initiating this degree, and also to David Murphy, Chris Seeley and David Ballard, who have joined us in its subsequent development.

arises from some perspective, I contest these claims of objectivity. The assumptions of economics, for example, are worthy of review in this light (Daly and Cobb 1990). Others question whether the planet is in environmental crisis (Meadows *et al.* 1992; Lomborg 2001). Still others debate whether challenges can be addressed by adapting current business and societal mind-sets (Lovins *et al.* 1999). Although it may be difficult, we must bring these debates into the classroom. Rather than acting as a deterrent, controversy should encourage us to consider *how* we educate and learn in relation to such issues, especially because they are as relevant to everyday behaviour as to intellectual understanding. We must ask, 'What is good practice in educating for sustainability?'

Current educational forms may be part of our ecological problems. Orr (1994), for example, critiques their propensity, *inter alia*, to divide the world by academic discipline, to advocate domination over nature, to promote individualism and rights rather than citizenship and responsibility and to separate rationality from feeling and valuing:

> The crisis we face is first and foremost one of mind, perceptions and values; hence, it is a challenge to those institutions presuming to shape minds, perceptions and values. It is an educational challenge. More of the same kind of education can only make things worse (Orr 1994: 27).

The introduction of electives about environmental, social and ethical issues into established programmes such as MBAs is valuable but it fails to meet Orr's challenge. It treats the issues as if they were discrete add-ons to mainstream philosophies of business and implies that such philosophies do not require fundamental reform.

In this chapter, I explore how issues pertaining to ecology, sustainability and social justice could be integrated into business education. I suggest that pedagogy matters, and that we need to generate educational forms and practices that are robustly congruent with the issues addressed. Seeking to match form to content in this way, I and my colleagues, Gill Coleman and Peter Reason, based our educational approach in action research and designed a new and innovative master's degree.

We chose action research (defined in Section 15.3) to provide students with a continual process of inquiry with which to engage in the challenges of considering sustainability and with disciplines for developing their practice in tandem with their intellectual understanding. We also designed the degree to provide ongoing, reflective, active learning opportunities so that we could show and enact issues relevant to sustainability and provide a forum to discuss them. Thus, action research has fundamentally influenced course design, the educational approaches, the subjects covered and participants' learning processes.

The Master's course in Responsibility and Business Practice is run by the Centre for Action Research in Professional Practice at the School of Management, University of Bath, Bath, UK, in partnership with the New Academy of Business (an independent educational organisation established in 1995 by Anita Roddick, founder of The Body Shop International [www.new-academy.ac.uk]). The degree was launched in 1996 to 'address the challenges currently facing those managers who seek to integrate successful business practice with a concern for social, environmental and ethical issues'.[1]

In this chapter, I outline key educational choices made in designing the degree, describe the teaching practices adopted and review some of the learning achieved, based on staff experience and extensive participant feedback.

15.1 Programme and participants

The Master's course in Responsibility and Business Practice is part-time and comprises eight intensive five-day residential workshops over two years. Most of these take place at the University of Bath campus, with the exception of the third workshop, which explores deep ecology, theoretically and experientially (Maughan and Reason 2001) and is held at Schumacher College in Devon, an International Centre for Ecological Studies close to a relative wilderness area that enables students to experience living systems (www.schumacher.org.uk).

Course participants range in age from about 25 to 60 years. They come from a wide range of job areas and organisations, including for-profit companies, consultancies, the public sector and non-governmental organisations (NGOs). Some people already have sustainability or corporate social responsibility remits. Others want to move their professional lives further in these directions. Many are change agents in some way and want to develop these skills as part of the programme. People come from various countries in addition to the United Kingdom, including Brazil, Canada, Finland, Kosovo, New Zealand, Portugal, South Africa, Sweden, Switzerland, the USA and Vietnam. This diversity is perceived by participants as a strength of the degree.

As of March 2004, 84 people have graduated from the degree, and 71 are currently registered. The eighth intake in March 2004 reached the current maximum capacity (in terms of learning environment and staffing pattern) of 25 participants.

15.2 Educational choices

The Master's is innovative in content and learning approach. Underlying its design was our intention to explore key issues relating to ecology, sustainability, social justice and business in a programme where these are declared and legitimate agendas—not hidden, tagged on or apologised for in a programme based on mainstream assumptions—and considered alongside each other to allow interrelationships and potential tensions to become apparent. To do this at all, and certainly to do this well, we believed that we had to devise forms of education and learning that

1 From a course brochure, which includes comments from graduates and can be found on our website: www.bath.ac.uk/carpp/msc.htm.

are congruent with the nature of the material that we encounter and that offer participants robust methods and skills for engagement. The nature and potential controversy of the areas required us to consider *how* we educate and learn: we realised 'information-based' teaching was not enough.

We therefore set out to provide adult education that was question-posing, critical and values-aware. We also wanted to encourage participants to engage reflectively with challenging, controversial, multi-dimensional and potentially disturbing issues and, consequently, to help them think and act differently. We thus chose action-research-based approaches because we saw these as flexible, inquiry-based disciplines able to contain and enable the learning of course participants and of ourselves. These approaches also support the development of practice with intellect and of experiential learning with propositional learning.

In the following sections, I explore how we implemented our intentions. I start in Section 15.3 with our foundations in action research. Then, in Section 15.4, I consider course content. In Section 15.5 I show how action research has shaped our educational practices. Finally, in Section 15.6, I discuss some of the challenges.

15.3 Learning approaches: part 1

As already indicated, action research has strongly influenced the course form and content. As tutors, we suggest that there are no simple solutions to the dilemmas posed by trying to integrate ecology, sustainability and social justice with successful business practice and so invite participants to become reflective, active explorers and pioneers.

Definitions of action research abound and have their merits. Here I offer just one definition for those unfamiliar with these approaches:

> Action research is a participatory, democratic process concerned with developing practical knowing in the pursuit of worthwhile human purposes, grounded in a participatory worldview which we believe is emerging at this historical moment. It seeks to bring together action and reflection, theory and practice, in participation with others, in the pursuit of practical solutions to issues of pressing concern to people, and more generally the flourishing of individual persons and their communities (Reason and Bradbury 2001:1).

Action research practices provide potential 'containers' from which course participants can address the challenges of course content and maintain a simultaneously appreciative and critical, question-posing approach in value-laden areas. Objectivity is not an option, so we seek to offer participants frames and grounded practices from which to develop critical subjectivity and the capacity for continual learning.

15.4 Course content

The Master's covers topics that are normally included only as marginal or optional courses in management degrees and collects these into one educational experience. Each workshop explores a content area in depth and incorporates other, ongoing, strands of learning and activity.

Theme	Description
1	Globalisation and the new context of business
2	New economics
3	Ecology and sustainable development
4	Sustainable corporate management
5	Humanity and enterprise
6	Corporate citizenship
7	Diversity and difference in a global context
8	Self and world futures

Table 15.1 **The Master's course in Responsibility and Business Practice, University of Bath, UK: the eight workshop themes**

A workshop week has four main streams of activity:

- Topic-based discussions exploring the theme of that workshop, including content reviews
- Auxiliary strands of learning ('cross-woven threads') that run throughout the degree (see Section 15.4.2)
- Learning groups
- Ongoing process reviews and a business meeting

15.4.1 Core course themes

The content of workshops and the learning resources are updated each time the sessions are taught. Our intention is to provide critical material that enables students to identify and engage with key issues, questions and challenges. Those who want to achieve a more detailed understanding of an area do so independently. The typical format for exploring the week's topic involves discussion of designated readings that participants have done in advance. This discussion is focused on the first day into a mapping session in which key themes and issues are identified as learning agendas for the week (flipchart notes on these will typically remain on the course room walls during the workshop as reminders). Tutors may also present topic overviews at this stage. Tuesday to Thursday we have sessions with visiting speakers and core staff tutors.

Visiting speakers who are leading authorities in an area or who are people working with innovative management or other practices provide many of the topic-based sessions. They are invited in to work *with* the course group, rather than only to lecture. We favour using active session formats, involved critical discussion, case-study examples and listening to invited speakers with divergent perspectives. For example, one workshop on Corporate Citizenship (June 2001) included: exploring Sky TV's 'Reach for the Sky' project (a nationwide social marketing venture helping young people develop self-esteem and career aspirations), the impact of Rio Tinto's mining explorations on communities and a moderated debate between representatives of Médecins sans Frontières and GlaxoSmithKline concerning affordable access to medicines in the developing world. Core staff facilitated discussions and related examples to relevant literature.

Course participants and graduates also contribute content from their expertise. As the programme proceeds, participants can see the interconnections and potential tensions between issues pertaining to ecology, sustainability, social justice, ethics and business rather than treating them as discrete problems to solve. Elkington (1997), for example, invites us to recognise that there are potential shear zones between economic, environmental and social bottom lines. Many, perhaps most, current challenges are not easily resolvable.

15.4.2 Cross-woven threads: auxiliary strands of learning

In addition to the designated workshop topics, we have identified other strands of theory and practice that we believe are important to facilitate people's learning. We call these 'cross-woven threads'. They enable participants to work with the content of the degree in question-posing, critical, reflective and applied ways. The main cross-woven threads are: inquiry (based in action research); systemic thinking; change and being an agent for change; power; gender; diversity; and leadership. Sessions on these topics are interspersed through the workshops with opportunities to revisit themes and issues for deeper engagement as the programme develops. Coverage includes introducing conceptual frameworks and offering exercises to apply them to course participants' practices and lives. In this, and other, aspects of the programme we work with respect for multiple ways of knowing, such as the experiential, practical and intellectual (Heron 1992; Goldberger *et al.* 1987).

These auxiliary strands of learning are important, because educating for sustainability is not just about offering information, although putting information (such as data on current ecological degradation) into systems where it has not been before (such as management education) is a vital aspect of systemic change (Meadows 1991). It is about how we 'think', and how we work with that information—it is about how we know. As Berman (1989: 312 [emphasis in original]) offers enigmatically: '*How* things are held in the mind is more important than *what* is in the mind, including this statement itself'.

Intellectual knowing, then, is insufficient. Moving towards sustainability requires people to act and think in new ways—hence our emphasis in the course on developing practice as well as understanding. Again, we find action research a robust, multifaceted medium for enacting and exemplifying course content and issues. Some course participants identify this stream of learning as a major aspect of their development during the course, especially in their abilities to be change agents in their organisations. Graduates' comments in the course brochure reflect this (see footnote 1 on page 198).

15.5 Learning approaches: part 2

The programme is designed to foster disciplined inquiry into issues and practices involved in seeking a more ecologically and socially just world. We use action research principles to achieve this. In Sections 15.5.1–4 I provide some examples.

15.5.1 Training in action research

Training in various forms of action research is offered, including training in: self-reflective, first-person inquiry (Fisher *et al.* 2000; Marshall 1999, 2001); co-operative inquiry, engaging in research with others (Maughan and Reason 2001); and third-person inquiry, seeking to spread inquiry capacities in a wider organisational system (Reason and Torbert 2001). We cover an array of action research practices and do not prescribe which ones participants should adopt. We require only that students *do* find some suitable forms of discipline (this is a coursework requirement). Participants are encouraged to develop these skills in their everyday engagement in the programme, individually and collectively, as well as in their individual inquiries. For example, we discuss how to communicate appropriately with visiting speakers, including how to ask probing questions without attacking the speaker if a student's perspective differs from that of the speaker. Such issues are identified by the group and considered when preparing for and debriefing after speaker sessions.

15.5.2 Cycles of action and reflection

Engaging in cycles of action and reflection—a key feature of action research methodology—to generate continual testing between tentative understanding and practice is incorporated into the course format in various ways. For example, all workshops include time for content and process reviews. Performance is therefore monitored as each workshop week and the course proceeds. This is a mutual activity, with course participants joining staff in taking responsibility for the generativity of the programme. Proposed changes are typically treated as experiments to be reviewed and, if necessary, readjusted.

Cycles of action and reflection are also built into the course to give shape to students' learning journeys. Course participants work in learning groups of four or five members (a tutor is assigned to each group, but much meeting time is self-managed). These meet on the Mondays and Fridays of the workshop weeks (i.e. on the first and last days). This scheduling deliberately introduces cycling between action and reflection into the structure and learning experience of the course. On the Friday, members set learning agendas to pursue during the coming months. Between workshops they engage in action, although this is likely to incorporate reflection too and is not limited to one cycle. Participants engage in more sustained reflection by writing learning papers (circulated before the next workshop) and reporting to their groups on the Monday of the next five-day workshop.

15.5.3 Congruence of assessment practices with territories of learning

An important feature of the learning design of the degree is the use of assessment processes that are congruent with innovative, inquiry-based forms of education and that adhere to established expectations of academic excellence. We provide clear guidelines to evaluate quality, but allow participants, in consultation with their staff tutors and learning groups, to interpret these in ways relevant to their own work. Four broad criteria of quality are used, covering: an intellectual dimension; the method of inquiry; a practice dimension; and a self-reflective dimension. These are discussed extensively with course participants. Students are required to select topics and issues of importance to them and to their practices. They establish, and continuously develop, self-guided learning agendas. Staff work with participants to identify their learning interests and devise inquiry strategies. Learning group peers are also highly important in this process.

The course format also provides frequent opportunities for feedback and discussion. During the first year, participants receive written and verbal feedback on their learning papers (see Box 15.1) from tutors and peers. After one year, there is an interim assessment, using the four criteria of quality, for which students submit their first three learning papers (revised if they choose) and a first-year learning review. Detailed feedback is given. Re-submission is required if the work is not satisfactory. (If a student consistently fails to submit satisfactory work during the first year, he or she may be required to withdraw.) During the second year, participants work on chosen projects, again engaging in research cycles, writing papers and receiving feedback. At the end of the degree they submit a project report and full course learning review for assessment. Successful work is graded as a pass or distinction. Regulations allow one re-submission if additional work is required.

In a programme that does not treat academic material as value-neutral and encourages students to develop practice as well as intellectual competence, some educators may be concerned about academic quality. As noted above, this is maintained by using the four criteria. In the UK system, each course has an external examiner from another institution, part of whose role is to advise on quality standards. The external examiner for the first four years of the degree, in his end-of-office report, said that the degree 'has matured rapidly to become well balanced in terms of theory, practice and critical reflection'.

First-year learning paper inquiries might:

● Take an area of sustainability practice to review, for example, how environmental, social and ethical auditing practices might be applied to the participant's company

● Explore ideas and literature relating to a chosen topic, such as deep ecology, transformative change or new economic theorising

● Track practice; for example, a consultant introducing notions of sustainability might explore what formats encourage client exploration and how to manage issues of credibility

Second-year learning projects tend to be grounded in participants' practice and must cover the four quality criteria. For example, an internal change agent seeking to raise consciousness of sustainability issues in his or her organisation might plan and track the initiatives with an action inquiry approach using multi-dimensional theories of power and literature about strategies for organisational change (Ainger 2001).

Box 15.1 The Master's course in Responsibility and Business Practice, University of Bath, UK: an illustration of course work

15.5.4 Using collaborative action research to manage course process

As already indicated, the course is managed by staff in strong collaboration with participants. There are some intrinsic dilemmas in the programme format that each course cohort has to address for itself. It would be restrictive educationally for staff to assume authority and impose resolutions. Two core dilemmas concern how much to focus learning through engaging with visiting speakers compared with how much to generate learning from within the course cohort, and what is an appropriate balance between sessions focusing on content and those addressing inquiry and other cross-woven threads. Again, action research informs our educational practice. We invite discussion of these choices as we run each workshop week and plan future workshop formats. This educational approach exemplifies and mirrors our course purposes: to raise issues relevant to sustainability and social justice—which we thus encounter, reflectively, in action rather than only learning 'about' them—and to practise the skills of collaborative action research.

15.6 Some of the issues and learning we have encountered along the way

In this section I consider some of the issues that have arisen from running the degree, drawing on staff experience and participant feedback.

15.6.1 Developing our practices for teaching action research

One dimension of our learning as staff has been how we can offer action research approaches and support people in this aspect of their learning. Although we explain this core feature of the course during marketing, at open days and during interviews with applicants, what it may really entail is not always apparent to people. Also, each participant must develop skills of inquiry in his or her own way. Typically, this learning is cyclic and takes time. We offer presentations, readings, workshop sessions and direct support to people implementing inquiry in their work and lives. We have learned that once is seldom enough to thoroughly ground inquiry practices and so we are now doing more recapping as the course progresses. The learning groups and peer support are vital to the development process. Typically, graduates report that their understanding of inquiry progressed with the course. Some were helped by engaging automatically at first in the required disciplines (such as 'cycling' between action and reflection) and then saw the learning this brought; others learned from experiencing ways in which the programme exemplifies and models action research. We continue to develop our practice on this aspect of the course.

15.6.2 How to position staff expertise in multidisciplinary education

One challenge is how to engage in integrative exploration when the tutors involved are unlikely to have expertise in all of the topic areas covered. What teaching approach is appropriate? How can question-posing be sufficiently robust? How can staff work together who have a diversity of content knowledge and, potentially, of epistemology? What types of learning strategies do course participants need to adopt?

We developed the staffing pattern during the initial years of the degree. Core staff act as intake tutors. Usually, two go through the degree with a cohort of students. They also act as learning group tutors. They have expertise in some fields, especially inquiry and other cross-woven threads, but are not subject experts across all topics covered on the degree; this would be impossible given the scope of material. Tutors must, however, have the ability to engage in and encourage critical questioning across topics. How to ensure quality of content engagement in a course that is wide-ranging and integrative rather than discipline-segmented is an important issue we have addressed. In some ways, we are using inquiry approaches to provide a 'meta-frame of expertise' which holds the programme together as a whole. The visiting speakers and reading materials are the primary means for introducing subject expertise within this structure. For specific workshops some tutors from the core team take a more content-related role in areas of their own specialisation, selecting and organising visiting speakers, chairing sessions and providing topic area input. This provides continuity and depth of grounding within the core staff team.

15.6.3 The challenges of seeking to encompass the world

Addressing globalisation from a specific base makes it challenging to engage with a wide range of perspectives if we are to seek to include potentially marginal voices from our society and from the developing or 'majority' world. The search for diversity has influenced our choice of visiting speakers and reading materials and is an issue we will continue to monitor. We do benefit greatly from the diversity of course participants. Also, it is of concern that potentially marginalised voices do not seem well incorporated into the rising tide of literature on corporate social responsibility. 'Mainstream' voices still seem to dominate.

15.6.4 How do we adequately contain and support education of this kind?

This programme, and indeed all similar education, makes significant demands on participants and, consequently, on staff. Thus, what kinds of competence do tutors require?

The Master's course in Responsibility and Business Practice involves engaging with potentially disturbing and upsetting issues, such as stark information about ecological degradation and global poverty, doubts about mainstream business assumptions and challenges to people's mind-sets and lifestyles. Most participants find their learning unsettling at some time. How do we 'contain' and work developmentally with such learning experiences?

Many graduates report that the degree has been a life-changing experience. Some come to learn primarily about the content and are surprised by the programme's wider impacts. Others come to re-examine their careers and life-paths. Even among the latter, some would certainly say that their learning and development through participation in the programme was more than they expected. So we must ask how, or perhaps if, the course can be sufficiently supportive. Data from the Quinquennial Course Quality Review (conducted during the academic year 2001/2002 as a University of Bath requirement) suggested that people generally feel supported by the course, staff and learning community. This is an aspect of the programme that needs ongoing attention. Some graduates want to continue the networking and action-research-based development they experienced during the degree. Although some activities are peer-generated, staff are also now offering alumni learning groups.

Another issue is how participants cope with education that foregrounds issues of sustainability and social justice when addressing these concerns may 'unfit' them for high-paying jobs in mainstream corporate life (an intent of management education, especially the MBA). Certainly, some graduates are reorienting their careers and taking the financial consequences of being in a learning phase in new, for them and for society, territories. How do course participants and staff work with such discord? The challenge is ongoing.

For all these reasons, and more, many participants engage in the programme with high levels of commitment but also with potential ambivalence, especially concerning how much change they want to encounter. They therefore expect a great deal, including in their relationships with staff. They do not approach this as an 'ordinary course'. Although this is the kind of education to which staff are committed, and with which they have experience, high expectations from participants, and the nature of those expectations, place considerable demands on tutors. Are faculty trained in, prepared for and sufficiently supported to do this kind of educational work? The short answer is probably 'not usually'.

Our programme requires the following as staff competences: academic capabilities in action research and other cross-woven threads; the ability to identify issues and engage in critical questioning in topic areas related to sustainability and social justice; the ability to facilitate group dynamics in a learning community; the ability to coach individual students in inquiry-based development that may be unsettling to those students; the ability to enact action research as a tutor engaging simultaneously in all the above; and the ability to judge appropriate boundaries—for example, by questioning how much to work with group process. Also, some expertise in one or several content areas is helpful.

In navigating my own way through some of these issues, I find it helpful to remember Heron's (1999) invitation to see facilitation as a circumstance-appropriate blend of exercising authority, joining in participation and creating space for autonomy. Educating for sustainability using appropriate forms is, then, challenging work for tutors.

At Bath, we hold regular staff meetings, which include discussions of the practices and crafts of working on the programme. We learn from each other, and from course participants, as we proceed. We recently held a more substantial staff development workshop, mapping areas of competence, conducting and comparing self-assessments and peer assessments and making development plans, individually and jointly.

15.7 Conclusions

In this chapter I have advocated the matching of form to content in educating for sustainability. I have showed how we designed and teach a programme founded in action research.

Action research has been a robust and pliable base from which to develop this Master's course in Responsibility and Business Practice. It helps us and course participants engage with, and experience, the challenges of sustainability and social justice in ways we could not do through more traditional forms of education. The first years have been an exciting and demanding journey for us as tutors. In this, too, action research, in its various guises, has been our resource.

References

Ainger, C. (2001) *MSc Project Report* (unpublished report; Bath, UK: University of Bath).

Berman, M. (1989) *Coming To Our Senses: Body and Spirit in the Hidden History of the West* (London: Unwin).

Bilimoria, D. (1998) 'What If We Taught As If "All Our Relations" Mattered?', *Journal of Management Education* 22.4: 449-51.

Daly, H., and J.B. Cobb (1990) *For the Common Good* (London: Green Print).

Egri, C., and K. Rogers (eds.) (2003) 'Teaching about the Natural Environment in Management Education', *Journal of Management Education* 27.2 (Special Issue): 139-270.

Elkington, J. (1997) *Cannibals with Forks: The Triple Bottom Line of 21st Century Business* (Oxford: Capstone Publishing).

Fisher, D., D. Rooke and W.R. Torbert (2000) *Personal and Organisational Transformations: Through Action Inquiry* (Boston, MA: Edge\Work Press).

Goldberger, N.R., B.McV. Clinchy, M.F. Belenky and J.M. Tarule (1987) 'Women's Ways of Knowing: On Gaining a Voice', in P. Shaver and C. Hendrick (eds.), *Sex and Gender* (Newbury Park, CA: Sage): 201-28.

Hawken, P. (1993) *The Ecology of Commerce* (New York: HarperCollins).

Heron, J. (1992) *Feeling and Personhood: Psychology in Another Key* (London: Sage).

—— (1999) *The Complete Facilitator's Handbook* (London: Kogan Page).

Lomborg, B. (2001) *The Sceptical Environmentalist* (Cambridge, UK: Cambridge University Press).

Lovins, A.B., H. Lovins and P. Hawken (1999) 'A Road Map for Natural Capitalism', *Harvard Business Review*, May/June 1999: 145-58.

Marshall, J. (1999) 'Living Life as Inquiry', *Systemic Practice and Action Research* 12.2: 155-71.

—— (2001) 'Self-reflective Inquiry Practices', in P. Reason and H. Bradbury (eds.), *Handbook of Action Research* (London: Sage): 433-39.

Maughan, E., and P. Reason (2001) 'A Co-operative Inquiry into Deep Ecology', *ReVision* 23.4: 18-24.

Meadows, D.H. (1991) 'Change is Not Doom', *ReVision* 14.2: 56-60.

——, D.L. Meadows and J. Randers (1992) *Beyond the Limits: Global Collapse or a Sustainable Future* (London: Earthscan Publications).

Orr, D.W. (1994) *Earth in Mind: On Education, Environment and the Human Prospect* (Washington, DC: Island Press).

Reason, P., and H. Bradbury (2001) 'Introduction', in P. Reason and H. Bradbury (eds.), *Handbook of Action Research* (London: Sage): 1-14.

—— and W.R. Torbert (2001) 'Toward a Transformational Science: A Further Look at the Scientific Merits of Action Research', *Concepts and Transformations* 6.1: 1-37.

Shrivastava, P. (1994) 'Greening Business Education: Towards an Ecocentric Pedagogy', *Journal of Management Inquiry* 3.3: 235-43.

—— (1995a) 'Ecocentric Management for a Risk Society', *Academy of Management Review* 20.1: 118-37.

—— (1995b) 'The Role of Corporations in Achieving Ecological Sustainability', *Academy of Management Review* 20.4: 936-60.

Starik, M., and A.A. Marcus (2000) 'Introduction to the Special Research Forum on the Management of Organisations in the Natural Environment: A Field Emerging from Multiple Paths, with Many Challenges Ahead', *Academy of Management Journal* 43.4: 539-46.

—— and G.P. Rands (1995). 'Weaving an Integrated Web: Multilevel and Multisystem Perspectives of Ecologically Sustainable Organisations', *Academy of Management Review* 20.4: 908-35.

Westley, F., and H. Vredenburg (1996) 'Sustainability and the Corporation: Criteria for Aligning Economic Practice with Environmental Protection', *Journal of Management Inquiry* 5.2: 104-19.

Part 3
Tools, methods and approaches

16
Making sense of corporate responsibility tools

Sasha Courville
Regulatory Institutions Network, Australian National University

In the past two decades, we have seen an exponential increase of tools for integrating social justice and environmental protection issues into business practices. These include environmental management systems, corporate reporting systems, codes of conduct, third-party certification systems and ethical investment. This proliferation can make it difficult for practitioners, government representatives and students to make sense of the different approaches. A conceptual framework in which the various business and sustainability approaches can be understood and contextualised would be a useful tool to help teach sustainability. In this chapter, I explain the rise of corporate sustainability, argue for the necessity of a conceptual framework for business and sustainability tools and then outline such a framework.

16.1 The rise of corporate sustainability and the mess of sustainability tools

With the decline of the social-democratic welfare state model and the rise of neoliberal thinking, governments have been relatively unable or unwilling to link economic activities such as production and consumption with social justice and environmental issues (Courville 2001; see also Arden-Clarke 1998 for a discussion of production and process methods in international trade law and Pearson and Seyfang 2001 for a discussion of the demise of statutory labour codes). Reasons are complex but include concerns about reducing national competitiveness in international trade by imposing stringent regulatory requirements and the high costs of enforcement of traditional top-down regulatory mechanisms.

With the globalisation of the economy, the power to integrate social and environmental objectives into economic activities is moving out of the realm of the nation-state and into new spheres. Frustrated by the lack of governmental progress toward sustainability, new actors such as social movements, non-governmental organisations (NGOs) and even private corporations are creating alternatives to fill this regulatory vacuum. As a result, a plethora of non-governmental initiatives, tools and projects that seek to integrate environmental and social issues into economic activities have been developed over the past two decades (Gereffi *et al.* 2001; Meidinger 1997). The diversity of these initiatives can be overwhelming for practitioners, researchers and students.

Even the terminology used to identify these activities is not clear. Triple bottom line (TBL) is one common expression used to capture activities that seek to integrate and balance economic, social and environmental objectives. Corporate social responsibility (CSR) is another, used to describe the incorporation of social issues such as human and labour rights or community relations into business practices. This term is also sometimes used to encompass environmental issues (see CPGMWG 2002: 4, 8).

Corporate sustainability tools have evolved through different stages over the past few decades. Frustrated by the lack of government enforcement on environmental and social justice issues since the 1980s, several NGOs, trade unions and other civil-society actors have questioned, using media and Internet campaigns, the performance of high-profile corporations (Bell 2002; Courville 2001; Karliner and Bruno 2002; SustainAbility 2002). In response, many targeted companies have tried to create a responsible corporate image by subscribing to codes of conduct or by establishing environmental management systems, for example. Motivation for these responses includes a desire for a 'green' image, a desire to reduce risk, wanting to address shareholder concerns and better employee relations and even a genuine concern by senior management for social and environmental improvement (Bell 2002; SustainAbility 2001; Houlder 2001).

Although some companies have significantly improved their practices, the credibility of many social and environmental claims of corporate self-regulation has been questioned. A 1999 study by the Office for Development and Transition Economies of Consumers International reported that inadequate or false environmental claims on products were found in all ten countries surveyed. Furthermore, in Australia, of 52 environmental product claims examined, only 11 were found to be valid (ODTE 1999). To address these concerns, new mechanisms have been developed. These include bilateral relationships between individual NGOs and corporations and broad multi-stakeholder coalitions underpinned by widely accepted standards and codes of ethics such as the conventions of the International Labour Organisation (ILO) and multilateral environmental agreements (see Pearson and Seyfang 2001).

The number of current tools and initiatives designed to integrate TBL thinking into the business sector is impressive and is likely to continue to grow. The tools that are being used worldwide encompass a spectrum of activity and range from the early self-regulatory approaches of companies to the most sophisticated private regulatory systems based on independent third-party certification. Certain initiatives are particular to a company whereas others are industry-wide initiatives developed at the national or international level, such as the cement industry initiative of the World Business Council for Sustainable Development (WBCSD 2002). Some initiatives focus on social and environmental certification of products (e.g. computers), services (e.g. eco-tourism) and facilities (e.g. apparel factories). Other softer approaches such as the Ethical Trading Initiative (ETI) in the United Kingdom or the United Nations Global Compact claim to be 'learning initiatives'. They seek to investigate how to improve and evaluate the social and environmental performance of companies (ETI 2001; United Nations 2003).

Consumers—be they supermarket shoppers, government procurement officers or corporate buyers—can have a hard time distinguishing among this dizzying array of tools. How can a consumer know that the claims being made are credible? Similarly, companies often struggle with choosing the 'most appropriate' tool to commit to or to require their suppliers to comply with. Companies operating in sustainability-sensitive sectors want to know what the most important TBL tool is, while pleading for harmonisation and co-ordination among the initiators of corporate sustainability initiatives.

There are no easy answers to the above questions. Clearly, new frameworks are needed to make sense of the options. Initiatives first must be understood in terms of their functions. For example, if they are designed mainly to improve the internal activities of an organisation, sustainability tools can be flexible and do not necessarily require the involvement of external actors. However, if such tools are to be used to communicate information about a product, service, facility or company to consumers or to supply-chain companies, then independent verification is recommended.

In the next section I outline a heuristic to help place different types of corporate sustainability initiatives in a context that examines their relationships. Although not exhaustive, this framework provides a guideline to explain how TBL tools can be chosen and used alone or together within a specific organisation.

16.2 Making sense of the complexity: a diagrammatic tool

Figure 16.1 shows how different TBL tools fit together. To improve social, economic and environmental performance and to communicate this achievement to external stakeholders, a company may go through several steps, represented in the central column, starting at the bottom and moving upwards. Although this is represented linearly for the sake of simplicity, in reality movement between the different stages is an iterative process. It should also be noted that not all companies will take all steps. Rather, they will pick and choose from among the TBL activities. The activities planned around each step can be accomplished as an internal corporate process, to communicate to external stakeholders or both.

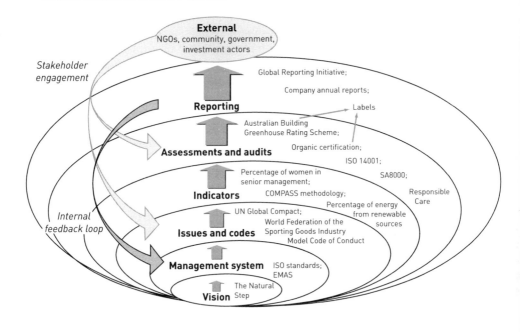

Figure 16.1 Relationships between triple-bottom-line tools

The first step is to outline company values and objectives with respect to sustainability. This requires a **visioning process** where senior executives or a wider range of employees identify core values that the organisation embodies or that it should adopt. Key long-term objectives for sustainability can also be outlined through this process. The Natural Step (www.naturalstep.org) is one TBL tool that starts from a visioning process.

Once the key values and long-term objectives are mapped out, a general operational framework for implementing them is needed: a **management system**. Management systems aid organisational learning and continuous improvement and generally include the following: company policy, as developed in the visioning process, compliance with legislation, a management review process of operations, clear definitions of roles and responsibilities, planning and implementation processes, implementation of corrective action procedures from feedback learned and outside communication of this process.

With the rise of corporate responsibility, several management systems designed for environmental management have been developed. Examples are the European Union Eco-Management and Audit Scheme (EMAS)[1] and the ISO 14000 series from the International Organisation for Standardisation (ISO).[2] Given the success of the ISO 14000 series standards and their quality management standard predecessor,

1 www.europa.eu.int/comm/environment/emas/index_en.htm
2 www.iso.ch/iso/en/prods-services/otherpubs/iso14000/index.html

the ISO 9000 series,[3] ISO is evaluating the feasibility and desirability of developing a corporate social responsibility management system standard. A company can undergo third-party certification for compliance to ISO 14001, but this does not necessarily provide information about concrete social or environmental performance benchmarks on issues such as waste minimisation or freedom of association, because management systems are based on continual improvement.

Key issues relevant to companies or industry sectors can be identified and formalised by using **codes of conduct** or **sets of principles**. These are sets of TBL issues that a company or industry association considers important to address (e.g. the Model Code of Conduct of the World Federation of the Sporting Goods Industry[4]). Certain codes or sets of principles, such as the Global Compact, are established more broadly through networks of NGOs, trade unions, businesses and international institutions.

Codes of conduct or sets of principles can be important TBL tools because they can represent a learning process through which a normative direction toward sustainability can be outlined, such as the process leading to the development of the Earth Charter. They also allow a company or industry to state publicly its commitment to adhere to, or to work toward, specific sets of values on particular issues.

Codes or principles are a critical, but preliminary, stage on the road to sustainability. After an organisation adopts codes or principles and/or installs an environmental management system, it must measure its performance against specific commitments in the code or the targets for improvement in the management system review.

To this end, **indicators** work as 'measuring sticks', helping to evaluate how well organisations are accomplishing their goals. Indicators can be considered a specific type of TBL tool but they usually are used as building blocks for higher-level tools. For example, the ISO 14030 series is dedicated to supporting the use of indicators within environmental management systems. Conversely, the COMPASS (Companies' and Sectors' Path to Sustainability) methodology from the Wuppertal Institute for identifying industry-specific indicator sets through stakeholder engagement is an example of an indicator that can be considered a tool its own right (Kuhndt *et al.* 2002).

As mentioned above, after companies have identified core social, environmental and economic issues through codes or principles, they must next assess their performance against the stated criteria. Indicators form the underlying mechanism for measuring performance within a broader framework of **assessment or audit**. Assessments or audits usually require code-based standards, specific indicators for each issue and a team that evaluates performance with respect to the standards. This may result in recommendations for improvement through corrective action plans or in a statement about the company's compliance to a particular standard or code.

---

3 www.iso.ch/iso/en/iso9000-14000/iso9000/iso9000index.html
4 www1.umn.edu/humanrts/links/wfsgi.html
5 www.earthcharter.org

Several possibilities for assessment exist. Where a company has developed its own set of issues and indicators and is in the initial stages of development, the assessment process may be done in-house by company staff. To ensure greater transparency, independent verification of the results could be obtained. Furthermore, if a widely accepted set of issues or codes are available and relevant the company may be audited or inspected by an independent third party. Systems such as the Social Accountability 8000 (SA8000) standard from Social Accountability International (SAI 2002), based on the ILO labour conventions and life-cycle-based eco-labelling systems of the Global Ecolabelling Network,[6] work this way. Some TBL tools, such as ISO 14001 or the Australian Building Greenhouse Rating Scheme,[7] can be used either as internal tools to improve performance or as tools to communicate to stakeholders via an optional independent verification process.

Figure 16.1 outlines clear steps or 'ideal type' stages, but many TBL tools fall between two steps or integrate elements of different stages. For example, the Responsible Care® initiative of the International Council of Chemical Associations[8] is placed at the intersection of the issues and codes level and the assessment level with the indicators stage between. This is because it comprises principles to be integrated into business practice while simultaneously providing procedures for company assessment and reporting practices. This initiative is evolving from what was a code of conduct into an assessment tool, although it stops short of consistent third-party assessment.

The final step is **reporting** the results. This can be directed either to external stakeholders or to internal management improvement processes, as shown by the arrows in the diagram. The reporting process will vary depending on the target audience, but a consistent main goal is to align more closely the values of the external community with those of internal company actors. As the lightly shaded, curved arrows show, this engagement is generally most appropriate during the stages of identification ('issues and codes') and assessment. An internal feedback loop (indicated by the darker-shaded curved arrow) integrates the results into the company's management system with the goal of improving performance against social, economic and environmental benchmarks credibly and transparently.

As in the other stages, several TBL reporting options are available. The most common is the production of annual reports. TBL issues are sometimes addressed within general annual reports, but specific social, environmental and sustainability reports are becoming more popular. The information these reports provide is critical for transparency and credibility. Harmonising frameworks such as the Global Reporting Initiative (GRI) have been developed to allow for comparison across companies while balancing this with flexibility in application to suit different corporate activities. This is accomplished in the GRI by emphasising core indicators that can be applied across a range of organisational environments and additional indicators for specific industry sectors (GRI 2002: 12).

Product certification and labelling are other ways to report TBL results to supply-chain clients and consumers (e.g. labels certifying the product as organic or labels giving the product an energy rating). Certificates and labels give users simple,

6   www.gen.gr.jp
7   www.abgr.com.au
8   www.icca-chem.org/section02a.html

independently verified information about the social or environmental performance of a product or company.

As certification systems become more popular, questions of who monitors the monitors arise. The most sophisticated systems also have accreditation systems to evaluate the certification body and, if successful, to accredit it to a higher-level organisation. The International Accreditation Forum provides one main accreditation platform.[9] Other international verification systems that operate accreditation programmes include SAI-accredited certification bodies to carry out verifications on the SA8000 standard,[10] the International Organic Accreditation Service[11] and the Forest Stewardship Council.[12]

In Figure 16.1, the expanding ellipses indicate the scope and relationship among TBL tools. As can be seen, the reporting stage theoretically can encompass all other TBL tools. Thus, sustainability reports can give information about a company's social and environmental performance achieved by using management systems, codes of conduct and auditing systems, among other TBL tools. For example, third-party certification obtained for social and/or environmental performance against a widely accepted standard can be noted in a sustainability report.

It should also be noted that, although outside the scope of an individual company, information given by sustainability reports and other tools is used by yet another TBL tool: ethical investment or SRI. SRI research groups rank companies' social and environmental performance. Most of this information is obtained either from the TBL tools that a company implements (i.e. sustainability reports or certification) or from questionnaires. This research forms the basis for screening companies for certain positive or negative characteristics.

16.3 Conclusions

The world of TBL initiatives is currently fraught with confusion; thus, it is imperative that we find relatively simple ways to understand and explain it. Consumers, regulators and students must be able to understand differences in the range of TBL tools based on the explicit purposes, scope of activity and concrete performance outcomes of those tools if we are to ensure that the integration of sustainability concepts and practices into businesses continues with the best possible outcomes.

Companies must be able to understand which TBL tools are best suited to their needs, which are most valued by clients and consumers and how tools can be combined to reduce costs, increase credibility and improve outcomes. Opportunities for harmonisation and complementarity are significant but hard to identify in the current sea of TBL initiatives. The heuristic outlined in this chapter offers a framework for understanding how various tools fit together. It does not capture all the complexities of the relationships between TBL tools but it does provide a

---

9 www.iaf.nu
10 www.SA8000.org
11 www.ifoam.org → Organic Guarantee System → Accreditation Programme
12 www.fscoax.org

roadmap with signposts to help the weary traveller through the world of TBL initiatives.

References

Arden-Clarke, C. (1998) 'Process and Production Methods', in D. Brack (ed.), *Trade and Environment: Conflict or Compatibility?* (London: Earthscan Publications): 72-78.

Bell, D. (2002) 'The Role of Government in Advancing Corporate Sustainability', background paper prepared by the Sustainable Enterprise Academy, York University, on behalf of Environment Canada for the G8 Environmental Futures Forum, Vancouver, March 2002.

Courville, S. (2001) 'Not Just Trade: Steps toward Incorporating Social and Ecological Costs into International Trade: Lessons Learned from "Better" Case Studies of Coffee Production to Consumption Systems', in *School of Resources, Environment and Society* (Canberra, Australia: Australian National University).

CPGMWG (Consumer Protection in the Global Market Working Group) (2002) *The Desirability and Feasibility of ISO Corporate Social Responsibility Standards* (Port of Spain, Trinidad and Tobago: ISO COPOLCO [Committee on Consumer Policy]).

ETI (Ethical Trading Initiative) (2001) *Learning Our Trade: Annual Review 2000-01* (London: ETI).

Gereffi, G., R. Garcia-Johnson and E. Sasser (2001) 'The NGO–Industrial Complex', *Foreign Policy*, July/August 2001: 56-65.

GRI (Global Reporting Initiative) (2002) *Sustainability Reporting Guidelines* (Boston, MA: GRI).

Houlder, V. (2001) 'Hard times put green business to the test', *Financial Times*, London, 4 June 2001.

Karliner, J., and K. Bruno (2002) *EarthSummit.biz: The Corporate Takeover of Sustainable Development* (San Francisco/Oakland, CA: Food First Books, Institute for Food Development).

Kuhndt, M., J. von Geibler and A. Eckermann (2002) 'Developing a Sectoral Sustainability Indicator Set Taking a Stakeholder Approach', in *10th International Greening of Industry Network Conference Goteborg, Sweden, June*.

Meidinger, E. (1997) 'Look Who's Making the Rules: International Environmental Standard Setting by Non-governmental Organisations', *Human Ecology Review* 4: 52-54.

ODTE (Office for Developed and Transition Economies) (1999) *Green Claims: Environmental Claims on Products and Packaging in the Shops: An International Study* (London: ODTE, Consumers International).

Pearson, R., and G. Seyfang (2001) 'New Hope or False Dawn?', *Global Social Policy* 1: 49-78.

SAI (Social Accountability International) (2002) 'SA8000', www.cepaa.org/SA8000/SA8000.htm.

SustainAbility (2001) *Buried Treasure* (Engaging Stakeholders Reports; London: SustainAbility).

—— (2002) *Good News and Bad: The Media, Corporate Social Responsibility and Sustainable Development* (Engaging Stakeholders Reports; London: SustainAbility).

United Nations (2003) *How the Global Compact Works: Mission, Actors and Engagement Mechanisms* (New York: Global Compact Office).

WBCSD (World Business Council for Sustainable Development) (2002) *The Cement Sustainability Initiative: Our Agenda for Action* (Geneva: WBCSD).

17
Teaching sustainability
Whole-systems learning

Molly Brown

Intermountain Synthesis Center, USA

Joanna Macy

Teaching sustainability to business people, or anyone else for that matter, requires more than additional data, more than a list of rules. It requires a fundamental shift in attitude, in the way people think and feel. We must address the root causes of our unsustainable practices, which lie deeply in our assumptions about the relationship of humans to the natural world and in our relative ignorance of the functioning of living systems, including human systems.

Many business people are coming to recognise the obvious: the goal of maximising profit must necessarily come second to the welfare of the living world, its human and non-human beings and its cycles of air, water and carbon that support life on Earth. They are coming to recognise that we must include *all* the costs of production—including the ecological and human costs—in our business accounting and responsibility. Externalising these costs, as we have been doing, wreaks havoc on our economy, our social fabric and our life-support system (for a fuller explanation of the externalisation of costs, see Hawken 1995). Sustainability requires whole-systems learning in order to see the wider context in which we function and the web of relationships on which all life depends.

17.1 The work that reconnects

In this chapter we present an approach to whole-systems learning that is helping citizens around the world find clarity, purpose and creativity in meeting the challenges of our time. More fully explicated in our book, *Coming Back to Life: Practices to Reconnect Our Lives, Our World* (Macy and Brown 1998), it is called the 'work that reconnects' and is entirely appropriate to business settings. Grounded in general systems theory, the 'work that reconnects' helps people experience their innate connections with the self-correcting, self-organising powers of all living systems. In our experience, this empowers people to seek out, create and apply sustainable business practices within the workplace and the larger world. The methods used are highly interactive, experiential and enjoyable, and we describe a few examples in this chapter.

The following goals serve the central purpose of the 'work that reconnects':

- To help people explore the effects of externalising ecological and human costs of production, so that they can register these effects as real, immediate and directly affecting their lives

- To provide people with the opportunity to share with others their inner responses to conditions experienced in their lives and work

- To reframe their distress about their lives and the world as evidence of their interconnectedness in the web of life and hence of their power to take an active part in its healthy functioning

- To provide people with concepts from systems science that illumine this power, along with exercises that reveal its play in their own lives

- To provide people with methods to experience their responsibilities to past and future human generations and other life forms, and the inspiration they can draw from those sources

- To enable people to support each other in clarifying their intentions and affirming their commitment to the health of the world

17.2 Understanding systems

Many of today's socially and environmentally unsustainable business practices arise from ignorance about the way in which living systems function. From the perspective of many systems thinkers, such practices seem to be based on the premise that humans can exist apart from nature. The notion of unlimited economic growth is one example. Johnson and Bröms, in their fine book, *Profit beyond Measure*, note that nothing in the universe grows endlessly without limits, stating that 'the issue we face in the business world is to transform our obsession with quantitative growth in size into a delight with qualitative growth in diversity, until that delight becomes the energising force in our lives' (Johnson and Bröms 2000: 200).

In our experience, general systems theory (GST), or systems thinking (Bateson 1972; Berman 1984; Buckley 1968; Capra 1996; Laszlo 1972a, 1972b; Macy 1991; Olds 1992; Sahtouris 1989; von Bertalanffy 1968; Wheatley 1992), seems basic to understanding sustainability and implementing sustainable policies and practices. It reveals the general principles at work in all open systems, be they biological, ecological or organisational. Instead of examining phenomena by breaking things down into component parts, GST views them as self-organising patterns woven and sustained by flows of matter, energy and information. The focus shifts from separate and static entities to the dynamic relationships from which they arise.

These life-sustaining flows are multi-directional. There is no single power source. No single authority rules from above. Instead, the collective membership of a system governs the whole through an intricate web of relationships and information exchange.

Open systems self-organise: that is, they are self-correcting and self-governing. Thanks to the flow-through of matter, energy and information, they can self-stabilise and evolve in response to changing conditions. As they weave larger patterns of collaborative behaviour, creating larger systems, new capacities emerge. In adaptive systems, these emergent properties are synergistic, allowing greater flexibility and variety of form.

The relationships forming an open system are external and internal. A system is a self-organising whole in its own right because of the dynamic interdependence of its parts. Because it depends on energy and information from its surrounding world, it is also a subsystem of larger systems, be they social, economic or ecological. Each system is a 'holon', meaning it is a whole as well as a part of a larger whole.

Feedback is the essential feature that permits an open system to maintain its form across time (homeostasis) and to adapt to challenges by changing (evolution). Alert to signals from within and without, an open system monitors its performance by matching it to existing goals or values acquired through previous learning. When a mismatch persists, the healthy system adapts by reorganising its internal structure and goals.

Information flow is of paramount importance, therefore, to the health of any living system or enterprise. Feedback from its component parts, and from the larger systems in which it operates, is essential to long-term survival. When feedback is blocked or discounted, the system cannot meet its own changing needs or respond to a changing environment. One of the problems with top-down decision-making, for example, is that valuable information from 'lower down' in the organisation is often suppressed or ignored.

Feedback from the biosphere—climatic disruption and loss of forests, fisheries and topsoil—is revealing that our present economy is unsustainable. The feedback indicates an urgent need to change the goals our system pursues and the values by which it measures success. Many systems thinkers and ecologists hold that the maximisation of corporate profits as our economy's highest priority is progressively destroying the interwoven fabric on which all life depends. When we block this feedback, our corporate economy, geared to a dysfunctional goal, spins out of control. In systems terms, it is on a 'runaway' course. Lacking vital information about the effects of its behaviour, it is caught in a vicious self-amplifying cycle, causing 'overshoot' in one area after another.

Because it runs counter to basic assumptions of the industrial growth society—especially assumptions about endless economic growth and that we have inexhaustible resources and sinks for our waste—this feedback is hard to countenance. In business settings, our awareness of this feedback can be hard to express, but it lurks in the soul, surfaces in dreams, feeds into free-floating anxieties. Yet to acknowledge it together opens the way to great adventure: that of using business experience and skills to create a new, sustainable economy. This is possible and necessary—and happening.

17.3 Unblocking feedback

We are assaulted with information from all sides about what is happening to people and other living beings around the planet, but we often block it because it is anomalous to our prevailing ways of thinking, to the assumptions that support our accustomed modes of functioning in the world. Moreover, this information may arouse feelings of fear, anger, grief and a sense of helplessness. These emotions are actually healthy: they inform us that something is amiss and that change is needed. Denial of anomalous information and uncomfortable feelings blocks our ability to think clearly and responsibly. Instead of responding to issues and dangers in a timely fashion, we seek reassurance that everything is okay and that we may continue with business as usual. We become apathetic.

To understand apathy, it is helpful to recall that the word derives from the Greek *apatheia*, meaning 'non-suffering'. Apathy is the inability or refusal to acknowledge suffering. It is widespread today, because to acknowledge the suffering we experience—or cause—could mean re-evaluating some of our most basic assumptions and goals; it could mean changing the way we do things and reducing our profit margin. Yet the very feedback that is blocked by apathy provides information essential to the sustainability of our enterprises and our economy.

The 'work that reconnects' is designed to overcome these blocks so that we and our enterprises, as open systems, can self-correct. It provides structures for spontaneous expression that help us tell the truth about what we know, see and feel is happening to our lives and our world. It helps us to realise that our felt responses arise not from some personal pathology but from our essential interconnectedness as living systems.

Our workshop participants report a profound shift in perspective and attitude: they see themselves as linked and mutually supported within the web of life; thus, their energies are freed for creative and collaborative action. Their minds return to a state of natural clarity. Concepts, which bring relatedness into focus, become vivid. Significant learning occurs because the individual system (an individual person or an organisation) is reorganising and reorienting, grounding itself in wider reaches of 'enlightened self-interest'. Because the approach is participatory, people arrive at new perspectives from their own experiences.

The work proceeds sequentially in four stages. Each unfolds from the previous and corresponds to the way healthy systems function: (1) recognising our mutuality, (2) integrating painful information (feedback), (3) expanding our perceptual horizons and (4) finding creative responses. We will now discuss each of these in turn.

17.3.1 First stage: recognising our mutuality

As we have said, whole systems operate through mutual give and take, in reciprocal relationships. Their viability depends on their ability to provide and receive support, even more than on their ability to 'compete' in the old, narrow sense of the word. Whole-systems learning involves perceiving this fundamental mutuality in our own lives and organisations so that the essential relationships of part to whole are clearly recognised and understood. We learn to see that, because a system cannot operate in isolation, neither can a business operate in isolation from the community and the natural world. Its adaptive self-organisation requires an appreciative awareness of its dependence on these larger systems, as well as on the unrestricted, mutually supportive interplay of its component parts (employees, customers and so on).

Gratitude plays a key role in heightening our awareness of systemic mutuality. It helps ground people in an appreciative, felt sense of how they are embraced and sustained by the larger natural and social systems in which they live. Gratitude also builds a sense of confidence and expanded capacity in preparation for the next stage. We begin the work, therefore, with exercises designed to evoke the expression of the gratitude that we all carry, often just below the surface of our immediate awareness. A sample gratitude exercise is described in Exercise 17.1.[1]

In pairs, small groups, or moving from one person to the next around the circle of the whole group, people are invited to describe four specific things: (1) something they love about their work, (2) a place they remember as magical to them as children, (3) someone who helped them believe in themselves and (4) some things they appreciate about themselves. People are urged to avoid generalisations and to speak of particulars, because there is more vitality when they do. Participants often discover a great commonality in what they appreciate in their lives and work, evidence of our essential interconnectedness. They perceive how deeply they are supported and nourished by the larger social and natural world around them

---

Exercise 17.1 First stage: gratitude exercise

Source: Macy and Brown 1998

---

1 A few of the exercises from our book, *Coming Back to Life: Practices to Reconnect Our Lives, Our World* (Macy and Brown 1998) are briefly described in this chapter. Business educators interested in incorporating the exercises into their programmes are urged to acquire the book. It offers a thorough explication of the theory, guidelines for facilitation and step-by-step instructions for 46 exercises, most of which can be adapted to a business setting.

17.3.2 Second stage: integrating painful information

All living systems adapt and evolve in response to feedback. However, in human systems, the very feedback a system most needs to receive may be filtered or screened out because it conflicts with assumptions. These include assumptions about the goals and values of an enterprise as well as about the difficulty of changing them. Such feedback may be experienced as pain and thus be suppressed. Yet pain is an essential form of feedback, designed to warn us of imminent or immediate threats to survival and well-being. Ignoring it is folly.

Because we are used to censoring certain feedback, the 'work that reconnects' does not deliver information about world or business conditions so much as encourage people to articulate it themselves from their experiences. As they speak about their experiences, they find that their thoughts and feelings are widely shared. Released from the illusion of separation, and the unconscious need to repress this vital information, people can receive and utilise more feedback. Their energy is freed and they find a strong sense of connection with others and with the larger world (see the sample exercise for this stage, Exercise 17.2, titled 'Open Sentences').

This exercise invites people to voice their responses to the condition of our world, as they experience them. Its structure helps people to listen closely and to express thoughts and feelings that are usually censored for fear of comment or adverse reaction.

People sit face to face in pairs, close enough to focus on one another. Each partner in turn responds to an 'open sentence' spoken by the guide, completing the sentence and continuing spontaneously for the time allotted. The sentences address what inspires people in their work, what they find difficult, their concerns about the larger world and thoughts and feelings that arise from all this. After both partners have responded to all the sentences, the whole group can explore common themes that emerged and how they may relate to more global concerns. Difficulties at work that people often mention include time pressures (that deadlines are becoming increasingly short), problems from the chain of command (that inadequate information is given to perform their jobs) and competitiveness. These pressures can be seen as the result of dysfunction in the larger system; individual inadequacy is seldom to blame. Systems thinking tells us that workers at all levels of unsustainable organisations suffer at the hands of the same assumptions and practices that are tearing apart the social fabric and destroying the environment. Recognising this relationship removes the self-blame that many people feel, freeing them to look more closely at the dysfunction of the whole system to discover how it can be changed.

Exercise 17.2 Second stage: 'Open Sentences'

Source: Macy and Brown 1998

17.3.3 Third stage: expanding our perceptual horizons

To incorporate feedback, systems must adapt their 'codes'—their values and goals—to include anomalous information. In this way, perceptual horizons can expand. The industrial society habitually ignores our embeddedness in the economy of the natural world. Ingrained cultural assumptions of 'us versus them', based on exaggerated individualism, have contracted our vistas. In order to maximise monetary profits and market share we externalise the environmental and social costs of production, blinding ourselves to the deleterious effects of our enterprises on other stakeholders in the larger 'household'. Our measurements of performance, such as quarterly reports and stock value, have too short a timeframe for much relevant feedback to occur, thus hindering self-correcting capacities of a system. We cannot perceive or respond to the unfolding consequences of our actions.

This stage of the 'work that reconnects' provides new conceptual and attitudinal tools to achieve sustainability, to help us understand the systemic, interactive, reciprocal nature of power and to help us to see our lives and work within the contexts of space and time.

Three sample exercises for this stage of the work are described below. 'Widening Circles' helps people consider important issues from perspectives other than their own (Exercise 17.3). 'The Systems Game' demonstrates systems principles through a lively physical game (Exercise 17.4). 'The Seventh Generation' facilitates the comprehension of our situation and actions through the eyes of future beings (Exercise 17.5).

This exercise helps people to consider an issue or situation of great concern from four perspectives. Thus participants widen the circle of their perception and understanding, bringing wisdom, compassion, flexibility and perseverance. The name of the exercise is taken from a poem by Rainer Marie Rilke, first published in 1905, 'I live my life in widening circles that reach out across the world' (Macy and Barrows 1996: 48).

Participants sit in groups of four. Each person chooses an issue or situation of concern. Then each person describes the issue from four perspectives, using in each case the first person ('I think', 'I feel' and so on). In this way, he or she describes: (1) his or her experience and point of view, (2) the perspective of a person whose views are different from and even adversarial to his or her own views, (3) the issue as seen by a non-human being (e.g. an animal, a plant, a river, a mountain and so on) that is involved in or affected by the situation and (4) the views of a future human whose life is affected by choices made now.

To speak on behalf of an other, and to identify even briefly with that being's experience and perspective, is an act of moral imagination. It is not difficult to do: as children we knew how to 'play-act'. People are not asked to 'channel' or be omniscient but simply to imagine another point of view. They are asked to treat each perspective with respect, avoiding caricatures or satire. This process can expand one's perceptual horizons, even beyond the specific issue addressed.

Exercise 17.3 **Third stage: 'Widening Circles'**

Source: Macy and Brown 1998

This lively, engrossing process provides a direct experience of the dynamic nature of open systems, especially: (1) that life is composed not of separate entities so much as of the relations between them and (2) that these relations are continually self-organising.

People begin in a large circle. Each participant mentally selects two other people in the group (without indicating their choice) and then moves so as to keep an equal distance between himself or herself and each of these two people. People begin to circulate to achieve this objective, each movement triggering many others in an active, interdependent fashion. Participants find they are, by necessity, maintaining wide-angle vision and constant alacrity of response. The process is purposeful, suspenseful and laced with laughter. It speeds up for a while, then may abate, accelerate and again slow down toward equilibrium, but it rarely comes to stasis. It continues for four or five minutes, then, as activity lessens, the guide invites people to pause where they are and reflect.

Participants' reflections usually bring out some key features of self-regulating systems, such as the interdependence of all parts and their continual activity in seeking and maintaining balance. Feedback, especially that from visual perceptions, is noted as necessary to fulfil the task. It also becomes obvious that no one from above or from outside could direct the complexity of movements necessary to keep this system in balance.

People also often articulate perceptual and psychological shifts they experienced, including a radically widened sense of context. A temporary eclipse of self-consciousness may be noted, as one's perceptions focus not on one's own actions so much as on those of others—that is, the focus is not on separate entities but rather on relationships among them.

Exercise 17.4 Third stage: 'The Systems Game'

Source: Macy and Brown 1998

This process expands people's sense of time, bringing them into imagined contact with human beings of the seventh generation from now. This helps them see and respect their current efforts.

Sitting in two concentric circles, people face each other in pairs, close enough to listen without distraction. Those in the outer circle (facing inwards) speak for themselves, out of their experience in the present time. They remain seated in the same place. Those in the inner circle (facing outwards) are people of the seventh generation, about 200 years from now. After each encounter, they move one place to the right, so that the inner circle moves slowly clockwise whereas the outer circle is stationary.

For each of the three encounters, the guide speaks for the representatives of the future and asks a question of the people of the present. Each present-day person responds by speaking to the future representative in front of him or her. The three questions: (1) is it really true what we hear about the wars and hunger and poverty at the beginning of the 21st century and, if so, what was that like for you? (2) What first steps did you and your colleagues take to transform society to a life-sustaining one? (3) Where did you find the strength to continue your efforts, despite all the obstacles and discouragement? As the present-day people respond, they may describe feelings they did not know they had or contributions they did not realise they were making.

After the questions, the people of the future can express their thoughts and feelings about what they have heard. Their reflections can be powerful in helping people to see their present lives and to work from the standpoint of the future. Respect and appreciation arise. In addition to expanding the concept of time, the exercise helps people imagine how they can make a difference and how they may already be contributing to a 'great turning' toward a more sustainable world.

Exercise 17.5 Third stage: 'The Seventh Generation'

Source: Macy and Brown 1998

17.3.4 Fourth stage: finding creative responses

In the last stage, we explore the synergistic power available to us as open systems as we move toward sustainability in our lives and enterprises. The experiences of the preceding stages—the recognition of our mutuality, the freeing-up of energy as we integrate previously repressed feedback and the widening of our perceptual horizons—provide a strong basis for our undertakings. In this final stage, we harness our understanding and imagination to envision a viable future; we assess our inner and outer resources and we practise planning appropriate actions in collaboration with others.

As we bring our hearts and minds together in this way—forming new systems—new possibilities and properties emerge. Hope arises as we develop visions and plans that will help us take concrete steps.

Two exercises provide a taste for this stage: 'Goals and Resources' and 'Planning Actions' (Exercises 17.6 and 17.7).

This practice helps people clarify their roles in creating sustainable businesses and brings into focus a path or project to pursue or to continue pursuing. It helps them recognise the many, often untapped, resources available and to identify steps to take.

People work in pairs. Each partner responds to the questions asked by the guide, while the other records the responses on paper. Then the speaker and scribe switch roles. People are asked to contemplate a change they want to help make in their organisations, workplaces or communities and what they could accomplish towards that vision in the coming year. They are asked to consider the inner and outer resources they have and those they need to acquire. They are asked how they may stop themselves and how they can overcome these blocks. Finally, they choose a first step to take in the next few days.

When both partners have scribed the other's responses, they take turns reporting to each other from the notes they have taken, using the second-person pronoun: 'You want to . . .', 'You have . . .', 'One way you might stop yourself . . .'. The other listens as if hearing, at long last, his or her orders from the universe.

Exercise 17.6 Fourth stage: 'Goals and Resources'

Source: Macy and Brown 1998

This exercise reveals how a group can work together and empower its members as it moves from a general or abstract goal to immediate and concrete action. The process unfolds in two stages: progressive brainstorming and role playing.

A group chooses a sustainability goal it wishes to focus on, which is posted at the top of a large sheet of newsprint. For about five minutes, the group brainstorms on what conditions this general goal would necessitate. Then the group chooses one of the ideas and brainstorms about the conditions this more specific goal would necessitate. This process continues in five-minute rounds until the goals are quite specific, so that each person could conceivably do something about one of them in the next 24 hours. From the distant goal, the group has moved to specific and immediate steps.

Now that the group has an immediate (though still hypothetical) action to undertake, people role-play the encounters this action might require such as requests that might be made, permissions that might be sought and support that might be elicited. Role playing helps move people beyond the blocks that keep some of the finest ideas trapped in the world of dreams. As the role play proceeds, participants are asked to switch roles and to continue talking, so that they experience the encounter from both points of view.

The exercise is as instructive as it is entertaining. It forces people to discover how well they can 'think on their feet' and what they need to know and say to be convincing. Moreover, role reversal in mid-conversation gives insight into the thoughts and feelings of the people one is trying to enlist. It breaks participants out of 'we–they' thinking, helps them to identify with others and enhances their confidence and effectiveness.

Exercise 17.7 **Fourth stage: 'Planning Actions'**

Source: Macy and Brown 1998

17.4 Conclusion

Countless groups of people all over the world—business people, professionals, artists, workers, college students, young and old—have engaged in the 'work that reconnects' during the past 25 years and have been inspired to work together for a more sustainable world. After the workshop, many report experiencing a visceral understanding of the interrelatedness of all life, an understanding that informs choices they make as individuals and within their various enterprises. We hope that sharing this work with business educators will enrich efforts to teach sustainability. We also hope that, whatever educational methods are employed, more attention is paid to the mental barriers we have erected to avoid painful feedback from the larger world and to the feelings that arise in response to global crises. We want to honour the deep caring and the desire to serve that exist within every human heart. For this, whole-systems learning is needed. The heart and mind together hold the key to a more sustainable way of life for everyone.

References

Bateson, G. (1972) *Steps to an Ecology of Mind* (New York: Ballentine).

Berman, M. (1984) *The Reenchantment of the World* (New York: Bantam).

Buckley, W. (1968) *Modern Systems Research for the Behavioural Scientist* (New York: Aldine).

Capra, F. (1996) *The Web of Life: A New Scientific Understanding of Living Systems* (New York: Anchor).

Hawken, P. (1995) *The Ecology of Commerce: A Declaration of Sustainability* (New York: HarperCollins).

Johnson, H.T,. and A. Bröms (2000) *Profit beyond Measure: Extraordinary Results through Attention to Work and People* (New York: Simon & Schuster).

Laszlo, E. (1972) *Introduction to Systems Philosophy: Toward a New Paradigm of Contemporary Thought* (New York: Gordon & Breach).

—— (1972) *The Systems View of the World* (New York: George Braziller).

Macy, J.R. (1991) *Mutual Causality in Buddhism and General Systems Theory: The Dharma of Living Systems* (Albany, NY: State University of New York Press).

—— and A. Barrows (1996) *Rilke's Book of Hours* (New York: Riverhead Books).

—— and M.Y. Brown (1998) *Coming Back to Life: Practices to Reconnect Our Lives, Our World* (Gabriola Island, BC, Canada: New Society Publishers).

Olds, L. (1992) *Metaphors of Interrelatedness* (Albany, NY: State University of New York Press).

Sahtouris, E. (1989) *Gaia: The Human Journey from Chaos to Cosmos* (New York: Simon & Schuster).

Von Bertalanffy, L. (1968) *General System Theory* (New York: George Braziller).

Wheatley, M.J. (1992) *Leadership and the New Science: Learning about Organizations from an Orderly Universe* (San Francisco: Berrett-Koehler).

18

Corporate education programmes for sustainable business
Communicating beyond the green wall

Trudy Heller
Executive Education for the Environment, USA

Environmental managers often speak of the need to disseminate sustainable business thinking throughout a company, of communicating beyond the 'green wall'. Some refer to this process as an organisational 'sea change'. Others have noted that the introduction of sustainable business thinking 'cannot be done by fiat. It must be top-down . . . *and* bottom-up' (Source 1).[1] In another's words, 'It's about [whole] organisational learning, not pockets of groups making progress and others not' (Source 2).

With these statements in mind, in summer 2001 I conducted a pilot survey of ten companies from a variety of industries (see Table 18.1). In addition, I interviewed a communications director at the Volvo Group headquarters in Gothenburg, Sweden. I set out to discover how companies were educating employees about doing business in an environmentally sustainable way. What activities and programmes were supporting the kinds of organisational changes cited above?

I discovered a range of educational programmes across industries and companies. These programmes varied in terms of the content and the delivery methods of the programmes and the extent of employee participation. I also found, significantly, that companies share common concerns about how best to achieve learning goals.

Sound educational rationales underlie these programmes. Corporate-sponsored educational programmes can send a message that top management believes in the importance of environmental initiatives. Employees who have some ecological

1   Details of sources are given at the end of the chapter.

Company	Classification[a]	Web address of environmental statement
Bethlehem Steel Corporation	Iron and steel mill	n/a
The Coca-Cola Company	Beverage and food manufacturing	www.environmentalreport2002.coca-cola.com
DuPont	Chemicals and plastics manufacturing, synthetic fibres, agricultural products	www.dupont.com → Social Commitment → Safety, Health and Environment
Electrolux AB	Household and commercial appliances	ir.electrolux.com/html/environmentalreport2002
Hewlett-Packard Company	Computer and peripheral equipment manufacturing	www.hp.com/hpinfo/globalcitizenship/ environment/index.html
Patagonia	Outdoor clothing, technical apparel and gear	www.patagonia.com/enviro/main_enviro_ action.shtml
Pfizer Inc.	Pharmaceutical preparation manufacturing	www.pfizer.com/ehs
Sunoco Inc.	Petroleum refineries and products	www.sunocoinc.com/health_env_safety
Starbucks Corporation	Coffee manufacturing	www.starbucks.com/aboutus/envaffairs.asp
Volvo AB	Transportation equipment manufacturing	www.volvo.com/group/global/en-gb/career/ volvovalues/environmentcare

a All industry designations, except that of Patagonia, are as listed in the North American Industry Classification System (US OMB 1997).

Table 18.1 Companies surveyed and industries represented

literacy can be more conscientious implementers of an environmental management system (EMS). Employees who are knowledgeable about the impact of their business on the environment can be engaged in the challenge of solving environmental problems in a way that also supports the bottom line.

I have constructed a prototype that combines elements of various programmes into a curriculum that is ideal for educators because it prepares participants to become active partners in achieving sustainable business practices (Barnes *et al.* 1994). It begins with the 'big picture' of the Earth and its carrying capacity. Then, the activities of the particular business and their impacts on ecosystems are placed in this context. Finally, the specific role of the employee in addressing environmental problems is spelled out. The description of this prototypical programme is followed by common challenges companies faced when implementing employee education.

18.1 Programme content

18.1.1 Prepare the ground

No one can learn in any basic sense from another . . . unless the learner is actively and imaginatively receptive.

Charles I. Gragg (1940), quoted in Barnes *et al.* 1994: 15

Questions posed

- Why the environment?
- Why now?

Overview

Harvard Business School educator Barnes and co-workers (Barnes *et al.* 1994) are clear that active participation of students is required for learning. The goal of education for sustainable business is for employees to learn new ways of thinking about connections between the natural environment and their business. Employees can be prepared by addressing obstacles to learning. Obstacles may come as scepticism—or downright denial—that environmental problems exist or as a viewpoint that sees business and environmental interests as incompatible. Companies in my sample create readiness for learning in their employees in various ways.

Volvo's Dialogue for the Environment programme (Volvo 1999: 5) confronts employees with the statement 'Working for the environment is not just a fashionable trend. It is a natural part of the work of many companies.' This statement acknowledges employees' scepticism that the training they are required to undergo may just be 'flavour-of-the-month' management. With this statement, trainers demonstrate that they are connecting to employees where they are—sceptical attitudes and all. Management thus begins to create a new vision of building a sustainable business—a process that will continue in the future—and scepticism about the environment theme as a passing fad diminishes.

Another company, Patagonia, holds a company-wide, worldwide workshop once a year on environmental issues. These events cover the company's core values and a statement of purpose as well as a current topic each year. Sessions are on-site in small groups. Attendance is mandatory. The widespread and mandatory attendance requirement announces the value that this company's management attaches to environmental performance. These events serve to reinforce environmental values as significant aspects of the company's culture.

Bethlehem Steel uses a video in which the CEO introduces training sessions on environmental initiatives. This strategy conveys the message that environmental performance is a priority of the top leaders of the company.

The CEO may, indeed, be in the best position to articulate a vision of sustainable development for the company. Lief Johansson, CEO of the Volvo Group, presents a vision of the future of transportation. He emphasises his belief that the developing world cannot be industrialised with the same technologies and making the same environmental footprint of the developed countries. 'History cannot be allowed to repeat itself,' Johansson states. 'The largest cities [of developing countries] need to develop a transportation industry without repeating bad history' (Source 3).

Johansson also noted his company's strategy of developing the next generation of transportation technology, stating, 'We refuse to sell the old technology of the West to the developing world. We are beginning to see demand for skill jumping in the developing world. There is no demand for old systems.'

Goal in preparing the ground

The goal of this introductory part of the programme is to create a vision of business as a partner working toward environmental sustainability. This positive vision sets the context for some of the gloomy material about the state of the environment in the next section.

18.1.2 Develop ecological literacy

> **We tend to focus on snapshots of isolated parts of the system, and wonder why our deepest problems never seem to get solved**
>
> Peter Senge (1990: 7)

Question posed

- Why should business be concerned about the natural environment?

Overview

An ideal programme progresses to 'environmental literacy'. This part of the programme reviews some of the basics of ecological science. Included may be material on ecosystems, carbon cycles, photosynthesis, the hydrological cycle and thermodynamics. This basic ecological literacy forms the foundation for understanding how human industrial activity may have disrupted natural cycles. Volvo, for example, includes information on some of the most publicised environmental problems, such as climate change, air and water pollution, acid rain and decline in biodiversity.

This material appeals especially to engineers and other technical or research personnel who may need to 'see the science' behind environmental initiatives. The lead trainer at Volvo noted that her background as a chemist lent credibility to this part of its programme. Other employees may benefit from a focus on the basic, least controversial aspects such as the notion that we are using natural resources at a rate that exceeds the Earth's carrying capacity. This idea reinforces the theme of part one: that the environment problem is real and will extend into the future. It is not a passing fad.

Striking a balance between informing and overwhelming participants with gloomy information about the state of the Earth is important. Volvo uses light-hearted cartoon-style drawings to illustrate its written material on 'Nature's ABCs' (Volvo 1999). Bethlehem Steel emphasised the importance of using face-to-face groups in order to assess reactions (including body language) of participants. Some companies use off-the-shelf tools such as The Natural Step or the CERES Principles for this part of the curriculum. The Natural Step is a framework that guides a company through a stepwise process from understanding the unsustainable nature of society's current condition to integrating sustainable business thinking into its strategy (Nattrass and Altomare 1999). CERES, the Coalition for Environmentally Responsible Economies, is an alliance of investor, environmental, labour and public-interest groups that works to enlist companies to adopt its ten principles of sustainable business practices (CERES 2002).

Other companies develop their own in-house materials. Volvo's programme, Dialogue for the Environment, covers environmental science topics, such as photosynthesis, cell respiration and ecosystems. Hewlett-Packard, Pfizer and Starbucks include material on environmental issues in orientation sessions for new employees. DuPont runs a one-day session for product stewards from each of 90 business units that focuses on stewardship of the Earth, life-cycle analysis and designing to eliminate environmental impact. Patagonia sends people out into the environmental community on voluntary internships. The interns then report back to Patagonia, keeping the company up to date on emerging issues.

Goal in developing ecological literacy

The goal of this part of the curriculum is to create awareness of the impact of human, industrial activity on the Earth and to stir in participants a sense of urgency to change industrial practices to lighten the environmental footprint of business activity (Holland 2003).

18.1.3 Relate environmental problems to the company's business

Question posed

- What is the environmental footprint of our business?

Overview

A second content area is more directly related to the particular company and industry in question. This part of the curriculum concentrates the focus on the more general knowledge of the previous section onto the particular environmental issues most relevant to the business at hand. Volvo's Dialogue for the Environment training manual, for example, notes, 'Transport accounts for one half of oil consumption', and that '[the] new situation calls for a new approach' (Volvo 1999: 32). It outlines the use of buses in developing countries, such as Mexico, India and Brazil. Starbucks teaches employees about shade-grown coffee and how sourcing this type of coffee bean helps to prevent loss of rainforests and the biodiversity supported by those ecosystems. Patagonia's employees learn how the growing of organic cotton avoids the problems created by pesticide use in the cultivation of inorganic cotton.

Goal in relating environmental problems to company business

The goal of this part of the curriculum is to enable employees to understand the rationale for the environmental initiatives they will be asked to implement. Also, this material may potentially engage employees in the process of dreaming up creative solutions to environmental problems that the business is now facing and that it will face in the future.

18.1.4 Provide information specific to an employee's role

Questions posed

- What systems are in place to lessen the footprint of our business?
- What specific role do I play in its implementation?

Overview

This part of the curriculum varies depending on the job of the employee. An engineer may need instructions for implementing an EMS. A marketing manager may need a briefing on the latest research concerning green consumers. New product developers need information on sourcing materials that can be recycled or biodegraded at the end of the product life-cycle. Messages may be tailored to the role of the particular employee.

At Hewlett-Packard, for example, an environmental strategy and business solution council brings together representatives from different business disciplines under a global manager:

> So to marketing we talk about customer expectations, to [an] R&D manager we talk about customers' concerns about energy performance, to services and support we talk about product take-back. We tailor the message to each group (Source 4).

Environment staff at Sunoco talk with maintenance people to initiate thinking about how to redesign equipment to prevent environmentally damaging leaks and spills. Pfizer has developed a matrix of 'jobs × information'. According to the type of job, employees will receive the information they need. Starbucks sends people to conferences relevant to their field of expertise. A design professional, for example, talked to peers in design. He came back with new 'green' specifications for the headquarters building.

Goal in providing information specific to an employee's role

The goal of this part of the curriculum is for employees to understand their role in diminishing the company's environmental footprint and to gain the specific knowledge they need to do their part.

18.2 Challenges

No well-worn roadmap exists for these programmes. Companies in the survey faced common dilemmas. In the following I highlight the most frequently voiced concerns.

18.2.1 Why not just skip to the last phase? Isn't that all you need?

Environmental managers participating at the 2001 Environment Conference[2] emphasise that technical training is not enough to inspire a 'culture change' and sustainable thinking among employees. Technical requirements of an EMS may be carried out in a perfunctory way when employees do not fully understand why they are being asked to help create a more sustainable business. Although technically trained, they may lack the motivation to 'go the extra mile'. Furthermore, they may not be thinking about how to improve environmental performance continuously.

18.2.2 How do you alter the content and delivery of programmes to accommodate employees at different levels of the organisation?

Most companies noted differences in programmes targeted for upper management and for 'rank-and-file' employees. Executive management programmes often had an off-site component. At DuPont, attendees at an annual management seminar

2 The conference, which took place in April 2001 in New York, was titled 'Sustainable Development and Corporate Power: Products as Change Agents' and was presented by The Conference Board and the World Business Council for Sustainable Development.

tour a site of environmental interest, such as a New England fishery, to learn about how another community solved its environmental problems. Luncheon speakers also provided a common delivery methods for executive education. Pfizer schedules luncheons for upper management with speakers on environmental topics. Managers at Starbucks are self-selected to receive training as a member of the company 'Green Team'.

For lower- and middle-level employees, Volvo and Bethlehem Steel used a 'train-the-trainers' strategy. Programmes were first developed at corporate headquarters by communications staff. Employees from different operating units were then trained by corporate staff to facilitate groups of employee learners.

18.2.3 Which works best? Face-to-face sessions or putting material on the intranet?

In the beginning, face-to-face contact is preferable. Educators and participating employees are on a steep learning curve at this stage. At Bethlehem Steel, for example, communications professionals quickly learned to avoid the term 'sustainable development' by watching the eyes of participants glaze over when these words were spoken—visual cues that would be lost with an intranet programme.

Later, when the programme is more established, a company's intranet may be used with successful learning outcomes. Electrolux, for example, relies on the company intranet for its environmental education programme, Eco Know How.[3] At Bethlehem Steel, learning modules are posted on the intranet *after* they have been presented in face-to-face sessions. Hewlett-Packard uses the intranet to post timely information rather than conceptual material and for manuals, such as environmental standards worldwide. Patagonia has an electronic bulletin board regarding the environment for posting current developments.

18.2.4 How do I know if my programme is effective? How can I assess learning outcomes?

Outcome assessment was on the wish list at some companies. Examples of assessment procedures were evident at others. At Starbucks, environmental concerns are part of the budget process. A budget review will ask, 'What are you doing to advance the goal of diminishing the environmental footprint?' Bethlehem Steel interviews employees after training sessions. It also has a link on the intranet website that allows employees to ask questions which are then used to revise the training curriculum. Sunoco uses pilot programmes to launch and fine-tune new educational initiatives. Volvo uses written assessments to compare participants' knowledge before and after its programme.

3   www2.electrolux.se/prod/public/c99ecweb.nsf

18.2.5 I don't have a programme.
Where is the best place to begin?

A large part of the art of instruction lies in making the difficulty of new problems large enough to challenge thought, and small enough so that, in addition to the confusion naturally attending the novel elements, there shall be luminous familiar spots from which helpful suggestions may spring.

John Dewey (1916), quoted in Barnes *et al.* 1994: 11

Begin with something that makes sense for your company. New ideas are more easily assimilated when connected to the familiar. Several companies found ways to connect ideas about sustainable business to existing core values and capabilities.

At Coca-Cola, environmental issues are discussed during training sessions for customer service employees that staff the 1-800-GET-COKE hotline. These employees must be prepared to answer callers' questions about recycling and other environmental issues. DuPont had a strong corporate value: safety. Its environmental initiatives have progressed from a focus on worker safety to include notions of the health of the planet. Other companies have well-developed programmes on corporate social responsibility. Environmental issues are approached first as one aspect of social responsibility along with the sponsoring of community events or philanthropic giving. As experience demonstrates that environmental initiatives can be healthy for business, the company may develop an independent focus on environmental goals and programmes.

Volvo used employee environmental education as preparation for and an adjunct to training for certification to ISO 14000 series standards. They believe that this was the best way to start. The Director of Core Value Communication at Volvo states:

> This [education] programme came before the start of the ISO 14000 process which I think is the right thing. If you have the facts [about environmental problems] and you have understood the facts, then you can start questioning what are we really doing. That questioning of what are we actually doing is an excellent start for the environmental management system (Source 5).

The experience at Volvo clearly suggests that the Dialogue for the Environment programme lay the groundwork for subsequent successful implementation of ISO (International Organisation for Standardisation) standards. Once every employee was versed in the state of environmental problems, this awareness remained in the company culture. Rather than repeat the entire programme for each new employee, Volvo continued to use the EMS within the ISO 14000 series as a diagnostic tool to determine what basic environmental education employees may need. Different units of the organisation may proceed differently. Basic environmental education materials are provided, and business units use them as they see fit. Since training for EMS implementation is mandatory, the simpler sustainable business educational materials are an easy adjunct.

18.3 Conclusions

The programmes studied in the survey suggest significant movement forward in teaching corporate sustainability and communicating beyond the 'green wall'. Although no single company has a programme that is ideal, exciting and promising, experimental trials are under way. The elements of an educationally sound programme are 'scattered about', but the outlines of a clear, relevant and effective curriculum can be discerned. The goal is to educate employees to understand the general, big picture of our unsustainable world and, more specifically, the roles to be played by themselves and their businesses in developing more sustainable practices. The ideal outcome is employees who are partners working together to solve the problem of enhancing business while diminishing its environmental footprint.

Two themes emerge from this that suggest guidelines for teaching sustainability to employees. First, the approach that a company takes must be consistent with its culture and values. The environment problem can be framed variously: as a matter of health and safety, as a way of expressing concern about the community, as focused on customers, as part of a global strategy, as preparation for ISO implementation and so on. The chosen framework must make sense for a particular company. Second, dilemmas in implementing strategies were common across the companies. The development of mechanisms to compare notes across companies would prevent the inefficiency of each company reinventing the wheel. Furthermore, this cross-fertilisation would help hasten the ultimate goal of organisations, individually and collectively, to achieve true and lasting change.

References

Barnes, L.B., C.R. Christensen and A.J. Hansen (1994) *Teaching and the Case Method* (Boston, MA: Harvard Business School Press, 3rd edn).

CERES (Coalition for Environmentally Responsible Economies) (2002) *CERES Performance Review of General Motors Corporation* (Boston, MA: CERES, January 2002).

Dewey, J. (1916) *Democracy and Education* (Macmillan, repr. 1944).

Gragg, C.I. (1940) 'Teachers Also Must Learn', *Harvard Educational Review*, January 1940.

Holland, L. (2003) 'Can the Principle of the Ecological Footprint Be Applied to Measure the Environmental Sustainability of Business?', *Corporate Social Responsibility and Environmental Management* 10: 224-32.

Nattrass, B., and A. Altomare (1999) *The Natural Step for Business: Wealth, Ecology and the Evolutionary Corporation* (Gabriola Island, BC, Canada: New Society Publishers).

Senge, P.M. (1990) *The Fifth Discipline: The Art and Practice of the Learning Organization* (New York: Currency Doubleday).

US OMB (US Office of Management and Budget) (1997) *North American Industry Classification System* (Washington, DC: US OMB).

Volvo (1999) *The Environment and Volvo* (www.volvo.com/group/global/en-gb/career/volvovalues/environmentcare/management).

Sources

Source 1: speaker at The Environment Conference on 'Sustainable Development and Corporate Power: Products as Change Agents', presented by The Conference Board and the World Business Council for Sustainable Development, New York, April 2001.

Source 2: speaker at The Environment Conference on 'Sustainable Development and Corporate Power: Products as Change Agents', presented by The Conference Board and the World Business Council for Sustainable Development, New York, April 2001.

Source 3: Lief Johansson, CEO of the Volvo Group, keynote speech at the International Greening of Industry Network Conference 2002, Gothenburg, Sweden.

Source 4: author's telephone interview with manager at Hewlett-Packard, 27 August 2001.

Source 5: author's interview with the Director of Core Value Communication, Volvo, Gothenburg, Sweden, 2002.

19
The neo-Socratic dialogue
A method of teaching the ethics of sustainable development

Beate Littig
Institute for Advanced Studies, Austria

19.1 Sustainability, ethics and business

Business enterprises are increasingly regarded as important actors in relation to sustainable development. Development towards sustainable business is fostered by the dissemination of business rankings based on corporate sustainability indices, which assess a corporation's overall sustainability performance. The sustainability indices demand sustainable products and services, ecological management, social and ecological reporting, codes of conduct, equal rights for men and women, non-discrimination and so on. Consequently, some business enterprises have started to establish sustainability groups or centres, sustainability reporting and corporate value management (Kitson and Campbell 1996; Wieland 2001) to cope with these challenges.[1]

These trends provoke the questions whether and how managers and business students are prepared and trained for the necessary shift of awareness of sustainability within business enterprises. There seems to be little research on these questions and, as recently reported by Baue (2002), the pictures painted by current studies on corporate social responsibility (CSR) in MBA programmes in the USA are rather conflicting:

> The National Social Venture Competition portrays an optimistic view, as MBA students from 31 business schools across the USA sub-

1 See e.g. www.globalreporting.org, www.corporateregister.com and www.sustainability-reports.com.

mitted business plans that redefine profitability to include social and environmental as well as financial returns.

The winners of the National Social Venture Competition, who received generous awards of seed capital, were announced in April 2002.[2]

A less rosy portrait of the treatment of CSR in MBA programmes emerged in a report entitled *Where Will They Lead? MBA Student Attitudes about Business and Society*, released in January 2002 as part of the Initiative for Social Innovation through Business (ISIB) of the Aspen Institute. The study reported that many MBA students are not taught what 'social responsibility' is and, furthermore, that they perceived a 'disconnect' between business priorities and social issues in MBA curricula. The students surveyed voiced interest in seeing social issues integrated into the core curriculum, instead of relegated to electives' (Baue 2002)

Taking the students' complaints seriously, one has to take a closer look at the question of how social responsibility—a core ethical issue of CSR and of sustainable development—can be taught? Or, more generally, we can say that, taking the ethical demands for sustainable corporate performance seriously, one must ensure that the practising and teaching of sustainability comprises ethical reflections on the relevant moral ideas of sustainable development. Since the concept of sustainable development is strongly bound to moral principles (e.g. social justice, human dignity, human rights, ethical concepts of a good life and of solidarity; Littig 2001; Pepper 1996), how can the ethics of sustainability be taught in a business context?

In this chapter I put forward neo-Socratic dialogue (NSD) as a didactic method to communicate fundamental ethical questions about sustainable development in business training and enterprises. Furthermore, I will give an overview on this method and its application to teaching the ethics of sustainable development. In addition to describing the conceptional background to the NSD I will present a case study of an NSD conducted with an interdisciplinary group of students at the University of Vienna, Austria.

19.2 What is a neo-Socratic dialogue?

19.2.1 General characterisation

An NSD is an inquiry into ideas that is intended to find consensus on some topic through a joint deliberation and weighing-up of arguments. The dialogue aims at visioning, explaining values and clarifying fundamental concepts. It implies a systematic investigation of our assumptions, reasons and viewpoints and a co-operative testing of their validity. In the dialogue, participants attempt to formulate legitimate principles and develop a shared and inspiring perspective (Nelson 1922, 1965; Heckmann 1993). Participants do not need specialised or expert knowledge of the question at stake.

---

2   For details, see www.socialvc.net.

A second aim of NSD is to improve dialogical capabilities (such as listening to each other, referring to each other, tolerance, striving for mutual understanding) of the participants. This requires adequate command of a number of dialogical roles, skills and attitudes, in particular the suspension of judgements and the need to keep a balance between taking a position and submitting to another view.

Both aims of the NSD are intimately connected to the development of strategy, organisational learning and knowledge management. These concepts demand the ability to set up dialogues or conversational inquiries to build shared visions of value systems, goals and missions rather than scientific knowledge (Kessels 1996). These aims are relevant in different contexts where the NSD has been applied successfully, such as in organisational learning (Kessels 1996), business ethics (Kessels 1997, 2001), medical ethics (Birnbacher 1999), university teaching (Birnbacher 1982; Gronke and Stary 1998; Heckmann 1993; Kleinknecht 1989; Littig 1999), participatory technology assessment (Grießler and Littig 2002) and in primary education (Murris 2000; Weierstraß 1967; Neisser and Saran 2004).

An NSD is focused on a single fundamental (ethical or philosophical) question. This question should concern basic, essential matters. It should be non-empirical—that is, it should be answerable purely by thinking. It must be formulated in a plain and simple way (not piling up complicated concepts). For the participants, something should be at stake in searching for an answer. The question needs to be an urgent one. It must be possible for the participants to find examples from their own experience in which the question plays a central role. An NSD is applied to a concrete experience of one of the participants that is accessible to all other participants. Systematic reflection on this experience is accompanied by a search for shared judgements and underlying reasons for these.

Note that, with reference to Senge (1990) and Kessels (1996), a dialogue is not to be confused with a discussion:

> In a discussion participants propound opinions, aiming at winning, convincing others, having one's view accepted by the group. A dialogue, on the other hand, is a real communication, an exchange of questions and answers, aiming at joint reflection. The purpose of a dialogue is to go beyond any one's individual understanding, and thereby gaining insights that simply could not be achieved individually. In a dialogue 'a new kind of mind begins to come into being, which is based on the development of a common meaning '(Kessels 1996: 55).

19.2.2 Socratic questions of sustainable development in a business context

As discussed above, the starting point of an NSD is a fundamental philosophical or ethical question. In the case of corporate sustainable development examples of such questions, and the reasons for the choice of these questions, are as follows:

● What does it mean to improve the quality of life? The social dimension of sustainable development is very often associated with improving the quality of life, including not only environmental conditions but also overall working and living conditions. Sustainable products and services contribute to higher standards of living. This relates, for example, to a company's product policy: looking for new (sustainable) commodities and reflecting more deeply on the meaning of the term 'quality of life' (usually a rather vague concept) can be helpful.

- Is luxury unnecessary? Sustainable development is very often associated with the idea of renunciation and of practising a lifestyle of simplicity—a way of living that is not appealing to many people. The reflection on the meaning of luxury can help to find adequate marketing strategies to sell sustainable products or services. (For the example of car-sharing concepts is it not luxurious to have the use of a car without the obligation to maintain it?) Alternatively, reflection on this question might help in the discovery of a corporate mission statement that focuses on the production of sustainable luxury instead of sustainable simplicity.

- What does participation in the context of business enterprises mean? 'Participation'—of all stakeholders—is one of the keywords of sustainable development. However, it is rather unclear as to what participation means. Is participation limited to information-sharing? Does it comprise certain decision-making rights of employees and workers and of customers too?

- Why should business enterprises seek solidarity with the 'weak'? CSR and to a certain extent solidarity with the weak—those having fewer resources and less power—are some of the underlying assumptions of many sustainable business indices, but what does it mean to act according to social responsibility or to solidarity? Why should it be aspired to?

- Under what circumstances does individual benefit justify collective risk? This question is fundamental for sustainable development. The question addresses the free-rider problem at all levels and scopes—in terms of individuals, organisations and corporations.

These questions concern tacit matters and fundamental beliefs that cannot be handled on an operational level. They cannot be answered by scientific investigation alone. They require thorough consideration and weighing of arguments in a dialogue such as the NSD (Kessels 1996). What is Socratic in the NSD is the method of rigorous inquiry into the thoughts, concepts and values we hold as true. The NSD is a joint investigation into the assumptions we make when we formulate our thoughts.

19.2.3 The course of the neo-Socratic dialogue

An NSD follows the procedure given below:

- Before the discourse begins, a well-formulated, general question is asked.

- The first step is to collect concrete examples experienced by participants in which the given question plays a key role.

- The group selects one example that will be the basis of the analysis and argumentation throughout the dialogue. This analysis usually starts with a concrete judgement based on the selected example and relating to the original question of the dialogue.

- In the course of the dialogue the participants examine this judgement or statement step by step with regard to its validity. This thorough examination of arguments is called 'regressive abstraction' and is explained below.

From an epistemological perspective, the NSD is guided by the idea of regressive abstraction. This means that individual reason is gained from a concrete judgement and personal experience (Nelson 1965). According to argumentation theory, concrete judgements must be backed by more general rules or principles at a higher level than the judgement itself (see e.g. Toulmin 1958). The idea of regressive abstraction can be illustrated by the hourglass model illustrated in Figure 19.1 (Kessels 1997, 2001: 205). The hourglass illustrates the change between different levels of abstraction: being rather general in phase 1, becoming increasingly concrete in phases 2 and 3, and becoming again more general in phases 4 and 5.

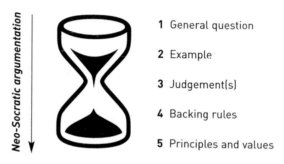

Neo-Socratic argumentation

1 General question

2 Example

3 Judgement(s)

4 Backing rules

5 Principles and values

Figure 19.1 Regressive abstraction: the hourglass model

The general question is the starting point and focus of the dialogue. The example gives relevant facts, circumstances and actions or decisions that have been taken in a given case. The judgement represents a standpoint to be examined. The rules give reasons for the judgement. The principles and values give reasons for the rule(s). The aim of this Socratic dialogue is to find out these backing rules and to discuss the validity of the rules and principles in relation to the particular example.

The NSD should be conducted by a trained facilitator.[3] This facilitator has the

3 Most authorised facilitators for NSD complete academic training before they start their training as facilitators (for further information on training, see www.philosophisch-politische-akademie.de, with links to training facilities in various countries all over the world). This training is based on a (minimum) of two years' experience as a participant in NSD. The practical and theoretical facilitator training lasts an additional two to three years and is supervised by an experienced facilitator (mentor). Qualifications emphasised in the training include: pedagogic competence, democratic attitude, discourse ethics, psychological sense, awareness of group dynamics and result orientation.

following tasks to carry out. She or he must: ensure that participants understand each other, refer to their own experience, proceed step by step, remain focused on the issue, participate equally in the dialogue, explain their contributions thoroughly, substantiate their judgements, strive for consensus and make progress in the dialogue. Moreover, the facilitator documents the reasoning of the dialogue, noting the steps of the argumentation on a flipchart. She or he does not contribute directly to the content of the dialogue. The number of participants is limited from a minimum of 5 to a maximum of 15.

The participants in an NSD must abide by the following rules:

- Each participant's contribution is to be based on what she or he has experienced, not on what she or he has read or heard.

- The thinking and questioning are to be honest. This means that only genuine doubts about what has been said should be expressed.

- It is the responsibility of all participants to express their thoughts as clearly and concisely as possible, so that everyone is able to build on the ideas contributed by others earlier in the dialogue.

- Participants should not concentrate exclusively on their own thoughts. They should make every effort to understand those of the other participants and, if necessary, seek clarification.

- Anyone who has lost sight of the question or the thread of the discussion should seek the help of others to clarify where the group stands.

- Abstract statements should be grounded in concrete experience in order to illuminate such statements.

- Inquiry into relevant questions continues as long as participants have not yet reached a point of clarity (either in terms of a shared position or in terms of clearly expressed differences of contradicting viewpoints).

19.3 Neo-Socratic dialogue in practice: a case study

The NSD described below formed part of a university seminar on environmental sociology at the University of Vienna in 2001. This course included units on risk theories, risk society and technology studies as well as covering basic ideas of sustainable development.[4]

One aim of the NSD is to give the students the chance to improve their cognitive capability regarding arguing by building up systematically and step by step an argumentation on the issues at stake. The NSD was also presented as a method for working on the ethical implications of sustainable development with philosophi-

---

4 Although the dialogue was not conducted with business students, it provides insight into the idea and course of an NSD.

cal laypeople (i.e. people who do not have specialised philosophical training or that do not hold an academic degree in philosophy). Six students and a Socratic facilitator participated (the rest of the group [i.e. those who were not present in the first session of the NSD], observed the dialogue with regard to the interaction, the process and the outcome of the dialogue). The NSD lasted nine hours (three sessions of three hours each). None of the participants had experienced an NSD before. The question that the students choose was: 'Under what circumstances does individual benefit justify collective risk?'

As usual, the dialogue started with personal examples from the participants' experiences. The list given in Table 19.1 includes the keywords of their examples.

Number	Example
1	Using public transport without buying a ticket
2	Riding a motorcycle while drunk
3	Smoking cigarettes at a private (non-smoker) party
4	Using the car to drive children a short distance to school
5	Sending kids to school despite the fact they have a cold
6	Driving a car without having a driving licence
7	Skiing in an area where snow-slip is highly probable

Table 19.1 Neo-Socratic dialogue: the examples given by the group, taken from their personal experience, in answer to the question 'Under what circumstances does individual benefit justify collective risk?'

Discussing the experiences with regard to their differences and similarities the list given in Table 19.2 of the individual benefit and the collective risk was made.

The example that was selected for further analysis—that of using the car for taking children a short distance to school—is illustrated Figure 19.2, showing the lines of argumentation that were elaborated throughout the dialogue.[5] This particular choice of example was made for two main reasons: the clarity of the situation and the easy comprehensiveness of the situation. All participants could easily imagine the situation described by the example-giver.

As can be seen from Figure 19.2, the analysis of the selected example commenced with the example-giver's judgement on his behaviour. The group decided to start with the issue of comfort and time-saving benefit in the judgement and then to proceed with the health component. During the dialogue the group divided into two camps: one following a more ecological line of argumentation (position A), the other following a more human-centred, pragmatic line (position B). Despite the different starting points both positions accepted the necessity of environmental protection on the one hand and the consideration of pragmatic constraints on the other. What could not be discussed further was the degree of admissible environmental damage with respect to everyday constraints. In a final step, the

---

5   The following analysis of the dialogue was carried out by Peter Brune and me.

Example number	Individual benefit	Collective risk
1	Saves money	Others have to pay more
2	Fun, comfort	Risk of accident
3	Smoking with relish, fun	Risk to health of oneself and others
4	Comfort, time-saving	Air pollution
5	Comfort, stress reduction	Risk to health of other children
6	Fun	Risk of accident
7	Fun	Risk of snow-slip and risk to health and property of others

Table 19.2 Selecting the individual benefit and the collective risk from the examples listed in Table 19.1

different lines of argumentation were applied to the other examples that were given at the beginning of the seminar (see Tables 19.1 and 19.2).

The result of the dialogue might appear trivial to the reader, but the success should not be judged by the content of the argumentation alone. It is unlikely that the NSD will lead to extraordinary new ideas (although this might happen). What is extraordinary about the NSD is its systematic way of common investigation and argumentation within a group of people. This process is consensus-oriented. Usually, consensus can be reached concerning single questions, sometimes also in the backing arguments or rules, but even if no consensus is reached the dialogue produces clear results: namely, systematic argumentation of the different views. Usually, this helps participants to gain new insights and to understand other positions better.

The students' comments on this NSD were very positive. The students greatly appreciated the process of thinking carefully through each statement in detail. They experienced a lively dialogue in which they systematically elaborated an argument, after being directly confronted with the comments of others. They also mentioned positively their emotional involvement and the respectful treatment they received in the discussion. They also gained self-assurance, in the sense that they trusted more in their capability to think on their own. Critically, they remarked that nine hours as planned for the dialogue was not enough. They wished to have one or two more sessions to discuss their examples in more detail.[6]

6   With regard to business applications of the NSD it has to be stated that time limits are often a problem (Kessels 1997, 2001; Grießler and Littig 2003). Once the dialogue has started, participants often get very sophisticated in investigating the questions and arguments presented in the group. Thorough investigation (even in a dialogical manner) needs time. Consequently, the NSD should last for at least three or four hours. To cope with time restrictions the facilitator can use some accelerating strategies, such as asking participants to prepare examples in advance according to a certain structure, limiting the number of examples, concentrating on one line of argumentation and so on.

Socratic question

Under what circumstances does individual benefit justify collective risk?

Experience or example

Yesterday I took my son J. to the car, which was parked five minutes' walking distance from our home. We collected my wife and my son L. from home and drove to the nursery school which is about 500 metres away from our house. We dropped our children at the nursery school. Then my wife and I drove about 700 metres to a parking area and took the public train to commute to work. I saved about 15 minutes (compared with walking). Beside the time-saving effect, comfort was another reason for my decision to take the car. I am aware of the environmental problems caused by short drives.

Concrete judgement

I think that my 'short-distance shuttle service' is justified because

a I would otherwise use public transport and not use the car very much.

b The time and co-ordination needed by parents is high, and time saving relieves pressure on parents.

c It is easier to go by car with two little children than to walk with them.

d I do not have to walk through the cold air with the children.

Rules and conditions

1. Comfort: (b) and (c) in the judgement

Position A:
Comfort does not justify the air pollution created through the example-giver's car drive. (The damage, resulting from the car drive in the reported situation is too big to justify the comfort.)

Position B:
Comfort justifies the short-distance car drive.

2. Health: (d) in the judgement

Position A:
Concern for children's health does not justify the air pollution.

Position B:
Acute risk to the children's health justifies my car drive.

Specifications

1. Comfort: (b) and (c) in the judgement

Position A:
Should not be done except in certain circumstances (e.g. it is really cold, or there is 'real' stress).

Position B:
Can be done until existing air pollution increases dramatically.

Explications

2. Health: (d) in the judgement

Position A:
Children's health could be strengthened through walking.

Position B:
There is a relevant difference between an 'acute risk' and a 'mere creeping risk' of catching a cold.

Backing rules and conditions

Position A:
Position A looks on the question from a strict environmental point of view: avoiding environmental damage is valued very highly in this position. Individual behaviour has in principle to be oriented towards this goal.

Position B:
Position B starts from the individual benefit side of the question: achieving individual benefit (comfort, health, time savings) is justified in principle (at least for parents of young children).

Explications

Specifications

Position A:
Only in a few, exceptional, cases can environmental damages be accepted.

Position B:
There are certain limitations through special thresholds of environmental pollution.

Figure 19.2 Case study of new-Socratic dialogue based on the question, 'Under what circumstances does individual benefit justify collective risk?': lines of argumentation for using the car for taking children a short distance to school

19.4 Concluding remarks on using neo-Socratic dialogue in teaching business sustainability

The example given in Section 19.3 does not come from a business teaching context but from a seminar in environmental sociology. What are the links, then, to business sustainability? In the following I will point out three connecting lines from the NSD and business sustainability, first on the thematic level, second on the level of individual learning and personal capacity-building and third on the level of CSR.

19.4.1 The thematic link

As mentioned earlier, the general ethical question of 'individual benefit versus collective risk' is relevant for many decisions, personal and professional. In the example given in Section 19.3 participants focused on their individual daily behaviour. (Since most of them were students of sociology a link to business sustainability was not necessary.) When teaching sustainability for business the focus could easily be on corporate decision-making and on weighing individual corporate benefit against collective risk (e.g. from environmental pollution).

In principle, there are two ways of linking NSD to a business context, depending on the participants' corporate working experience. If they do have personal experience with corporations, the area of the example (given in the first phase of the NSD) can be limited to the corporate or business field. Consequently, the dialogue deals from the beginning with business issues. If the participants do not have their own experiences within corporations to relate, which will tend to be the case for most business students, the examples can come from their everyday experience. In this case the second procedure of linking the NSD to a business context can be used. The dialogue would start with a collection of concrete situations and problems from the corporate world that relate to the general question (e.g. an environmental scandal caused by an enterprise). The NSD would then proceed as described in the case-study example. The final step is to transfer the results from the dialogue to the business examples by looking for parallels and contrasts.

19.4.2 Learning and human capacity-building

The NSD strongly takes into account the 'subjective factor' of knowledge and human capacity-building that is increasingly required in the business context (Wieland and Grüninger 2003). The knowledge gained in the NSD increases not only cognitive capabilities (conceptual and perceptual) but also affective and sociodynamic capabilities. These capabilities are trained through the dialogical procedure of the NSD (note the difference between dialogue and discussion, as discussed in Section 19.2.1). The techniques used to aid mutual understanding train participants to better perceive and comprehend others' statements. They also help participants to improve on expressing ideas and thoughts clearly. By encouraging participants to comprehend the situation and actions of the example-giver, one thoroughly trains their affective skills, especially empathy. Socio-dynamic capabilities, such as giving room to the beliefs and viewpoints of others, tolerance, mutually relating and listening to each other and so on are, are taught through the overall process of the NSD (Gronke and Stary 1998). These different skills are important elements of successful teamwork, which must be absorbed and can be trained with use of the NSD (Kessels 1996). Effective training requires that the participants be personally interested in taking part. Thus, it is not recommended to oblige people to attend an NSD but rather to give them the choice. Under these conditions, the NSD can be a useful instrument to carry out ethical reflections on the concept of sustainability in a business context.

19.4.3 Corporate social responsibility

At the World Summit on Sustainable Development in September 2002 in Johannesburg, business enterprises were again endorsed as key actors of sustainable development.[7] The calls demanding corporations to take extended societal and environmental responsibility were renewed. These proposed responsibilities go far beyond the responsibility to shareholders for financial performance, with proponents stating that business should be accountable to all stakeholders for its economic, environmental and social impacts. Some enterprises have already taken up this challenge, installing new forms of corporate governance such as sustainability centres or sustainability reporting, and some have revised their corporate guidelines to integrate sustainable principles. But if business organisations convincingly want to take up the challenge of sustainable development then their implicit ethical values have to become part of the moral constitution of the entire business enterprise (Wieland and Grüninger 2003). For reasons of credibility and implementation, values relevant to sustainable development must be shared by the managers, the employees and the teams 'running the mill'. NSD can be a helpful tool for achieving this goal.

Today, universities, academic training centres, business schools and academies are core actors in the dissemination of the principles of sustainable development. In this chapter I have proposed use of NSD as a useful instrument for teaching ethical questions of business sustainability. I started from the viewpoint that the ethical implications of sustainable development are a necessary component of teaching programmes on sustainability. The objective of these courses is to enhance positive attitudes towards sustainable development and environmental protection. Another objective is to provide the needed working knowledge to apply sustainability approaches in professional (business) practice, policies and strategic guidelines. Finally, they aim to prepare and develop in students, or in representatives of industries, or business personnel, the professional and organisational skills necessary to implement practically the principles of sustainable development. These goals can be deepened through philosophical reflection. As noted, the NSD has been applied internationally in different contexts, in business enterprises and

7 See 'The Johannesburg Declaration on Sustainable Development',
   www.johannesburgsummit.org.

in university settings. So far there has been no documented application of the NSD in teaching sustainable business, but the experiences gathered in other, related, fields make NSD a promising instrument in this field too.

References

Aspen Institute (2002) *Where Will They Lead? MBA Student Attitudes about Business and Society* (Queenstown, MD: Aspen Institute).

Baue, W. (2002) 'The Progress and Stagnation of Corporate Social Responsibility in MBA Programme', 2 May 2002, www.socialfunds.com.

Birnbacher, D. (1982) 'Review of Heckmann: Das sokratische Gespräch. Erfahrungen in philosophischen Hochschulseminaren', *Zeitschrift für Didaktik der Philosophie* 4: 43-45.

Birnbacher, D. (1999) 'The Socratic Method in Teaching Medical Ethics: Potentials and Limitations', *Medicine, Health Care and Philosophy* 99.2: 219-24.

Gronke, H., and J. Stary (1998) ' "Sapere aude!" Das Neosokratische Gespräch als Chance für die universitäre Kommunikationskultur', in *Handbuch Hochschullehre, Informationen und Handreichungen aus der Praxis für die Hochschullehre* (loose-leaf supplement number 19, Chapter 2.11; Bonn, Germany: Raabe): 1-34.

Heckmann, G. (1993) *Das sokratische Gespräch: Erfahrungen in philosophischen Hochschulseminaren* (ed. Philosophisch-Politische Akademie; Frankfurt am Main, Germany: Dipa-Verlag).

Grießler, E., and B. Littig (2003) 'Participatory Technology Assessment of Xenotransplantation: Experimenting with the Neo-Socratic Dialogue', *Practical Philosophy* 6.2: 56-67.

Kessels, J. (1996) 'The Socratic Dialogue as a Method of Organisational Learning', *Dialogue and Universalism* 6.5–6: 53-67.

—— (1997) *Socrates op de markt: Filosofie in bedrijf* (Amsterdam: Boom, Meppel)

—— (2001) *Die Macht der Argumente* (Weinheim, Germany: Beltz).

Kitson, A., and R. Campbell (1996) *The Ethical Organisation: Ethical Theory and Corporate Behaviour* (London: Macmillan).

Kleinknecht, R. (1989) 'Wissenschaftliche Philosophie, philosophisches Wissen und Philosophieunterricht', *Zeitschrift für Didaktik der Philosophie* 11: 18-31.

Littig, B. (1999) 'Die Analyse von (Fall-)Beispielen: Gemeinsamkeiten und Unterschiede zwischen sokratischer Methode und interpretativ-hermeneutischen Verfahren der qualitativen Sozialforschung', in D. Krohn, B. Neißer and N. Walter (eds.), *Schriftenreihe der Philosophisch-Politischen Akademie* (vol. 6; Frankfurt: Dipa Verlag): 159-73.

—— (2001) *Feminist Perspectives on Environment and Society* (London: Pearson Education).

Murris, K. (2000) 'Can Children Do Philosophy?', *Journal of Philosophy of Education* 34.2: 261-79.

Neisser, B., and R. Saran (eds.) (2004) *Enquiring Minds: Socratic Dialogue in Education* (Stoke on Trent, UK: Trentham Books, forthcoming).

Nelson, L. (1922) 'Die sokratische Methode', in L. Nelson, *Gesammelte Schriften* (vol. 1; Hamburg: Meiner, repr. 1970): 269-316.

—— (1965) 'The Socratic Method', in L. Nelson, *Socratic Method and Critical Philosophy: Selected Essays by Leonard Nelson* (New York: Dover): 1-40.

Pepper, D. (1996) *Modern Environmentalism: An Introduction* (London: Routledge).

Senge, P.M. (1990) *The Fifth Discipline: The Art and Practice of the Learning Organization* (New York: Doubleday).

Toulmin, S. (1958) *The Uses of Argument* (Oxford, UK: Oxford University Press).

Weierstraß, K. (1967) 'Über die sokratische Lehrmethode und deren Anwendbarkeit beim Schulunterricht', in K. Weierstraß, *Mathematische Werke* (vol. 3; Hildesheim, Germany: Olms, repr.): 315-29.

Wieland, J. (2001) 'The Ethics of Governance', *Business Ethics Quarterly* 11.1 (Special Double Issue: 'Loyalty and Corporate Governance'): 73-88.

—— and S. Grüninger (2003) 'Ethics Management Systems and their Auditing: The Instruments of a Governance Approach to Business Ethics', in J. Wieland (ed.), *Standards and Audits for Ethics Management Systems: The European Perspective* (Berlin: Springer): 119-47.

20
Sustainability in a business context

Kathleen Wood, Maria Bobenrieth
and Faye M. Yoshihara

The notion of introducing and embedding sustainability in a business environment, where demands frequently exceed resources, can be challenging at best. With much to do, little time and a level of cynicism about its usefulness, teaching sustainability in a traditional way will not work. Pulling people into a classroom where an expert will lecture them while they are separated from the reality of their businesses and expecting them to return and change their corporations is a recipe for failure. As adults, learning is accelerated by our ability to make direct connections to what we know and direct applications to what is relevant to us. Thus, following a strategy to make learning relevant and applicable increases success as defined by measurable progress in products and processes. Teaching that wants to embed new thinking into a business must be done with seamless integration. In this chapter, we describe an innovative method that addresses these challenges.

The teaching of sustainability should be aligned with the needs and directions of a business and should focus on the pragmatic imperative (only that which is essential to the business). Use of sustainability as a new lens through which to view existing processes can also be a means of initiating and supporting desired long-term organisational change (such as innovation or efficiency) and can further ground the application in business relevance. Thus, success in helping people embed sustainability in the organisation is found by connecting learning goals with the stated strategic objectives of the business that are articulated as measurable outcomes (see Fig. 20.1).

The flow of the process is continuous and initiates a loop where strategic business objectives lead. From these objectives, linked and focused learning outcomes (e.g. to deliver compelling business results, cultivate sustainable thinking and

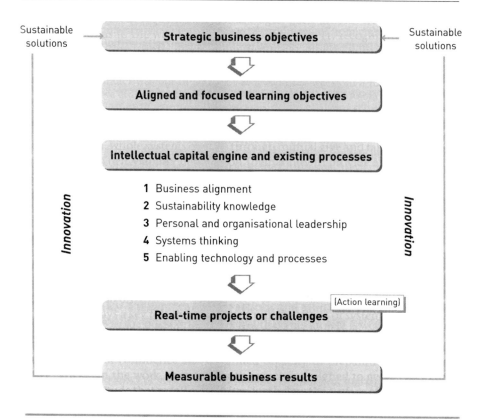

Figure 20.1 Process diagram of the integration of sustainability into strategic business objectives

create internal leadership capacity) are derived as outcomes of the learning programme.

This model is highly dependent on the ability of the designated project manager to understand, interpret and articulate the stated business objectives and transform them into relevant learning objectives. Accessing the intellectual capital of the entire organisation, especially true champions and detractors, can help.

Champions are senior-level supporters and members of the organisation who are doing sustainability or environmental work but calling it something else (quality, efficiency and so on) or they are visionaries who see the importance of implementing sustainability. They are a source of intellectual capital that often requires more thorough investigation and are critical to making sustainability relevant to the business. Conversely, the important role of detractors should not be ignored or avoided. Although they may not be easy to talk with, experience shows that detractors actually provide valuable input and are a good test of success criteria—they often point to the elephant in the middle of the room—and of impending organisational challenges. Moreover, early engagement with detractors creates more opportunities to create buy-in. In this model, the importance of system-wide internal expertise in creating the learning plan cannot be emphasised enough.

Likewise, the use of existing internal processes, such as strategic planning and project management, which are familiar to the participants provides a more relevant and credible framework. The challenge is to expand and add a sustainability lens to these familiar processes. For example, during Nike's Sustainability Initiative the emerging leaders selected projects that were aligned with the business plans already existing and they created objectives for the project that contributed to these plans.[1] People were also asked to ensure, with their manager, that their time, energy and learning were written into their performance appraisals. Seamless integration into existing procedures and processes is key. Our experience has shown that this approach is less disruptive and thus more effective than immediately attempting to introduce new tools or methodologies.

Sustainability learning is embedded in organisations through the systemic approach and the strategic application of the 'five pillars':

- Business alignment

- Sustainability knowledge

- Personal and organisational leadership

- Systems thinking

- Enabling technology and processes

Learning is applied to real-time projects or challenges, called 'action learning' (Dotlich and Noel 1998). These activities deliver measurable and reportable results. This process initiates a continuous innovative loop that allows the re-examination of strategic business objectives and moves forward from there (see Fig. 20.2).

20.1 The five pillars of sustainability: learning in a business context

The premise of the five-pillars model is that sustainability cannot be learned as a separate discipline as can accounting or marketing strategy. To embed sustainability into a business one must use a systems approach. A system is a set of components that work together towards the objectives of the whole, where the whole is greater than the sum of its parts. Systems thinking is about looking at the whole, not just the parts, for patterns and relationships to find high-leverage (connecting) points that reinforce or change these patterns. In this model, sustainability learning is actually the convergence of several disciplines that, when applied, can create high-performing teams that provide innovative sustainable solutions. This model challenges teams to apply their knowledge to real-time projects—action

---

1 The Nike Sustainability Initiative, 1999–2000, Nike Inc. The authors were consultants to the project.

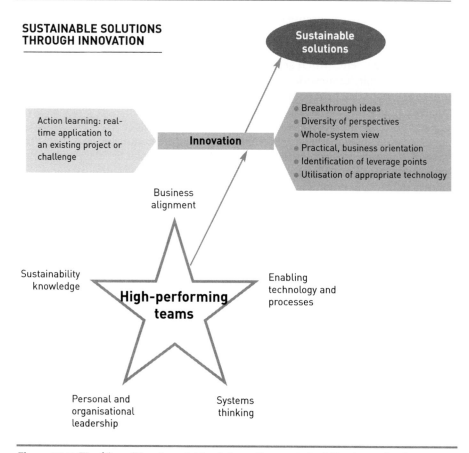

Figure 20.2 The 'five pillars' model for integrating sustainability into a business

learning—using sustainability as an additional 'lens' through which to gauge success. The tools within each 'pillar' are not limited to any list contained in this chapter. They are continuously expanding and, typically, are customised to groups, based primarily on key stakeholder feedback. Moreover, the design process is fluid. Additional relevant information or tools may be introduced at any time during the programme, as needed.

As noted, application of this model requires buy-in from key business champions and stakeholders to design a relevant and effective customised learning programme. It is important to assess each of the pillars and identify the level of competence, openness and need within an organisation. Often, this is greatly influenced by corporate culture and the tone set by the programme champions. Although it is not possible to create a programme that looks at all five pillars in detail, it is important to be aware of how focusing on one pillar can affect the others. A balanced approach provides more lasting support for success. The absence of building skills in the construction of one pillar can limit the effectiveness of the others. In Sections 20.1.1–5 each of the five pillars is described in detail.

20.1.1 Business alignment

Key components include:

- Strategic leadership
- Effective communication
- Fact-based decision-making
- Expanded finance
- Expanded markets

Strategic leadership

A business must continually attract new investment capital by demonstrating financial viability to its shareholders. This continuous stream of financial returns is also what allows a business to invest in positive environmental and social return for its broader set of stakeholders. In a competitive business environment, with a primary focus on financial returns, many managers want to 'do what is right', yet the standard business model does not adequately value non-financial returns. A few visionary companies, such as SC Johnson and Nike, are beginning to develop models that view core business strategies and decision-making processes through a sustainability lens.[2]

However, until a sustainable business model is widely accepted, practitioners of sustainability must find points of entry within the current system. A critical look at the strategic initiatives of a business often uncovers opportunities. The more aligned sustainability initiative is with the strategic plan the more likely it is to receive resources and senior-level support. Furthermore, if sustainability is seen as an innovative solution to a core strategic business issue it is more likely to be included in key metrics and in the incentive pay of managers. In either case, meaningful measurements, such as impact on cost of goods sold or changes in brand strength, should be considered essential to any sustainability programme.

Effective communication

In most large organisations, work teams and departments routinely communicate daily with their own members but only weekly or monthly with the rest of the company. The lack of timely and complete communication and interaction across departments may become evident when undertaking a sustainability initiative that involves many functional areas of the business. Often, one will find that information needed by one function unknowingly exists in another part of the

---

2 SC Johnson Sustainability projects, SC Johnson Company, 2000–2002. The authors were consultants to the projects. See also footnote 1 on page 225.

organisation. A sustainability initiative can become a vehicle to help identify gaps and to develop a communication framework across work team and functional areas to ensure that intellectual capital in sustainability knowledge is captured and used effectively.

Fact-based decision-making

Like any other strategic decision, a sustainability initiative should make a compelling business case, supported by facts instead of assumptions, speculative threats or the generic banner of corporate responsibility. Practitioners of sustainability can raise the credibility of their proposals and make a better case for investment by using the same decision-making model, with appropriate modifications, already used by the organisation. This should include dialogue and analysis with market-research, product-research and consumer-insight teams, which track early trends and leading indicators. It also means early engagement with the finance team, which can provide an analysis of scenario plans and financial impacts. These fact-based decision tools can become critical levers to justify the undertaking of a sustainability initiative.

Expanded finance

Finance teams are charged with the role of monitoring, evaluating and ensuring that controls exist to protect and enhance the profitability of the company. The chief finance officers (CFOs) or financial controllers can be excellent champions, able to make the connection between long-term shareholder value and a sustainability initiative, especially when considering investments that may improve efficiency or environmental performance. They often recognise the need for a broader view of financial health because they see the shareholder-value impacts of decisions, such as the total cost to clean up an environmental spill. They may see a sustainability initiative as a risk-management strategy, especially if they have dealt with legal costs arising from non-compliance, or reputation costs resulting from the public's perception of irresponsible corporate behaviour. As markets move from a product orientation to a service orientation in search of differentiation and competitive advantage, intangible assets such as brand value and reputation become important drivers in shareholder value and further build the case for a sustainability initiative.

Expanded markets

Businesses undertaking initiatives are often market leaders in their industry sector that are seeking new ways to create competitive advantage. To continue to grow, they must either take share from competitors or expand their markets. Sustainability can be a platform for innovation and continued market expansion. Reframing the customer's needs and bringing novel solutions to the market differentiates them from their competitors. A well-executed and -aligned sustainability initiative can become the platform from which the company can launch its innovative growth model.

Summary

In summary, the following checklist pertaining to business alignment should be considered:

- Does the initiative align with strategic and business planning processes?
- Does the initiative work with or change current processes?
- Does the initiative address innovation, cost savings or risk management?
- Does the initiative value non-financial capital by adding sustainability decision-making criteria?
- Does the initiative create outputs and easy-to-track indicators and measures that are relevant to the business and key outside stakeholders?
- Does the initiative provide an early warning system for emerging threats?
- Does the initiative provide a holistic view of the business?

20.1.2 Sustainability knowledge

As the 'field' of sustainability develops and matures, an increasing, sometimes daunting, number of theories and frameworks emerge. Much of the material is innovative and relevant, but it is easy for learners to become overwhelmed and drowned in the theory. Our experience shows that it is best to identify early on what is most relevant for the learning audience so that participants can 'operationalise' concepts. Then, one should limit the introduction of sustainability material to what is applicable in achieving the objectives and outcomes of the learning programme.

It is also important to make available additional material (in the form of resource or supplemental tools) to interested learners. This is particularly true of recent articles that run parallel to or support the theory being applied and that are relevant to the industry of the participants. In our experience, a tool that has consistently helped turn theory into action is that of case studies that illustrate how sustainability knowledge is applied.

A balance of internal and external case studies creates relevance and supports best business practices. Moreover, most organisations have many internal case studies that have been overlooked or that have not been framed in the context of sustainability. For example, an innovative partnership between SC Johnson's manufacturing facility and Goodwill Industries creates jobs for the unemployed while recycling facility 'waste'.[3] A tour of the facility provided an instructive case study for participants in a sustainability learning programme.

Most participants need very little information to understand and apply basic sustainable business principles. What is needed are relevant real-life examples and practical tools in a format and context that inspires action.

3 See footnote 2 on page 257.

20.1.3 Personal and organisational leadership

Introducing sustainability into an organisation is about introducing change to people. Embracing change effectively requires personal and organisational leadership about how to learn and think differently. For sustainability to be successfully embedded in an organisation there must be significant effort and attention paid to the system from an organisational development and leadership standpoint.

One factor in bringing about lasting organisational change is being able to link people's ability to lead and think differently with awareness of how it will enhance their business or project. If they can align (a) the market imperatives, (b) the organisation's direction, (c) their job responsibilities and (d) what *they* care about they will naturally develop leadership that is purpose-driven, with the greatest chance of being lasting and effective.

The following elements support the ability of participants and organisations to learn and integrate sustainability:

- Purpose-driven leadership
- Visionary foresight
- Personal mastery

Each of these is discussed in turn below.

Purpose-driven leadership

Purpose-driven leadership requires the following.

- The leader must understand what the market imperatives are: that is, he or she must know the market drivers relevant to the business and to the issue of sustainability and then link the two within the business case.

- The leader should be able to identify a strong link between market imperatives and what participants must do. This means asking, 'Do I understand what role our organisation plays identifying the market needs and how sustainability can address that? Do I know how my job helps to support that?'

- The leader must feel passion for the objectives beyond the business case, asking, for example, 'How do I, as an individual and as a leader, connect those pieces to what I care about?' If a leader clarifies and makes a link to the subject beyond the business case (e.g. the answer may include statements such as 'my children will be affected' or 'it is the right thing to do') ,then the company will have a greater chance of creating lasting change.

Visionary foresight

Markets, people and organisations will be radically different in 20 years. Part art, part science, the ability to make predictions about these requires the skill of weaving future views into daily thinking and planning. This is the essence of personal and organisational visionary foresight. The ability of individuals and organisations to think in this way will be vital in creating the desired outcomes. One tool used successfully is scenario planning. The use of learning sessions in which participants engage in scenario planning for the organisation and the use of scenario planning to identify needs at the beginning of projects are ways in which to build a visionary skill set. This activity can also identify future needs for embedding sustainability into the systems (computer, financial, supply chain and human resource processes) that will help support individual efforts to bring about change.

Personal mastery

Certain levels of self-mastery are essential to bring new ways of thinking into organisations. Being a 'change agent' requires a high level of self-awareness and the ability to work on personal developmental. These skills include the following.

- Effective communication. Learning and practising the articulation of the business case clearly and succinctly is critical to the organisational sell-in process. The goals are to communicate effectively, consistently and openly. Also, learning to balance genuine inquiry with passionate advocacy is a skill that greatly enhances effective presentation of the business case.

- Learning agility. Learning requires an ability to adapt to constant change. Change agents are pioneers on the front line. This means being confident, using persuasion and being aware of when to relent when pushing further would be counter-productive. An effective change agent develops formal and informal influencing skills while working across the system to inspire others and create change.

- Self-renewing behaviour. Preventing personal or professional burnout, knowing when to stop and using practices that are revitalising increase the ability to remain focused and effective. This includes physical and emotional self-renewal.

20.1.4 Systems thinking

In this section we have borrowed concepts from many great systems thinkers. Sources are *The Art of Systems Thinking* (McDermott and O'Connor 1997); *The Systems Thinking Playbook* (Sweeny and Meadows 2001); *The Dance of Change* (Senge *et al.* 1999); The Center for Strategic Management (www.csmintl.com); and papers by Carol Sanford (1997).

Systems thinking requires moving beyond linear, and even lateral, thinking to seeing the world as many parts connected through relationships. When we try to look at each part separately without considering the effects of the surrounding relationships, a system loses the properties and values it had as an intact whole. Thus, it would be ineffective to work towards sustainable practices in one department without working on the relationships that the department has with other departments, suppliers, customers and clients. Systems thinking approaches recognise that sustainability cannot happen in a vacuum and are essential to effective learning programmes. Systems thinkers are able to:

- See the whole through connections and complex cause-and-effect relationships
- Recognise that all systems are evolving
- Consider how mental models create the future

Seeing the whole

- Leaders must see relationships as integral to understanding and changing the system. The building of relationships across departments is more important than are the departments themselves.

- Leaders must have an internal and external view of relationships. Looking at the individual, the department and the division from a systems perspective can help broaden one's decision-making skills. For example, the creation of a large systems map at Nike helped participants see themselves as a part of the whole and to identify the leverage points and relationships needed to create change.[4]

- Sometimes small changes produce big results. Areas of highest leverage are frequently the least obvious. Some guidelines are to:
  - Look for and pay attention to unanticipated consequences
  - Create a high-feedback learning environment to offset resistance to change

Recognising that all systems are evolving

Objective goals, outlined milestones and success indicators support a learning environment in the context of an evolving system. Systems thinkers are able to:

- Create structures to help keep the system in balance (e.g. through communication and through use of time-lines, project management tools, defined goals and milestones); the processes for evaluating progress must also be able to adjust to unanticipated changes

- Identify, understand and clearly define the limitations of what is realistic, whether pertaining to process or product, through self-assessment and examination of expectations

- Know that 'where you end up will not be where you thought you would'; they expect considerable learning to take place that will affect and possibly change the goals

- Pay attention and give voice to the long term; this may require holding creative tension and paradox in the short term

4   See footnote 1 on page 255.

Considering how mental models create the future

In *The Dance of Change*, Peter Senge *et al.* (1999) encourage us to develop awareness of attitudes and perceptions that influence thought and interaction—looking at our mental models. Becoming skilled at this can open new ways of thinking through:

- Suspending judgement long enough to allow for other input and ideas
- Being flexible and adaptive: for example, by searching for multiple outcomes rather than for one 'best' way (either/or)
- Recognising that internal shifts in one part of the system affect the entire system and that resistance to change creates challenges for the entire system
- The encouragement of evolution (innovation) instead of natural decline

20.1.5 Enabling technology and processes

The ever-evolving world of science affects sustainability initiatives. We believe the 'duelling science' surrounding sustainability issues will continue in flux and, as with many other elements of a business, this means leaders must make decisions with imperfect information. An organisation must have a mechanism to continue to monitor technical advances externally and must erect a framework internally that encourages or mandates the use of sustainability guidelines. These may be called, respectively, technical leadership and literacy.

Business teams, especially product designers, formulators and developers, need access to tools that help them make better-informed decisions. A 'to-do list' from the sustainability or environmental department is not good enough. To encourage environmentally progressive behaviour, SC Johnson has implemented a 'Green List'™ process.[5] This unique tool is linked directly to its business plan and wraps strategy and goal in one easy-to use process. It gives formulators timely information so that they can make the best possible choices as they develop new products.

Another 'enabling process' that is receiving more attention is cross-sector partnerships among the private sector, public sector and non-governmental organisations (NGOs). These partnerships are becoming an important strategic approach to tackle complex social and environmental challenges. Partnerships, process-specific or product-specific, can be an effective route to social cohesion, environmental stability and equitable economic growth. The Prince of Wales International Business Leaders Forum and Cambridge University in the United Kingdom have created successful frameworks for cross-sector partnerships (Tennyson and Wilde 2000). They state key partnership principles which include:

- Equity: partners are given due respect and status
- Transparency: partners are open and honest in their dealings with each other

5 See footnote 2 on page 257.

● Mutual benefit: interdependences among partners are understood and connected

20.2 Implementing the five-pillar model

The five-pillar model is executed through a series of modules organised into workshops. The series is delivered to a group over 3–12 months. The number of workshops and the configuration of participants is determined by an assessment process sensitive to organisational culture and constraints. Identifying the audience and articulating the depth of information to achieve the objectives is done with internal champions. Programmes that allow participants to learn new skills, return to their jobs and apply action-learning principles in real-time settings and then return to share experiences last longest. A summary of the execution of the programme is illustrated in Figure 20.3.

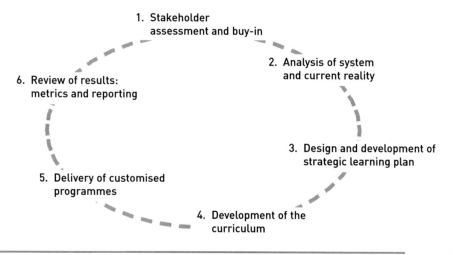

Figure 20.3 Executing the five-pillar sustainability learning model

20.2.1 Stakeholder assessment and buy-in

The primary objective of the assessment is to add value to the business while connecting with its time-lines. This requires front-loading the design process with input from relevant stakeholders to support and complement business teams and learning programmes. To ensure buy-in and maximum effectiveness, stakeholders will (a) continue to contribute input to curriculum design, development and delivery and (b) actively engage in a review and follow-up to identify areas needing revision.

20.2.2 Analysis of the system and current reality

Business alignment should be based on a review of business and sustainability objectives. The focus is on the pragmatic imperative, which addresses only what is meaningful and adds value.

20.2.3 Design and development of strategic learning plan

The strategic learning plan is the blueprint that shows how to achieve the objectives. These are customised to each organisation, but generally are related to the following:

- Delivery of compelling business results
- Development of internal leadership capacity
- Cultivation of sustainable thinking

The customised learning plan balances a long-term vision with a short-term value-adding proposition that is holistic and organic in nature. The learning plan should focus on using sustainability as a catalyst to take care of a business mandate, such as a need for innovation or breakthrough thinking. The plan must deliver meaningful and actionable results that add value. Therefore, continued input from stakeholders is vital. The ability to adapt to changing business objectives as well as to review and redesign the curriculum and materials based on feedback from the business is critical. Appropriate changes assure buy-in and relevance.

20.2.4 Development of the curriculum

One must customise a detailed curriculum design for each workshop that:

- Is aligned with strategic business objectives and delivers business results
- Identifies and articulates SMART (specific, measurable, actionable, realistic and timely) learning objectives that support and complement current programmes
- Taps into the 'intellectual capital engine' of the organisation
- Addresses the alignment of personal values with corporate values
- Applies an action-learning approach (real-time), as coined by David Dotlich in his book *Action Learning* (Dotlich and Noel 1998)
- Integrates five-pillar learning, providing some learning in each area
- Is *not* linear but a 'living' loop that reinforces itself

Participants are required to work on project(s) that align with their everyday work and with the business objectives of their group. We suggest that each participant sit with their manager and create a learning plan for themselves and for furthering the goals of the business unit. Optional pre-workshop and post-workshop reading materials enhance the curriculum and learning.

20.2.5 Delivery of customised programmes

Although acknowledging the limitations of resources, including time, we have found that one-off training sessions rarely accomplish lasting results. Participants need time to reflect and test the learning between sessions and to return to upgrade their learning with the whole group.

Modules are arranged and delivered in a series of four to six workshops (ideally four to six weeks apart) with a group of high-leverage participants. The length of each workshop varies according to what is most effective for the business and the objectives the programme is trying to accomplish. Nike held four-day workshops, with the first day open to a larger audience and the last three focused on in-depth learning of the five pillars.[6] At SC Johnson, the workshops were half a day in length and held over a period of a year.[7]

We believe it is important to have the same group go through the series together. This builds camaraderie and additional leverage in embedding sustainability. Our experience has also shown us that clearly identified work projects needing attention between workshops expands learning and supports the application of concepts to real-time projects. At Nike, participants in the nine-month programme engaged with their sustainability project teams outside of the workshops and reported their progress and learning at each session. This accomplished two objectives: it involved more people in the process of embedding sustainability and kept the learning tied to a relevant business issue.

20.2.6 Review of results: metrics and reporting

Modules and workshops are reviewed and revised with input from stakeholders and are measured for effectiveness. Measures are qualitative and quantitative and are selected with stakeholder input. Although this six-step process for creating meaningful and inclusive learning programmes has been successful in launching sustainability learning programmes, it is important to recognise that there is often a time lag between delivery of the programme and visible results. This is partly because business time-lines tend to be focused on the short-term, whereas some results from a sustainability initiative take longer to happen. Often, participants are not able to apply sustainable business principles until a new fiscal year, for example. Long-term tracking of participants yields the most accurate measure of effectiveness and results.

20.3 Conclusions

Living in a world where businesses measure success by peering through social and environmental lenses as well as through an economic lens can happen only if

---

6 See footnote 1 on page 255.
7 See footnote 2 on page 257.

people and systems reconceptualise their roles. Designing and executing learning opportunities for embedding sustainability into a business is critical if we are to realise this vision. Traditional models do not work because they do not account for the challenges of teaching sustainability.

The teaching of sustainability requires addressing the challenges, such as limited time and cynicism, that hold people back from learning. It also requires seamlessly integrating the business systems in place with the new, sustainable objectives of the business and the personal lives of participants. Doing this systematically and strategically over time allows a business to reap the rewards associated with new ways of thinking and being as an organisation, renewed motivation to implement sustainable practices in the short term and a better grasp of the long-term importance of being sustainable. As shown here, an innovative method, the five pillars of sustainability learning (business alignment, sustainability knowledge, personal and organisational leadership, systems thinking and enabling technology and processes) addresses these challenges and is an effective method of teaching sustainability.

References

Dotlich, D.L., and J.L. Noel (1998) *Action Learning: How the World's Top Companies Are Recreating Their Leaders and Themselves* (San Francisco: Jossey-Bass).

McDermott, I., and J. O'Connor (1997) *The Art of Systems Thinking* (London: Thorsons Publishers).

Senge, P., A. Kleiner, C. Roberts, G. Roth, R. Ross and B. Smith (1999) *The Dance of Change* (Redfern, NSW, Australia: Currency Press).

Stanford, C. (1997) *Systems: A Hierarchy of Types* (unpublished papers).

Sweeny, L.B., and D. Meadows (2001) *The Systems Thinking Playbook* (PSSR/UNH [Institute for Policy and Social Science Research/University of New Hampshire]).

Tennyson, R., and L. Wilde (2000) *The Guiding Hand: Brokering Partnerships for Sustainable Development* (Price of Wales Business Leaders Forum and United Nations).

21
Teaching sustainability in business schools
Why, what and how

Bob Willard
University of Toronto, Canada

Business is the direct or indirect cause of most ecological challenges, but it is becoming increasingly evident that it is also the only institution left on the planet large enough, well managed enough and resourceful enough to solve the problems facing us. However, business leaders usually turn a deaf ear to well-researched, affordable solutions that would help restore a balance between the growing human population, rising levels of consumption and threats to natural systems. Their training has indoctrinated them to prioritise increasing bottom-line profits and shareholder value, not saving the world. The benefits of implementing social and environmental initiatives must be quantified and expressed in business language as bottom-line benefits relevant to the short- and long-term priorities of the business in order to engage executives. My premise is that core courses in business schools must quantify the bottom-line benefits of corporate social responsibility (CSR), also known as sustainable development, and educate corporate leaders to believe that adopting restorative strategies for a healthy planet is a win–win–win proposition for companies, the environment and society.

How are business schools doing on sustainable development today? One of the best barometers is the *Beyond Grey Pinstripes 2001* survey by the World Resources Institute (WRI) and the Aspen Institute for Social Innovation Through Business.[1] They surveyed 463 MBA schools, 400 of which were in the USA. Of the 82 that responded, 58 were in the USA and 24 were elsewhere. They found that students

---

1 The 2003 survey is available from the Beyond Grey Pinstripes website at www.beyondgreypinstripes.org.

who seek sustainable development coursework rate MBA programmes a D+ on how often social and environmental concerns were raised by faculty in required courses. Dedicated faculty, who were 'going it alone' integrating CSR into their courses, rated social and environmental courses as A– in importance but rated their MBA schools only as C+ in incorporating sustainable development issues in their core MBA curriculum. The key words are **required** and **core**. Sustainable development is relegated to optional ethics classes, volunteer and philanthropic extracurricular activities or electives that are not linked to core business strategy. There is a clear message that sustainable development is a tangential issue in MBA curricula at best.

That is, business leaders are good people, but they have been educated to think of the economic well-being of their companies as being at odds with, or irrelevant to, the environmental and social health of the planet. Business schools encourage their students to comply with environmental, labour and human rights regulations but seldom suggest that there are significant benefits to be gained from going further. Their maxim is that 'the business of business is business'—governments or philanthropic organisations should worry about ecological and social issues. They see CSR and profits in terms of 'either/or' instead of 'both/and'.

The *Beyond Grey Pinstripes* findings show that business schools are overlooking one of the most compelling win–win business opportunities available. They can support the profit orientation of companies *and* show how a well-executed sustainable development strategy can be a large contributor to savings, revenue, productivity, competitiveness, lower risk and new markets. Convincingly quantifying the bottom-line benefits of CSR is possible, should be included in required business school courses and would be useful to help convince corporate leaders to embrace sustainable development.

In my book, *The Sustainability Advantage: Seven Business Case Benefits of a Triple Bottom Line* (Willard 2002) I show how addressing sustainability issues in a systematic way provides new profit opportunities. It includes a template of potential business benefits of sustainable development that can be used as a sustainability business case simulator. This chapter is a condensation of the sustainability benefits quantified in the book, to reinforce that the economics of sustainability is a legitimate component of core MBA courses.

To illustrate the financial benefits of sustainability, I use a hypothetical company from the computer industry—a composite of the five largest high-technology companies based on *Fortune* 500 1999 data (*Fortune* 2000).[2] The fictitious 'Sustainable Development Inc.' or 'SD Inc.' is assumed to have revenues of US$44 billion, profits of US$3 billion and 120,000 employees. The average employee's salary is US$60,000 per year, and the average manager's salary is US$70,000 per year. If SD Inc. is much larger than a particular company of interest, just divide the assumed size by 10, 100, 1000 or another suitable factor, as the logic used is scalable. Figures for any specific company can be substituted into the business case simulator and are intended to be so.

2   The data used is from 1999, but as it is used only to derive the financial information for a hypothetical company, SD Inc., it does not matter that it is not current. SD Inc. is a composite of five companies: International Business Machines (IBM), Hewlett-Packard, Compaq Computer, Dell Computer and Xerox.

Some benefits may appear more qualitative than quantitative at first. However, by making explicit assumptions about the 'so what?' of these benefits, the bottom-line impact can be estimated. Using the Sustainability Advantage Worksheets, business leaders can play out 'what if?' scenarios using their assumptions. By tuning the assumed values according to their experience and good judgement, executives can 'custom-fit' the business case.

To capitalise on the seven areas of benefit, every manager and employee must be empowered, educated and motivated to contribute to the sustainability effort. A five-year plan of company-wide sustainability education must be deployed so that everyone understands environmental and sustainability principles, current global ecological and social issues, life-cycle assessment and costing, design for environment, the company's environmental and social track record and the company's business, environmental and social plans. The sessions would be sponsored and attended by senior leaders, to reinforce the company's commitment to this strategy and to empower employees to suggest innovative ways that the company could benefit financially from environmental and social initiatives.

For example, the 3M Company started its employee-based Pollution Prevention Pays (3P) programme in 1976 with similar encouragement. By 2000, 4,650 employee projects had saved 3M US$810 million, conservatively counting just the first-year savings from the projects (3M 2004). The recommended education could be done in classroom sessions, integrated with other business education, provided through self-study CD-ROMs or delivered via online training modules. If the equivalent of two days of education were given to every employee in the first year, and one day of education in each of the next four years, the five-year investment for increased environmental education for 120,000 employees and managers in our SD Inc. sample company would be about US$372 million. To be conservative, this expense includes the lost productivity of employees during this time, although that allowance is usually not included in companies' traditional training-cost equations. In the financial model, this is considered to be the only investment that the company needs to make. The costs of improvements required to reap the claimed benefits are assumed to be paid off by savings before the benefit is claimed. The savings are assumed to take effect only after the payback period.

When a company such as SD Inc. makes the internal communications and educational investment in sustainable development, it lays the foundations for significant savings, revenue and employee productivity opportunities in seven areas of potential benefit:

- Easier hiring of the best talent
- Greater retention of top talent
- Increased employee productivity
- Reduced expenses for manufacturing
- Reduced expenses at commercial sites
- Increased revenue and market share
- Reduced risk and easier financing

The first three areas (hiring, retention and productivity) are about people. The next two (reduced expenses for manufacturing and at commercial sites) are primarily about initiatives that help the planet. Combined with the last two areas (increased revenue and lower risk), each of these contributes to profits: people, planet and profits—an integrated win–win–win case. I will now briefly quantify the benefits for SD Inc. in each of the seven areas.

21.1 Seven benefits of sustainable development

21.1.1 Easier hiring of the best talent

Surveys show that, despite the economic slowdown and the end of the dot.com boom, the war for talent is intensifying (Axelrod *et al.* 2001; Herman Group 1999; Mercer/Angus Reid 1999[3]). Findings from the Millennium Poll on Corporate Social Responsibility (Environics 2000)—with results accurate to within 3%, 19 times out of 20—suggest that about 20-40% of potential recruits would care enough about the environmental image and reputation of a company to let it influence their decision to accept a job offer. A more recent poll in late 2001 showed a 15-point increase in these numbers, with 60-70% of respondents in the USA, Great Britain, Australia and Canada saying they had rewarded or punished a company in the last year because of its corporate social responsibility reputation (Environics 2002). To be conservative, the lower estimate of 20% is assumed. Only a 5% savings of recruiting costs for this group is used, assuming the need for recruitment will be slightly less because retention will be higher, as explained in Section 21.1.2, and that word of mouth and a higher acceptance rate may also reduce hiring costs.

Therefore, if SD Inc. were to have a well-communicated, exceptional sustainable development reputation, the recruiting cost would be 5% lower for about 20% of those it is competing to hire, yielding a **1% saving** on recruiting costs. Admittedly, this is not a big saving—consider it a placeholder that could be tuned higher, depending on company senior management's comfort level with less conservative assumptions. The real benefit of attracting the best talent that values sustainability is not to save on recruitment costs—the aim is the increased retention and productivity of these talented employees after they are hired; the figures for these are calculated next.

21.1.2 Greater retention of top talent

Hiring top talent is one challenge; keeping it is another. The issue of retaining top talent is a serious problem that is getting worse. A detailed accounting of the costs of losing a good person, hiring a new person and training that replacement can

---

3   The Mercer/Angus Reid poll was of 307 Canadian CEOs.

add up to three times the employee's salary.[4] These are not soft costs; these are real dollars.

If we assume that each year the company loses just 1% of those employees that it does not want to lose and then has to replace them, the real question is how would a well-communicated and credible corporate sustainable development agenda affect the retention of these good people? Money is definitely important—informal surveys worldwide indicate that 40% of information technology (IT) professionals will seriously consider leaving their enterprise for a 20% greater salary (McNee *et al.* 1998). Would some care enough about their company's sustainability focus to stay? In *First Break All the Rules*, Marcus Buckingham and Curt Coffman (1999) say that one of the top 12 questions that determine whether employees stay is: 'Does the mission of my company make me feel like my work is worthwhile?' In his studies of 'meaning at work', Tom Terez (2002) found that of 22 keys to meaningful work and retention the most important is purpose—the sense that what the employee is doing as an individual, and what the organisation is doing collectively, truly matters. Also, an Arthur D. Little study found that Novo Nordisk, a company that has won awards for its commitment to honesty, values and stakeholder engagement, had a turnover of only 5% of staff at the end of 1998 compared with a biotech industry average of 10%.[5]

The magnet of an inspiring vision of sustainability with an empowering environment to help make it a reality may be strong enough that some people would want to stay with a company more than they would otherwise. I conservatively assume that 20% of the 10% of people leaving would indeed change their minds and stay if their company had a vibrant sustainable development mission that added purpose and meaning to their work. This leads to a **2% saving** on attrition costs, which flows as pure profit to the bottom line.

21.1.3 Increased employee productivity

The research by James Collins and Jerry Porras in *Built to Last* (1994) and by others shows that talented people are more committed when working for companies in which the missions inspire worthwhile work (leadership 'gurus' who support the claim that a higher purpose increases commitment include Bennis and Namus 1985; Blanchard and Bowles 1998; Clemmer 1999; Hesselbein *et al.* 1996; Jensen 1992; Kouzes and Posner 1995; Leider 1985; Pritchett 1994; Senge 1990). Zero emissions, self-sufficient energy production, zero waste and helping to restore the social and environmental health of the planet would be powerful vision elements for a company. The value chain from vision to empowerment to commitment to productivity suggests that corporations embracing a sustainable development goal as a higher purpose will energise and motivate at least part of their workforces to be more productive. To be consistent with the proportion of people assumed to be

---

4   This is a rule of thumb used by human resource professionals. It is also backed up with detailed calculations and assumptions in my book, *The Sustainability Advantage* (Willard 2002).

5   Colin Leduc, private correspondence, 13 December 1999, giving excerpts from an Arthur D. Little Inc. presentation on the business case for sustainable development.

attracted by SD Inc.'s environmental and social responsibility image, assume that 20% of employees will resonate with a sustainable development vision. Conservatively assuming these employees would then be 25% more productive, this works out to an average 5% increase in productivity for the whole workforce (25% of 20%), which is conservatively lower than the average 9–23% higher annual returns for visionary companies found by Collins and Porras (1994).[6]

So far, only the productivity of individuals has been considered. The impact of a powerful sustainable development vision on cross-functional team productivity should also be considered. In most large organisations, a major challenge is teamwork among departments that do not know or understand each other. Case studies (Nattrass and Altomare 1999) show that sustainable development programmes across multiple departments provide an excellent team-building opportunity, with a beneficial spillover effect on how the departments continue to work as a team on other business solutions. Assume the resulting productivity from improved company-wide teamwork is only 2%, another conservative assumption— it would certainly be greater than zero.

The above two productivity elements are based on people being inspired and drawn together by opportunities for environmental and social projects that transcend departmental boundaries. There is a third potential contributor to productivity benefits driven by environmental initiatives: increased productivity from improved workplace conditions.

Let us suppose the company decides to retrofit buildings to capitalise on energy efficiencies so that lighting systems are converted to more energy-efficient bulbs and small-task lighting, and clever ways are found to bring natural light throughout the workplace, thus reducing glare. Workers gain more control over the light, heat and air in their environment by means of occupancy sensors and workstation controls. Surprising to many companies that have made these kinds of changes to reap ongoing savings in energy costs, an unanticipated ancillary benefit becomes evident—their people are more productive in the upgraded facilities. Joseph Romm, author of *Cool Companies* (1999), uses case studies to show how firms that converted to energy-efficient lighting reaped productivity improvements of 7–15%. He also found a drop in sick leave and absenteeism. Again, to be conservative, I will assume only a 7% gain in productivity for half the employees, for an average of 3.5% across the company.

The power of sustainability initiatives to engage and unleash employee productivity is too big to ignore. The productivity improvements at the individual and team level, plus improved productivity from better workplace design, add up to a **10.5% increase** in employee productivity, enabling growth without additional staff. Companies ignoring this potential are leaving money on the table.

---

6 Collins and Porras discovered that visionary companies had 65-year cumulative stock returns between 1926 and 1990 that were over 6 times (600%) greater than those of comparative companies and 15 times (1,500%) greater than those of the general market. Crudely averaging the difference over the 65 years, the returns were 9–23% better each year.

21.1.4 Reduced expenses for manufacturing

Business reformer Paul Hawken estimates that 99% of the original materials used in the production of, or contained within, goods made in the USA become waste within six weeks of sale (quoted in von Weizsäcker *et al.* 1997). If the term 'waste' were to be replaced by 'squandered corporate assets', corporations might be pressured by their shareholders to use this opportunity to save money. The business imperative to stop squandering these assets has environmentally beneficial by-products—a true win–win proposition. Even if a company does not care about the environment, it can get substantial savings within today's operations. Some examples are: (1) substitution of less expensive, more environmentally friendly raw materials and energy sources for those currently being used, (2) reducing the amount of material, energy and water used per product, even if this means redesigning the product or manufacturing process, (3) reducing, re-using and recycling scrap material and wasted energy, turning them into useful products instead of throwing them away and (4) re-using and recycling parts and materials from returned products that have been designed for disassembly. These are the 'low-hanging fruit' of eco-efficiency that excite companies in their first blush of enthusiasm for environmental concerns.

Assume that hardware sales account for half of a company's annual revenue, with the remaining revenue generated from services. Hardware materials, energy and water costs are assumed to be 30% of hardware sales. Now for the big question: how much of the hardware cost would be saved by a more aggressive blend of eco-efficiency, process redesign and take-back initiatives? Even a small proportion yields a big number, so let us choose a conservative net saving of 5%—that is, net savings counted after the cost of retrofits or other measures are repaid. Let us further assume that half (50%) of these savings is reserved in a capital pool to invest in other sustainability projects that may exceed company payback period norms. We add the remaining **2.5% saved** to our annual profit.

21.1.5 Reduced expenses at commercial sites

Potential savings at commercial stores, staff and field location office buildings, distribution centres and storage facilities come from: (1) employee discretionary consumables, (2) improved handling of waste, (3) greater energy efficiencies, (4) conservation of water, (5) lower costs for landscaping, (6) reduced need for office space and (7) less business travel. Assume the cost of selling, general and administrative (SG&A) expenses are about 15% of total revenue and that energy costs are 2% of that. Let us 'lump' the costs for water and consumables into that amount, to be extra-conservative. How much of this annual expense could be saved? Amory Lovins describes how old wooden-frame buildings, glass-walled office towers, university buildings and masonry row houses can be retrofitted to save up to 90% of their energy consumption—and the payback occurs within months or a few years (von Weizsäcker *et al.* 1997). Let us assume **20% savings** in our company's facilities, again after the cost of the retrofit has been repaid.

21.1.6 Increased revenue and market share

Let us assume that our company gains favourable publicity for its environmentally friendly operations, products and services. More revenue is generated from new 'green' customers. These customers continue to purchase the company's products. The company adds a new revenue stream by leasing its products instead of selling them, launching a business to perform the services of its products and charging a premium for its environmentally friendly products. Given these diverse new revenue opportunities, let us conservatively assume a **5% increase**, which translates into big money. If we assume the proportion of this incremental revenue that flows to the bottom line is the same as that of today's revenue, then we can add 7% toward profit—for SD Inc., today's US$3 billion of profit is 7% of today's US$44 billion of revenue.

21.1.7 Reduced risk and easier financing

Sustainable approaches to a company's manufacturing processes and operations can (1) lower the market risks of regulatory bans on sales, reduced demand or customer boycotts, (2) lower the balance-sheet risk of remediation liabilities, harm to property values, damage assessments and 'toxic torts', (3) lower the operating expense risk of cleaning up spills, of worker safety measures and of escalating energy and material costs, (4) lower the capital cost risks of product redesign to meet new regulations and new waste-treatment facilities and (5) lower the sustainability risk from energy and material inefficiencies, take-back legislation and fossil-fuel taxes. A derivative of these lower risks is the ability to raise capital in the marketplace more easily as the impact of these risks spills into market valuation.

The sum of the financial benefits of reduced risk is a 'fruit salad' of cost avoidance, lower insurance premiums, reduced legal and regulatory costs, preferred rates on loans, greater investor appeal and avoidance of lost revenue from consumer actions. Depending on the accounting techniques used, these would be accounted for in the operating expenses listed on annual income statements or in the liabilities listed on balance sheets. Quantification of the benefits of risk reduction is difficult. In an extreme case, a disaster could wipe out the business. Even if it is not possible to quantify all the risk factors, just thinking through which ones are important helps.

Robert Repetto and Duncan Austin, in *Pure Profit: The Financial Implications of Environmental Performance* (2000), describe a way to quantify multiple risks. They use a scenario-planning approach to aggregate the financial exposure of 13 US pulp and paper companies to several pending environmental issues. Their assessment of the companies' exposure in 1998–2010 ranged from +2.9% to –10.8% of the companies' market value, with 12 of the 13 companies affected negatively and most of the companies facing a loss of up to 8% of share value. Some companies were poorly positioned for the issues in the scenarios and would face relatively high capital costs to meet regulations or to mitigate other risks. This would put them at a competitive disadvantage if they were to cover the costs with price increases or would make them unable to afford other capital expenditures if they were to absorb the costs.

This is an important point. Companies sometimes mislead themselves, believing that their relative competitive position will be protected if potential regulatory or other risks actually happen, as their competitors will be subject to the same statutes to a similar degree. Think again. The above study showed a wide range of financial impacts on companies in the same industry, depending on how well positioned they were for the impending environmental issue. That is why Repetto and Austin favour a scenario-based comparison of companies rather than a checklist approach when assessing the attractiveness of each company as an investment. Business schools would do well to reinforce the value of scenario-based risk assessment in MBA programmes.

Having said that, at least a placeholder is required to complete our calculation of the seven benefit areas. Since risk will ultimately hit expenses or revenues, when and if it happens, I will bundle the financial benefit of reduced risk into savings and cost avoidance. Previously (Section 21.1.5) I calculated SG&A expenses to be 15% of total revenue. Assume just 5% of the SG&A expenses are risk-related, and 5% of that amount would be reduced by more proactive company social and environmental initiatives. This small amount avoids accusations of inflating benefits and helps more rigorous estimates to be inserted instead.

21.1.8 Summary of benefits

Table 21.1 summarises the savings or increases in the seven benefit areas. Some benefits are small proportions of large numbers and some are large percentages of small numbers. The absolute contributions are shown in Figure 21.1, revealing that the two highest contributors are increased employee productivity and increased revenue. Since traditional business case efforts to justify sustainability initiatives have typically focused on cost savings in manufacturing and at commercial sites (the middle two benefits illustrated in Fig. 21.1) it is unsurprising that the business case has been weak. The case becomes more compelling with a more holistic view of the benefits. For SD Inc., total benefits in all categories yield a **38% increase in profit**.

Source of savings	Change (%)
Reduced recruitment costs	−1
Reduced costs of attrition	−2
Increased employee productivity	+10.5
Reduced manufacturing expenses	−5 (−2.5)
Reduced expenses at commercial sites (for energy, water and consumables)	−20
Increased revenue and market share	+5
Reduced risk and easier financing	−5

Table 21.1 **Percentage savings from sustainable development**

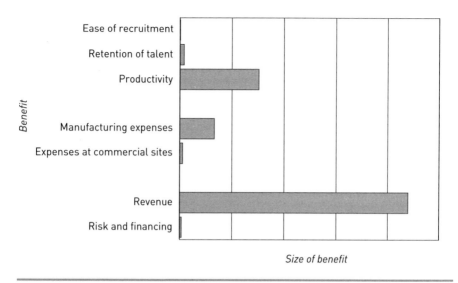

Figure 21.1 Relative size of beneficial contributions

Suppose realising the full benefit of these savings takes five years. Some benefits associated with 'low-hanging fruit' are immediate, but the full benefits take longer. I assume that during the first year only 30% of the full benefits are realised, 50% in the second, 70% in the third, 90% in the fourth and 100% in the fifth. Even so, return on the annual environmental education investment ranges from 714% in the first year to 5,327% in the fifth year. Not bad. That is why a company creating a sustainable development profit centre, led by a respected senior executive or visible 'up-and-comer' to make this happen makes sense. The centre's mandate is to ensure that financial benefits are realised as soon as possible. If the five-year allowance can be compressed, all the better.

Not all benefit areas need be pursued—just a few will help. Executives can inject their own parameters into the spreadsheet model rather than accept the well-researched ones that are built into the template. If they do so, they can prove to themselves that sustainable development will yield hard-nosed business benefits for their company and prioritise which to pursue first. For example, if their gut feeling based on their company's situation and experience is that a 5% increase in revenue is too optimistic, they may want to see what a 2% increase would yield instead. In this case, profit would drop only 3%. Similarly, if executives are more comfortable with a 5% increase in productivity, rather than the 10.5% of the template, they would still see increased profit of 25%.

If executives tailor the business case to their situations they may find that using sustainability performance as a competitive weapon will help them compete smartly. The benefits are there for the taking, and knowing executives will take them before their competitors do. Companies that lead will win. Business schools can help them discover this advantage.

21.2 **Leadership opportunity for business schools**

The idea of integrating the sustainability business case in the core business school curriculum is original and important in three ways. First, a compelling and credible business case for sustainability has been the 'Holy Grail' of consultants, business schools and corporations for years. The relevance of the cause to the decision-maker's day-to-day priorities must be evident—if it does not help the business, it is not on leaders' radar screens. A financial business case approach would focus on the hard bottom-line benefits stressed in core MBA courses, not on the seemingly soft altruistic societal and environmental results that are often relegated to elective ethics courses. Environmental and social benefits can be a happy by-product, even if they are not the initial motivators. No field-authenticated, comprehensive, generic sustainability business case worksheets have been available before. Use of a sustainability business case simulator would be a first for whichever business school seizes the opportunity.

The second reason why this approach is a breakthrough is that it quantifies three human resource benefits—the ability to attract, retain and increase the productivity of top talent—in the sustainability business case. In fact, this quantification is a breakthrough in the leadership and organisational development arenas too, because it helps answer the question 'How much is a vision worth?' The leadership, culture change and learning organisation literature is largely silent on this question. By substantiating the links in the chain from a compelling vision to a bottom-line benefit, executives would be encouraged to display the visionary leadership that is highly correlated with business success. Business schools would be able to support literature rhetoric about the benefits of visionary leadership with hard numbers.

A third reason why the simulator approach is important relates to transformational learning and organisational development. Use of the Sustainability Advantage Worksheets is based on a powerful principle of organisational and personal change. As executives interactively tailor the computerised worksheets by using their assumptions and their company's parameters, or as MBA students do this for companies they are studying, they will see how compelling the business reasons are for aggressively embedding sustainable development approaches in strategy. This 'see-for-yourself' approach supports the wisdom of using inquiry over advocacy when attempting transformational learning with senior business leaders. The methodology is not prescriptive; it is suggestive. It asks, not tells. As senior leaders give the answers in the sustainability business case simulator, they convince themselves. It is an action-learning experience for aspiring change agents.

21.3 Positioning sustainability content in business school curricula

Terminology matters. Colonel Sanders understood this. He instinctively knew that 'finger-licking good' chicken would attract more customers than 'fried dead bird'. Both are descriptive and accurate but one is repulsive. Effective marketing requires getting inside customers' heads, understanding their priorities and positioning products effectively. Features and characteristics of the product that are unrelated to a customer's needs are interesting but irrelevant to that customer. Marketing 101[7] teaches that you have to talk the customer's language.

Convincing business schools to embrace 'sustainable development' works in the same way. If a business school has built a reputation for corporate finance, breakthrough business strategies or creative corporate leadership, then use of language that suggests that it should now also save the world would not be an effective sales technique. What should we call a course about the business benefits of strategies based on the trinity of economic, environmental and social stewardship that we are encouraging business schools to adopt? 'Sustainability'? 'Corporate Social Responsibility'? 'Sustainable Development'? 'The Triple Bottom Line'? These titles are descriptive, but do they talk the language of business schools?

Here is a lateral-thinking thought. Forget course titles that imply sustainability is an end in itself. Instead, use titles that describe what sustainability strategies enable. The key is not what sustainability is but the 'so what?' of it. We should focus on 'leadership', 'innovation', 'productivity', 'competitive business strategies', 'profits' and 'shareholder value' as the end results, with sustainability initiatives as the means to those ends. Going further, rather than risking marginalising the sustainability business case as an additional, separate consideration covered in a special 'Productivity, Profits, Innovation: The Sustainability Trinity' course, ideally the business case would be integrated into existing core courses. It would not be an add-on course; rather, it would be an add-in theme in existing required courses on finance, strategy and leadership.

21.4 Conclusions

Using real case studies, business schools can show how leading sustainable development companies are 'doing well while doing good'. Current and future business leaders can learn from these case studies, can consider how the rationale and methods used by those leading sustainable development companies might apply to them and can accelerate their sustainable development journeys. More importantly, they can use a sustainability business case simulator as a decision-making tool, tailored to their particular situation.

7 'Marketing 101' is a generic term for a basic marketing course.

The business case for sustainable development should be the cornerstone of an enlightened curriculum in business schools. The compelling business case shows how advancements in environmental and social performance also result in improvements in the bottom line, including competitive differentiation and gains in market advantage. By integrating the business case into their core curriculum, business schools can help convince corporate leaders to want to capitalise on the sustainable development proposition. Thus they would be educating business leaders as if the bottom line *and* the world mattered.

References

3M (2004) 'More about Pollution Prevention Pays', www.3m.com/about3m/sustainability/policies_ehs_tradition_3p.jhtml

Austin, D., and R. Repetto (2000) *Pure Profit: The Financial Implications of Environmental Performance* (Washington, DC: World Resources Institute).

Axelrod, E., H. Handfield Jones and T. Walsh (2001) 'The War for Talent, Part Two', *The McKinsey Quarterly* 2Q 2001; www.mckinseyquarterly.com.

Bennis, W., and B. Namus (1985) *Leaders: The Strategies for Taking Charge* (New York: Perennial Library).

Blanchard, K., and S. Bowles (1998) *Gung Ho! Turn On the People in Any Organisation* (New York: William Morrow & Co.).

Buckingham, M., and C. Coffman (1999) *First Break All the Rules: What the World's Greatest Managers Do Differently* (New York: Simon & Schuster).

Clemmer, J. (1999) *Growing the Distance: Timeless Principles for Personal, Career and Family Success* (Kitchener, ON, Canada: TCG Press).

Collins, J., and J. Porras (1994) *Built to Last: Successful Habits of Visionary Companies* (New York: HarperCollins).

—— (2000) 'The Millennium Poll on Corporate Social Responsibility', conducted by Environics in co-operation with the Prince of Wales Business Leaders Forum and The Conference Board, www.mallenbaker.net/csr/CSRfiles/ Resources.html, accessed March 2004.

Environics (Environics International Ltd) (2002) *Corporate Social Responsibility Monitor 2002* (Toronto: Environics).

Fortune (2000) 'Fortune 500 Archive', www.fortune.com/fortune/subs/500archive/search/0,19391,,00.html, accessed March 2004.

Herman Group (1999) 'Trend Alert: Where Have All the Students Gone?', in R. Herman and J. Gioia (eds.), *Trend Alerts* (Greensboro, NC: Strategic Business Futurists, www.herman.net/alert/archive_8-24-99.html, 21 August 1999).

Hesselbein, F., M. Goldsmith and R. Beckhard (eds.) (1996) *The Leader of the Future* (sponsored by the Peter F. Drucker Foundation; San Francisco: Jossey-Bass).

Jensen, P. (1992) *The Inside Edge: High Performance through Mental Fitness* (Toronto: Macmillan Canada).

Kouzes, J., and B. Posner (1995) *The Leadership Challenge* (San Francisco: Jossey-Bass).

Leider, R. (1985) *The Power of Purpose* (Toronto: Fawcett Gold Medal Books).

McNee, B., C. Smith Ardito, D. Tunick Morello and E. Zidar (1998) *IT Staff Retention and Recruitment: Addressing a Critical Problem for the IS Organization* (Stamford, CT: The Gartner Group, 28 September 1998).

Mercer/Angus Reid (1999) *Beyond the Bottom Line: What CEOs Are Thinking* (Toronto: William M. Mercer Company).

Nattrass, B., and M. Altomare (1999) *The Natural Step for Business: Wealth, Ecology and the Evolutionary Corporation* (Gabriola Island, BC, Canada: New Society Publishers).

Pritchett, P. (1994) *Firing Up Commitment During Organisational Change* (Dallas, TX: Pritchett & Associates).

Romm, J. (1999) *Cool Companies: How the Best Businesses Boost Profits and Productivity by Cutting Greenhouse Gas Emissions* (Washington, DC: Island Press).

Senge, P. (1990) *The Fifth Discipline: The Art and Practice of the Learning Organization* (New York: Doubleday Currency).

Terez, T. (2002) 'Key Findings', www.meaningatwork.com/akeyfind.html, accessed March 2004.

Von Weizsäcker, E.U., A.B. Lovins and L.H. Lovins (1997) *Factor Four: Doubling Wealth, Halving Resource Use. The New Report to the Club of Rome* (London: Earthscan Publications).

Willard, B. (2002) *The Sustainability Advantage: Seven Business Case Benefits of a Triple Bottom Line* (Gabriola Island, BC, Canada: New Society Publishers).

22
Population, business and sustainability

David K. Foot

University of Toronto, Canada

Population is part of the external environment for all business. The size and growth of the population cannot be readily influenced by business decisions, yet the size and growth of the market is a crucial determinant of the success of any business. Moreover, the workforce is also drawn from the population, so population developments influence the ability of business to produce goods and services.

The study of people, or human populations, is called demography. Since people are both customers and workers demography plays an important part in all business decision-making. In this chapter I present an introduction to demography and its relevance to business and sustainability. I outline the determinants of the size and growth of populations and the applicability to markets, workforces and sustainability. The globalisation of many businesses requires not only an understanding of local demographics but also, increasingly, an awareness of demographic developments elsewhere in the world. This chapter includes a discussion of world demographic developments.

Population size and growth is almost always at the core of most sustainability issues, whether they relate to environmental, economic or social sustainability. Sustaining an increasing population in a world with limited resources characterises the essence of the sustainability challenge. This challenge is not new. It was recognised over two centuries ago by Thomas Malthus, the British cleric whose pessimism has endured even if his forecasts have not, at least in the developed world. To Malthus the inevitable growth in population occasioned by human's proclivity to procreate would always come into conflict with the slower growth in food supplies, thereby setting humanity on a course of long-term poverty (see Weeks 2002: ch. 3).

Although this vision is characteristic of much of the world today, some regions have escaped this pessimistic destiny. It was as if Malthus ignored the major technological advances that were occurring in his lifetime. The Industrial Revolution in Britain enabled production to outstrip population growth, thereby leading to an increase in the standard of living over time. This fact has led many observers to the conclusion that technological change can overcome the sustainability challenge posed by demographics. Many others do not share such optimism, pointing out that the world must have a limited carrying capacity for humans much as the seas, forests and lakes have for all living species.

The remainder of this chapter is arranged as follows. First, in Section 22.1, the fundamentals of population growth are presented with a 'discussion, to diagrams, to mathematics' format.[1] This multiple representation approach has been shown to be a successful teaching technique. This approach clearly identifies and reinforces the key demographic relationships and develops the concept of population dynamics. Next, in Section 22.2, the connections of population dynamics to sustainability analysis are outlined. This is followed, in Section 22.3, by the implications of population dynamics for business decision-making. Finally, in Section 22.4, an examination of the global marketplace from a demographic perspective is presented. The chapter concludes, in Section 22.5, with a summary of lessons for teaching demographics, especially to business students.

22.1 Population dynamics

Analysis of demographics and sustainability frequently starts with a focus on world population. In this context the world is sometimes referred to as 'spaceship Earth' to emphasise its isolation from the rest of the universe.[2] This is also a conve-

---

1   There is nothing rigid about this order of presentation, only that teaching experience has shown that this works best in a general class setting. Students with strong mathematical backgrounds may prefer to reverse the order, whereas those with weaker mathematical backgrounds may choose to skim the mathematical material. What is important, however, is that the links between each format be carefully outlined so that students with different learning styles or preferences can focus not only on the learning technique best suited to their needs but also can also use this format to understand and integrate the alternative formats into their analysis. This multiple representation approach provides the basis for the cross-pollination of these learning formats. It also facilitates the understanding of alternative communication strategies, thereby reducing inhibitions, building confidence and improving discussion. These are important characteristics of any successful business leader.

2   Although it is useful to focus on the world to establish the essential characteristics of population size and growth, it is important to remember that international discussions and negotiations of sustainability issues have repeatedly recognised the interrelationships of individual countries in contributing to a sustainability strategy for the world. National strategies are, therefore, important in contributing to this global perspective. The increased education of women (from the 1992 United Nations Conference) and decreased energy use (the Kyoto Protocol) provide two examples. Nonetheless, spaceship Earth is a good place to start any discussion of global sustainability.

nient way to introduce demographic concepts for subsequent business applications.

How has the world population grown over time? Table 22.1 provides a summary of world population growth over human history. In 1999 it was estimated that the world population passed six billion people, a fivefold increase in numbers since the first billion people was reached around 1800 AD. Historically, world population has followed a path that is similar to the Malthusian postulate of compound growth, although since the third billion people arrived in 1960 the population growth rate has been decreasing over time.[3]

Year	Population (billions)	Years per billion growth	Average growth rate (percentage per year)
1800	1		
1930	2	130	0.53
1960	3	30	1.36
1974	4	14	1.21
1987	5	13	1.17
1999	6	12	1.14

Table 22.1 World population growth, 1800–1999

Source: Deevey 1960, with updates by the author

22.1.1 Discussion

From a population growth perspective, the world is a very convenient focus for analysis. Migration is not relevant when considering the world population since, to date, Earth has not knowingly accepted residents from other planets nor sent Earthlings to other planets. World population growth, therefore, is simply the difference between global births and deaths, with births adding to population size and deaths reducing population size. Consequently, if births exceed deaths in any period the population will increase, whereas an excess of deaths over births will reduce the population size over that period. An unchanging or stable population means that births exactly match deaths over the period of stability. This situation corresponds to zero population growth (ZPG; note that for ZPG it does not matter what rates are, only that they are equal).

Demographers, the professionals who study population developments, have devised key concepts to understand the determinants of births and deaths over time (and across countries). The birth rate is defined as the number of births in any

3 The year 1960 conveniently coincides with the peak of the postwar baby boom and the beginning of the commercial introduction of the birth control pill in many developed countries (see e.g. Foot and Stoffman 1996).

period (usually a year) divided by the population size.[4] Often, this number is multiplied by 1,000 so that the rate is expressed per 1,000 of population. By the end of the 20th century there were approximately 22 births per year per 1,000 people on the world.

Not surprisingly, a similar calculation can be carried out for the death rate, which is defined as the number of deaths in any period divided by population size. By the end of the 20th century there were approximately 9 deaths per year per 1,000 people on the world.

If the birth rate exceeds the death rate, global population will grow, whereas a death rate above the birth rate will cause global population decline. Population stability (or ZPG) requires that the two be equal. The difference between the birth rate and the death rate determines the rate of population growth. At the end of the 20th century this difference was 13 (22 – 9) per 1,000, which translates into an annual global population growth rate of 1.3%.

Historically, rising birth rates and falling death rates have both contributed to increasing rates of population growth on spaceship Earth. In the second half of the 20th century, with the increased use of family planning methods, including the birth control pill, birth rates declined and so did the rate of world population growth. Improved health and nutrition contributed to declining death rates, but at slower pace,[5] so that the gap between birth and death rates narrowed, resulting in slower population growth. This accounts for the slower population growth rates since 1960 as shown in Table 22.1.

22.1.2 Diagram

A visual presentation of the above discussion can contribute to understanding and analysis. In Figure 22.1 the square box represents the population size, which is measured at a point in time. As indicated in Table 22.1, the population size changes over time. For these reasons, population size is called a stock variable. It is a stock like the amount of oil reserves or the amount of physical capital. These are measured at a point in time but can change over time depending on the additions and deletions to the relevant stock.

A circle in Figure 22.1 represents a flow. A flow is anything that must be measured over a period of time rather than at a point in time. The measured value can change over time (and, therefore, is also a variable). The number of births and deaths are

---

4   The beginning, mid-period or end-period population can be used, although the beginning population is preferred. For accuracy, this concept is called the crude birth rate since it ignores the age structure of the population. The same caveat applies to the death rate. Ignoring age structure simplifies the presentation. See Weeks 2002 for more details on demographic concepts.

5   Much of the reduction in the death rate was attributable to reduced infant mortality rather than increased longevity over this period. Slower population growth results in the ageing of a population, as there are proportionally fewer people in the younger ages and proportionally more of the population in the older ages. Ultimately, population ageing can result in a decrease in the birth rate, as older people are less likely to bear children, and in an increase in the death rate, as older people are more likely to die. This further reduces population growth.

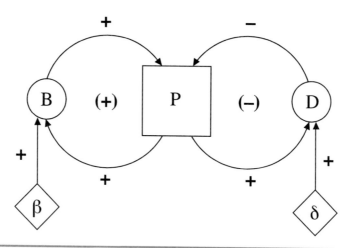

Figure 22.1 **Population dynamics**

examples of flow variables. They must be counted over time, such as a year or a decade, and the observed numbers can change over time.

Of particular relevance in Figure 22.1 are the arrows and the signs (plus and minus) on the lines. The arrows show the direction of causation. The top half of the figure shows that births and deaths cause a change in population size. The signs indicate the direction of change. A plus sign indicates a positive relationship and a minus sign designates a negative relationship. Births add to the population so the arrowed line from births to population carries a positive sign, whereas deaths reduce the population size so the associated sign is negative.[6]

Births always add to population, so the sign is always positive. However, a reduction in the number of births over time will reduce the increase in the population over time. This is what the growth data in Table 22.1 is suggesting. In addition, slower population growth can reflect an increase in the number of deaths over time.

However, the population 'story' does not stop there, since more people are likely to have more children (when they reach maturity) and there are more people to die. Ignoring, for simplicity, the issue of timing, there is also causation from population size to births and deaths. The relationship is positive in each case: that is, more people lead to more births and more deaths. These relationships are indicated in the bottom half of Figure 22.1, with the associated positive signs.

The combination of these relationships produces 'feedback loops'. An increased population will result in more births, and more births will increase the population. This is called a positive feedback loop and is indicated in Figure 22.1 by a plus sign in a circle in the middle of the left-hand (or birth) loop in the figure. At the same time, an increased population will result in more people dying (a positive relation-

---

6   For the mathematically inclined, these are the signs of the derivatives of the destination variable with respect to the source variable in the line.

ship), but more deaths reduce the population size (a negative relationship). The combination (or multiplication) of a plus and a minus sign produces a negative loop, as indicated in the middle of the right-hand (or death) loop in Figure 22.1.[7]

The significance of these signed loops is paramount to the way a variable such as population size changes over time. This is called dynamic analysis. Positive feedback loops contribute to growth, whereas negative feedback loops contribute to decay. In this example, the birth loop leads to population growth, whereas the death loop leads to population decline. For a growing population, such as the world population summarised in Table 22.1, the positive loop is more powerful than (or dominates) the negative loop and therefore is called the dominant loop. This is a complicated way of saying that births must have been higher than deaths or the population would not have grown over this period!

Although Figure 22.1 may look unnecessarily complicated, this diagrammatic approach leads to insights regarding population dynamics and the rate of growth of the population. If the rate of population growth is slowing, as it has in the world since 1960, then the dominance of the birth loop must be gradually waning. Another way of saying this is that the difference between world births and deaths, or between the birth rate and the death rate, must have been getting smaller over recent decades.

Since there is nothing preventing deaths from being greater in number than births, this gradual shifting of dominance from the birth loop to the death loop signals not only a decline in the growth of population but also, perhaps, the ultimate decline in the size of the population. Whether this will actually happen to world population remains to be seen, but Figure 22.1 provides a visual representation of how it may come to pass.

The advantage of feedback diagrams is that they provide a visual representation of the important relationships underlying any observed outcome, whether it can be measured or not. They can provide a useful foundation for mapping all the likely relationships in any analysis and identifying the dominant causes of growth and decay for any variable, including important stock variables, such as population size, and many environmental indicators, such as forest area. For real-world problems such as sustainability these diagrams can become extremely complicated (a good example can be found in Meadows *et al.* 1992).

22.1.3 Mathematics

The important features of demographic analysis—population size, births and deaths—can also be captured in mathematical equations. An equation shows the relationship between variables. Since population size varies over time (see Table 22.1), the determinants of population size, namely the number of births and deaths, must also vary over time. These are the key variables in any mathematical representation of population growth (such mathematical representations are often called models).

7 As in multiplication, two negative signs produce a positive sign (as do two positive signs), whereas a negative and a positive sign always produce a negative sign regardless of the order in which they occur.

In the equations that follow, population size is represented by P, and the number of births and deaths by B and D, respectively (recall that P is a stock variable whereas B and D are flow variables; see Section 22.1.2). Population growth, whether positive or negative, is measured by a change in the size of the population over time. To indicate this it is necessary to introduce time (represented by t) into the equation. Traditionally, this is done by using a subscript. In this notation, P_t denotes the population size at the end of time-period t.

The change in the population over time-period t is then represented as the difference between the population size at the beginning of the period and that at the end of the period. Since the population size at the beginning of the period is, by definition, the population size at the end of the previous period (which is represented by P_{t-1}), the change in population is mathematically represented by the difference between P_t and P_{t-1}.

This change in population size is caused by births, which increase the population size, and deaths, which decrease the population size. The definitional relationship or equation is:

$$P_t - P_{t-1} = B_t - D_t , \qquad [22.1]$$

which can be rewritten as:

$$P_t = P_{t-1} + B_t - D_t . \qquad [22.2]$$

Note that Equation [22.1] represents the top half of Figure 22.1.

In all equations the direction of causation is from the right-hand side to the left-hand side. Hence, the change in population size is caused by the difference between births and deaths (Equation [22.1]), or the population today is the population yesterday plus the difference between births and deaths over the intervening period (Equation [22.2]).

Equations [22.1] and [22.2] express population growth in terms of absolute numbers of people. However, as noted in Table 22.1 and discussed above, population growth is often referred to in relative terms: that is, relative to the population size. This is called a growth *rate* (denoted here by g) and is defined as:

$$g = \frac{P_t - P_{t-1}}{P_{t-1}} , \qquad [22.3]$$

which is often multiplied by 100 and expressed as a percentage (as in Table 22.1). Note that this equation can be rewritten as:

$$P_t = (1 + g) P_{t-1} . \qquad [22.4]$$

It is useful to remember that Equations [22.3] and [22.4] are equivalent ways of stating the same relationship.

Population growth is determined by the number of births and deaths, so the next step is to introduce equations for the number of births and deaths. The simplest postulate is that the number of births and the number of deaths are directly proportional to the size of the population entering the period; that is:

$$B_t = \beta P_{t-1} , \qquad [22.5]$$

and

$$D_t = \delta P_{t-1},$$ [22.6]

where β and δ are parameters of proportionality (for simplicity, the parameters are assumed here to be constant, but in more complicated analysis the parameters of proportionality can change over time). These equations simply state that the bigger the population the greater the number of births and deaths, and vice versa. Demographers call P_{t-1} the population 'at risk' over time-period t. Note that Equations [22.5] and [22.6] represent the bottom half of Figure 22.1, with the parameters entering the birth and death circles.

Equations [22.2], [22.5] and [22.6] represent three equations in three unknowns (P_t, B_t and D_t). The fourth variable (P_{t-1}) is called a predetermined variable since its value is known entering period t. These related equations, which together are often referred to as a model, can be summarised by substituting Equations [22.5] and [22.6] into Equation [22.2] as follows:

$$\begin{aligned} P_t &= P_{t-1} + \beta P_{t-1} - \delta P_{t-1} \\ &= (1 + \beta - \delta)\, P_{t-1}. \end{aligned}$$ [22.7]

Note that Equation [22.7] is identical to Equation [22.4] with

$$g = \beta - \delta.$$ [22.8]

To understand the meaning of this mathematical equivalence note that Equations [22.5] and [22.6] can be rewritten to define β and δ as follows:

$$\beta = \frac{B_t}{P_{t-1}},$$ [22.9]

and

$$\delta = \frac{D_t}{P_{t-1}}.$$ [22.10]

In demographic analysis these are, respectively, the definitions of the birth rate and death rate (see footnote 4 on page 285). Mathematical analysis has now made it clear that, just as the absolute growth in population size is determined by the difference between births and deaths, so the relative growth in the population (or population growth rate) is determined as the difference between the birth rate and the death rate. This is a mathematical confirmation of the results of both the discussion and the diagrammatic treatment (Sections 22.1.1 and 22.1.2).

The definition of the population growth rate as according to Equation [22.8] shows that population growth will be positive if the birth rate is higher than the death rate (β is greater than δ, written as $\beta > \delta$), zero if the birth rate equals the death rate ($\beta = \delta$) or negative if the birth rate is lower than the death rate (β is less than δ, written as $\beta < \delta$). These three possible outcomes of the population model outlined above can be derived by solving Equation [22.4] or Equation [22.7]. The solution can then be used to illustrate and understand the history of world population growth within this framework. It can also be used to investigate the impact of population growth in a world with limited resources, which underlies most sustainability analysis.

22.1.4 The compound growth solution

In mathematical parlance, Equation [22.4] is called a first-order difference equation (it is first order because P_{t-1} is a one-period lag). This is the simplest of all dynamic models. Although mathematicians have well-defined solutions for such models, non-mathematicians must solve them by more mundane techniques. This means deriving values for P_t associated with different time-periods so that the trajectory of the population can be tracked over time.

The starting or initial population size at $t = 0$ is denoted P_0. The population size in the next period ($t = 1$) is then related to the initial population by using Equation [22.4]; namely,

$$P_1 = (1 + g) P_0 . \tag{22.11}$$

For the next time-period ($t = 2$) the same relationship applies, or:

$$P_2 = (1 + g) P_1 . \tag{22.12}$$

By substituting the previous solution for P_1, the equation for P_2 becomes:

$$\begin{aligned} P_2 &= (1 + g) (1 + g) P_0 \\ &= (1 + g)^2 P_0 . \end{aligned} \tag{22.13}$$

Successive substitutions leads us to the general solution to this model; that is:[8]

$$P_t = (1 + g)^t P_0 . \tag{22.14}$$

If $g = 0$ in Equation [22.14] (which is equivalent to $\beta = \delta$ in Equation [22.8]), the population will be stable, with $P_t = P_0$ for all values of t; that is, for all time. This is the ZPG solution. Population growth occurs when g is positive (or $\beta > \delta$), in which case the solution will exhibit the familiar trajectory of compound growth. The third possible solution, where g is negative, is less familiar. In this case $(1 + g)$ is less than one so that compounding leads to ever-smaller population numbers as t gets larger. Under these conditions, P_t declines and heads towards zero as t gets larger. Note: in mathematical language this is expressed as:

$$P_t \rightarrow 0 \text{ as } t \rightarrow \infty$$

(read as 'P_t tends to zero as t tends to infinity').

When the birth rate is higher than the death rate and hence the growth rate is positive, the compounding effect of positive growth is readily apparent. As the population growth rate decreases, perhaps as a result of a declining birth rate, the trajectory of P_t moves towards the flat line of stable or zero population growth. Further decreases in the population growth rate below zero, perhaps as a result of an increasing death rate in an ageing population, moves the population trajectory gradually towards zero. This analysis can be used to understand the trajectory of the world population as summarised in Table 22.1.

---

8 The format of Equation [22.14] should be familiar to most business students since it is analogous to the compound growth formula used in financial analysis to calculate the return (principal and interest) by investing a principal P_0 for time-period t at an interest rate r; that is, $P_t = (1 + r)^t P_0$.

The simple most probable explanation of the increase in the world population growth rate up to 1960 is an increase in the birth rate as a result of increased living standards made possible by the Industrial Revolution. A coincident decline in the death rate made possible by better health and sanitation, resulting in increases in life expectancy, further supported the increase in the population growth rate over this period. An increasing birth rate supported by a more modestly decreasing death rate increased the difference between the birth and death rates, thereby increasing population growth. Since 1960, rapidly decreasing birth rates facilitated by more effective birth control and the changing role of women in society in many countries has had the opposite impact on global population growth. This trend has dominated the continued more modest declines in the death rate, thereby leading to a reduction in the difference between the birth and death rates and the consequent reduction in world population growth. Demographers refer to this explanation as the theory of demographic transition (see e.g. Beaujot 1991: ch. 3).

How can these changes be combined with the compound growth solution to explain world population growth as summarised in Table 22.1? The observed world population data lies on different compound growth paths that reflect the changing values of the underlying growth parameters: namely, the birth and death rates, over time[9] Continuation of this slower growth trend, perhaps as a result of increasing death rates from population ageing in the developed world, could result in eventual population decline on spaceship Earth. This is unlikely within the 21st century.

22.2 Population dynamics and sustainability

Slowing world population growth may be explained by decreases in birth rates and/or increases in death rates, but what causes these changes in human behaviour? Changes in technology, standards of living and attitudes are undoubtedly major reasons for observed changes in human behaviour throughout human history, but perhaps there is another even more fundamental force at work.

A common feature in many discussions of sustainability is the concept of a maximum sustainable population (MSP), or maximum carrying capacity. Usually, this concept is applied to non-human populations where a lake, forest or bio-zone is estimated to have a maximum carrying capacity for certain species of fish, animals or birds. A population approaching that carrying capacity will experience slower growth, usually as a result of an increased death rate reflecting reduced food per individual. Reductions in carrying capacity as a result of pollution, deforestation or other ecosystem 'unfriendly' activities will result in sharp reductions in the population of the affected species, for the same reason.

Such concepts apply equally to human populations. Spaceship Earth provides an ecosystem in which humans live. Given human needs and behaviour the Earth

---

9 Note that these population growth rates are all measured from the same initial population (P_0 in Equation [22.14]).

probably has a maximum carrying capacity for humans beyond which famine and starvation would be widespread and population growth would cease. On the path to this situation population growth would slow down. Perhaps the slowing world population growth reflects humanity beginning to approach the habitable limits of spaceship Earth. Any such limits may not be fixed and could potentially be extended by creative use of new technologies or new behaviour. Nonetheless, a growing population on a fixed planet with no emigration release-valve is likely to face resource constraints on its activities sooner or later.

The concept of an MSP can be conveniently incorporated into the population growth model by making the growth rate dependent on how close the population is to the maximum sustainable population (represented by $P^\star$; see MacIntyre 1999). The closer the population is to $P^\star$ the slower the growth. This can be conveniently accomplished by modifying Equation [22.4] in the following way:

$$P_t = \left(1 + g\left[1 - \frac{P_{t-1}}{P^\star}\right]\right) P_{t-1}.$$
[22.15]

Note that if there is no MSP then $P^\star = \infty$, so

$$\frac{P_{t-1}}{P^\star} = 0,$$

and Equation [22.15] reduces to Equation [22.4]. Where $P^\star$ is a finite number, the closer P_{t-1} gets to $P^\star$, the closer the expression

$$1 - \frac{P_{t-1}}{P^\star}$$

gets to zero, so the smaller the expression

$$g\left(1 - \frac{P_{t-1}}{P^\star}\right)$$

becomes. What this framework leaves unexplained is whether the decrease in

$$g\left(1 - \frac{P_{t-1}}{P^\star}\right)$$

is reflected in the birth rate or the death rate of the population. The solution to this problem is not nearly so straightforward as above, although the time trajectory of the population can be readily calculated for any particular situation. It starts out like the compound growth curve when the population is far from $P^\star$ but then gradually approaches $P^\star$ as P_t gets closer to the MSP. In mathematical terms, $P^\star$ is called an asymptote.

This approach to the problem can be further extended to incorporate variable MSPs. It is possible for $P^\star$ to increase as a result of research and development (R&D) and the implementation of new technologies. An example is the use of trace elements to bring previously infertile land into production. However, a more likely scenario is for $P^\star$ to decrease over time. This situation would arise if continuing unsustainable behaviour were to erode the eco-base for the population. For example, as has been demonstrated only too well in many regions, rapacious over-fishing can destroy habitat and reduce fish stocks to levels from which they can never recover. Deforestation resulting in soil erosion can mean that the forest can never be re-established at that location, implying a permanent loss of the resource with a consequent reduction in $P^\star$. Examples in non-renewable resources are even more poignant since, when used, they are, by definition, gone forever (although, of course, this might not be important if new technology presents a suitable substitute).

In the case where the population is increasing and the MSP is decreasing, it is possible for P_{t-1} to be higher than the reduced $P^\star$ (this is sometimes termed overshooting in the simulation literature; see Meadows *et al.* 1992). This makes the ratio

$$\frac{P_{t-1}}{P^\star} > 0 ,$$

in Equation [22.15] greater than one, which makes

$$g \left(1 - \frac{P_{t-1}}{P^\star} \right)$$

negative and results in a rapid decline in the population. This is what may have happened to the population of Easter Island as a result of the deforestation of the island (for more information on population growth on Easter Island, see Foot 2005).

The introduction of an MSP is a simple and convenient way to incorporate environmental sustainability (and technological change) into a population growth framework. However, it cannot adequately reflect economic and social sustainability issues in population growth. To do this it is necessary to combine the population growth with a model of economic and social change.

The standard of living of a population is some measure of output per person. For Malthus, this measure was food per person. In modern societies it is often some measure of income per person. Note that, although focused on some measure of output or income, there is no inherent reason why the standard of living measure could not include some measure of leisure or happiness in its construction.

The economic theory of output uses the concept of production that relates output or production to inputs such as land, labour, capital and technology. Since spaceship Earth is fixed in size and has a limited supply of resources, 'land' in this context acts as a proxy for all resource inputs that are limited in supply. Economic theory argues that, if an input such as land is fixed in quantity, then application of additional amounts of the remaining inputs will, sooner or later, result in diminishing returns to production. Output will not grow as fast as the growth in the other inputs, including the population input (labour) because of the constraining influence of the fixed or limited input. As output continues to increase, more demands are made on the input in limited supply and it becomes increasingly difficult to maintain output growth, unless new technology can be introduced to economise on its use. With unchanging technology, diminishing returns takes effect.

A growing population makes ever more demands on fixed or limited resources over time. Under the economic theory of production with diminishing returns there will be increasing challenges in maintaining output per person let alone in increasing it. Without new technologies being continually introduced, output per person will, sooner or later, peak and start to fall. Economic sustainability will suffer. Ultimately, social sustainability will suffer as well (for more information on social sustainability, see Chapter 7).

How can this outcome be avoided? There are two main ways to sustain standards of living in a world of resource constraints. One is to lower the population curve and the other is to raise the production curve. Lowering the population curve implies decreased rates of population growth. This means reducing the difference between the birth rate and the death rate. In practice, this means reducing the birth rate, since increasing the death rate is not a palatable option (although it is worth mentioning once again that increasing death rates can be a characteristic of ageing populations).

In a world of unchanging technology, the only solution to the sustainability challenge posed by binding resource limits is zero population growth (ZPG). Even then the population must be at a level that does not result in resource erosion (called the maximum sustainable population [MSP]). As shown above, a reduction in the MSP ($P^\star$) can have catastrophic consequences for a population over time.

The other option is the sustained introduction of new technologies, so that the output grows with population over time, thereby resulting in an output per person that does not decrease over time (note that new technologies may raise $P^\star$ in Equation [22.15]). This highlights the importance of R&D and new technology implementation in sustainable development.

Moreover, this brings the analysis back to the debate outlined in the introduction. In a world of no technological change Malthusian pessimism was justified. Continued population growth in a world of limited resources would ultimately destine humanity to poverty (low output per person). This is viewed through today's lens as an unsustainable condition. However, technological change can ameliorate or, if fast enough, offset the impact of resource limitations, resulting in a world of unnecessary economic, environmental and social sustainability. Such optimism is justified provided that the population does not surpass the MSP established by the resource limits and the available technology. Populations that grow beyond the MSP for any sustained period are likely to face precipitous decline both because population growth will become negative (reflecting falling birth rates and/or rising death rates) and because the MSP will tend to decrease, thereby further intensifying the challenge to reduce population below the current MSP. Overshooting the MSP can have dire consequences for humanity.

22.3 Population dynamics and business

A growing population means a growing market for goods and services and, usually, a growing workforce. Generally, these demographics would be considered desirable by a business focused on growth. It is certainly easier to attain growth targets for sales when the potential customer base is growing than when it is stagnant or declining. This is true whether sales are directly to the customer or are indirectly to the customer through other businesses.

Recall, however, that a growing population is not automatically associated with growing incomes, especially in terms of income per capita. As has been noted in Section 22.1, technology and resources play defining roles in the ability of a society to pursue sustainable growth. Consequently, population growth is not an automatic guarantee of sales growth, but it is a prime indicator.

Population structure may also be important in achieving sales targets. Demography also studies the structures of populations with reference to such characteristics as age, gender, education, region, religion, ethnicity, marital status and a host of other potential market segmentation variables. Although the plethora of possible business applications is too numerous to be considered here (see the market segmentation section of any marketing text for elaborations and applications), one particular variable can be considered as illustrative of the demographic approach to marketing and sales.

The age structure of the population is an important demographic characteristic for many businesses. Just as products have life-cycles, so too do people. A population dominated by young people will need products and services associated with childcare, schooling and other common pursuits of the young such as sporting facilities and cinemas. A population dominated by elderly people is likely to need products and services associated with leisure and healthcare, including package travel tours, pharmaceuticals, home care and hospital facilities. Because of these largely predictable life-cycle needs of different age segments of the population, the potential success of any business product or service is potentially influenced by the age structure of the population. Moreover, market segmentation around age can influence advertising and marketing strategies as well as a host of other strategic decisions in business, including human resource strategies.

People are also employees. Growing populations generally deliver an expanding and dynamic workforce to business. This provides business with flexibility, since new workers are more mobile and often are better trained. It can also result in a surplus of workers, thus keeping a downward pressure on wages (although this can be a two-sided sword, since too much unemployment can lead to social instability, which is not a desirable environment for business). Conversely, slower-growing populations usually reflect ageing workforces, where workers are less mobile, their skills are frequently less up-to-date and their average wages are higher.

Once again, the age structure of the workforce is relevant in human resource applications. First, in most societies young people are excluded from the workforce by tradition or by legislation. Consequently, the population under 15 years old is excluded from the source population of the labour force in many countries. A growing labour force, therefore, usually requires a growing population in the source ages (note that increasing labour-force participation rates are the other source of a growing labour force). Second, very few people in the retirement ages participate in the workforce. Once again, the retirement age varies across countries, but the age of 65 years tends to be a widely used and accepted definition of a typical retirement age. People of 65 years and over tend to participate much less in the labour force. This means that a growing labour force typically requires a growing population between the ages of 15 and 64 years. Finally, for this group there are the inevitable recruitment, retention and retirement strategies that affect every business. Even these decisions tend to be connected to the human life-cycle, with recruitment generally focused on younger workers, retention focused on middle-aged workers and retirement focused on older workers, although most strategies are designed to cover all workers.

Population growth impacts every business, either through the growth in the customer base or through the growth in the workforce, or, more likely, through both channels. However, because of human life-cycle considerations, population growth does not automatically feed into growing sales or growing employee availability. Understanding the age structure of the population is an additional demographic characteristic that can reap important rewards for business. Other demographic characteristics may also be relevant, depending on the type of business, its location and its strategic direction.

Finally, as noted in Section 22.1, populations do not always grow. If deaths dominate births in the population, growth will become negative and the population will shrink.[10] Labour-force growth may also become negative. Output growth will also slow and may become negative but, if output growth remains above population growth, output per person can still increase in a declining population. Nonetheless, this is not an external environment that is favourable to a growing business, unless the market is a well-identified niche market. Population ageing in the developed world may create these conditions in some countries, and businesses producing healthcare products for senior citizens can still be successful in these niche markets.

22.4 Globalisation

So much of world trade is in goods and services that occur between the countries of the developed world. As a result, most businesses in the developed countries produce either for their domestic market or for markets in other parts of the developed world. This includes the countries of Europe (possibly excluding East Europe), North America, Japan and the newly industrialised countries (NICs) of South-East Asia (Hong Kong, Singapore, South Korea and Taiwan). Recent interest in free trade and globalisation have expanded business awareness of markets outside of this sphere (such as Brazil, China, India, Malaysia and Mexico) but to date successful business ventures into these markets appear to be limited.

Obviously, there are obstacles to penetrating unfamiliar business environments, especially with respect to language, laws, customs and institutions. Nonetheless, limited or focused marketing with appropriate products and services in selected markets could yield good results, especially if the market is large enough. So, how large is this market, both in terms of people and in terms of income? The business case for a globalisation strategy requires an understanding of the demographics of the target countries and the associated markets if they are to be tapped to

---

10 This is true in the absence of migration. Note that migration from one region to another may stimulate growth in the receiving region but intensifies population decline in the sending region.

contribute to sustainable business growth in both the developed world and in the businesses located in the rest-of-world (ROW) marketplace.

22.4.1 Population size and composition

The populations of individual countries and regions reflect migration in addition to births and deaths, so birth and death rates are no longer sufficient to characterise market size and growth for sub-world populations. Therefore, in this section I concentrate on population size alone. The source for the data is the Population Reference Bureau (PRB 2003).

By mid-2003 6.31 billion people were estimated to populate spaceship Earth. Of these 1.20 billion (19.4%) were in the developed countries of Europe, North America, Japan, Australia and New Zealand. This means that over 80% of the people of the world are not in the developed world. This 'ROW population' represents a market potential of over 5 billion people.

The population of China (1.20 billion) alone matches the population of the entire developed world. This is why China is such an attractive potential market to many businesses: 6.5% of the Chinese population is larger than the population of the biggest country in Europe (Germany); 5% is larger than the population of United Kingdom, France or Italy; 25% of the Chinese population is equivalent to a population larger than all of East Europe combined. Together, China and the developed world constitute almost 40% of the world's population.

The world's second most populous country, India, contains 1.07 billion people. Even 10% of India's population, which could well be a reasonable estimate of the country's 'middle class' by developed-nation standards, is equivalent to a potential market larger than the population of all but the top 10 most populous countries in the world. It is larger than Mexico, for example; 15% of the population in Indian is greater in number than the populations of Russia or Japan.

The ROW market excluding the world's two most populous countries (China and India) comprises 2.75 billion people. If the 301 million people in East Europe are added to this total, the ROW market excluding China and India totals over 3 billion people, or 48.4% of the world's population. Of these, 21.3% are in Asia, 13.6% in Africa and 8.6% in Latin America. The remaining 4.9% are in East Europe (4.8%) and Oceania (0.1%).

A total of 30% of the world's population is under the age of 15 years, and 7% is 65 years and older (see Table 22.2). These are often considered the populations most dependent on those of prime working age (15–64 years) for their economic support. In the developed world these two shares are much closer—18% and 15%, respectively—indicating that the developed world is older than the average world population. In West and South Europe the shares are very close—around 16% to 17% in both groups—indicating that these are the oldest regions in the world. However, Japan is the oldest country by this measure, with 14% under 15 years old and 19% 65 years and older. North America is younger, with 21% under 15 years old and 13% 65 years older.

In comparison, the ROW population is much younger, with 33% under 15 years old and only 5% 65 years and older. The population of China is somewhat older, with 22% under 15 years old and 7% 65 years and older. Consequently, the ROW

Country or region	Age-structure of population (%)	
	less than 15 years	**65 years or more**
Developed world	18	15
Europe	17	15
North	19	16
West	17	16
South	16	17
East	18	13
Japan	14	19
North America	21	13
ROW	33	5
ROW, excluding China	36	4
Africa	42	3
Asia	30	6
Asia, excluding China	34	5
China	22	7
India	36	4
Latin America	32	6
Oceania	25	10
World	30	7

ROW = rest of world

Table 22.2 Percentages of world populations aged under 15 years or aged 65 years and over

Source: PRB 2003

population excluding China is even younger, with 36% under 15 years old and 4% 65 years and older.

Within this ROW population, the youngest region clearly is Africa, with 42% aged under 15 years and only 3% 65 years and older. This is followed by Asia (excluding China) with 34% and 5%, respectively. India is slightly younger than average, with 36% and 4%, respectively. Close behind is Latin America, at 32% and 6%, respectively. East Europe is much older, with 18% and 13%, respectively. Oceania includes both developed countries (Australia and New Zealand) and ROW countries, with over 70% of the population coming from Papua New Guinea, with 39% and 4% shares, respectively.

22.4.2 Income

Market size is often measured in terms of total income, which combines population size with per capita income. International comparisons of income are difficult at best and inaccurate at worst. The most important consideration is the choice of exchange rate at which the various currencies are converted. Current exchange rates are often subject to considerable volatility and/or manipulation, so economists prefer a purchasing power parity (PPP) rate. Quite often, appropriate national data on income is not available so estimates must be made. Consequently, the following figures should be considered as indicative rather than definitive.

By 2003, average PPP gross national income (GNI) per capita for the world was US$7,160 (see Table 22.3). In the developed world this figure was much higher, at US$22,030, whereas in the ROW the estimated amount is US$3,660 per person. This comparison suggests that incomes in the developed world were over six times those of the ROW. If China (at US$3,950 per person) is removed, the ROW figure drops to US$3,570 per person.

Not surprisingly North America has the highest per capita incomes, at US$33,510, followed by Europe, at US$16,270. The figures for countries of North and West Europe are much higher, at US$23,620 and US$25,430 per person, respectively. (Income in East Europe is estimated to be US$7,170 per person, which is probably why it should not be included in the developed world.) In the remaining countries of the developed world, Japan's GNI is measured at US$25,550 per person, Australia is reported at US$24,630 and New Zealand at US$18,250. Finally, the NIC Hong Kong is at US$25,560, Singapore is at US$22,850 and South Korea at US$15,060.[11]

Africa has the lowest per capita incomes in the ROW (US$2,120), followed by Asia (excluding China: US$4,470) and Latin America (US$6,820). The Asian figure is reduced by the figure for India (US$2,820) and is therefore higher if India is removed (US$5,670).

Despite these comparatively low incomes, the ROW market potential is considerable. To provide an estimate of market size, per capita incomes can be multiplied by population size. These calculations suggested that world GNI is slightly over US$45 trillion, of which Europe generates 26.2% and North America 23.9%; that is, over 50% of world income is generated in these two regions. Japan adds an additional 7.2%, and the remaining developed countries (Australia, New Zealand and the NICs) another 4.2%. The entire developed world accounts for 61.5% of global income. Presumably, this is why business concentrates on the developed world. One-fifth of the world's people generate over three-fifths of the world's income.

Nonetheless, that still leaves 38.5% of income generated outside the developed world. Currently, China is responsible for 11.3% and India for 6.7% of this total. Alternatively, Asia including these two countries, but excluding Japan and the NICs, accounts for slightly over one-quarter of world income. This offers a considerable opportunity for business. Of the remainder, Latin America accounts for

11 There are other individual countries with a GNI per capita slightly higher than that of South Korea, such as the Bahamas, Bahrain, Barbados, Cyprus, French Polynesia, Israel, Kuwait and New Caledonia, but these countries are too small to make any difference to the overall results. Results for Taiwan are not available.

Country or region	PPP GNI per capita (US$)
Developed world	22,030
Europe	16,270
North	23,620
West	25,430
South	18,610
East	7,170
Japan	25,550
North America	33,510
Hong Kong	25,560
Singapore	22,850
South Korea	15,060
Australia	24,630
New Zealand	18,250
ROW	3,660
ROW, excluding China	3,570
Africa	2,120
Asia	4,290
Asia, excluding China	4,470
Asia, excluding India	5,670
China	3,950
India	2,820
Latin America	6,820
World	7,160

Table 22.3 Average purchasing parity power (PPP) gross national income (GNI) per capita for selected countries and regions

Source: PRB 2003

8.1% and Africa for 4.0% of world income.

22.4.3 Future population

Population projections are, by their very nature, uncertain. The future can never be known today, so demographers base projections on current trends of demographic variables (births, deaths and migration). The extrapolation of recent trends, however, provides a glimpse into likely future developments. The source for the following population projections is the Population Reference Bureau (PRB 2003).

By 2025 the world's population is projected to reach 7.91 billion persons, of whom 15.9% (1.26 billion) will be in the developed world (12.3% excluding East Europe). This is a reduction from 19.3% (14.4% excluding East Europe) in 2001. Although the developed world's population is projected to continue to grow in size (despite declines in Europe and Japan), its share in the global population is projected to decline.

This means that the ROW market can be expected to grow significantly. China and India are projected to grow to 1.46 billion and 1.36 billion persons, respectively, in 2025. However, their projected population share of the ROW population is projected to decrease, from 46.5% in 2001 to 42.4% in 2025, primarily because of slower population growth in China.

The remaining ROW population (including East Europe) is projected to add over a billion people, increasing from 43.2% (2.86 billion) to 48.4% (4.11 billion people) of the world's population. This is primarily attributable to rapid population growth in Africa and Asia, which together account for 38% of the world's population (up from 33% in 2001). Unfortunately, these projections suggest that the most rapid population growth will take place in the poorest regions (Africa, Asia and India).

By 2050, projections show a world population of almost 9.2 billion people. The developed world population remains unchanged, but its share of the world population shrinks even further, to 13.7% (11% without East Europe). This implies that the ROW population share continues to increase, to 86.3% (up from 80.7% in 2001). China's population and share is projected to decline, and India is projected to surpass China as the world's most populous nation, with 1.63 billion persons (compared with 1.39 billion for China). Together, their share of world population is projected to continue to decline to 32.9%. Meanwhile, the remainder of the ROW population adds yet another billion persons, to reach 4.92 billion, or 53.5%, of the world's population. Again, Africa and Asia account for most of the increase (594 million and 373 million, respectively). Latin America adds another 100 million persons between 2025 and 2050.

22.5 Conclusions

In this chapter I have focused on demographic analysis and its applicability to business decisions and sustainability analysis. A model of population dynamics has been developed using a multiple representation approach to population growth. The multiple representation approach uses discussion, diagrams and mathematics to illustrate the key concepts and to show the connections between the different learning styles. This is an inclusive approach to learning that fosters the understanding of different communication techniques and respect for different learning strategies. These are important lessons for business students.

The solution to the simple model of population dynamics presented in this chapter is a compound growth equation that is familiar to any student of financial analysis. In this application, the 'interest rate' is the population growth rate that equals the difference between the birth rate and the death rate for the population. The population trajectory over time reflects a 'tug of war' between a birth feedback loop that causes population to increase and a death feedback loop that causes population to decline over time. The changing dominance of interconnected feedback loops captured in this simple model of population dynamics is at the core of the 'limits-to-growth' literature that first explored the possible conflicts between population and economic growth and environmental sustainability (see e.g. Meadows *et al.* 1992).

The challenges posed by population growth in a world of limited resources has an illustrious history. Popularised by Malthus at the beginning of the 19th century, the debate over whether humanity is destined for poverty or prosperity remains as relevant today as when it was first introduced. This chapter shows how the integration of population dynamics with simple economic production theory highlights the important features of the sustainability debate. Of particular interest are the concept of a maximum sustainable population and the important role played by technological advances in dealing with the diminishing returns to fixed resources that determines the economic and, ultimately, the social sustainability of the external environment for business.

Demographic analysis is not only important for understanding sustainability and the external environment for business but also impacts decision-making units within business. Demography is about people, and people are both customers and employees. The success or failure of sales and marketing strategies are influenced by demographic developments, as are human resource strategies and outcomes. Whether it is advertising or recruiting, acquisitions or retention, or strategic planning of any kind, demographics can play an influential role.

Demographers also study the characteristics of populations. Just as products can experience a life-cycle, so can people. As a result, the age structure of the population is especially important in influencing the growth potential of individual products and the success or otherwise of recruiting, retention and retirement policies. The age structure of the population also determines the size and growth of the workforce, which has important implications for business.

Currently, the developed countries dominate the world's trade. Even though they account for only 20% of the world's population they account for over 60% of the world's income. However, the population of the developed world is much older than that in the remainder of the world, and this has major implications for current and future business growth strategy. Population projections indicate a decline in the populations of many of the countries of the developed world in the future. Although population growth in North America maintains the population size of the developed world at around a billion persons, its share is projected to shrink to under 15% of the world's population by 2050.

In contrast, despite slowing population growth and then population decline in China, the ROW population is expected to continue to expand, from 5 billion persons in 2001 to 8 billion persons in 2050. Sustained business growth in the future can be achieved only by tapping into this currently largely untapped market. Demographics is one of the drivers for globalisation. For this reason, the developed world has an important stake in the continuation of globalisation, and businesses interested in pursuing a global strategy must be fully aware of global demographic developments.

References

Beaujot, R. (1991) Population Change in Canada: The Challenges of Policy Adaptation (Toronto: McClelland & Stewart).

Deevey, E.S. (1960) 'The Human Population', *Scientific American* 203.195: 195-204

Foot, D.K. (2005) 'Easter Island: A Case Study in Non-sustainability', in C. Galea (ed.), *Teaching Business Sustainability*. II. *Case Studies* (Sheffield, UK: Greenleaf Publishing, forthcoming).

—— with D. Stoffman (1996) *Boom, Bust and Echo: Profiting from the Demographic Shift in the New Millennium* (Toronto: MacFarlane, Walter & Ross).

MacIntyre, F. (1999) 'Is Humanity Suicidal? Are There Clues From Rapa Nui?', *Rapa Nui Journal* 13.2: 35-41.

Meadows, D., L. Meadows and J. Randers (1992) *Beyond the Limits* (London: Earthscan Publications).

PRB (Population Reference Bureau) (2003) *World Population Data Sheet* (Washington, DC: PRB).

Weeks, J.R. (2002) *Population: An Introduction to Concepts and Issues* (Belmont, CA: Wadsworth, 8th edn).

23

Teaching sustainability
Challenges, methods and tools

Darcy Hitchcock and Marsha Willard
AXIS Performance Advisors Inc., USA

Implementing sustainability requires teaching everyone in the organisation about its principles and practices. It is not enough that only the executive team 'get it'. Everyone in the organisation must understand sustainability, because the best opportunities are often uncovered by 'front-line' employees (see Box 23.1).

Yet teaching sustainability in business presents a number of unique challenges. The task is more complex than a typical corporate change effort, because the goals are arguably more complex: to change how people see the world, convince them that they can make a difference in a global problem and to give them tools that they can use in their daily lives. Educators must manage high expectations, because employees may become impatient with the pace of corporate change when they understand the magnitude of the problem. They must also plan the implementation so that the organisation's profitability is maintained while it researches and tries to develop new methods. The leaders of the organisation must be able to envision the end-game so that they do not invest in dead-end technologies. Few of us are adept at thinking at the scale or in the time-frames needed for sustainability.

Further complicating the process, people often become confused and overwhelmed by the honest and not-so-honest debate that swirls around many environmental issues. It is also often difficult for people to grasp an abstract concept such as sustainability and to adopt the necessary systems perspective of business practices. Given that sustainability is still a new movement, educators must also overcome the inertia of a business community that is still largely oblivious to the strategic importance of sustainability.

The task, however, is not impossible. We have uncovered strategies that work (and have abandoned some that do not) as we have worked with organisations to

At C&A Floorcoverings, for example, employees challenged the prevailing tenets of their business, ignoring the advice of the 'experts', to achieve a major breakthrough. They found a way to turn old carpet into new carpet that performed *better* than the original carpet and cost a little less to make! Dobbin Callahan, general manager of government markets, is adamant that C&A Floorcoverings could not not have achieved this without full participation of its employees. He believes the management team and engineers could not have figured it out themselves. As he puts it, the operators succeeded because 'they didn't know it couldn't be done'.

Box 23.1 Case study: C&A Floorcoverings

Source: Sustainability Series™ booklets, AXIS Performance Advisors

overcome these obstacles. This chapter represents the results of our experience. We provide solutions for the most common challenges likely to be encountered as educators help people understand and implement sustainable business practices. We have also included a number of our learning exercises in the companion volume (Hitchcock and Willard 2005a, 2005b). One key to success is to translate the concepts into models or visuals that communicate well. Thus we have included many of our time-tested examples in this chapter.

For simplicity and clarity, we have separated the subject into three objectives:

- Getting it: helping learners to understand the science and principles behind sustainability

- Selling it: preparing them to enlist support for implementing sustainability in their organisations

- Applying it: showing them how to integrate sustainability into organisational practices and policies

We present the challenges of each, provide solutions, then offer training resources and activities that can be used to help overcome the challenges.

These issues transcend training. Teaching sustainability involves more than just taking workshops. If educators want learning to translate into action, then they must look outside the classroom. Accordingly, this chapter covers issues that go beyond what happens during formal training and provides links to the 'real world'.

23.1 Getting it: helping learners understand the science and principles behind sustainability

Learners new to the concept of sustainability need a grounding in its definition and underlying scientific principles. Teaching the science, even to non-scientists, is not that difficult. Overcoming the learner's misconceptions, prejudice, disinformation and guilt are the challenges. This section addresses these specific training hurdles. Some resources are listed in Box 23.2.

In the body of Section 23.1 we allude to a number of training exercises. Here are some additional resources:

- In the companion book of exercises (Hitchcock and Willard 2005a, 2005b), we have provided a set of Science and System Condition Discussion Cards that are designed to make important distinctions and help people understand some of the subtleties (e.g. some metals are worse than others from an environmental perspective).

- *Making Sense of Sustainability* by Darcy Hitchcock (2001, www.pacifier.com/~axis) provides an employee overview of sustainability, including exercises. It can be used as the basis for meeting discussions or handed out as reading in new employee orientations.

- The Union of Concerned Scientists has published a set of Eco-System Services toolkits that include activities, communication tools and reports on pollination, water purification and flood damage. At the time of writing, not all of these toolkits are yet available (www.ucsusa.org).

- Joanna Macy's book, *Coming Back to Life: Practices to Reconnect Our Lives, Our World* (1998), is filled with activities that reconnect people to their feelings. These need to be used judiciously in a work setting, but they can be powerful motivators.

Box 23.2 Resources for teaching the science and principles of sustainability

23.1.1 Finding a term that works

'Sustainability' as a label has significant drawbacks. First, people often misconstrue it to mean sustaining their own organisation. When they realise that it is more than that, they then have to grapple with a concept that is complex, abstract, intellectual and sometimes fuzzy on specifics. Also, *sustaining* something rarely has the same emotional appeal as *creating* something; sustainability has a feel of levelling out the carnage instead of inspiring a 'renewal'. Although 'sustainability' is the term that is recognised globally, sometimes it is necessary to use a different term inside your organisation to make the subject more approachable. For example, in manufacturing, 'zero waste' might resonate well. Companies that have had a strong total quality programme may find it easiest to frame this as 'quality plus', an expansion on a familiar concept that includes the environment (and perhaps also society). People in the building or architectural profession might find 'green building' (or, more recently, 'high-performance buildings') a more meaningful term. Think about your own audience. If you are worried that 'sustainability' may turn more people off than on, review some of the other options we have provided in Box 23.3.

23.1.2 Understanding a whole-system view

To understand sustainability, you must understand the interconnections; you must be able to see the whole system. The video *Mind Walk* (Capra 1991) proposes

If the term 'sustainability' won't fly in your organisation, at least not yet, find another 'bridging term' such as those below, which can get you most of the way toward sustainability without raising unnecessary resistance.

- Zero waste
- Green building
- Community health
- Green chemistry
- Safety
- Risk management
- Product stewardship

- Social responsibility
- Triple bottom line
- Resource efficiency
- Product certification
- Enlarged definition of 'quality'
- Stakeholder management
- Economic renewal
- Smart growth

Box 23.3 Alternatives to the term 'sustainability'

that the primary problem is our mechanistic thinking, dating back to Descartes, seeing the world as divisible parts. Instead, everything is interconnected. In defining sustainability, we often use the 'three Es': economy, environment and (social) equity. We talk about how these are often traded off in our society instead of being collectively optimised. For example, Congress decides not to increase the CAFE (corporate average fuel economy) fuel efficiency standards for cars (which would help the environment) because it might hurt the economy. We treat these elements as if they were independent; we are blind to the interconnections—air pollution from cars contributes to asthma and other lung problems, which makes people sick so they are not at work but instead driving up business healthcare costs, thus hurting the economy.

A systems diagram helps people see the interconnections among the three aspects of sustainability (see Fig. 23.1), showing them as interlocking gears.

One example we have found useful examines the 'heat island effect'. It explores the interplay among the three Es using a situation with universal relevance. The heat island effect is the tendency for urban areas to be significantly warmer than the surrounding countryside because of their heat-absorbing surfaces. This leads to a downward cycle in all three 'Es'.

We explain that sustainability is about turning each of these 'gears' in the opposite direction, coming up with solutions that simultaneously improve the economy, the environment and the health of our society. When we ask people for an action that could turn all the gears in a positive direction, they often say, 'plant trees'. Trees help the environment because they sequester carbon and provide habitat. Trees help the social realm by cleaning the air (leading to better health) and providing a more aesthetically pleasing view. Trees help the economy by cooling the buildings so that businesses spend less money on energy and on slowing stormwater run-off thus reducing the amount of money a city has to spend on waste-water treatment. Sustainability involves taking actions that turn all three gears in a positive direction.

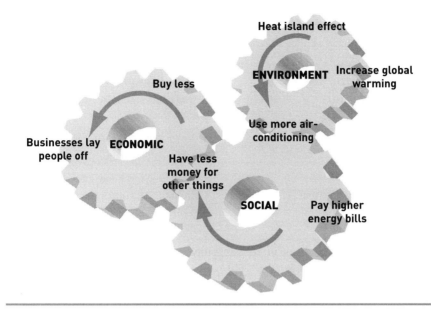

Figure 23.1 The interconnections between economics, environment and social ethics: the heat island effect

23.1.3 Thinking they have done all they can

Some organisations think they are doing all they can with regard to the environment. They may have an environmental department and be in compliance with all applicable regulations. Service organisations often do not believe there is anything they can do beyond recycling their office paper. The challenge is to get them to see all that they are *not* doing, to acknowledge that they are still 'light years' from a sustainable state. So we use the diagram in Figure 23.2 to help people distinguish sustainability from the other, necessary but lower, forms of corporate efforts.

At the low end are organisations that are still focused only on regulatory compliance. Organisations at this level are concerned primarily with avoiding legal liabilities and may view environmental issues as a source of additional costs and 'headaches'. Organisations focusing on eco-efficiencies have discovered that saving resources not only helps the environment but also their financial bottom line. Thus they are interested in saving water, energy, raw materials and so on. Here the focus is internal. At some point, many organisations realise that being 'green' can attract new customers or make their community more attractive. They then use green marketing to differentiate themselves from others.

The acts of green marketing and concentrating on eco-efficiencies are focused on 'doing better'. However, when organisations understand sustainability, they begin to wonder, 'Are we doing enough?' Just 'doing better' may not be enough to live within the limits of nature. When organisations reach the level of sustainability,

Figure 23.2 Steps toward sustainability

they understand in their hearts the need to significantly change what they are doing, that becoming 'less bad' will never be good enough to achieve sustainability; and they also understand in their heads the incredible business opportunity sustainability presents, that this is not so much an issue for the environmental department as an issue for the executive team. Duke Castle, a co-founder of the Oregon Natural Step Network, says:

> The breakthrough in sustainability thinking seems to come when an organisation moves beyond incremental 'green' thinking to one of imagining their organisation being fully sustainable and then 'backcasting' from that vision to their current situation.[1]

Some businesses go beyond even sustainability (which balances our demands on nature with what it can provide) to restoration—rebuilding what we have degraded.

These distinctions help people understand not only how sustainability is different from other things they have been doing but also that it is a logical extension of those activities. After defining each level for your audience, ask learners to indicate which level represents their current position and which level describes where they think they should be in five years. Since there is a human tendency to want to be 'above average', this diagram also creates a desire in many to move further up the steps and creates the need to learn more.

23.1.4 Making it seem possible

One thing that holds people back is the fear of failure. If the problems are so huge and overwhelming, why even try? To businesses, the social aspects of sustainability are particularly confounding.

We find it is often useful to translate sustainability into the logical responsibilities the organisation should assume. We use the diagram in Figure 23.3 for businesses to explain their responsibilities.

We talk through an example from another industry. For example, what might a restaurant do over a ten-year period? It could:

1 Personal communication.

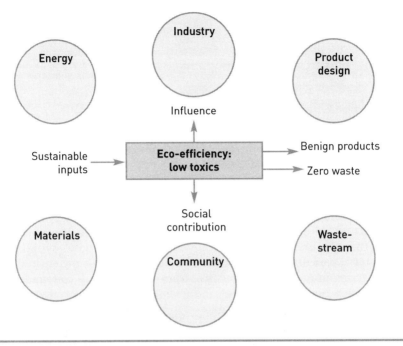

Figure 23.3 **Vision of a sustainable organisation**

- Buy green power and organic produce (sustainable inputs)
- Use waste heat from its ovens to heat water to wash tablecloths and other linen (eco-efficiencies)
- Find alternatives to toxic cleaners (low toxics)
- Donate all leftovers to homeless shelters (social contribution) and compost all food scraps (zero waste)
- Advocate fair wages and living conditions for migrant labour (industry influence)

Using an example such as this makes sustainability seem attainable. We then ask learners to come up with possible initiatives for their own organisation.

23.1.5 Dealing with negative perceptions associated with environmentalism

Although many people may view themselves as environmentalists, others have negative associations with the environmental movement. For some audiences, it can be important to distance sustainability from these negative connotations. Here are tactics we have used to avoid this problem:

- Pitch sustainability to your audience's own interests. You can emphasise the economic benefits to business people and the human interests to social-service organisations.

- Avoid using common environmentalist terminology, such as ecosystem, Earth, planet and so on.

- Avoid overwhelming them with doomsday statistics about the environment.

- Openly acknowledge the mistakes that some in the environmental movement have made: being adversarial, appearing to care more about other species than people and so on.

- Explain how sustainability is different from past 'green' efforts: it is non-political, it is collaborative, it does not place blame, it acknowledges the need for a healthy economy and profitability and so on.

23.1.6 Getting past 'science phobia' and technical jargon

Not everyone enjoyed their science classes at school, and certain audiences can be turned off by technical, scientific jargon. With such audiences, it is important to find terms, examples and demonstrations that connect with their experience. Props, demonstrations and examples linked to everyday situations can help. We have explained evolution by using someone's arm as a time-line, hanging props (using toy dinosaurs, soda bottles to represent carbon dioxide and so on) at the appropriate points along it. People may not be familiar with the laws of thermodynamics, but they understand that if you put a drop of ink in a bathtub the ink will evenly disperse making both the ink and the water unusable. We have explained bioaccumulation and biomagnification by tracing pesticide up the food chain to the dinner table. We have introduced The Natural Step system conditions by using little more than a picture of the Earth and four easy-to-remember icons.

23.1.7 Motivating reluctant learners

It is possible that some in your presentations or classes may not be there willingly. The best way to approach reluctant learners is to engage their interest. We have found the following strategies helpful:

- Tap into their concerns. When people introduce themselves, ask them to mention a problem in their community that worries them. These will almost always fit into one or more of the three Es of sustainability: economy, environment and social equity (or livability). Make the connection for them so they can see sustainability as a way of solving a problem that they care about.

● Give them the chance to express their doubts and scepticism (e.g. environmentalism costs jobs, makes things more expensive and means I cannot drive my car). Show them that sustainability need not be about sacrifice or a reduced standard of living but of finding new solutions that work for everyone.

● Plan lots of activities and group interaction to keep the learning interesting.

● Do not let the topic depress people. Introduce humour and hope where possible.

● Use lots of stories and examples. These draw people in.

23.1.8 Managing guilt and defensive behaviour

One of the biggest psychological barriers is despair and helplessness. Many people feel guilty about their lifestyles and choices. They know about environmental problems, but they do not know how to fix them so they push them out of their mind. They may also be overwhelmed with the plethora of environmental and social issues—global warming, the ozone hole, pesticides, cancer rates, species extinction, acid rain, poverty and so on. If people miss the overall relationship between these problems, they may feel as if there are too many plates to keep spinning in the air, especially for busy people. Here are some ways to handle some of these challenges:

● Declare a guilt-free zone at the beginning of your presentation. Explain that none of us is sustainable yet. Explain that sustainability should not be about not having what you want; it should be about getting what you want sustainably.

● At the beginning of your presentation, ask people to list environmental and/or social problems that worry them. Write these on a flipchart. Make a long, messy list. Add your own if the process stalls or they need prompting. Then point out that all these problems can be tied back to a handful of mistakes we made in designing our society. We like using The Natural Step system conditions because they provide four easy-to-understand principles that encompass all the issues. The three Es work well also. You can go back to your learners' list and show how all these disparate problems can be tied back to these principles.

● Include an activity that shows them how to apply the system conditions (or whatever framework you choose) to everyday decisions. Many companies have found that employees want to try out some of the concepts at home, in lower-risk decisions, before they implement them at work. We made up a set of cards representing a host of everyday decisions (buying juice at the grocery store, landscaping the garden, ordering at a restaurant, choosing a form of exercise, planning a holiday and so on). Using pictures from magazines and newspaper advertisements we present three options to participants. Students assess each option in light of each system condition and select the best and worst choice based on The Natural Step framework. This activity has been important for anchoring the concepts and for building students' confidence in their ability to make a difference.

23.1.9 Avoiding arguments about the data

Sometimes defensiveness pushes people to denial and they refute the basic data (e.g. the pace of species extinction, topsoil or rainforest decline and whether global climate change is actually happening). In these situations, it is important not to get into a my-data-is-better-than-your-data argument or to embarrass the individuals raising the issues. We have found the following strategies can help you get out of these quagmires:

- Agree as much as you can with what the person has said (e.g. acknowledge that there is still a lot of uncertainty about the rate of species decline).

- Cite the sources for your data. Ideally, you are using widely accepted sources for your data (e.g. the UN Intergovernmental Panel on Climate Change). In these situations, we often mention that the media, in their attempt to tell 'both sides of a story', frequently do not do a good job of explaining that one perspective is backed up by, for example, thousands of the world's leading climatologists, and the other represents a handful of scientists often paid by industry.

- If there is any reason to suspect that the data you are referencing is not entirely objective, acknowledge that. For example, non-profit organisations can benefit by making things look worse than they are just as industry groups may have an interest in making things look better. In these situations, you can often go on to say, 'Let's assume for a minute that their estimates are overstated by a factor of two. That still doesn't eliminate the basic problem. We're still not sustainable; the rate of degradation is just slower.'

- Express interest in reviewing their sources. Tell them once you have had a chance to look it over, you would be glad to comment. In some cases, ask experts in the field to respond and forward their comments.

23.2 Selling it: preparing learners to enlist support for implementing sustainability in their organisations

Once people are excited about sustainability, they face the tough job of selling it to others in their organisations. Experience teaches that passion for the subject is not only insufficient in converting an organisation, it is often counter-productive if others view the missionary as over-zealous. In this section we discuss how to prepare learners to take the message back and effectively sell it in their organisations by planning responses to these challenges. Some resources are listed in Box 23.4.

In the body of Section 23.2 we allude to a number of training exercises. Here are some additional resources:

- 'Innovating Our Way to the Next Industrial Revolution', by Peter Senge and Goran Carstedt (2001), is an excellent overview of sustainability from the perspective of business strategy.

- Joanna Macy's book, *Coming Back to Life: Practices to Reconnect Our Lives, Our World* (1998), is filled with activities that reconnect people to their feelings. These need to be used judiciously in a work setting, but they can be powerful motivators.

- Alan AtKisson's book, *Believing Cassandra: An Optimist Looks at a Pessimist's World* (1999: ch. 9), describes an interesting activity called the Innovation Diffusion Game that can teach people principles for spreading sustainability throughout the organisation.

Box 23.4 Resources for selling sustainability

23.2.1 Establishing the urgency and relevance of sustainability

We know from diffusion-of-innovation theory that it is harder to sell a programme that avoids a possible future scenario (e.g. insurance) than one that addresses an immediate felt need. For many, sustainability will seem like a nice-to-have initiative, one that can be addressed when things are less hectic (i.e. never), so it is critical that employees leave your training able to demonstrate the urgency. Here are some approaches we have found to help:

- The Natural Step 'funnel' diagram[2] or the $I = PAT$ formula (where $I =$ impact, $P =$ population, $A =$ affluence and $T =$ technology) frame the issues in clear, compelling ways. Find local or industry examples of problems that could have been predicted by these models (e.g. the collapse of a fishing community, products regulated out of existence, customer or community pressure and so on).

- Where possible, raise relevant and imminent threats: new regulations, a competitor's new product, a change in customer requirements, increasing price of materials.

---

2 www.naturalstep.org/learn/understand_sust.php

- Cite respected businesses, especially any in their own industry, that are pursuing sustainability. Describe why these businesses thought it was important to pursue sustainability and the benefits they gained. Better yet, invite speakers from those businesses to share their stories in person.

- Provide copies of relevant articles from respected business journals: *Harvard Business Review*, MIT *Sloan Management Review*, *Wall Street Journal*, *Scientific American*, *Journal of the American Medical Association* and so on. (One of our favourites to share with executives is Peter Senge's and Goran Carstedt's article, 'Innovating Our Way to the Next Industrial Revolution' in the *Sloan Management Review*, 2001.)

23.2.2 Overcoming resistance

People are busy, so, when someone comes out of your training and tries to enlist the support of others, they are likely to encounter resistance. Trying something new is like swimming upstream. New options must be analysed; perhaps new vendors must be sought; new procedures may need to be written. It is no wonder others do not greet our eagerness with the same enthusiasm, so make sure your trainees understand how to enlist the support of others:

- Start by learning about the people you are selling to, their work and their needs. Do not lead off with your desire for them to change. Instead, find out what they have already done, what makes their work hard and so on. Through this you may discover a problem that sustainability could help solve. For example, a janitor might complain about rashes and itching caused by caustic cleaning products. This opens a door to talk about green purchasing practices.

- Soft-sell using hard data. Sometimes all that people need are some startling statistics to get them motivated, so share relevant data. This might include a chart on the growth of human population, the rate of decline in your local aquifer, the acres of trees you would have to plant each year to offset your energy use, the number and cost of sick days attributable to chemical exposure, and the cost of protective equipment, training and regulatory reporting associated with the hazardous substances you use. However, also share positive stories: about energy efficiencies gained with new technology; money saved in process efficiencies, employee productivity and quality improvements from daylighting and so on.

- Involve them in establishing criteria for future options. Environmental impact should be one of many criteria, including quality, performance, safety and so on.

- Do a lot of the legwork for them. Remember, this was originally your idea, so gather some of the data, find alternative products or vendors and so on.

- Suggest an experimental pilot period. Do not ask people to abandon something that has worked for a long time for something untested. Instead, enlist them in doing a comparison test for a few weeks or months.

23.2.3 Getting support from top management

Top management needs a clear business case to pursue sustainability instead of their plethora of other possible initiatives, so you must show a potential for a healthy financial return. But do not stop there: think about the potential for competitive advantage, innovations or an inspiring vision for the future. Help your learners to develop, in effect, four different business cases: focused on the long term and the short term as well as internally and externally focused (see Table 23.1).

		Focus	
		Internal	*External*
Focus	**Short term**	**Design** *What is the breakthrough innovation that will dramatically improve your sustainability?* ● Pursue product stewardship and take-back policies ● Dematerialise your product ● Use biomimicry (designs mimicking nature) ● Convert products to services	**Vision** *What inspiring role could you play in creating the new, sustainable economy?* ● Restore ecosystems ● Develop synergies with other sectors to solve social and/or environmental problems ● Transform your industry ● Serve disadvantaged markets
	Long term	**Efficiencies** *Where could you save money, time or resources?* ● Reduce waste and find markets for waste-streams ● Conserve energy ● Substitute materials ● Reduce the regulatory burden ● Reduce health and safety costs	**Competitiveness** *Where are the opportunities to improve your competitiveness?* ● Create new products and/or services ● Improve your corporate image ● Attract new customers ● Avoid new regulations or legal liabilities ● Attract and retain key talent as a result of your inspiring mission

Table 23.1 Four elements of a robust business case

Organisations must develop at least some answers to put into each of these four quadrants. You do not need to have a finished product, but to sell sustainability inside the organisation you should come up with at least a couple intriguing examples. If all you focus on are the short-term efficiencies, you will never get to sustainability. Another advantage to exploring all four dimensions is that different people will be motivated by different 'pitches'. Perhaps your facilities manager will be most convinced by the potential for internal efficiencies; the marketing manager may be intrigued by the competitive advantage; engineers are likely to find the design innovations stimulating; and the visionaries in your organisation will be motivated by the long-term vision for your company and industry. Your top-management team is likely to need to look at all four perspectives to be convinced. For each person you aim to enrol choose examples from the most appropriate quadrant.

23.2.4 Building critical mass

To create change in an organisation, not everyone has to be 'on board', but the 'right people' have to be. The sequence with which you approach people can make a difference. In developing a national outreach strategy, Karl-Henrik Robèrt, the founder of The Natural Step, was a master at this. In a 'daisy chain' of conversations, he went to one person after another, lining up commitments (Robèrt 2002). Teach your audience to be savvy about whom to approach. One useful tool is a stakeholder diagram with which people analyse who is in the best position to make a difference (positive or negative) and what it would take to shift them in the right direction (see Table 23.2). We ask learners to first list all the critical stakeholders associated with their ideas. Then, for each stakeholder, they must indicate where that stakeholder stands on sustainability: are they likely to want to make it happen, help it happen, let it happen, resist it or try to stop it? They should think through where they need each person or group to be and then strategise over what it would take to move their stakeholders in the appropriate direction on the chart. Note that sometimes you need to move people to the right (of Table 23.2), to let go of some of the ownership, for the implementation to be successful.

23.2.5 Preparing the pitch

Sometimes the hardest part about selling sustainability is getting an opening to start the conversation. Few people are trained in sales and fewer still are comfortable making pitches. We help prepare your trainees to talk about sustainability by helping them create short, three-point 'presentations' for each of their target audiences—what we call the 'elevator pitch'. You encounter your CEO in the elevator (lift) and have three floors to get him or her interested in hearing more. What do you say?

We break the elevator pitch into three segments:

- The 'hook': a couple of sentences that will get your stakeholder's attention
- The 'message': two to four key points tailored to the needs, interests and style of your stakeholder
- The 'action': a clarification of what you want your stakeholder to do to move you one step toward your goal

It is important to help participants be clear about what they want as a next step. Do they want a stakeholder to read an article, agree to a longer meeting where they

Stakeholder	Stance					Role	Suggested action
	Make it happen	**Help it happen**	**Let it happen**	**Resist it**	**Stop it**		
CEO	←——————		•			Champion	Share trend analysis with him or her; build a business case with him or her
Maintenance manager	←——————		•				Clarify his or her needs and the performance expectations of the products he or she uses
Union			←——————	•		Planning team	Make it a partner in the process; guarantee no changes in job levels
Employees	• —→					Planning team	Back off a little until CEO is convinced; focus on projects that have clear financial returns

• = where they are now; —▶ = where you need them to be

Table 23.2 Stakeholder diagram: approaches to stakeholder stances on sustainability

can discuss the concept, leave time for a presentation on sustainability at the next management meeting or attend a forthcoming breakfast meeting?

23.3 Applying it: showing learners how to integrate sustainability into organisational practices and policies

Possibly the biggest challenge in teaching sustainability is helping people translate the concepts and principles into actions and strategies. In this section we describe strategies for overcoming the barriers and helping learners see the possibilities for implementation. Some resources are provided in Box 23.5.

23.3.1 Making the abstract actionable

There is no point in doing training if people do not apply what they learn 'on the job'. But the gap between learning and action can be a chasm when you are teaching something as abstract as sustainability. Here are some strategies that make sustainability real:

In Section 23.3 we allude to a number of training exercises. Here are some additional resources:

- We have submitted a Business Simulation in the companion volume (Hitchcock and Willard 2005a, 2005b) which shows people how to apply sustainability in a variety of industries. Doing this in a hypothetical town prepares them psychologically to find similar opportunities in their own organisation.

- The Oregon Natural Step Network Toolkit includes samples and case studies from companies that have pursued sustainable business practices (www.ortns.org).

- The *Sustainability Series™* booklets show you how to implement sustainability into your organisation. They provide background reading, step-by-step instructions, lessons learned and resources for each task: making a business case, establishing an implementation strategy, identifying environmental impacts, establishing metrics, greening your supply chain and purchasing decisions, reducing greenhouse gases and so on (www.pacifier.com/~axis).

Box 23.5 Resources for applying sustainability

- Work in the hypothetical first. It is usually easier for people to redesign someone else's workplace, as they are often too close to their own situation to see the possibilities. Thus it can be very helpful to present a hypothetical case first and then let the participants translate the results to their own workplace (See the Business Simulation in the companion volume [Hitchcock and Willard 2005a, 2005b].)

- Use real examples and problems. Gather situations from your learners and use these situations to increase the applicability of your training. As an activity, have the learners do an informal analysis of their own organisation's environmental and social impacts and then set them to work on identifying the 'low-hanging fruit'.

- Do just-in-time training. Do not blitz people with a long training programme and expect them to go off and do it. You are much better off breaking the tasks into bite-sized pieces and leading the students through each step over time. A consortium approach, where you bring several organisations, teams or departments together to lead them through the analysis, can not only be a cost saver but also can help cross-pollinate ideas and build relationships across organisations.

- Provide worksheets, templates and a process. Few people are trained in effective group processes, and you do not want them to flounder. Therefore, lay out a flexible process and provide the students with sample worksheets, analytical tools and so on. Consider providing a professional facilitator to keep them on track (see the *Sustainability Series™* booklets for, example, from AXIS Performance Advisors listed in the resources at the end of this chapter).

23.3.2 Managing the complicated trade-offs in implementing sustainability

What is the most sustainable option? Answering that question can confound the best of us! One option might use less energy but more water. Another might produce a smaller quantity of waste but use a more toxic chemical. Should you factor in the transportation to your site or impacts associated with the customers' use of the product? What happens at the end-of-life of the product? It is easy to get stuck in analysis-paralysis. Here is some advice:

- In the early rounds, coach your learners to keep it simple. Sacrifice some of the nuances to making progress. For example, instead of weighting the toxicity of various compounds on a complex scale, encourage your learners to use a binary (yes/no) analysis or some other simpler scale (e.g. a three-point scale such as lethal, has some long-term health consequences, benign). The subtleties can come later when the students are more mature in their understanding.

- Encourage learners to start by focusing within their own site rather than the full life-cycle impacts. Eventually, they may want to tackle the 'cradle-to-cradle' impacts of their business but, when just beginning, it is often more productive to focus on what happens within the bounds of their own location. They will have more influence and experience less frustration.

- Begin with products or processes that are relatively simple—these will turn out to be complicated enough, trust us! The students should get some successes under their belts before they take on the full life-cycle costs of the entire operation.

23.3.3 Identifying appropriate starting places

Sometimes the first step seems the biggest. Once participants leave training, they should have a clear sense of where best to begin. There is no pat answer. The strategy will vary from organisation to organisation. If they have top-executive support for sustainability, they may already have a path laid out. If your trainees are trying to start something from where they are in their organisations, help them to develop a low-profile approach. We have identified at least five ways to bring sustainability into an organisation (Fig. 23.4). Use these ideas to help your learners understand and select a path that will work for them:

- Some organisations embed sustainability into their strategic planning process as one of many issues to consider. This is a good way of introducing the concept to executives as one of many interesting business trends they should consider as they lay out long-term plans.

- Others fold sustainability principles into their existing environmental management systems. Sustainability can be written into their policies and can be used as a basis for setting objectives and targets.

Figure 23.4 Pathways to sustainability

- Some begin work on their supply chain. This may run the gamut, from choosing 'greener' products, or including sustainability language in requests for proposals and contracts, to collaborating with vendors, to redesigning organisational processes and relationships. Some have used the construction of a new building or another capital project as an opportunity to include sustainability criteria in decision-making.

- Organisations that have well-established team structures to make improvements in the organisation (e.g. quality improvement teams) can use these teams to work on sustainability-related projects.

- Some organisations, especially those with executive support, choose to implement sustainability as a new, separate effort.

23.3.4 Aligning existing business systems to support sustainability

People frequently underestimate the impacts of the changes they want to make and, in doing so, set themselves up for disappointment or frustration. If you are training people to help them get sustainable practices implemented, provide them with guidance on how to anticipate the ripple effects of their ideas.

Our work suggests that most organisational changes eventually come up against various business systems. Have your trainees consider how many existing systems might be affected by the implementation of their ideas. Provide them with the checklist in Box 23.6 and uncover the potential ripple effects and unintended consequences of their plans. Identify specific changes that will need to be made to these systems and assign responsibilities for carrying them out.

How will your idea impact the following systems in your organisation?

- Information systems
- Training
- Job duties
- Purchasing
- Shipping and receiving
- Business systems
- Warehousing
- Accounting
- Maintenance
- Compensation
- Research and development
- Sales and marketing

Box 23.6 Checklist

23.4 Conclusions

Guiding people through their learning is a complex process in any situation, but it is particularly difficult when your topic is sustainability. Sustainability is a large, abstract topic and a new field. We are all feeling our way on this journey. In this chapter, we have outlined the major challenges you are likely to face:

- Getting it: helping learners understand the science and principles behind sustainability. Here the challenge is to avoid tapping into sources of resistance. This requires a good understanding of the audience: their points of view, existing knowledge base and desires.

- Selling it: preparing them to enlist support for implementing sustainability in their organisations. This requires a solid grounding in organisational development principles. There is a need to know how to nurture new ideas inside an organisation, how to decide when to go public, how to line up support of key stakeholders and how to create a compelling vision that overcomes inertia.

- Applying it: showing them how to integrate sustainability into organisational practices and policies. This requires a practical framework and tools for moving forward. A management system for compiling and choosing from among all the possible ideas is required, and a flexible implementation process is needed so that people do not repeatedly reinvent the sustainability wheel.

Although it may be hard, the task of teaching people about sustainability is incredibly rewarding. Once people understand sustainability principles, these tend to filter into all facets of their life. People cannot pretend they do not know any more. As Bill McDonough, co-founder of McDonough Braungart Design Chemistry and author of *Cradle to Cradle* (2002), likes to say, 'Negligence starts tomorrow.'

References

AtKisson, A. (1999) *Believing Cassandra: An Optimist Looks at a Pessimist's World* (White River Junction, VT: Chelsea Green Publishing).

Hitchcock, D., and M. Willard (2005a) 'Business Simulation', in C. Galea (ed.), *Teaching Business Sustainability*. II. *Case Studies* (Sheffield, UK: Greenleaf Publishing, forthcoming).

—— and —— (2005b) 'Science and System Condition Discussion Cards', in C. Galea (ed.), *Teaching Business Sustainability*. II. *Case Studies* (Sheffield, UK: Greenleaf Publishing, forthcoming).

McDonough, W. (2002) *Cradle to Cradle* (New York: North Point Press).

Macy, J. (1998) *Coming Back to Life: Practices to Reconnect Our Lives, Our World* (Gabriola Island, BC, Canada: New Society Publishers).

Robèrt, K.-H. (2002) *The Natural Step Story* (Gabriola Island, BC, Canada: New Society Publishers).

Senge, P., and G. Carstedt (2001) 'Innovating Our Way to the Next Industrial Revolution', *MIT Sloan Management Review*, Winter 2001.

Resources

Capra, Bernt (1991) *Mind Walk* (video; Paramount Home Entertainment).

Hitchcock, D., and M. Willard (2001–2004) *Sustainability Series*™ (booklet series; Portland, OR: AXIS performance Advisors; www. pacifier.com/~axis).

The Natural Step, Oregon, Oregon Natural Step Network Toolkit; available from www.ortns.org.

Union of Concerned Scientists, Eco-System Services toolkits; available from www.ucsusa.org.

•

Abbreviations

AA	AccountAbility
AACSB	Association to Advance Collegiate Schools of Business
ABS	Australian Bureau of Statistics
ACF	Australian Conservation Foundation
AGSM	Australian Graduate School of Management
AIDS	acquired immuno-deficiency syndrome
AMN	*Academy of Management News*
ANOVA	analysis of variance
APN	American Political Network
ASIC	Australian Securities and Investments Commission
BBC	British Broadcasting Corporation
BELL	Business–Environment Learning and Leadership (North America)
BEP	HRH the Prince of Wales's Business and the Environment Programme
BSE	bovine spongiform encephalopathy
BSR	Business for Social Responsibility
CAFE	corporate average fuel economy
CBC	Canadian Broadcasting Corporation
CDCAC	Canadian Democracy and Corporate Accountability Commission
CD-ROM	compact disc–read-only memory
CEEFHE	Committee on Environmental Education in Further and Higher Education (UK)
CEMP	Corporate Environmental Management Program (University of Michigan)
CEO	chief executive officer
CEP	Council on Economic Priorities
CERES	Coalition for Environmentally Responsible Economies
CFC	chlorofluorocarbon
CFO	chief finance officer
CIDA	Canadian International Development Agency
CMSIG	Critical Management Studies Interest Group
COMPASS	Companies' and Sectors' Path to Sustainability (Wuppertal Institute)
CPGMWG	Consumer Protection in the Global Market Working Group

CSR	corporate social responsibility
CSSS	Center for Sustainable Systems Studies (Miami University)
DfE	design for environment
DJSGI	Dow Jones Social Group Index
DJSI	Dow Jones Sustainability Indexes
EC	European Commission
EDF	Electricité de France
EEC	Environmental Enterprise Corps (World Resources Institute)
EH&S	environmental, health and safety
EMAS	Eco-Management and Audit Scheme
EMS	environmental management system
ETI	Ethical Trading Initiative
EVOSTC	*Exxon Valdez* Oil Spill Trustee Council
FDI	foreign direct investment
FTSE	Financial Times Stock Exchange
GNI	gross national income
GRI	Global Reporting Initiative
GST	general systems theory
HIV	human immunodeficiency virus
IBLF	International Business Leaders Forum
IES	Institute of Environmental Science
IFC	International Financial Corporation
ILO	International Labour Organisation
IM	Institute of Managers
IMAP	International Multidisciplinary Action Project (University of Michigan Business School)
IoD	Institute of Directors
ISEA	Institute of Social and Ethical AccountAbility
ISIB	Initiative for Social Innovation through Business (Aspen Institute)
ISO	International Organisation for Standardisation
IT	information technology
LA–BELL	Latin America Business–Environment Learning and Leadership
LCA	life-cycle assessment
LDC	less-developed country
LP	liquefied petroleum
MBA	Master of Business Administration
MDGs	Millennium Development Goals
MEB	Management Institute for Environment and Business (USA)
MIT	Massachusetts Institute of Technology
MMSD	Mining, Minerals and Sustainable Development
MSP	maximum sustainable population
MUBS	Middlesex University Business School
MUSP	Miami University Sustainability Project
MW	megawatt
NEON	National Ecological Observatory Network (USA)
NGO	non-governmental organisation
NIC	newly industrialised country

NOAA	National Oceanic and Atmospheric Administration (USA)
NSD	neo-Socratic dialogue
NWFCCC	National Wildlife Federation Corporate Conservation Council (USA)
ODA	official development assistance
ODTE	Office for Developed and Transition Economies (UK)
OHSAS	Occupational Health and Safety Assessment Series
ONE	Organisations and the Natural Environment
PDF	portable document format
PPP	purchasing power parity
PRB	Population Reference Bureau
PVC	polyvinyl chloride
Q&A	question and answer
R&D	research and development
RMIT	Royal Melbourne Institute of Technology
ROW	rest-of-world
SA	Social Accountability
SAI	Social Accountability International
SAP	structural adjustment programme
SEEG	La Société d'Energie et d'Eau du Gabon
SEP	Sustainable Enterprise Program (formerly MEB)
SG&A	selling, general and administrative
SIF	Social Investment Forum
SIR	Shell International Renewables
SMART	specific, measurable, actionable, realistic and timely
SME	small or medium-sized enterprise
SSD	La Société de Services Décentralisés (Mali)
TBL	triple bottom line
TQEM	total quality environmental management
TV	television
UNAIDS	Joint United Nations Programme on HIV/AIDS
UNCED	United Nations Conference on Environment and Development
UNDP	United Nations Development Programme
UNESCO	United Nations Educational, Scientific and Cultural Organisation
UNSW	University of New South Wales
US OMB	US Office of Management and Budget
WBCSD	World Business Council for Sustainable Development
WCED	World Commission on Environment and Development
WLPGA	World Liquefied Petroleum Gas Association
WRI	World Resources Institute
WSSD	World Summit on Sustainable Development
WTO	World Trade Organisation
ZPG	zero population growth

Biographies

Kariann Aarup is a social entrepreneur, educator, writer and facilitator. Above all, she is a change agent. Kariann holds a BA Economics and MBA from McGill University (Montreal, Canada), where she has been a sessional instructor in the faculty of management since 1999, and is PhD (ABD) from HEC-Montréal. Kariann is also co-founder of Community Experience Initiative (www.cei-iec.ca), a national internship programme that matches management students with voluntary-sector-organisation learning/work opportunities. More details on her facilitation and writing projects can be found at www.divertika.ca and www.lighthousemedia.ca.
kariann@divertika.ca

Tom Abeles is president of Sagacity Inc., a firm that consults, internationally, in renewable energy and sustainable enterprises. A former tenured professor of environmental and interdisciplinary studies, he also consults on second-generation e-learning and edits *On the Horizon*, an international academic journal on higher-education futures. He is on the editorial board of *Foresight, The Journal of Sustainable Agriculture* and *The International Journal for World Peace*. He has provided workshops and keynotes on areas ranging from knowledge management and complex dynamics to watershed management and distance education.
tabeles@attglobal.net

John Adams is Director of the Organisational Systems PhD programme at Saybrook Graduate School, USA. He is also Executive Director of Eartheart Enterprises, an international consulting practice specialising in sustainability, work–life balance and large-scale change implementation.
jadams@saybrook.edu

Dan Anderson is the Leslie P. Schultz Professor of Risk Management and Insurance at the School of Business at University of Wisconsin–Madison. He teaches and publishes widely in the area of environmental risk management. He is the leader of a faculty group promoting the development of courses in environmental strategy and sustainability.
danderson@bus.wisc.edu

Bobby Banerjee is Professor of Strategic Management at the International Graduate School of Management, University of South Australia, Adelaide. He has taught at the University of Massachusetts, where he received his PhD in 1996; at the University of Wollongong, where he headed the doctoral programme; and RMIT University, where he was Director of the Doctor of Business Administration programme. His research interests are in the areas of sustainable development, corporate environmentalism, socio-cultural aspects of globalisation, post-colonial theories, and indigenous ecology. His work has appeared in several journals, including *The Journal of Marketing, Organization Studies, The Journal of Management Studies, Organization, The Journal of Advertising, The Journal of Business Research, Advances in Consumer Research, Management Learning, The Journal of Corporate Citizenship, The Journal of Environmental Education, Media, Culture and Society*, and *Organization and Environment*.
apache@unisa.edu.au

A consultant with McKinsey & Company in Copenhagen, **Pepukaye Bardouille** has previously worked on energy and sustainable development issues with the United Nations Development Programme in New York. She has a background in mechanical engineering (BSc) and environmental management (MSc) and holds a PhD in environmental and energy systems studies from Lund University, Sweden.

Suzanne Benn is a lecturer and researcher with the Corporate Sustainability Project at University of Technology, Sydney. She is the co-author of the book *Organisational Change for Corporate Sustainability*, published in 2003 by Routledge, London. Her research on local and regional networks for sustainability, corporate sustainability and teaching for sustainability has also been published in a number of international journals and edited publications.
suzanne.benn@uts.edu.au

Maria Bobenrieth is an independent consultant focusing on helping organisations create strategies and programmes to effectively integrate corporate responsibility into business practices. She holds a master's degree in International Management, and a certificate from Cambridge University in the Cross-Sector Partnership Initiative and the Partnership Brokering Accreditation Scheme. She spent 20-plus years in international sales and marketing in the private sector. Born in Chile, raised in the US, she now lives in Amsterdam.
Mariabobenrieth@earthlink.net

Molly Young Brown, MA, MDiv, is an internationally recognised teacher and writer in the fields of ecopsychology, ecoliteracy and psychosynthesis, presenting talks and workshops across North America and Europe. She is co-author with Joanna Macy of the highly acclaimed *Coming Back to Life: Practices to Reconnect Our Lives, Our World* (New Society Publishers, 1998), and author of three other published books, including *Growing Whole: Self-realization on an Endangered Planet* (Hazelden, 1993). She is a founding director of Intermountain Synthesis Center in Mt Shasta, California, offering professional training in the region and online. (See www.mollyyoungbrown.com.)
molly@mollyyoungbrown.com

David Bubna-Litic is currently a Lecturer in Strategic Management at the School of Management at the University of Technology, Sydney. He is the author of several book chapters and journal articles on organisation theory and strategy, and has presented conference papers in North America, Europe and the Pacific Rim. Prior to entering academia he worked for seven years as a management consultant. His research interests traverse ethics, East-Asian philosophy and cognitive science to form social ecological understandings relevant to organisation theory, economics and strategy.
david.bubna-litic@uts.edu.au

Polly Courtice is a Director of the University of Cambridge Programme for Industry, the university's department specialising in leadership and organisational development. She is a co-director of the Business and the Environment Programme and the Sustainability Learning Networks Programme, an advanced diploma in sustainability for business from the University of Cambridge. She has research interests in organisational learning and sustainable development.
Polly.Courtice@cpi.cam.ac.uk

Dr **Sasha Courville** is a Research Fellow at the Regulatory Institutions Network (RegNet), Australian National University. In linking theory with practice, Dr Courville is involved with a number of Australian and international initiatives in the areas of the regulation of organic agriculture, ensuring credibility of private certification systems and supply chain relationships. She is the co-ordinator of the Social Accountability in Sustainable Agriculture (SASA) project of four international social and environmental verification initiatives (SAI, FLO, SAN and IFOAM) which examines how to improve social auditing methodologies and standards as well as fostering convergence between the four initiatives.
sasha.courville@anu.edu.au

Tom Eggert is a lecturer at the School of Business of University at Wisconsin–Madison. He is also an honorary fellow with the Gaylord Nelson Institute for Environmental Studies, University of Wisconsin–Madison. In addition to developing and teaching the class discussed in Chapter 14, he also has developed and teaches Ethics, Values and Sustainability for the MBA programme at the Business School. He also teaches Sustainability and the Corporate Response as a complement to the class described in Chapter 14.
teggert@bus.wisc.edu

Steven R. Elliott is Assistant Professor of Economics at Miami University. Dr Elliott's doctoral training was at the University of Colorado at Boulder, and he has done post-doctoral work at the University of Arizona with Dr Vernon Smith and Oak Ridge National Laboratory. He has taught also at the University of Colorado and Michigan Technological University. His fields of interest include applied microeconomics, environmental economics in particular valuation of non-market goods and industrial organisation.
elliotsr@muohio.edu

O. Homer Erekson is Dean and Harzfeld Professor of Economics and Business Policy at the Henry W. Bloch School of Business and Public Administration at the University of Missouri–Kansas City. His research and teaching interests centre on various policy areas, including corporate and public policy, environmental economics and management, economics of education finance, and business ethics. Dr Erekson holds a PhD in Economics from the University of North Carolina at Chapel Hill (1980) and BA degrees in Economics and Political Science from Texas Christian University (1974). He has over 40 publications appearing in professional journals and books.
ereksonh@umkc.edu

David K. Foot is Professor of Economics at the University of Toronto in Canada. Since his doctorate in economics from Harvard University, Professor Foot's research and teaching interests have increasingly focused on economic–demographic interactions, particularly the economic and policy implications of population ageing. He is author of the Canadian best-selling books under the *Boom, Bust and Echo* title. Professor Foot is a recipient of the national 3M Award for Teaching Excellence and is a two-time winner of the undergraduate teaching award at the University of Toronto. He is a much-sought-after speaker to businesses, associations and governments on the implications of demographic change, both nationally and globally.

foot@chass.utoronto.ca

Chris Galea is a father, educator, outdoor enthusiast, builder, sailor and entrepreneur. He currently teaches at the Gerald Schwartz School of Business at St Francis Xavier University in Antigonish, Nova Scotia. He was also part of the founding faculty of the Sustainable Enterprise Academy at the Schulich School of Business at York University in Toronto. Much of his doctoral and current research is in the area of management learning as it relates to sustainability. Chris lives by the ocean surrounded by land he cherishes and people he cares about.

cgalea@stfx.ca

Dr **Raymond F. Gorman** is Associate Dean for Curriculum, Richard T. Farmer School of Business, and former director of the Center for Sustainable System Studies, Miami University. His academic background is in corporate finance and mathematical economics. His environmental research interests include studies of the relationship between financial and environmental performance. Other research interests are in the areas of corporate finance, specifically capital structure, the effect of regulation on the financial aspects of regulated firms, and behavioural finance. He served recently as editor of the *Mid-American Journal of Business*. His training includes AB, Brown University; MBA, Duke University; and DBA, Indiana University.

gormanrf@muohio.edu

Trudy Heller is the founder and president of Executive Education for the Environment. She has over 20 years' experience as a consultant and business educator. She conducts seminars and gives presentations on Business and the Natural Environment for businesses, universities and government agencies internationally. Her current writing focuses on sustainable business education and innovation of environmentally sensitive products. Her writing on sustainable business appears in *Research in Corporate Sustainability* (ed. Sharma; Edward Elgar, 2003), and her research on new technology development in the journals *Organization Science*, *Entrepreneurship: Theory and Practice* and *The IEEE Transactions on Engineering Management*. Ms Heller holds a PhD in Management from the Wharton School of the University of Pennsylvania and a PhD in Organisational Development from Temple University.

Heller97@aol.com

Darcy Hitchcock and **Marsha Willard** are founders of AXIS Performance Advisors, a consulting firm that has been in business since 1990. They apply their management consulting, training and facilitation skills to help organisations find responsible solutions that meet all stakeholder needs: for owners, customers, employees, the community and the environment. They have co-authored five popular business books on such topics as teamwork, trust, work redesign and quality. They are recognised experts in the implementation of sustainability inside organisations. Their *Sustainability Series*™ booklets show organisations how to simultaneously improve their financial, social and environmental performance. They designed and facilitate a professional certificate programme on Implementing Sustainability for Portland State University. Darcy teaches and does presentations for the Oregon Natural Step Network. She advises the Oregon Sustainability Board. Marsha facilitates multi-stakeholder consensus processes. Their clients span all industry sectors and include the Oregon Department of Environmental Quality, adidas, Oregon State University, Bonneville Power Administration and Metafore. (See www.pacifier.com/~axis.)

darcy@axisperformance.com
marsha@axisperformance.com

Diane Holt is a senior lecturer in environmental management at Middlesex University Business School, UK, and is programme leader of the BA degree in international management. She is a member of the Centre for Interdisciplinary Strategic Management Research. Her research areas are green supply chain management, greening small businesses and environmental education.
D.Holt@mdx.ac.uk

H. Gregory Hume is a Lean Product manager at TechSolve, Inc. He worked as a graduate assistant for the Miami University Sustainability Project and received a Master of Environmental Science in 1995. Prior to graduate school, he worked for General Electric in its appliance, nuclear fuel and aircraft engine businesses. His BS training was at the University of Kentucky.

Dr **Timothy C. Krehbiel** is Professor of Decision Sciences and Management Information Systems at Miami University. His research interests include experimental design, quality improvement and statistical education. His environmental research has explored the application of total quality environmental management in applied business decision-making. His MS and PhD degrees are from the University of Wyoming.
krehbitc@muohio.edu

Ass. Prof. Dr habil. **Beate Littig** is a senior researcher at the Department of Sociology, Institute for Advanced Studies, Vienna (since 1996). In addition, she is lecturer at the University of Vienna and at the University of Economics in Vienna. Her teaching and research activities are in the field of environmental sociology, innovation research, technology assessment and the sociology of ethics. She has co-ordinated several national and international research project related to these fields. She is an authorised Socratic facilitator in the tradition of Nelson/Heckmann.
littig@ihs.ac.at

Dr **Orie L. Loucks** taught botany, zoology and environmental science at Miami University. Earlier, he taught at the University of Wisconsin, 1962–78, and headed the Holcomb Research Institute, 1978–89, Indianapolis, IN, working on global carbon sequestration and air pollutant effects. Dr Loucks is the author or co-author of five books and some 250 peer-reviewed papers and book chapters. At Miami he initiated links between business and science, seeking common principles of sustainable development. He served on the National Academy of Sciences Board on Water Science and Technology in the 1980s (co-chairing the 1986 review of the Great Lakes Water Quality Agreement), as a member of the Science Advisory Board, International Joint Commission, and on the national Board of Governors of The Nature Conservancy.
loucksol@muohio.edu

Joanna Macy, PhD, has developed a diverse international following over the course of 40 years as a speaker and workshop leader on systems theory, sustainability, deep ecology and Buddhist philosophy. She is the author of seven books including *Coming Back to Life: Practices to Reconnect Our Lives, Our World* (New Society Publishers, 1998; co-authored with Molly Young Brown), *World as Lover, World as Self* (Parallax Press, 1991) and her recently published memoir, *Widening Circles* (New Society Publishers, 2000), as well as numerous journal articles. She currently lives and teaches in Berkeley, California. (See www.joannamacy.net.)
joanna@joannamacy.net

Judi Marshall is a Professor of Organisational Behaviour in the School of Management, University of Bath, Bath, UK. Her research interests have included managerial job stress, women in management, organisational cultures, organisational change and career development. She contributes to action research practices by developing self-reflective, action-oriented inquiry approaches. She teaches on a range of academic courses, and is Director of Studies for the Master's course in Responsibility and Business Practice.
j.marshall@bath.ac.uk

Ron Meissen is Senior Director of Engineering within the Environment, Health and Safety Group at Baxter International. He is a strong advocate for sustainability initiatives within Baxter, a regular guest lecturer on sustainable development at the Illinois Institute of Technology, Chicago, IL, and is currently completing his PhD thesis in this subject area.
ron_meissen@baxter.com

Jonathon Porritt is a co-director of the Business and the Environment Programme. He also co-directs the Sustainability Learning Networks Programme, an advanced diploma in sustainability for business from the University of Cambridge. He is a leading writer, commentator and broadcaster on sustainable development and is Programme Director of Forum for the Future, a leading UK charity on sustainable development. He is also chairman of the UK government Sustainable Development Commission.

Gillian Rice is Associate Professor at Thunderbird, The Garvin School of International Management, where she teaches International Marketing. She obtained her PhD from the University of Bradford and has taught at various institutions in the UK, USA and Canada. In 1996 she taught at the University of Bahrain as a Senior Fulbright Scholar. Her current research interests lie in the areas of the cultural impact on organisational creativity, cultural models of environmental attitudes and behaviour, and the Islamic perspective on marketing and business ethics.
riceg@t-bird.edu

Susan Ross is a consultant for Golder Associates in Calgary, Canada, specialised in economic and social management and implementation issues at the organisational and project level, in North America and internationally, working with multiple stakeholders to achieve their respective objectives. She advises on and undertakes socioeconomic impact assessment, public consultation, resettlement planning, community development planning, project impact evaluation, skills transfer and capacity-building. Work is undertaken in the context at the institutional level of effective management of sustainable development, and at the project level of achieving sustainable outcomes.
siross@golder.com

Verie Sandborg retired from Baxter International in June 2002. She was co-founder and co-chair of the Environment, Health and Safety Sustainable Development Team at Baxter. With the company for 23 years, Verie Sandborg was an early proponent of sustainability initiatives at Baxter. She was responsible for producing the company's first full sustainability report in 1999.
sandborg@sbcglobal.net

Michael Schaper, PhD, is Professor of Small Business and Entrepreneurship within the Graduate School of Business at Newcastle University, Australia. His research interests include ecopreneurship, the greening of small and medium-sized enterprises, indigenous entrepreneurship, business advisory services for small and new firms and sustainability education in business.
michael.schaper@newcastle.edu.au

Amy Sprague joined the World Resources Institute's Sustainable Enterprise Program in August 2000. She works with the New Ventures programme and co-ordinates the Environmental Enterprise Corps. Prior to coming to WRI, Amy received an MA in Latin American Studies and a Master of Public Affairs from the University of Texas at Austin. While at UT, she co-ordinated the University's Center for Environmental Resource Management in Latin America and worked at the Texas Department of Housing and Community Affairs. Amy was a State Department Intern at the US Embassy in Caracas, Venezuela, and had previously worked for a food distributor in Caracas. She holds a BA in Anthropology and Spanish from the University of Notre Dame.
amys@wri.org

Dr **Allan M. Springer** is Emeritus Professor of Paper Science and Engineering, Miami University. He completed a doctorate in chemical engineering at the Institute of Paper Chemistry, and has had extensive experience in the pulp and paper industry overseas as well as in the US. He is the author of the textbook *Industrial Environmental Control: Pulp and Paper Industry* (TAPPI Press, 2nd edn, 1993). Springer's research has focused on pollution abatement through process modification and on measures of sustainability for the pulp and paper industry.
sailor37@aol.com

Bob Willard is the author of *The Sustainability Advantage: Seven Business Case Benefits of a Triple Bottom Line* (New Society Publishers, 2002). He is a leading expert on the business value of corporate sustainability strategies, and in the last two years has given over 70 keynote presentations to corporations, consultants, academics and non-governmental organisations. Bob applies business and leadership development experience from his 34-year career at IBM Canada to engaging the business community in proactively avoiding risks and capturing opportunities associated with sustainability issues. He has served on the advisory boards of the Certificate in Corporate Social Responsibility programme at the University of Toronto, the Ontario Sustainable Energy Association (OSEA) and Eco-Energy Durham. He is currently on the advisory boards of The Natural Step, Canada, and the Certificate in Adult Training and Development offered by the University of Toronto.
www.sustainabilityadvantage.com

Kathleen Wood is an independent consultant whose work for the last 15 years has focused on organisational learning and development. During the past five years she has worked with companies looking to integrate triple-bottom-line thinking into their business practices, and presently she is focused on bringing together organisations across sectors (business, government and non-profit) to address critical issues they haven't been able to solve on their own. Her educational background is in environmental science, training and development, intercultural relations and brokering cross-sector partnerships. Kathleen calls Portland, Oregon, USA home.
Kathwood@earthlink.net

Faye Yoshihara is an independent consultant, specialising in the integration of sustainable business practices, cross-sector partnerships and sustainable enterprise start-ups. For over two decades, she was employed by multinational corporations, focusing on business management in emerging economies. She holds degrees from Oregon State University and the Kellogg Graduate School of Management, Northwestern University. Faye currently lives in Portland, Oregon, USA.
fayeyoshihara@earthlink.net

Index